This is a smart and timely contribution on a key di[...] Dr. Panda, one of India's foremost scholars of East [...] lent group of analysts to probe the place of the Ko[...] and fast-changing region. This volume will make for [...] interested in contemporary Asia, and in international relations on the whole.

Michael Kugelman, Deputy Director, Asia Program, Woodrow Wilson Centre for International Scholars, Washington DC

Brings India back in, on Asia-wide issues where its perspective is very much needed. The editor assembles a fine group of scholars from throughout the continent and beyond. Creative, original theme and high-quality papers.

Kent E. Calder, Director, Edwin O. Reischauer Center for East Asian Studies, Johns Hopkins School of Advanced International Studies, Washington DC

The Korean Peninsula have overlooked the space for many potential regional actors for long. However, the changing power dynamics post the DPRK-US bilateral summits has allowed many regional actors to step in and aim to play different roles in the region. This book fills a very interesting research gap, particularly as the Indo-Pacific region has not been addressed as a third-party actor in the Korean Peninsula sufficiently. Therefore, this book makes a very relevant contribution to a dynamic and potentially unstable region of the world.

Niklas Swanstrom, Director, Institute for Security and Development Policy, Sweden

This is a magnificently comprehensive volume on a topic of vital importance. The diverse chapters are accessible to general readers but will also provide unique insights to experts. Highly recommended.

Richard Weitz, Senior Fellow and Director, Center for Political-Military Analysis, Hudson Institute, Washington DC

This volume provides keen insight into the Korean Peninsula's role in shaping Northeast Asia and the Indo-Pacific's emerging dynamics. Through linking peninsula security and diplomatic dynamics to broader geopolitical trends in the Indo-Pacific, the contributors to this volume have demonstrated that the Korean Peninsula is an important stakeholder in contributing to stability, security, and a rules-based order in the region.

Stephen R. Nagy, Senior Associate Professor, International Christian University, Japan, & Distinguished Fellow, Asia-Pacific Foundation, Canada

In his edited volume *The Korean Peninsula and Indo-Pacific Power Politics: Status Security at Stake*, Dr. Jagannath P. Panda has compiled chapters of immediate relevance that are at the same time remarkably diverse in both the geographic spread of focus and authors. The Republic of Korea may remain sceptical about the Indo-Pacific as a construct, however, it is clear from this work that the Indo-Pacific as a region is deeply interested in and important to Korea.

Gordon Flake, CEO, Perth USAsia Centre, The University of Western Australia, Perth

The Korean Peninsula and Indo-Pacific Power Politics

This book assesses the strategic linkages that the Korean Peninsula shares with the Indo-Pacific and provides a succinct picture of issues which will shape the trajectory of the Korean Peninsula in the future.

This book analyses how critical actors such as the United States, China, Russia and Japan are caught in a tightly balanced power struggle affecting the Korean Peninsula. It shows how these countries are exerting control over the Korean Peninsula while also holding on to their status as critical actors in the broader Indo-Pacific. The prospects of peace, stability and unity in the Korean Peninsula and the impact of this on Indo-Pacific power politics are explored as well as the contending and competing interests in the region. Chapters present country-specific positions and approaches as case studies and review the impact of power politics on stakeholders' relationships in the Indo-Pacific. The book also argues that the Korean Peninsula and the issue of denuclearization is of primary importance to any direction an Indo-Pacific Partnership may take.

Bringing together scholars, journalists and ex-diplomats, this book will be of interest to academics working in the field of international relations, foreign policy, security studies and Asian studies as well as audiences interested in policy and defence in Northeast Asia and Indo-Pacific dynamics.

Jagannath P. Panda is a Research Fellow and Centre Coordinator for East Asia at the Institute for Defence Studies and Analyses, India. An expert on China, Indo-Pacific and East Asian affairs, he is the series editor for *Routledge Studies on Think Asia*.

Routledge Studies on Think Asia
Edited by Jagannath P. Panda

This series addresses the current strategic complexities of Asia and forecasts how these current complexities will shape Asia's future. Bringing together empirical and conceptual analysis, the series examines critical aspects of Asian politics, with a particular focus on the current security and strategic complexities. The series includes academic studies from universities, research institutes and think-tanks and policy oriented studies. Focusing on security and strategic analysis on Asia's current and future trajectory, this series welcomes submissions on relationship patterns (bilateral, trilateral and multilateral) in Indo-Pacific, regional and sub-regional institutions and mechanisms, corridors and connectivity, maritime security, infrastructure politics, trade and economic models and critical frontiers (boundaries, borders, bordering provinces) that are crucial to Asia's future.

1 **India and China in Asia**
   Between Equations and Equilibrium
   Edited by Jagannath P. Panda

2 **Northeast India and India's Act East Policy**
   Identifying the Priorities
   Edited by M. Amarjeet Singh

3 **The Korean Peninsula and Indo-Pacific Power Politics**
   Status Security at Stake
   Edited by Jagannath P. Panda

4 **Conflict and Cooperation in the Indo-Pacific**
   New Geopolitical Realities
   Edited by Ash Rossiter, Brendon J. Cannon

URL: https://www.routledge.com/Routledge-Studies-on-Think-Asia/book-series/TA

The Korean Peninsula and Indo-Pacific Power Politics

Status Security at Stake

**Edited by
Jagannath P. Panda**

Routledge
Taylor & Francis Group

LONDON AND NEW YORK

First published 2020
by Routledge
2 Park Square, Milton Park, Abingdon, Oxon OX14 4RN

and by Routledge
605 Third Avenue, New York, NY 10017

First issued in paperback 2022

Routledge is an imprint of the Taylor & Francis Group, an informa business

© 2020 selection and editorial matter, Jagannath P. Panda; individual chapters, the contributors

The right of Jagannath P. Panda to be identified as the author of the editorial material, and of the authors for their individual chapters, has been asserted in accordance with sections 77 and 78 of the Copyright, Designs and Patents Act 1988.

All rights reserved. No part of this book may be reprinted or reproduced or utilised in any form or by any electronic, mechanical, or other means, now known or hereafter invented, including photocopying and recording, or in any information storage or retrieval system, without permission in writing from the publishers.

Trademark notice: Product or corporate names may be trademarks or registered trademarks, and are used only for identification and explanation without intent to infringe.

Publisher's Note
The publisher has gone to great lengths to ensure the quality of this reprint but points out that some imperfections in the original copies may be apparent.

British Library Cataloguing-in-Publication Data
A catalogue record for this book is available from the British Library

Library of Congress Cataloging-in-Publication Data
A catalog record has been requested for this book

ISBN: 978-1-03-240064-8 (pbk)
ISBN: 978-0-367-36423-6 (hbk)
ISBN: 978-0-429-34585-2 (ebk)

DOI: 10.4324/9780429345852

Typeset in Baskerville
by codeMantra

*In Memory of My Grandfather,
Bapa*

Contents

List of illustrations   xi
List of contributors   xiii
List of abbreviations   xix
Preface   xxiii
Acknowledgements   xxvii

Introduction: the Korean Peninsula and Indo-Pacific power politics: *Status security at stake*   1
JAGANNATH P. PANDA

PART I
Critical perspectives   19

1 America's conflicted strategy for the Korean Peninsula: from "fire and fury" to "denuclearisation"   21
DONALD KIRK

2 China's relations with North Korea: surmounting the "Great Wall"   39
ANURAG VISWANATH

3 Japan's security pledge in the Korean Peninsula   57
KOHTARO ITO

4 The twists and turns of Russia's relations with North Korea   72
GEORGY BULYCHEV AND VALERIIA GORBACHEVA

PART II
Contending perspectives   85

5 Denuclearisation and peace regime on the Korean Peninsula: perspectives of the two Koreas   87
JINA KIM

6 Korean Peninsula and the evolving Sino-US strategic stability in the Indo-Pacific   106
KUYOUN CHUNG

7 DPRK's proliferation activities and the denuclearisation talks: security in the Indo-Pacific and beyond   121
LAMI KIM

8 Russia and the two Koreas   137
ARCHANA UPADHYAY

9 Mongolia and the North-East Asian peace process   149
ALICIA CAMPI

10 India and the Korean Peninsula: between dialogue, diplomacy, and denuclearisation   165
JAGANNATH P. PANDA AND MRITTIKA GUHA SARKAR

PART III
Competing and cooperating perspectives   191

11 Unification of Koreas and North Korea's changing political system: models and movements   193
JIN SHIN

12 Negotiating mechanisms in the Korean Peninsula: what has worked? Any lessons for the Indo-Pacific?   209
MANPREET SETHI

13 Geoeconomics of the Indo-Pacific: competing economic architectures and South Korea   225
SEONJOU KANG

14 Between security and insecurity: resource politics in North-East Asia   242
ATMAJA GOHAIN BARUAH

Index   253

Illustrations

Figures

5.1	North Korea's pattern of behaviour	95
5.2	References to denuclearisation	95
5.3	National policy initiatives of the Moon Jae-in government	98
9.1	East Asia Railway Community Initiative among China, Mongolia and Russia	152
10.1	Total trade between India and South Korea	176
10.2	Total trade between India and North Korea	178
11.1	State's preference model	195
11.2	Conflict policy	197
11.3	Dynamics of decision-making in conflict policy process	199
11.4	Leadership change of N.K's political system	204
11.5	Strength-pressure curve	205

Tables

5.1	North Korea's intentions and related hypotheses	89
5.2	Policy objectives of the Moon Jae-in government	97
10.1	India's stance on major UN resolutions and sanctions	169
10.2	India's discussions on denuclearization with major stockholders in the Korean Peninsula	182

Contributors

Atmaja Gohain Baruah is pursuing her doctoral programme at the National University of Singapore (NUS) in comparative Asian studies, focussing on exploring the connection between climate variability, ecological migration, and inequality in India and China. She is a recipient of the President's Graduate Fellowship at the NUS. Apart from environmental governance in China, her research interests are non-traditional security threats facing Asia, Sino-Indian relations, Chinese foreign policy, and East Asia's geo-politics. She has published widely in *The Pioneer, Asia-Pacific Issues, East Asia Forum*, and *Megatrend*.

Georgy Bulychev is professor of economy at the Russian Academy of Science and a researcher at the Russian National Committee, Council for Security Cooperation in the Asia Pacific, Moscow. As an envoy extraordinary and minister plenipotentiary, he has had postings to Pyongyang and Seoul. He has authored and co-authored numerous books and articles, and presented many papers on Korean and East Asian affairs at various international forums. He also taught at Moscow State Institute of International Relations (MGIMO University).

Alicia Campi is a China/Mongolia specialist and researcher on North-East Asian security. She was a US State Department officer for 14 years, serving in Singapore, Taiwan, Japan, Mongolia, and the US Mission to the United Nations (USUN) in New York. Since 2013, she has been a research Fellow and lecturer at the Reischauer Center, School of Advanced International Studies (SAIS), Johns Hopkins University. She received her BA in East Asian history from Smith College (1971), MA in East Asian studies from Harvard University (1973), PhD in Central Eurasian and Mongolian studies from Indiana University (1987), and honorary doctorate from the National University of Mongolia (2007). In 2004, she received the "Friendship" Medal from Mongolian president N. Bagabandi, and in 2011 she was awarded Mongolia's "Polar Star" for contributions to US-Mongolian relations from Mongolian president Ts. Elbegdorj. She has been the president of the Mongolia Society for 12 years. Her book *Mongolia's Foreign Policy: Navigating a Changing World* was published in April 2019.

Kuyoun Chung is assistant professor at the Political Science Department in Kangwon National University, Republic of Korea. She currently serves as a member of the Policy Advisory Committee of the Ministry of Foreign Affairs, the Korea Institute of Nuclear Non-proliferation and Control, the Unification Education Commission, and the National Unification Advisory Council. Previously, she was a lecturer in the Department of Political Science at the University of California, Los Angeles (2011–2012); visiting professor at the Korea National Diplomatic Academy (2014–2015); and a research Fellow at the Korea Institute for National Unification (2015–2018). She received her Ph.D. in Political Science from the University of California, Los Angeles in 2011. Her research focusses on American foreign policy and Indo-Pacific security issues. Her papers "Geopolitics and a Realist Turn of US Foreign Policy toward North Korea" and "Gray Zone Conflict and Evolving US Maritime Strategy" are recently published in 2019, and another one "Wartime Reliability of the US-led Coalition of the Willing: The Case of the Iraq War, 2003–2011" is forthcoming in 2020.

Valeriia Gorbacheva is GR-director of the Russian National Committee on BRICS Research in Moscow, a legal entity created under the auspices of the Russian government for Track II activities. She is also a researcher at the Asian Strategy Center, Institute of Economics of the Russian Academy of Sciences, and is pursuing her PhD in world economy. Her research focusses on global governance, world economy, public diplomacy, NGOs, civil society, and BRICS countries.

Kohtaro Ito is a research Fellow at the Canon Institute for Global Studies (CIGS), Tokyo, Japan. He received his bachelor's and master's degrees in policy studies from Chuo University in 2001 and 2004, respectively. He also went to Korea University as an exchange student in graduate school. During 2004–2006, he worked at the office of Member of the House of Representatives and the Japan Center for International Exchange (JCIE). He was also a junior research Fellow at Ilmin International Relations Institute, Korea University (Korean Government Scholarship Programme). From 2015 to 2017, he served as deputy counsellor at the National Security Secretariat (NSS), Cabinet Secretariat, dealing with North-East Asian diplomatic and security issues, especially Korean affairs.

Seonjou Kang is professor at the Institute of Foreign Affairs and National Security-Korea National Diplomatic Academy (IFANS-KNDA). Most of her research centres on global governance, geoeconomics of Asian regionalism, and technological changes (4th Industrial Revolution). She received her PhD in political science from Michigan State University in 2000. Her widely cited papers include "The US Indo-Pacific Strategy and Geo-economics", "Implications of the US Withdrawal from the TPP", "U.S. President-Elect Trump's Foreign Economic Policies with Focus on Their Feasibility and Implications", "Assessing the 2nd-Year Performance of the Asian Infrastructure Investment Bank: China's Economic Statecraft or a Multilateral Development Bank?", and "Big Data: Current State and Its Use in Foreign Affairs and Security". Her academic research has been published in the *Korean Journal of International Studies* (2015), *European Journal of Political Research* (2007), *The Journal of Politics* (2005), and *Journal of Peace Research* (2004).

Jina Kim is a research Fellow at the Korea Institute for Defense Analyses, specialising in US-North Korea relations, nuclear non-proliferation, and North-East Asian security. She holds a PhD in international relations from the Fletcher School of Law and Diplomacy at Tufts University and teaches at the Yonsei Graduate School of International Studies. She is a member of the Advisory Committee for the Blue House, Ministry of National Unification, and US-ROK Combined Forces Command. She also serves at the Policy Review Board for the Ministry of Foreign Affairs and the Blue House's Public Information Committee. She has authored *The North Korean Nuclear Weapons Crisis* (2014) and co-authored *North Korea and Asia's Evolving Nuclear Landscape* (2017), *Maritime Security and Governance* (2014), *The North Korea Crisis and Regional Responses* (2014), and *The North Korean Military Secret Report* (2013). Her recent publications in academic journals include "Issues Regarding North Korean Denuclearization Roadmap with a Focus on Implications from the Iran Nuclear Deal" (2018), "Assessing Export Controls of Strategic Items to North Korea" (2017), "North Korea's Strategic Alliance towards Becoming a Nuclear Weapons State" (2017), and "Nuclear Brinkmanship on the Korean Peninsula and the Effects of Cognitive Variables in Crisis Decision Making" (2016).

Lami Kim is a lecturer at the Department of Politics and Public Administration, University of Hong Kong and an adjunct fellow at Pacific Forum. Her research interests include nuclear non-proliferation regimes, nuclear export controls and politics and security on the Korean Peninsula and in East Asia. Previously, Dr Kim served as a South Korean diplomat and a research fellow at Harvard's Belfer Center, Pacific Forum, and Stimson Center. She has taught at Harvard University and Boston College. Her works have been published in *The Washington Quarterly*, the *Bulletin of the Atomic Scientists*, *The Diplomat*, *PacNet*, and *Stimson Center*, among others. Dr Kim holds a master's and a PhD degree in international affairs from the Fletcher School of Law and Diplomacy at Tufts University, and a master's degree in Middle Eastern studies from Harvard University.

Donald Kirk is an author and journalist based in Washington and Seoul. He first visited Seoul in 1972 as a *Chicago Tribune* correspondent covering the "Red Cross talks" and since then has been reporting on Korea for the *International Herald Tribune*, the *Christian Science Monitor*, *Forbes Asia*, and the *Daily Beast*, among others. He has authored several books on Korea: notably *Korean Dynasty: Hyundai and Chung Ju Yung*; *Korean Crisis: Unraveling of the Miracle in the IMF Era*; *Korea Betrayed: Kim Dae Jung and Sunshine*; and *Okinawa and Jeju: Bases of Discontent*. He has been a Fulbright scholar and Edward R. Murrow press Fellow at the Council on Foreign Relations in New York.

Jagannath P. Panda is a research Fellow and heads the East Asia Centre at the Institute for Defence Studies and Analyses (IDSA), New Delhi, India. He is in charge of East Asia Centre's academic and administrative activities, including the Track-II and Track 1.5 dialogues with the Chinese, Japanese, and Korean think-tanks and institutes. His research areas include India-China relations, Indo-Pacific security, Indian foreign policy, and the Korean Peninsula, among others. He has been a visiting Fellow to the United States, Sweden, China, Taiwan, South Korea, and Japan, and was Japan Foundation and Korea Foundation Fellow in 2018. He is a recipient of the V.K. Krishna Menon Memorial Gold Medal (2000) from the Indian Society of International Law & Diplomacy in New Delhi. Dr Panda has authored *India-China Relations: Politics of Resources, Identity and Authority in a Multipolar World Order* (Routledge, 2017) and *China's Path to Power: Party, Military and the Politics of State Transition* (Pentagon Press, 2010). He has also edited several books and is the series editor of *Routledge Studies on Think Asia*. Dr Panda is a member of the editorial board of the *Journal of Asian Public Policy* (Routledge). He has published in leading peer-reviewed journals, such as *Rising Powers Quarterly*, *Journal of Asian Public Policy* (Routledge), *Journal of Asian and African Studies*, *Asian Perspective*, *Journal of Contemporary China* (Routledge), *Georgetown Journal of Asian Affairs*, *Strategic Analyses* (Routledge), *China Report*, *Indian Foreign Affairs Journal*, and *Portuguese Journal of International Affairs*.

Mrittika Guha Sarkar is a research scholar at the Centre for East Asian Studies, School of International Studies, Jawaharlal Nehru University (JNU), New Delhi. Her research areas are India-China relations; East Asia's geopolitics; and security studies focussing on regional affairs of China, Japan, and Korea. She writes for several journals, newspapers, and magazines, such as *Business Today*, *East Asia Military Monitor*, *World Focus*, *Defense and Security Alert (DSA)*, and *The Pioneer*. Her recent publications include "The Big Picture: US Ban on Huawei", "Shifting Sino-US Military Relations", "Changing Trends between India and Nepal", "Dalai Lama Holding Tongue on Doklam?", and "India-Vietnam Outreach: Strengthened Ties". She has been a project assistant and an intern with the East Asia Centre at the Institute for Defence Studies and Analyses (IDSA), New Delhi. She is also an editorial assistant for *Routledge Studies on Think Asia*.

Manpreet Sethi is a recipient of the prestigious K. Subrahmanyam award, an honour conferred for excellence in strategic and security studies in India by the premier think-tank Institute for Defence Studies and Analyses (IDSA), New Delhi. Dr Sethi is a Distinguished Fellow at the Centre for Air Power Studies, New Delhi, where she heads the project on nuclear security. Over the last 20 years, she has been researching and writing on nuclear energy, strategy, non-proliferation, disarmament, arms and export controls, and BMD, and has been published in several reputed journals. Her book *Nuclear Strategy: India's March towards Credible Deterrence* (2009) is deemed essential reading for many courses. She is also the author of *Code of Conduct for Outer Space: Strategy* *for India* (2015) and *Argentina's Nuclear Policy* (1999); co-author of *India's Sentinel* (2014) and *Nuclear Deterrence and Diplomacy* (2004); and editor of *Towards a Nuclear Weapons Free World* (2009), *Global Nuclear Challenges* (2009), and *Nuclear Power: In the Wake of Fukushima* (2012). She lectures regularly at establishments of Indian Armed Forces, Police, and Foreign Services. As a member of the prime minister's Informal Group on Disarmament in 2012, she has been a part of the country's Track II initiatives. She has been a member of the Executive Board of Indian Pugwash Society and is a consultant with the Global Nuclear Abolition Forum and Asia Pacific Leadership Network.

Jin Shin is president of the Institute for Peace Affairs in Seoul, South Korea. He is professor at the Department of Political Science & Diplomacy, and director of the National Strategy Institute, Chungnam National University, Korea. He is also the recipient of numerous academic awards, including the Global Peace Award, Leadership Award from the US Congress member, Senate and General Assembly Award and Joint Legislative Resolution Award from the State of New Jersey, Fulbright scholarship, and Korea Research foundation scholarship. He was also a visiting scholar at Columbia University and the Johns Hopkins University. Dr Shin taught Asian culture at Farmingdale State College, State University of New York, in 2008, and North-East international security at South Dakota State University in 1997. He has published many books on contemporary Korea, North Korea and international relations, and Korean political culture, including *Regional Trust and Prejudice as a Social Capital* (CNU Press, 2015), *International Politics and Security* (2011), *Sociable Negotiation* (2011), *The Vortex of N. Korea and US-Korea Foreign Policy* (2004), *Party and Electoral System Reformation* (2004), *Political Culture in Korean Rural Areas* (2006), *Elites in Korean Rural Areas* (2006), *Political Participation in Korean Rural Areas* (2006), and *NGO's in Korean Rural Areas* (2006).

Archana Upadhyay is professor at the School of International Studies, Jawaharlal Nehru University, New Delhi, India. She previously taught international relations and foreign policy in the Department of Political Science, Dibrugarh University, Assam (India). She received her PhD from the School of International Studies, Jawaharlal Nehru University. She has been a Commonwealth Visiting Fellow at the International Policy Institute of King's College, London, and received a Fulbright Visiting Lecturer Fellowship. Her research interests include international relations with a special focus on South Asian, Russian, and Eurasian issues; insurgency and terrorism; and conflict and conflict management. She has published several articles in reputed national and international journals. She has authored two books – *Multiparty System in the Russian Federation: Problems and Prospects* and *India's Fragile Borderlands: The Dynamics of Terrorism in North East India* – and a monograph on human rights.

Anurag Viswanath is a Singapore-based independent writer and China analyst. She is also an adjunct Fellow, Institute of Chinese Studies, New Delhi, India. While she has written about Thailand, India, and Singapore, her main focus is contemporary China. Her book, *Finding India in China* (2015), has received a lot of interest – she was invited to the Beijing Bookworm Literary Festival, Singapore Writers Festival, Foreign Correspondents Club (Shanghai and Hong Kong), Siam Society (Bangkok), Royal Asiatic Society (Shanghai), Hopkins Forum (Shanghai) and National Institute of Advanced Studies (Bangalore). Anurag has written prolifically over the years for the *Bangkok Post*, *Nation & Prachatai* (Thailand), *Far Eastern Economic Review* (Hong Kong), *Journal of Contemporary Asia* (Manila), *Channel News Asia* (Singapore), *Economic and Political Weekly* (Mumbai) and *Global Affairs* (Mumbai). She was a regular writer for *Business Standard* (2007–2011). She did her Ph.D in Political Science from the University of Delhi. Her thesis was on Chinese economic reforms and she spent a year at Fudan University, Shanghai. Anurag has received research fellowships from the Government of India, Ford Foundation and Indian Council for Social Science Research (ICSSR).

Abbreviations

A2AD	Anti-Access and Area-Denial
ACCC	ASEAN Connectivity Coordinating Committee
ADB	Asian Development Bank
ADMM	ASEAN Defence Ministers' Meeting
AEP	Act East Policy
AI	Artificial Intelligence
AIIB	Asian Infrastructure Investment Bank
AN/TPY-2	Army/Navy Transportable Radar Surveillance
APEC	Asia-Pacific Economic Cooperation
ARF	ASEAN Regional Forum
ASEAN	Association of Southeast Asian Nations
BCP	Business Continuity Planning
BMD	Ballistic Missile Defence
BRI	Belt and Road Initiative
BUILD	Act Better Utilisation of Investment Leading to Development Act of 2018
CBMs	Confidence Building Measures
CDB	China Development Bank
CEP	Cultural Exchange Programme
CEPA	Comprehensive Economic Partnership Agreement
CIA	Central Intelligence Agency
CKFTA	China-South Korea Free Trade Agreement
CMF	Combined Maritime Forces
CPC	Communist Party of China
CPTPP	Comprehensive and Progressive Agreement for the Trans-Pacific Partnership
CVID	Complete, Verifiable, Irreversible, Denuclearisation (sometimes, Dismantlement)
DMZ	Demilitarised Zone
DoD	Department of Defence
DPRK	Democratic People's Republic of Korea
DTT	Defence Trilateral Talks
EANET	Acid Deposition Monitoring Network in East Asia

EARC	East Asian Railway Community
EAS	East Asia Summit
ECNEA	Intergovernmental Collaborative Mechanism on Energy Cooperation in North-East Asia
EDD	Extended Deterrence Dialogue
EDGE	Enhancing Development and Growth through Energy
EDPC	Extended Deterrence Policy Committee
ESPO	East Siberian Oil Pipeline project
EU	European Union
EWG	Energy Working Group (of APEC)
FDI	Foreign Direct Investment
FE	Foal Eagle
FFVD	Final, Fully Verified Denuclearization
FMCT	Fissile Material Cut-off Treaty
FOIP	Free and Open Indo-Pacific
FOIPS	Free and Open Indo-Pacific Strategy
FTA	Free Trade Agreement
GDP	Gross Domestic Product
GLF	Great Leap Forward
GPPAC	Global Partnership for the Prevention of Armed Conflict
GRIPS	National Graduate Institute for Policy Studies
GSOMIA	General Security of Military Information Agreement
IAEA	International Atomic Energy Agency
ICAS	Institute for Corean [sic] American Studies
ICBM	Intercontinental Ballistic Missile
ICCSR	Indian Council of Social Science Research
IMF	International Monetary Fund
IMSS	India's Maritime Security Strategy
IORA	Indian Ocean Rim Association
ITAN	Infrastructure Transactional Assistance Network
JADIZ	Japan's Air Defence Identification Zone
JASDF	Japan Air Self-Defence Force
JASSM	Joint Air-to-Surface Standoff Missile
JGSDF	Japan Ground Self-Defence Force
JMSDF	Japan Maritime Self-Defence Force
JSDF	Japan Self-Defence Forces
KCNA	Korean Central News Agency
KEDO	Korean Peninsula Energy Development Organisation
KGB	USSR Committee for State Security
KIC	Kaesong Industrial Complex
KOEC	Korea Oil Exploration Corporation
KPA	Korean People's Army
KR	Key Resolve
kt	Kilotons
LWR	Light Water Reactor

MDB	Multilateral Development Bank
MFA	Ministry of Foreign Affairs
MOU	Memorandum of Understanding
MTCR	Missile Technology Control Regime
NAM	Non-Alignment Movement
NATO	North Atlantic Treaty Organisation
NDRC	National Development and Reform Commission
NEAC	Northeast Asian Conference on Environmental Cooperation
NEASPEC	North-East Asian Sub-regional Programme for Environmental Cooperation
NEAT	Northwest Pacific Action Plan Eutrophication Assessment Tool
NEO	Non-combatant Evacuation Operation
NGO	Non-Governmental Organisation
NOC	National Oil Company
NOWPAP	Northwest Pacific Action Plan
NPT	Treaty on the Non-Proliferation of Nuclear Weapons (or Non-Proliferation Treaty)
NSC	National Security Council
NSG	Nuclear Suppliers Group
NSP	New Southern Policy
NSS	National Security Strategy
NWFZ	Nuclear Weapons Free Zone
ODA	Official Development Assistance
OPCON	Operational Control
OPIC	Overseas Private Investment Corporation
PAC-3	Patriot Advanced Capability
PLA	People's Liberation Army
PLAN	People's Liberation Army Navy
POW/MIA	Prisoner of War/Missing in Action
PMD	Possible Military Dimension
PPP	Purchasing Power Parity
PRC	People's Republic of China
PVA	People's Volunteers Army
Quad	Quadrilateral grouping of Australia, India, Japan, and the US
RAAF	Royal Australian Air Force
RBIO	Rules-Based International Order
RCEP	Regional Comprehensive Economic Partnership
ReCAAP	Regional Cooperation Agreement on Combating Piracy and Armed Robbery against Ships in Asia
ROK	Republic of Korea
ROKMC	Republic of Korea Marine Corps
RSEZ	Rason Special Economic Zone

SAR	Special Administrative Region
SDF	Self Defence Forces
SLBM	Submarine-Launched Ballistic Missile
SLOCs	Sea Lines of Communication
SM-3	Standard Missile-3
SOEs	State-Owned Enterprises
SSBN	Strategic Submarine Ballistic Nuclear
STOVL	Short Take-Off and Vertical-Landing
TAES	Trans-Asia Energy System
TCS	Trilateral Cooperation Secretariat
TEMM	Tripartite Environment Ministers Meeting
THAAD	Terminal High Altitude Area Defence
TPNW	Treaty on the Prohibition of Nuclear Weapons
TPP	Trans-Pacific Partnership
UFG	Ulchi-Freedom Guardian
UN	United Nations
UNC	United Nations Command
UNESCAP	United Nations Economic and Social Commission for Asia and the Pacific
UNSC	United Nations Security Council
US	United States
USAID	United States Agency for International Development
USFK	United States Forces Korea
USIDFC	United States International Development Finance Corporation
USINDOPACOM	United States Indo-Pacific Command
USMC	United States Marine Corps
USPACOM	United State Pacific Command
WMD	Weapons of Mass Destruction
WPK	Workers' Party of Korea

Preface

The history of Korean Peninsula was always dominated by numerous invasions by empires. Following the end of Japanese imperial rule over Korea, the Peninsula underwent a partition, dividing the region into two administrative zones along the 38th parallel line. Over the next three years (1945–1948), the Soviet Union set up its communist regime in the northern part, and the United States set up in the southern part of the Peninsula.

Ironically, one of the countries on the Peninsula today poses serious and imminent perils to its surroundings and beyond, while the other advocates peace and stability. North Korea is seen as a threat to international peace and security because of its active nuclear weapons programme, track record of weapons proliferation, and an aggressive ruling regime. South Korea, on the other hand, is trying to play a greater role in regional peace and diplomacy through its economic and technical prowess. The scenario has been further complicated by their alliances with opposing powers during Cold War (the Soviet Union/China and the United States, respectively) as well as post-Cold War (China and the United States, respectively).

In recent years, the region has become the hub of great power rivalry between the United States, China, Russia, and to an extent Japan. Furthermore, since the Peninsula is situated adjacent to the Korea Strait – an important maritime trade passage – it has also become a crucial part of the region of Indo-Pacific. Thus, the Korean Peninsula remains a critical arena for the power politics in Indo-Pacific. Most importantly, no debate is likely to continue to dominate Asia's strategic spectrum as much as the issue of the denuclearisation of the Korean Peninsula and the prospect of reunification of the two Koreas. The issues are further convoluted by the distinct, and often divergent, perspectives of the critical stakeholders, namely South Korea, the United States, China, Japan, and Russia, on denuclearisation and the potential for Korean reunification.

In this regard, the historic meeting of June 12, 2018, between the American president Donald Trump and North Korean leader Kim Jong-un, and the inter-Korean summits in 2018 have heightened the prospects of peace and stability in the Korean Peninsula. Notwithstanding these positive trends, a denuclearised Peninsula still remains far-fetched, owing to the contentious power plays in the region. Further, despite the improved relations between Trump and Kim, the United States and North Korea continue to disagree on the process and definition of "complete" denuclearisation. While the United States, with a non-incremental approach, persists in treating the issue of denuclearisation through maximum pressure and diplomatic force, North Korea is adamant on a more flexible US approach while intending to denuclearise "when the time is right". At the same time, resolving historical misunderstandings between the two Koreas requires patience and time. In this context, South Korea has persistently called for resolving the crisis through peace and diplomacy. China is supporting the phased manner desired by North Korea, while Japan, another important actor in North-East Asia, is supporting the US demand for "Complete, Verifiable and Irreversible Dismantlement" (CVID).

Similarly, the inter-Korean summits held in 2018 enhanced the prospects of peaceful reunification of the two Koreas. Both the Koreas have repeatedly professed their commitment towards national unification, and over the last 70 years, countless words have been written and spoken about this commitment. However, the aim to achieve the reunification of the Korean Peninsula remains distant. Moreover, over the years, the political and ideological cleavages between the two Koreas have widened. Nonetheless, the role of the critical stakeholders in the reunification process should not be disregarded.

South Korea has vowed to work towards the reunification of the two Koreas by 2045. North Korea has welcomed such a pledge, but it hopes that the reunification happens without the interference of any external forces. As for the other stakeholders, Russia has been officially supporting peaceful, secure, and stable reunification. Japan, too, officially supports peaceful reunification, and though it may not be able to play a proactive role in the peace process, its long-term ambition to play a role in economic aid assistance after the reunification should not be discounted. China, on the other hand, while supporting Korean reunification, pursues an uncertain approach. It has essentially been supporting a "two Korea policy", acknowledging that the political, economic, and security threats of reunification would be far greater. No matter what each of these actors' official pronouncement on reunification appears to be, none of them would like to put their national interests at stake by losing the stamp of being a critical actor in the region. Hence, the genuine template of each of their stances on the reunification of the Koreas is subject to debate.

Nevertheless, a scenario is fast emerging in which world leaders are engaging with Pyongyang in contrast to the earlier stance, where the major powers sought to isolate North Korea and hoped for the collapse of its regime. This has been demonstrated by Kim Jong-un's regular meetings with the Chinese president Xi Jinping, South Korean president Moon Jae-in, and US president Donald Trump. Russian president Vladimir Putin's meeting with Kim Jong-un in April 2019 has further strengthened this assertion. Furthermore, the Trump-Kim summits being held in third countries, Singapore and Vietnam, is an indication that the world as a whole, sensing new trading opportunities, is now more receptive to engaging with North Korea. Further, all its neighbours and several other powers appear amicable to remove the UN sanctions on North Korea if its nuclear sites and stockpiles are completely dismantled. This finely poised dynamic makes it possible for many non-critical actors, such as India, the Association of Northeast Asian Nations (ASEAN), the European Union (EU), Australia, and Mongolia, to play a greater role in restoring peace and security while enhancing their strategic interests in the region.

Consequently, the critical issues of denuclearisation and reunification are increasingly being discussed among critical and non-critical stakeholders as well as in the bilateral, trilateral, quadrilateral, and even multilateral discussion forums and mechanisms. In other words, the power rivalries in the Korean Peninsula are no more restricted to the region but have expanded into the Indo-Pacific region, where the United States is a major security provider. It is important to note that the fate of denuclearisation in the Korean Peninsula would act as a litmus test for the legitimacy of US's economic, political, and strategic influence within and beyond Asia. Further, foreign assistance has so far aided the DPRK's (this volume uses the nomenclature of DPRK and North Korea, and RoK and South Korea, interchangeably) development of nuclear and missile capabilities. North Korea has had proliferation linkages with nuclear aspirants in West and South Asia, which, if expanded, would pose serious threats to international peace and security.

Undoubtedly, the Indo-Pacific is also likely to witness a similar coalescence or clash of interests. For instance, the United States and China, through their geo-economic strategies – "Indo-Pacific Strategy" and the "Belt and Road Initiative", respectively – are already turning the Indo-Pacific into a competing economic as well as strategic landscape. Moreover, other major actors are also engaging in the Indo-Pacific with connectivity initiatives, such as Security and Growth for All in the Region (SAGAR) by India, "Free and Open Indo-Pacific" vision by Japan, and the New Southern Policy (NSP) by South Korea. Nonetheless, it is in the interest of the littoral and non-littoral states of the Indo-Pacific to prevent miscalculations and misperceptions, especially when it comes to nuclear powers, in order to ensure a free, open, and prosperous international environment.

Surprisingly, literature on the Korean Peninsula has not addressed the complexity of the region from the perspective of the Indo-Pacific power politics. This volume, therefore, examines not only the prospect of peace, stability, and unity in the Korean Peninsula but also the contending and competing interests in the region and its impact on the Indo-Pacific. It further explores the contours and characteristics of major power politics on the Peninsula and the critical and non-critical perspectives of the various stakeholders therein in the larger context of the balance of power in the Indo-Pacific region. Moreover, such a volume, involving international subject experts with the lead of an Indian scholar from a prominent think-tank of India, makes it a rare and one of the prelude exercise.

This work is a sincere endeavour and has endured a rigorous review process. Any remaining omissions, mistakes, or unforeseen errors are the sole responsibility of the respective authors. The editor, the institute for which the editor works, and the publisher are not responsible either.

Dr Jagannath P. Panda

Acknowledgements

This book had its genesis during my stay in Seoul as a Fellow for the Korea Foundation for a period of two months (July–August 2018.) The stint offered me an excellent opportunity to hone and formulate my understanding of not just the Korean Peninsula but also the dynamic interplay between it and the major powers. I am, therefore, indebted to the Korea Foundation and its members for their generous support of this endeavour. A special thanks to Choi Hyunsoo, director, Korea Foundation, and Kim In Hyuk, senior program officer, Invitation and Fellowship Department, Korea Foundation.

My affiliation with the Hankuk University of Foreign Studies (HUFS) in Seoul during the Korea Foundation Fellowship was a rewarding experience. I specially thank Professor Chanwahn Kim and Dr Rajiv Kumar of HUFS for their support during my stay in their university as a visiting Fellow.

I am also thankful to Amb. Sujan R. Chinoy, director general, Institute for Defence Studies and Analyses (IDSA), for his continuous support. His encouragement as well as analysis of Korean affairs and East Asian dynamics in a larger geo-political context from an Indian perspective was a value addition to this research study.

This book would not have been possible without timely suggestions, critical comments, and constant encouragement by Cho Hyun, former vice minister of RoK; Dr Haksoon Paik, President, Sejong Institute, Korea; Professor Chanwahn Kim, director, Institute of Indian Studies, HUFS; Professor Wooyeal Paik of the Yonsei University; Dr Jaeho Hwang and Dr Jae Jeok Park of the Hankuk University of Foreign Affairs; and Professor Wongi Choi and Professor Seonjou Kang of the Institute for Foreign Affairs and National Security (IFANS) of Korea National Diplomatic Academy (KNDA). Thanks also to Dr Hyoungmin Han, Ms ChiHyun Yun, and Ms Jungmi Lee of the Korea Institute for International Economic Policy (KIEP) for their generous support throughout the study.

A special note of thanks to Kyle Ferrier, director of Academic Affairs and Research, Korea Economic Institute of America, Washington, DC, and Daniel Wertz, program manager, National Committee on North Korea, Washington, DC, for their useful interactions on issues relating to Korean affairs.

I am eternally grateful to all the scholars who contributed chapters for this book for their commitment. I am certain that they must have encountered countless obstacles in the form of securing reliable and accurate information on various sensitive political, economic, and social issues, especially with regard to the highly politicised nature of information available on North Korea. Their sincere effort in prescribing to the theme and their timely submission deserves much appreciation.

I would also like to express my gratitude to Ms Atmaja Gohain Baruah, Ms Mrittika Guha Sarkar, Ms Nivedita Kapoor, and Mr Jyotishman Bhagawati for their research assistantship, which helped concretise this study. A special mention of Ms Mrittika and Ms Atmaja, who have contributed enormously to the preparation of this book. I am also thankful to Ms Nidhi Pant for her excellent editing work.

Above all, I thank my wife, Madhu, whose reassuring presence has always been a strength; I am indebted for her patience and continuing support.

Introduction

The Korean Peninsula and Indo-Pacific power politics:
Status security at stake

Jagannath P. Panda

Debate over the state of affairs in the Korean Peninsula has dictated the strategic spectrum of world affairs for some time now. Much of the debate has transcribed the strategic orientation of the Democratic People's Republic of Korea (DPRK) emerging as a nuclear power, the authoritarian conduct of its regime and the behavioural pattern of North Korea surviving as a relevant actor or country amidst the current international sanctions and pressures. Similarly, critical actors in the region such as the United States, China, Russia, and Japan are caught in a tightly balanced power struggle to shape the trajectory of the Korean Peninsula in order to not only exert control over the Peninsula but also hold on to their status as a critical actor in the region.

Amidst the alliance politics, the two Koreas – North and South – are entangled in a complex computation to prevent the Korean Peninsula from losing its indigenous character as a "single Korea". Hence, *reunification* of the Koreas has emerged as a dominating subject. Moreover, with North Korea at the forefront, matters pertaining to the Korean Peninsula have emerged to become as the epicentre of North-East Asia for some time. The three Ds – *denuclearisation, demand for reunification,* and *dialogue diplomacy* – have been central to many of the political discussions on the region in recent times, making it the most strategically significant hotspot of the world. Therefore, each of the actors in the region is cautiously manoeuvring a range of politics that are key to their status as a critical actor in the region. The following four sections explore the critical facets at stake in the region: namely 'nuclear security standings', 'test for the alliance management status in the region', 'the identity of Korea', and 'regime survival and the state security of North Korea'. In other words, this volume provides a broad account of the state of affairs in Korean Peninsula by reviewing the critical powers perspectives and their status in the region.

Nuclear security standings at stake

Developments in the Korean Peninsula are indispensably linked to the Indo-Pacific power politics. The reasons are quite explicit. The Korean Peninsula has emerged as a "critical nuclear zone". Out of all the members of the Six-Party Talks (which abruptly ended with the non-participation of North Korea in

2009),[1] four are nuclear powers at present, while two – South Korea and Japan – hold adequate capabilities to emerge as nuclear powers. It is no secret that South Korea possesses adequate nuclear energy resources and is a leading technology-exporting country at present.[2] Since the 1970s, Seoul has possessed nuclear capability as part of its energy strength.[3] As a national strategic priority, nuclear energy has emerged as one of the important resource facets for the Republic of Korea (ROK), even though President Moon Jae-in has pledged to phase out ROK's nuclear power gradually. Its current strength of 24 reactors enable almost one-third of the country's electricity plants.[4] Further, Seoul is currently engaged in building four nuclear reactors in the United Arab Emirates under a US$20 billion contract.[5]

Japan, however, is trying to strike a balance between seeking reliable and affordable power sources and battling the psychological aspects of the nuclear debate.[6] In recent years, the question of possessing nuclear power versus its critical consequences has dictated Japanese public consciousness and revived the debate around the three 3Es: energy security, economy, and environment.[7] The Fukushima nuclear disaster might alarm many in Japan, and the anti-nuclear sentiment might still be prevalent in the country. However, it is unreasonable for Japan to avoid nuclear energy as a resource, since it needs to import 90 per cent of its energy requirement in order to meet its economic needs.[8] The Japanese dependency on nuclear energy resources is aptly reflected in Shinzo Abe's statement that "Japan cannot do without nuclear power to secure the stability of energy supply while considering what makes economic sense and the issue of climate change".[9]

The other four nuclear actors – the United States, China, Russia, and North Korea (with its newly acquired nuclear status) – are locked in the complex computation of *denuclearisation* vis-à-vis *complete denuclearisation* of the Korean Peninsula. And even though South Korea and Japan are somewhat part of these negotiations, the debates over North Korea, its capabilities, and how to make Pyongyang denuclearise have mostly involved the two major actors, the United States and China. The proliferation linkages of North Korea beyond the region of the Korean Peninsula are not clandestine anymore, highlighting that *complete denuclearisation* of the Korean Peninsula is more complex than it appears to be. In fact, at this juncture, no debate dominates the strategic landscape in Asia as much as the issue of North Korean *denuclearisation*. The US-DPRK summits, the inter-Korean meetings, and the other actors' outreach, including China's, to North Korea in the recent past may have heightened the prospects of peace in the Korean Peninsula, but there will be plenty of tests to come as Asia's military and strategic landscape is redrawn.[10]

Undoubtedly, *denuclearisation* is a complex chapter in the history of the Korean Peninsula. As Lami Kim, in one of the chapters of this volume, argues, that the external assistance from both state and non-state actors made debates about a nuclear North Korea an international affair long ago. Further, in spite of the recent overtures, the Americans and North Koreans will continue to differ on the very process and definition of "complete" *denuclearisation*. China will continue to back North Korea for a phased denuclearised process, while Japan will continue to hold on to its stand supporting the demand of its alliance partner, the United States, for "Complete, Verifiable and Irreversible Dismantlement" (CVID). What is, however, important to note is that the current logjam in the negotiations is more in terms of the *denuclearisation of North Korea* vis-à-vis the *Korean Peninsula*, rather than the *complete* denuclearisation of North Korea.

Pyongyang has been quite vocal about the distinction between *denuclearisation of the Korean Peninsula* and *denuclearisation of North Korea*. For the Kim Jong-un administration, *complete denuclearisation of the Korean Peninsula* will apparently lead to *complete denuclearisation in North Korea*. The North Korean stance is strongly reiterated in their official statement:

> When we talk about the Korean Peninsula, it includes the territory of our republic and also the entire region of (South Korea) where the United States has placed its invasive force, including nuclear weapons. When we talk about the denuclearization of the Korean Peninsula, it means the removal of all sources of nuclear threat, not only from the South and North but also from areas neighbouring the Korean Peninsula.[11]

For North Korea, the denuclearisation of the Korean Peninsula also means a Nuclear Weapon Free Zone. In other words, the denuclearisation debate will test the stature and standing of all the major actors in the region, particularly that of the United States, China, and the two Koreas, irrespective of their competing interests, priorities, and modalities for negotiations.[12]

Further, the debate over complete denuclearisation is not entirely limited to the Korean Peninsula. North Korea's illegitimate nuclear technological nexus with countries such as Pakistan, Syria, Libya, and Iran have been a matter of international debate and scrutiny. Moreover, India's consistent efforts, as a non-critical actor, have enabled the international community to take cognisance of the nuclear technological nexus between North Korea and Pakistan, and thus provide the crucial link between North-East Asia and South Asia. More importantly, what makes the Korean Peninsula tactically significant to the Indo-Pacific security calculus is how the mixed nuclear and economic character of wider North-East Asia impacts world politics. Kent Calder and Min Ye in their book *The Making of Northeast Asia* rightly contend that the converging interests of the three major nuclear and economic actors in North-East Asia make the Korean Peninsula an "unstable pivot".[13] In other words, North-East Asia's economic significance for the United States, China, Japan, and South Korea makes this region a pivotal point of global geostrategy and a high-status volatile zone in the Indo-Pacific.

Test for the alliance management status

The Korean Peninsula is a critical alliance frontier of the Indo-Pacific. All the alliances – Sino-DPRK, US-ROK, and US-Japan – in the Korean Peninsula have constituted the core of world politics for decades. Yet, the status of each of these alliances has undergone severe tests and trials amidst the (re)balancing approaches that their respective relationships have taken in recent times.

Take the Sino-DPRK alliance, for instance. This alliance has faced a lot of international scrutiny ahead of North Korea's emergence as a nuclear power, especially with continuous missile and nuclear testing. The relevance of the historic 1961 "alliance treaty" between China and the DPRK, known as the "Treaty of Friendship, Cooperation, and Mutual Assistance", has been strongly debated, especially keeping in view that its validity is up for renewal in 2021. Formally, it would necessitate China to come to North Korea's aid in case of attacks, though Beijing had stated clearly in 2017 that this clause is only applicable if Pyongyang does not attack first or provokes the attack.[14] Speculations further abound on whether China would still like to maintain its alliance with North Korea when Pyongyang has emerged as a nuclear power.[15] It is most unlikely that China would like to abandon or make any substantial revision to the 1961 treaty in 2021. This is partly because the Chinese leaders believe that a stronger nuclear North Korea not only strengthens its alliance framework in the region but equally weakens the United States' alliances in Asia.[16] After all, North Korea's emergence as a nuclear power was only possible in the past decade with the Chinese consent, assistance, and shield that was provided to counter the mounting international pressure on Pyongyang.

Moreover, Beijing has always been Pyongyang's best ally, especially after the fall of the Soviet Union. Even with North Korea emerging as a nuclear power and the United Nations (UN) imposing sanctions on it, China continued to conduct trade – of seafood, textiles, and minerals for oil from North Korea – while also routinely condemning the nuclear tests. In fact, if Chinese reports are to be believed, their trade relations were actually improving prior to the imposition of sanctions in the latter half of 2017. It had increased by 37.4 per cent in the beginning of 2017, as compared to 2016.[17]

Further, since the Korean War that began on June 25, 1950, China has played one of the most defining roles not only in promoting alliance politics but also in leading non-Western bloc in global affairs.[18] The *Panmunjom* and *Pyongyang declarations* arising out of the inter-Korean summits in 2018 might appear to overlook the Chinese partaking in the peace process: as China's role is passingly mentioned in the Panmunjom declaration. However, it is futile to think that China, a resident power in the Korean Peninsula, and most importantly, an alliance partner of North Korea and a strong economic partner of South Korea in the region, does not have the same clouts today that it has enjoyed since the Korean War period.

Though many would argue that North Korea has become a "strategic liability" for China, Beijing would like to strengthen its ties with Pyongyang, keeping in view that the security of the Korean Peninsula is in China's interest. As a country that shares a border with North Korea, China would like to ensure that a nuclear North Korea does not cross its limit and become erratic, affecting the regional security calculus. To Beijing, North Korea's status as a nuclear power serves the Chinese calculus to check American pressure tactics. Hence, China would like to renew the China-North Korea Treaty of Friendship in 2021. Articles II and VI of the Treaty guarantee China's role as a protector of North Korea; the Treaty emphasises China's role as a key "strategic ally" and, importantly, as a peacemaker in the Peninsula. However, President Xi is also wary of the changing geopolitical scenarios and the importance of military balancing, especially with the United States. Therefore, military-to-military action that was discussed in the four US-China bilateral dialogues at Mar-a-Lago in 2017 was by and large restricted to North Korea. While talks related to trade and economics took much precedence, the urgency of denuclearising North Korea was also highlighted.[19] From the North Korean point of view, it appears that Pyongyang would not perhaps move ahead to forge any significant understanding with South Korea or with the United States by breaking away from this historic accord that it still enjoys with China.

Likewise, the US-South Korea and US-Japan partnerships, characterised often as the security alliances in North-East Asia, have faced significant challenges. These two alliances have gone through anxious moments amidst Donald Trump's bold and unpredictable approach towards both the alliance partners. The United States' withdrawal from the Trans-Pacific Partnership (TPP) and the Trump administration's demand for a cost-sharing deal with Japan and South Korea for stationing military troops in their respective territories had put in doubt the United States' military commitments in the Indo-Pacific.

In fact, despite a long-standing alliance, cracks had started to appear in the US-South Korea ties on the broad aspects of how to deal with a nuclear North Korea when both Moon Jae-in and Donald Trump were new to power in their respective countries. Also, managing China's role and interest in the Korean Peninsula seems to have emerged as big challenge in their alliance. Seoul, under Moon Jae-in, has been careful in its China policy. In fact, unlike his predecessor, Moon has always appeared to pursue a more balanced approach towards both China and the United States. Importantly, Moon has been quite consistent with his approach towards China. Although he did not reverse the decision on the deployment of the Terminal High Altitude Area Defence (THAAD) anti-missile system, Moon has been quite categorical about improving relations with China and has acknowledged Beijing's importance as resident power in North-East Asia. However, Moon's approach to China was not really seen that positively by the Trump administration.

Further, Trump's business or corporate-oriented sharing of the security mandate cost in the region has been a new challenge to this alliance. For example, South Korea has shouldered nearly 90 per cent of the US$10.8 billion cost of building the new Pyeongtaek military base, which is being built after formally ending the 73-year-old historical Yongsan Garrison base in Seoul. Even though the Pyeongtaek military base is often seen as a security insurance for the US-RoK alliance, the disagreement over its cost sharing to troops stationing, including the geographical location of the base, seems to be the differing points.[20] This development has been a part of the American Global Defence Posture Review, which is essentially a military realignment programme to offer greater flexibility to the posturing and operations of the United States Forces Korea (USFK). Though this decision to shift the military base was made in 2003, it confirms Donald Trump administration's selective and business-oriented military strategy towards its alliance partner.

Additionally, the United States and South Korea also signed a one-year "Special Measures Agreement" in February 2019, slated till December 2019, which would divide the cost of keeping the US troops there. The agreement further raised South Korea's expenses by 8 per cent to $924 million.[21] There are differences between the two countries on policies regarding concessions on North Korea and the need to launch preventive strikes. Relations between the two Koreas have deteriorated recently owing to the US-ROK military activities, and South Korea fears that launching preventive strikes can spark off a North Korean retaliation. Further, though much of the US-ROK alliance is hinged on the existential threat posed by North Korea in the region, balancing China is also crucial for the United States. South Korea, however, is impassive about holding an anti-China rhetoric. Such differences combined with Trump's repeated pressure for greater contributions have raised apprehensions in South Korea.[22]

Nonetheless, the present US administration's military approach appears to be more positive towards South Korea than Japan. With Trump coming to power in the United States, there have been doubts over the United States' commitment towards Japan's security. Japan's intention, under Prime Minister Shinzo Abe, to revisit the pacifist Constitution, including Article 9, and strengthening of its self-defence capabilities are additional factors that have contributed to these doubts. Tokyo wants to become more independent in military posturing, even though it obviously will continue to rely on the United States. A new uneasiness was noticeable in the US-Japan alliance.

It is important to note that US military assistance to South Korea is to protect US interests in North-East Asia, while to Japan it is intended more towards protecting US interests in the Indo-Pacific region. US troops on the Korean Peninsula roughly number around 28,500. This might decline or increase depending upon the understanding that the US administration has with the ROK. The US military will also like to consider this with its rotational policy. In Japan, around 40,000 troops were stationed as of the end of 2017. The Seventh Fleet of the United States is headquartered in Japan and is the largest sea force with approximately 20,000 sailors, 145 aircraft, and about 60–70 ships and submarines.[23] These large numbers have forced the Trump administration to rethink the cost-sharing mechanisms with Japan, creating distrust between the two alliance partners.

The most pressing concern for the United States now is the denuclearisation of North Korea, for which maintaining the regional stability in North-East Asia is of vital importance. With relations between Japan and South Korea becoming bitter on historical to economic issues, primarily after South Korea deciding to scrap the General Security of Military Information Agreement (GSOMIA) – an intelligence-sharing pact about North Korean missiles it has with Japan – the onus falls somewhat on the US military to facilitate this process.[24] Therefore, the United States has been emphasising on holding bilateral training activities and trilateral security trainings to strengthen the resilience of their trilateral alliance.[25] Japan and South Korea have been identified as crucial alliance partners by the United States in the Indo-Pacific, not just to deter North Korea but also to keep China and Russia in check. What these countries require now is to de-escalate tension, put forward pragmatic approaches to facilitate denuclearisation negotiations, and come up with a sustainable strategy to strengthen the alliance.

The identity of Korea is at stake

Although both of the Koreas emphasize the significance of a unified Korea, the reality trumps the aspirations by juxtapositioning two contradicting visions for a common home. More ironically, the idea of Korean unification is focussed not on the two Koreas alone but on the major stakeholders, such as the United States, China, Japan, and Russia, whose divergent perceptions towards unification has transformed the region into a hub of power politics. It is in this regard that peaceful reunification of the Korean Peninsula seems rather infeasible at the moment and a unified Korea so far has been an abstract idea only. While the two sides have committed to "reconnecting the blood relations of the nation and bring forward the future of co-prosperity and independent reunification led by Korean", the quest for unification remains marred with uncertainties and challenges.[26] Thus, while the need for unification is recognised, there is yet no consensus on the exact process to achieve it.

One of the most important causes of the unification impasse has been the two totally different perceptions of a unified Korea by Seoul and Pyongyang. While both the Koreas aspire for a unified Korea, it is unlikely that either of them would give up their respective national interests for the cause.[27] While the South is a thriving, democratic market-based economy, the North is impoverished and ruled by a bellicose communist or an authoritarian regime. However, under the circumstances of a peaceful unification of the two Koreas, where the term "unification" defines the integration of the economy, governance, as well as defence, both the Koreas would require striking a compromise by pursuing a two-way approach. In this regard, unification through this approach still seemed possible just after the "Panmunjom Declaration for Peace, Prosperity and Unification of the Korean Peninsula" in September last year, in which both the Koreas agreed to cooperate through dialogue and diplomacy.[28] However, in the purview of current developments, unification seems far-fetched as the possibility for South and North Korea to make adjustments to their democratic and *juche*[29] ideologies respectively seems diminishing. Therefore, a peaceful unification in the Korean Peninsula has not been successful so far; instead, the differences between the two Koreas have made the situation further irreconcilable.

Consequently, while peaceful unification through compromise seems unviable, unification might be considered through conflict.[30] In such a scenario, South Korea might triumph in a battle with the military assistance of the United States and take control over the Northern side, or North Korea might come out to be victorious through its growing nuclear might and possible intervention by China. However, such a scenario might lead to an occurrence of yet another Korean war, with significantly more destruction on both the sides due to the possible use of nuclear weapons, thus, defeating the purpose of unification.

A third scenario, which is often debated to be the most workable approach to achieve unification, remains the collapse of North Korean regime.[31] Kim Jong-Un's vigour to continue enhancing its nuclear powers irrespective of the UN Security Council (UNSC) economic sanctions has been leading the fate of North Korea towards more sanctions, and hence a blow is expected to an already impoverished economy.[32] Further, Kim's undemocratic executions of not just the commoners but also many high-rank officials and elites have resulted in the waning of Kim's regime popularity.[33] In this regard, a regime collapse might expedite the unification negotiation process and result in a South Korea-led governance in the region. However, while some experts argue that North Korean regime's collapse can lead the way, it is likely to upset most North Korean elites as it would not be sustainable in the long run.[34] Moreover, while the United States might readily support a South Korea-led government in Korea, China, the strongest ally for North Korea, might intervene and even condemn such a move or act.

Moreover, while the negotiation for unification of the two Koreas is still caught in stalemate, the South and the North Koreas are not the only players. It is imperative to understand that unification of the two Koreas cannot be achieved in vacuum and the participation of the stakeholders has become equally significant. In this case, the United States would prefer a South Korean democratic model of governance in the Korean Peninsula, which would not just enhance its market outreach and strategic footprint in the region but also transform the Peninsula as a buffer zone to balance China.[35] China, on the other hand, though it officially supports the Korean unification, approaches the issue through uncertainty. China essentially supports a "Two Korea" policy, acknowledging that a unified Korea might have far more political, economic, and strategic threats.[36] Most importantly, a unified Korea might have the potentials to undermine China's influence in the region and prevent the latter from realizing its "Chinese Dream". In similar context, the positions of Japan and Russia too deserve scrutiny as none of the stakeholders would be willing to forgo their respective vested interests to ensure the Korean Unification.

Thus, divergent perceptions and major power plays in the region have exacerbated the already convoluted unification scenario in the Korean Peninsula. What is, however, being compromised within this whole scheme of negotiation is the indigenous character of "Korea" – the identity of Korea is compromised amidst major power politics and their vested interests. Korean reunification will have repercussions far beyond its geographical vicinity, but more so for its immediate and more powerful neighbours – China and Japan. In view of the European Union (EU) experience, building trust and a credible institutional arrangement would be more successful than forceful reunification.

Regime survival to state security at stake

For North Korea, regime survival has been one of the more pressing matters in recent times, compared to denuclearisation and alliance management in the Korean Peninsula. Much has been written on the future of the Kim Jong-un regime. The international perception of the North Korean regime has persistently become stronger – a "hermit kingdom"[37] or a "rogue state"[38] that generally prefers possessing nuclear weapons to feeding its population. Even in the face of global condemnation, North Korea has not seemed to comply and is, in fact, engaging in more provocative behaviour. Such behaviour by Pyongyang has led to multidimensional challenges in the region, from the deadlock on denuclearisation to the destabilisation of the region. In such a complex context, a systematic deconstruction of North Korean state's behaviour or its regime's bellicose attitude, from its military-first strategy to the self-reliance ideology to parallel development of military and economic growth strategy, has become a strategic necessity.

Besides, the international standpoint of achieving peace and stability in the Korean Peninsula begins with the denuclearisation of North Korea, to which Kim Jong-un has defiantly retorted that the world must discuss the denuclearisation of the Korean Peninsula as a whole. For North Korea, having a nuclear umbrella is what is going to ensure regime survival, mainly with a hostile United States at its tail.[39] Kim Jong-un can be said to be pursuing the grand strategy of military and economic development concurrently.[40] He has repeatedly focussed on how the Middle East has become a "victim of aggression" due to the absence of "powerful self-defence capabilities".[41] In Kim's contestation, therefore, in order to understand and facilitate discussions on denuclearisation, his regime's actions should not be considered irrational and erratic. Rather, in Kim's perception, his country should be treated as a rational actor, seeking to leverage diplomacy through Intercontinental Ballistic Missile (ICBM) capabilities.

As mentioned earlier, North Korea essentially identifies the Korean Peninsula with not just the two Koreas but also the surrounding areas where the external actors have substantial physical presence. It implies that North Korea's decision to denuclearise depends on the withdrawal of the United States' extended military services from the region, which are a part of the US nuclear umbrella that covers its regional allies.[42] Such a stance has not gone down well with the US administration. There is a long-standing mistrust between the United States and the North Korean regime – Washington has been insisting that Pyongyang relinquish all weapons of mass destruction (WMD) following a maximum-pressure strategy or engagement; on the other hand, Pyongyang has been striving to obtain security assurances while insisting on giving up its weapons in a gradual manner.[43]

While both Washington and Pyongyang seek continued negotiations, their deliberations have not shown enough flexibility, which is reflective of their inability to arrive at a common diplomatic understanding. There is also much certitude regarding the connotations of the "security guarantees" that Kim is demanding.[44] For the United States, North Korea's continued military provocations and repeated violations of the UNSC resolutions have made it into a capricious state which cannot be trusted with security guarantees until it is completely denuclearised. For North Korea, on the other hand, US policies are not very credible – it has already withdrawn from Afghanistan, the Iran nuclear deal, the TPP, and the Paris Climate Agreement. So, North Korea is aware that denuclearising without attaining certain tangible security guarantees might allow the regime to collapse or the state of North Korea to fall at the mercy of other major powers.

The *dialogue diplomacy* in the region, mainly the Trump-Kim summits and the inter-Korean summits, so far has been more of a spectacle rather than carrying much substance, though it certainly demonstrates progress towards rapprochement. In the absence of a credible multilateral security institution that could address the security impediments in the Korean Peninsula, it is difficult to have any real negotiations. Advancing any scope of cooperation will surely involve navigating between the growing interdependencies between countries, which has been by far quite asymmetrical. North Korea holds much less economic weight than any of the other negotiating partners but holds somewhat more sway in international nuclear talks. Moreover, all of these negotiating partners have vested interests in dealing with North Korea. Therefore, conflict resolution in North Korea should involve surpassing these individual differences; fostering mutual interests; and, most importantly, being willing to compromise.

What is important to note is that actors in the region are yet to find common ground on the North Korean impasse. This could be because the dynamics North Korea shares with its negotiating partners is hinged on various historical and domestic constraints. The economic and geopolitical influence of China on the Korean Peninsula is already very high. All the while, China's top priority has been to prevent the region from destabilising, which would invariably also have a spillover effect on China's neighbouring region.[45] As Pyongyang's military alliance partner, Beijing foresees many opportunities in advancing cooperation, though it has not been very persuasive in helping North Korea denuclearise.

Russia, too, has been advocating "security guarantees for North Korea", though it is vague about what constitutes such propositions.[46] Further, despite the call for cooperation and unification, the relationship between the two Koreas at present is in a limbo. North Korea's ICBM launches have worsened the situation. For Kim, South Korea should do away with the THAAD and other joint military exercises with the United States and engage more in coming up with a constructive road map for rapprochement.[47] For South Korea, denuclearisation is the key priority – the issue of unification comes somewhat later. While Moon Jae-in hopes for unification by 2045, there is very little enthusiasm among the general population for a united Korea.[48] Moreover, addressing the issues related to the UNSC sanctions resolutions against North Korea, its ICBM manufacturing capacity and its human rights violations take precedence for South Korea.

Just because the North Korean regime has survived for so long does not mean its survival in the coming years is ensured. Kim Jung-un, being a rational man, understands that his policies are not sustainable in the long run – they will and already have crippled the economy. While in the past, fanatic Korean nationalism and various forms of repression brought some economic aid, treading along the same route will lead to a systemic crisis. Instead, what multilateral institutions and the international community should strive for is not just denuclearising North Korea but assisting it in the transformation of its decaying economy. If and when North Korea opens to the outside world, the global economy should be receptive enough to accommodate its economic and social change. This receptivity may, in future, help to reunify the Korean Peninsula, achieve peace and stability in the region, and lift the current atmosphere of threat facing North-East Asia.

The book at hand

This volume addresses the strategic linkages that the Korean Peninsula shares with the Indo-Pacific and provides a succinct picture of the critical issues that will shape the trajectory of the Korean Peninsula in times to come. It brings together trained scholars, journalists, and ex-diplomats with substantial policy experiences. Besides, this volume draws on primary sources of materials, particularly language sources, and field experiences, which makes it an invaluable resource for researchers, graduate students, scholars, and policy makers.

This book is divided into three sections. The first section, "Critical Perspectives", talks about the role of critical actors in Korean Peninsula, highlighting their distinct, and often divergent, views on denuclearisation as well as national reunification. In Chapter 1, Donald Kirk argues that the US strategy on the Korean Peninsula rests on the principle of the status quo and is aimed to preserve the historic alliance between the United States and the ROK. The author explores the United States' shifting policy on the two Koreas in the last few years and wonders if Trump, first by threatening North Korea and then by pursuing a diplomatic tack, might be getting somewhere. He observes that the lingering threat is that the United States' patience is wearing thin as North Korea is avoiding "complete denuclearisation", as promised in the Singapore summit, and that the absolutist CVID no longer dominates the conversation post the summit.

Anurag Viswanath, in Chapter 2, discusses the "great game" that has transformed North-East Asia into a geo-spot riven with politics and polarisation, cooperation and contestation, manoeuvres and maritime disputes, triumvirates and tensions – a mass of entangled relationships that has made it one of the most volatile regions in the world. She argues that China was, is, and shall remain a critical player in the region. However, China has to balance its old responsibilities as a socialist power and new global responsibilities as the second most important power, keeping in view its economic, political, and strategic interests. She contends that the future road map for the region seems elusive because of the divergent interests of all the stakeholders.

In Chapter 3, Kohtaro Ito argues that the confrontation between Japan and China in the Senkaku Islands after the 2000s and the continued military provocations by North Korea have increased the threat perception for Japan.

As a response, Japan has not only fostered military relations with the US and Australian forces but also strengthened formerly weak military relations with other countries, such as Britain, Canada, and France. The author contends that Japan's Korean Peninsula strategy will function as a deterrent for not only North Korea but also China. However, what Japan fears is that the reduction or withdrawal of the USFK will be decided by the United States alone or between the United States and South Korea. In Chapter 4, Georgy Bulychev and Valeriia Gorbacheva argue that Russia's relationship with North Korea has experienced quite a few highs and lows in the three post-Soviet decades, in keeping with the policy changes. The authors trace the Russia-North Korea relations from 1991 until present times, through seven phases, discussing the prospects of cooperation and the challenges therein.

The second section of the volume, "Contending Perspectives", talks about how the critical yet contradictory approaches of the important actors have resulted in a power rivalry in the Korean Peninsula. In Chapter 5, Jina Kim explains that the dialogue on denuclearisation, which started as a bilateral issue between the United States and North Korea, has now transformed into a multi-party negotiation. The chapter also asserts that achieving consensus on a denuclearisation road map is impossible because political, technological, and diplomatic issues must be considered together. Nonetheless, it argues that facilitating mutual exchange and cooperation is one of the ways to incentivise North Korea and that maintaining a sustainable peace environment when North Korea renounces its nuclear arsenals requires a holistic approach and institutionalised practices within an agreed framework.

In Chapter 6, Kuyoun Chung argues that the strategic environment in the Indo-Pacific will evolve dramatically over the course of North Korea's denuclearisation. The author also asserts that any endgame of the denuclearisation on the Korean Peninsula is expected to shift the strategic interests of regional powers in the Indo-Pacific, influencing not only regional strategic stability but also the extended deterrence that has long sustained the US strategic dominance in the region. Therefore, it is necessary to discuss the strategic aspects of current denuclearisation negotiations and how they will interact with the Sino-US strategic competition that will define security environment in a foreseeable future.

In Chapter 7, Lami Kim illustrates how foreign assistance has so far aided the DPRK's development of nuclear and missile capabilities, as well as its rise as a proliferator. The author then discusses, from a global non-proliferation perspective, the implications of the success and failure of ongoing denuclearisation negotiations. In Chapter 8, Archana Upadhyay discusses the fast-changing global strategic environment that requires Russia to reset ties with the two Koreas, keeping in mind the far-reaching historical trajectory. The author analyses how the "Korea factor" in Russia's foreign policy strategy is crucial for its North-East Asia outreach and overall stability.

The remaining two chapters in this section analyses two non-critical – Mongolian and Indian – perspectives. In Chapter 9, Alicia Campi argues that Mongolia's multifaceted ties to the DPRK, which stem from its present non-threatening status and communist-era commonalities, can be useful in the Korean Peninsula peace process. She also discusses how Mongolia is uniquely placed to not only play the role of a mediator in the North-South Korean dispute, by being an active force in the North-East Asian peace process, but also create new mechanisms that contribute to regional connectivity. In Chapter 10 – the last chapter of the second section – Jagannath P. Panda and Mrittika Guha Sarkar assess India's approach to the Korean Peninsula keeping in view the current developments in the Indo-Pacific. They argue that India's dialogue and diplomacy approach is responsible for its enhanced partnership with South Korea and sustained diplomatic relations with North Korea. This very approach, they reason, is key to India being seen as a prospective facilitator or mediator to promote peace in the Korean Peninsula.

The last section of the book, "Competing and Cooperating Perspectives", discusses power politics in the Korean Peninsula, analysing the critical undercurrents that shape the competing and cooperative perspectives of the Korean Peninsula vis-à-vis Indo-Pacific. In Chapter 11, Jin Shin argues that the divergent political systems of the two Koreas will have serious implications for the global political order. The author further throws light on Kim's governing philosophy and strategies, as well as his undermined status in North Korea, and looks at the future trajectory of the country's nuclear policy and how it determines Korean unification.

In Chapter 12, Manpreet Sethi briefly traces the evolution of the various negotiating mechanisms in order to understand what has worked in the past and could be used again to make it work in the future. The chapter also provides an overview of the limited achievements of the negotiating mechanisms at different points of time. It concludes by drawing some inferences from these negotiating mechanisms in the Korean Peninsula for the situation in the Indo-Pacific. In Chapter 13, Seoujou Kang explores how the US Indo-Pacific Strategy, starting as geopolitics, is transforming itself into a geo-economics construct in the face of rising China. The author also compares the two competing economic architectures, led by the United States and China, in the Indo-Pacific region and analyses their effects on the region as a whole, and South Korea in particular.

Finally, in Chapter 14, Atmaja Gohain Baruah argues that North-East Asia is in a critical space in international politics, where resource competition and geostrategic rivalry between the neighbouring countries have stirred more conflict than cooperation. The chapter addresses three areas of growing resource insecurity: namely environmental concerns, maritime disputes, and energy security. The author contends that while resource insecurity has intensified economic and political rivalry between some of Asia's key economic powers, it has also created the conditions that encourage cooperation. However, the absence of cooperating mechanisms and political motivation is a challenge. Therefore, identifying areas for resource cooperation between these countries will not only achieve energy security and reduce regional tension but also encourage environmentally sustainable policies.

Overall, this volume addresses the critical facets of Korean Peninsula and its undercurrents that will continue to shape the future of the region. Given the

14 *Jagannath P. Panda*

fluidity of the politics in the region, the assessment made in this volume are certainly not constant. Yet, it goes without stating that the assessments made in this volume offer critical judgements on the future directive of the region that will certainly be a referring point for readers, especially policy makers and scholars.

Notes

1 Choe Sang-Hun, "N. Korea Threatens to Restore Plutonium Plant," *The New York Times*, August 28, 2008, at www.nytimes.com/2008/08/27/world/asia/27korea.html?mtrref=www.armscontrol.org&gwh=07D1FF3EC721DF83892F219C9C8DF07C&gwt=pay&assetType=PAYWALL. (accessed on September 24, 2019); "Statement by the President of the Security Council," United Nations Security Council, April 13, 2009, at www.un.org/en/ga/search/view_doc.asp?symbol=S/PRST/2009/7 (accessed on September 24, 2009).
2 "Nuclear Power in South Korea", World Nuclear Association, September 2019, at www.world-nuclear.org/information-library/country-profiles/countries-o-s/south-korea.aspx (accessed September 15, 2019).
3 Jack Unwin, "Nuclear Power in South Korea: Past, Present, Future", *Power Technology*, August 1, 2019, at www.power-technology.com/features/south-korea-nuclear-power/ (accessed September 15, 2019).
4 "Nuclear Power in South Korea", No. 2.
5 Ibid.
6 Rowan Hoopar, "Psychology Is Where Real Radiation Risks Lie", *The Japan Times*, August 15, 2015, at www.japantimes.co.jp/news/2015/08/15/national/science-health/psychology-real-radiation-risks-lie/#.XYrAIi2B3fY (accessed on September 25, 2019); "Nuclear Power in Japan", World Nuclear Association, September 2019, at www.world-nuclear.org/information-library/country-profiles/countries-g-n/japan-nuclear-power.aspx (accessed September 15, 2019).
7 Sumiko Takeuchi, "Is There a Future of Nuclear Power in Japan?" *The Japan Times*, July 16, 2019, at www.japantimes.co.jp/news/2019/07/16/business/future-nuclear-power-japan/#.XX2zUS2B3fY (accessed September 15, 2019).
8 "Nuclear Power in Japan", No. 6.
9 "Shinzo Abe Says Japan 'Cannot Do Without' Nuclear Power, on Eve of Fukushima Disaster", *South China Morning Post*, March 10, 2016, at www.scmp.com/news/asia/east-asia/article/1922953/shinzo-abe-says-japan-cannot-do-without-nuclear-power-eve (accessed on September 15, 2019).
10 Read, Jagannath Panda, "What Would a Denuclearized North Korea Mean for the Balance of Military Power in Asia?" *Independent*, June 17, 2018, at www.independent.co.uk/voices/north-korea-nuclear-kim-trump-summit-asia-power-balance-china-india-a8403356.html (accessed September 15, 2019).
11 "US Envoy Optimistic About N. Korea Despite Latest Friction", Press Trust of India, December 21, 2018, at www.ptinews.com/news/10259807_US-envoy-optimistic-about-N-Korea-despite-latest-friction (accessed September 15, 2019).
12 Duyeon Kim, "Negotiating Toward a Denuclearization- Peace Roadmap on the Korean Peninsula", *Centre for New American Security*, June 27, 2019, at www.cnas.org/publications/reports/negotiating-toward-a-denuclearization-peace-roadmap-on-the-korean-peninsula (accessed September 15, 2019).
13 Kent Calder and Min Ye, "Northeast Asia in Global Perspective", in *The Making of Northeast Asia*, Stanford University Press, Stanford, 2010, p. 3.
14 Glyn Ford, *Talking to North Korea*, Pluto Press, London, 2018, p. 250.
15 Anny Boc, "Does China's 'Alliance Treaty' with North Korea Still Matter?", *The Diplomat*, July 26, 2019, at https://thediplomat.com/2019/07/does-chinas-alliance-treaty-with-north-korea-still-matter/ (accessed September 15, 2019).

16 Gilbert Rozman (ed.), "Introduction", in *The East Asian Whirlpool: Kim Jong-Un's Diplomatic Shake-Up, China's Sharp Power, and Trump's Trade Wars, Joint U.S.-Korea Academic Studies*, Vol. 30, Korea Economic Institute of America, Washington, 2019, p. 7.

17 Jane Perlez and Yufan Huang, "China Says Its Trade with North Korea Has Increased", *The New York Times*, April 13, 2017, at www.nytimes.com/2017/04/13/world/asia/china-north-korea-trade-coal-nuclear.html (accessed September 15, 2019).

18 This section draws on, Jagannath Panda, "Chinese Revisionism in the Korean Corridor", *The Asian Age*, May 13, 2018, at www.asianage.com/360-degree/130518/chinese-revisionism-in-korean-corridor.html (accessed September 15, 2019).

19 Glyn Ford, No. 14, p. 251.

20 Shifting from its earlier approach, US is utilizing a selective approach keeping its military and strategic interests ahead of anything else under its 'America First' policy. The new Pyeongtaek base by US signals the same. However, this development has built a few disagreements between US and ROK. The US, through this approach is establishing a 'sharing' model of security mandate; however South Korea covering 90 per cent of the cost of the base has ensured some feuds in the US-ROK alliance, irrespective of the base being a strategic deterrent against China and North Korea. Please see, Jagannath P. Panda, "Pyeongtaek Expounds 'Corporate' Military Strategy," *Korean Herald*, July 3, 2018, at www.koreaherald.com/view.php?ud=20180703000543 (accessed on September 26, 2019).

21 The new "Special Measures Agreement" between ROK and US focusses on Seoul's contributions to hosting of the American troops after several strained negotiations. This step was taken in relation to the US president Trump's universal desire for allies to pay a greater amount for their defence. In this regard, the Trump administration proposed a 50 per cent increase in the 40 per cent of the amount paid by the Korean side to host American troops in 2018. The negotiation came down to 16 per cent increase in January this year, however not accepted by ROK. The negotiations were finally agreed upon at an 8 per cent increase just before the Trump-Kim meet in Hanoi this year, worth $924 million but with a condition for renegotiation every year by the Trump administration. These developments considerably put the US-ROK partnership into the shadow of a doubt. Please see Kyle Ferrier, "What Does the Signed Cost Sharing Agreement Mean for the US-South Korea Alliance?" *The Diplomat*, February 15, 2019, at https://thediplomat.com/2019/02/what-does-the-signed-cost-sharing-agreement-mean-for-the-us-south-korea-alliance/ (accessed on September 24, 2019).

22 Mark E. Manyin et al., "South Korea: Background and U.S. Relations", Congressional Research Service, 2019, at https://fas.org/sgp/crs/row/IF10165.pdf (accessed September 15, 2019).

23 "What Is the US Military's Presence Near North Korea?", *The Guardian*, August 9, 2017, at www.theguardian.com/us-news/2017/aug/09/what-is-the-us-militarys-presence-in-south-east-asia (accessed on September 24, 2019).

24 Justin McCurry," South Korea Cuts Intelligence Ties with Japan, Raising Fears over North Korea", *The Guardian*, August 23, 2019, at www.theguardian.com/world/2019/aug/23/south-korea-cuts-intelligence-ties-with-japan-raising-fears-over-north-korea (accessed September 15, 2019).

25 Randall Schriver, "The Importance of U.S.-Japan-Korea Trilateral Defense Cooperation", Transcripts from Center for Strategic and International Studies, at https://csis-prod.s3.amazonaws.com/s3fs-public/publication/190828_importance_us_japan_korea.pdf (accessed September 15, 2019).

26 "Panmunjom Declaration for Peace, Prosperity and Unification of the Korean Peninsula," Ministry of Foreign Affairs, Republic of Korea, September 11, 2018, at www.mofa.go.kr/eng/brd/m_5478/view.do?seq=319130 (accessed on September 24, 2019).

27 Bruce W. Benette, "Potential Paths to Korean Unification," *RAND Corporation*, November 14, 2018, at www.rand.org/multimedia/audio/2018/11/14/potential-paths-to-korean-unification.html (accessed on September 24, 2019).

28 Ministry of Foreign Affairs, Republic of Korea, No. 26.
29 Juche is North Korea's official philosophy, which roughly translates into "self-sufficiency", "independence", and "autonomy". Juche defines the ideology of the communist country which believes that North Korea as a power should remain separate from the rest of the international community, depending solely on the strength of its own and its god-like leader. Please see Zack Beauchamp, "Juche, the State Ideology that Makes North Koreans Revere Kim Jong Un, Explained," *Vox*, June 18, 2018, at www.vox.com/world/2018/6/18/17441296/north-korea-propaganda-ideology-juche (accessed on September 24, 2018).
30 Chung Min Lee and Kathryn Botto, "Reconceptualizing U.S.-ROK Cooperation in Korean Unification: A Stabilization Framework," *Carnegie Endowment for International Peace*, April 30, 2019, at https://carnegieendowment.org/2019/04/30/reconceptualizing-u.s.-rok-cooperation-in-korean-unification-stabilization-framework-pub-78737 (accessed on September 24, 2019); Bruce W. Benette, No. 27.
31 Quanyi Zhang, "Wide-Ranging Views on Korean Unification," *International Journal of World Peace*, 33 (3), 2016, pp. 76–77.
32 "North Korea's Kim Jong-un Oversaw Test of 'Super Large Multiple Rocket Launcher", *The Guardian*, August 25, 2019, at www.google.com/search?q=kim+tests+missile&rlz=1C5CHFA_enIN852IN852&oq=kim+tests+missile&aqs=chrome.69i57.8529j0j4&sourceid=chrome&ie=UTF-8 (accessed on September 24, 2019).
33 "Whispers of Dissent in North Korea Suggest Waning Loyalty to Kim Jong-un," *The Guardian*, June 4, 2015, www.theguardian.com/world/2015/jun/04/north-korea-kim-jong-un-popularity-waning (accessed on September 24, 2019).
34 Bruce W. Bennett, "Preparing North Korean Elites for Unification", *RAND Corporation*, 2017, at www.rand.org/pubs/research_reports/RR1985.html (accessed September 15, 2019).
35 Evans J. R. Revere, "Korean Reunification and US Interests: Preparing for One Korea," Brookings, January 20, 2015, at www.brookings.edu/on-the-record/korean-reunification-and-u-s-interests-preparing-for-one-korea/ (accessed on September 24, 2019).
36 Sukjoon Yoon, "China's Changing Role on the Korean Peninsula," *The Diplomat*, May 31, 2019, at https://thediplomat.com/2019/05/chinas-changing-role-on-the-korean-peninsula/ (accessed on September 24, 2019); Eleanor Albert, "The China-North Korea Relationship," Council on Foreign Relations, June 25, 2019, at www.cfr.org/backgrounder/china-north-korea-relationship (accessed on September 24, 2019); Please read Chae-Jin Lee and Stephanie Hsieh, "China's Two-Korea Policy at Trial: The Hwang Chang Yop Crisis," *Pacific Affairs*, 75 (3), 2001, pp. 321–341.
37 The term "Hermit Kingdom" has increasingly been used in the context of North Korea. A "hermit kingdom" usually implies that a country or a regime willingly tries to wall itself off, by maintaining a communication distance from the rest of the globe, physically or metaphorically. North Korean regime's behaviour has more or less replicated such a case, inviting many observers to allude to it as a "Hermit Kingdom". Read, Wilson Strand, "Opening the Hermit Kingdom", *History Today*, 54 (1), January 2004, at www.historytoday.com/archive/opening-hermit-kingdom (accessed September 15, 2019).
  Some others defy this by stating that it is a myth to call North Korea a "Hermit Kingdom". Read, Joel S. Wit and Jenny Town, "It's Not a Hermit Kingdom, and 4 Other Myths About North Korea", *The Atlantic*, March 29, 2013, at www.theatlantic.com/international/archive/2013/03/its-not-a-hermit-kingdom-and-4-other-myths-about-north-korea/274488/ (accessed September 15, 2019).
38 Many in the West, mainly in the United States, have called North Korea a "rogue state", to which the Kim Jong-un administration has reacted time and again, stating

that the United States wants to overthrow the regime in the DPRK by calling it a "rogue state". Read, Patrick Goodenough, "North Korea Bristles at Being Called a 'Rough State'", cnsnews.com, June 7, 2019, at www.cnsnews.com/news/article/patrick-goodenough/north-korea-bristles-being-called-rogue-state (accessed September 15, 2019); Kirk Spitzer, "5 Reasons North Korea Is a 'Rough Regime'", *USA Today*, January 6, 2016, at www.usatoday.com/story/news/world/2016/01/06/5-ways-north-korea-rogue-regime/78349910/ (accessed September 15, 2019).
39 Glyn Ford, No. 14, p. 7.
40 David W. Shin, *Rationality in the North Korean Regime*, Lexington Books, Maryland, 2018, p. 17.
41 Ibid., p. 271.
42 Bruce Klingner, "Would a U.S. Security Guarantee Achieve Guaranteed North Korean Denuclearization?" *The National Interest*, September 3, 2019, at https://nationalinterest.org/blog/korea-watch/would-us-security-guarantee-achieve-guaranteed-north-korean-denuclearization-77716 (accessed September 11, 2019).
43 Read, Benjamin Katzeff Silberstein, "The North Korean Economy and U.S. Policy: Stability Under 'Maximum Pressure'", in Gilbert Rozman (ed.), No. 16, pp. 276–303.
44 "North Korea's Kim Told Other Leaders He Seeks Security Guarantees Instead of Sanctions Relief: Sources", *The Japan Times*, July 13, 2019, at www.japantimes.co.jp/news/2019/07/13/asia-pacific/north-koreas-kim-told-leaders-seeks-security-guarantees-instead-sanctions-relief-sources/#.XX5H_y2B3fY (accessed September 15, 2019).
45 Thomas Fingar, "China's Growing Presence in the DPRK: Origins, Objectives and Implications", in Choe Sang-hun, Gi-Wook Shin, and David Straub (eds.), *Troubled Transition: North Korea's Politics, Economy, and External Relations*, The Walter H. Shorenstein Asia-Pacific Research, Stanford, 2013, p. 197.
46 Patrick M. Cronin and Ryan Neuhard, "Guaranteeing Peace with North Korea", *The Diplomat*, August 22, 2019, at https://thediplomat.com/2019/08/guaranteeing-peace-with-north-korea/ (accessed September 11, 2019).
47 Glyn Ford, No. 14, p. 218.
48 Ibid., p. 245.

Part I
Critical perspectives

1 America's conflicted strategy for the Korean Peninsula

From "fire and fury" to "denuclearisation"

Donald Kirk

Crossroads

In an era in which the future of both Koreas, and North-East Asia, hung in the balance, US policy on the Korean Peninsula at the outset of the presidency of Donald Trump seemed confused, uncertain, and dangerously ambivalent. Some of America's most knowledgeable, influential, and powerful officials were at odds with Trump over his unpredictable decisions. They also battled one another over what policies to pursue and feared for the future of US relations with North and South Korea as well as with other countries in the region, the rest of Asia, and the world.

America's shifting policy on Korea during the Trump administration ranged from threats and counter-threats to summits and deal making, inspiring moods and responses from roseate optimism to deep scepticism relating to the near, mid-, and distant future of the Korean Peninsula. From hovering on what seemed to be the brink of war in 2017, the year in which Trump threatened to unleash "fire and fury" on North Korea and referred to North Korea's Leader Kim Jong-un as "rocket man", the two Koreas in 2018 veered towards rapprochement and dialogue on a scale never witnessed since the division of the Peninsula between the Soviet-backed North and the Americanised South on either side of the 38th parallel after the Japanese surrender on August 15, 1945.[1]

To superficial appearances, the process reached what was widely described as "a historic milestone" on June 30, 2019, when Trump and Kim staged their third meeting – this time in the dramatic setting of the heavily fortified Demilitarised Zone (DMZ) between North and South Korea. In an atmosphere of mounting excitement, Trump clapped Kim on the shoulder as they shook hands on the North-South line. The greetings between them seemed portentous, laden with hope that this time, perhaps, the yearning for reconciliation would survive recriminations and intimidation.

"Nobody had expected this moment", said Trump. "It's significant", said Kim, talking in Korean, an interpreter at his side. "We want to bring an end to this unpleasant past and create a new future". It was not just that Trump met Kim in the truce village of Panmunjom, or for a few seconds stepped across the line into

North Korea, then made his way with Kim through besieging cameramen and security people on the southern side to Freedom House. There was no denying the whole occasion was "a very historic moment", as Trump proclaimed before he and Kim settled down behind closed doors for 50 minutes of serious talking.[2]

Trump emerged from that conversation, away from the pervasive cameras and microphones of the media, saying that he and Kim had "agreed to have teams set up" to return to talks that had simply not been happening since their disastrous second summit in Hanoi on February 28, 2019. However, if the two said a word about "denuclearisation", as promised during their first summit in Singapore the previous June, neither talked about it publicly. There was no mention of US demands for shutting down the North's main nuclear complex at Yongbyon 60 miles north of Pyongyang or for a full accounting of where the North was hiding other facilities for making nuclear weapons and missiles. Nor, apparently, was anything said about lesser issues, including return of more remains of those missing in action from the Korean War.

Nonetheless, by his own account of what he called "a very productive meeting", Trump "outlined the tremendous prosperity" that would befall North Korea "when this whole thing gets settled". In other words, if Kim would just get rid of his warheads and missiles, he could be sure of massive rewards for an economy hobbled by sanctions imposed after missile-and-nuclear tests last staged in 2017. The hope was that the economic bait would outweigh Kim's perceived need for a nuclear programme for defence against enemies, notably the United States.

A day after the president had tweeted the idea of seeing Kim while in South Korea meeting Moon, the burst of publicity surrounding the occasion at the DMZ enabled him yet again to lay claim to have come up with the solution to North Korea. "When I came into office, it was a fiery mess", he said. "Nothing was happening. In two and a half years we have had peace". In fact, he declared, standing beside South Korea's president Moon Jae-in before they flew up to the DMZ between the two Koreas for the meeting with Kim, that if Barack Obama had remained as president, "we would have been at war with North Korea".[3]

Trump was at pains, before and after seeing Kim at the DMZ, to defend the record of his previous two summits with Kim, in Singapore on June 12, 2018, and in Hanoi on February 28, 2019, even though the North Koreans had done nothing to get rid of their nuclear programme – and were assumed to have added several warheads to the 60 or so they were believed to have fabricated up to the Singapore summit. Standing with an American army officer at Observation Post Ouellette below the North-South line, he said, "You have 35 million people within range of their weapons". He did not say, of course, that hundreds of North Korean artillery pieces remained in place above the DMZ – not a topic of consideration in demands for the North to get rid of its weapons of mass destruction, biological, chemical, and nuclear.

The meeting at the DMZ, if nothing else, offered respite from the mood generated on the last day of February 2019 when Trump, in Hanoi, announced the failure of his second summit with Kim. "We'll end up being very good friends", he said after breaking off the conversation, but the fact was that the talks had come to a halt after it had become obvious that both sides were getting nowhere with their basic demands.[4] The Hanoi meltdown came as a shock after predictions that the two would surely issue a statement, however meaningless, pledging cooperation beyond the vague commitment to "denuclearisation" that each of them had signed after their first summit in Singapore the previous June. The most that Trump could take away before walking out of the meeting in Hanoi's historic Metropole Hotel was an impression – not a guarantee – that Kim would not test nuclear warheads and long-range missiles as previously conducted in 2017.

The Hanoi summit failed over the basic issue of sanctions versus denuclearisation. Kim demanded an end to most of the sanctions imposed by the United States and United Nations (UN) after those tests, while Trump refused to budge without a firm agreement that North Korea would actually close down its nuclear programme. Trump put on the table the US call for closure of the North's central nuclear site at Yongbyon, 100 kilometres north of Pyongyang, and surrender of the North's nuclear weapons, probably a few dozen. He also wanted a list of other sites in North Korea where engineers and technicians had been fabricating or testing warheads and missiles.

"To me it's pretty obvious, they have to denuclearise", Trump said at a press conference.[5] Maybe so, but Kim's father, Kim Jong-il, who died in December 2011, had rejected the South Korean offer of massive aid in return for denuclearisation.

Unlike his father, however, Kim Jong-un had indeed given the impression that he had given up his nuclear ambitions and was ready to talk. In his New Year's speech in early 2018, he announced he was basically done with testing nuclear warheads and missiles and would henceforth focus on the economy. Next, he agreed that North Korea would send athletes to the Winter Olympic Games to be held in Pyeongchang, nestled in the mountains in the South Korean portion of Kangwon Province, divided at the 38th parallel in 1945 and then again in the Korean War that ended with American and South Korean forces wresting still more of the province from the North. Finally, Kim made the grand gesture of sending his younger sister, Kim Yo-jong, to the Olympics, where she concluded her stay by presenting South Korea's president Moon Jae-in with a letter from Kim inviting Moon to the first summit held between North and South Korean Leaders since October 2007 when Moon had gone to Pyongyang as chief of staff to the late South Korean President Roh Moo-hyun's summit with Kim's father, Kim Jong-il.[6]

The United States seemed unsure how to respond. There was no way that Trump or any member of his administration could appear to be less than supportive of the obvious desire of President Moon to open up a wide range of contacts and relationships with the North. The Pyeongchang Olympics would mark an important step, but Trump's advisers and aides were far from certain how to behave. Vice President Mike Pence and his wife had seats in front of Kim's sister in the VIP reviewing box for the opening ceremony, but Pence avoided looking at her, much less shaking hands with her. Nor did he applaud as North Korean athletes walked with South Koreans in the opening parade on the field below – many North Koreans carrying the North Korean flag while athletes from both Koreas held aloft the unification flag featuring all Korea in blue on a white field.[7]

The succession of events undermined two of the most often heard clichés – one of them just an expression, the other a long-standing policy. The cliché – often uttered by Trump's defence secretary Jim Mattis and his secretaries of state, first Rex Tillerson and then his successor, Mike Pompeo – was that US and South Korean relations were so tight, "There's no daylight between us". The message was that the Americans and South Koreans agreed on everything, especially the second cliché, a long-standing policy position, "Complete, Verifiable and Irreversible Dismantlement" (CVID) of the North's nuclear programme, including all its nuclear warheads and long-range Intercontinental Ballistic Missiles (ICBMs). It was to maintain the military alliance between the two countries that the Americans professed to support Moon's efforts relating to inter-Korea relations, viewing them as not necessarily harmful or contrary to the alliance.

In that spirit, the Americans made a show of accepting just about anything Moon wanted in terms of reconciling with the North. They applauded the summit between Moon and Kim at Panmunjom on April 27, 2018, hailing the outcome as an important step en route to reconciliation. At the same time, they argued for persisting with the sanctions imposed by both the United States and the United Nations. The gesture by Kim Jong-un of stepping across the military demarcation line at Panmunjom, "the truce village" where the Korean War armistice was signed in July 1953, and then inviting Moon to step into the northern side before they walked between rows of South Korean troops to Peace House on the southern side, did not seem to jeopardise historic ties between the US and the Republic of Korea.[8]

In fact, the prospects for vastly improving relations between the United States and North Korea brightened in the minds of Koreans and Americans alike as Trump and Kim agreed to hold their own summit. Moon was delighted at the prospect of the Leaders of the United States and North Korea meeting for the first time, overcoming the long and tortuous history of American troops fighting to save South Korea in a war that had raged up and down the Korean Peninsula from June 1950 to July 1953.

The idea of a meeting between American and North Korean Leaders assumed the aura of an international spectacle, an opportunity for the mass media of the world to record history in the making. There was intense speculation as to where they should meet. Panmunjom, on the North-South line, the scene of sporadic talks between military and civilian officials from both sides over the years, seemed like a logical choice. Some Americans, however, objected to Panmunjom, saying there had been too many nasty episodes there over the years, notably the "axe murder" in 1976, in which two US army officers had been killed by North Korean soldiers while leading a detail of troops on a mission to cut down a tree obscuring the view across the Joint Security Area.

Road to Singapore

In the end, Singapore emerged as the preferred choice, not only because of its modern facilities but also because of Sentosa, a small outlying island reachable across a bridge. There the two Leaders could meet at the Capella Hotel in splendid isolation, away from the rest of the island city state, noted for its cleanliness, efficiency, and neutrality. Delegations from the United States and North Korea chose the finest hotels – the Americans at the Shangri La, the venue of the annual Shangri La dialogue on defence and other issues, the North Koreans at the St. Regis, ten minutes away by foot along a tree-shaded avenue.

Several thousand foreign correspondents, including this writer, were given accreditation after a vetting process in which they had to show letters of assignment, in my case from CBS News, for whom I was filing radio reports while writing mainly for the *Daily Beast*. Journalists watched the comings and goings of the North and South Korean delegations on huge screens on June 12, the day of the summit, at a press centre set up in an enormous building that normally housed garages, offices, and dining facilities for F1 car racing.

After waiting in excitement for the document that Trump and Kim had signed, one recoiled in shock at the vacuity of a joint statement that only showed how style had triumphed over substance in a deluge of imagery and optics. Had we all come to Singapore to stare at TV screens as these two, defined by their distinct hairstyles, "committed to cooperate for the development of new US-DPRK [Democratic People's Republic of Korea] relations and for the promotion of peace, prosperity, and the security of the Korean Peninsula and of the world"?[9] Afterwards Trump in a rambling press conference justified the exercise "as good for the US as for North Korea", but the statement contained no promises or commitments, no guarantees, nothing that changed the state of play between the two Koreas.[10]

If Trump during his presidential campaign had said that he would like to sit down with Kim for a hamburger, he and Kim appeared instead to have shared a nothing-burger. Perhaps the most remarkable aspect of the statement was what it did not say. It neglected to mention CVID. That omission marked a triumph for Kim, who would not have considered any formulation that committed him to denuclearisation.

Trump did not appear fazed by this omission. He had got Kim to make a "commitment to complete denuclearisation" that was good enough for him to claim a breakthrough. Sceptics, as Trump had tweeted, were "haters and losers".[11] There was, however, reason to be sceptical considering Kim's success in preserving the North Korean nuclear programme that had long been enshrined in the country's constitution. Kim's desire all along had been to join the elite club of the eight nations already armed with nuclear warheads.

But what about the 28,500 US troops still in South Korea? If North Korea was not going to engage in hostile acts, much less start a second Korean War, why have them in Korea at all? Trump agreed and said he would like to pull them back but not yet. In the meantime, he would call off the "war games", i.e. annual US-South Korean military exercises that he believed were not only "provocative" but costly and the North denounced as preparations for invasion. The decision marked the end of decades of joint exercises – none so upsetting to the North Koreans as mock "decapitation" raids staged in 2017 when US and South

Korean marines and special forces simulated landings and attacks against the Leader. The message had been clear — a "pre-emptive strike" on his nuclear and missile facilities was not the only option.

Trump's decision to cancel the exercises with South Koreans was probably the most important real news of the summit. Speed, he suggested, was of the essence. With that goal in mind, he said he would indeed like to meet Kim again.[12]

Pyongyang's Korean Central News Agency (KCNA) provided the version that Kim wanted the world to accept. Kim "clarified the stand", said KCNA, "that if the US side takes genuine measures for building trust in order to improve the DPRK-US relationship, the DPRK, too, can continue to take additional goodwill measures of next stage commensurate with them". At the heart of the discussions were the sanctions imposed by the United States and United Nations in retaliation for the North's missile and nuclear tests. "Trump expressed his intention to halt the U.S.-south Korea joint military exercises", said KCNA, putting the "south" in South Korea in lower case. The United States, said the dispatch, should also "offer security guarantees to the DPRK and lift sanctions ...".[13]

The North Korean state media harked back to the need to "implement the Panmunjom Declaration" but said nothing about denuclearisation. Thousands of artillery pieces constantly threatened the Seoul-Incheon megalopolis from above the DMZ, while half the North's armed forces consisting of 1.2 million troops remained within 40 to 50 miles of the North-South line, mostly well out of sight.[14]

If Trump really believed that Kim was about to take the first steps towards "complete denuclearisation", he was in for a rude awakening. Considering that North Korea had repeatedly resisted and avoided deals for jettisoning its nukes, no one should have been surprised that KCNA did not mention the word "nuclear" in its report on the meeting. The biggest surprise was the consternation and confusion among American military personnel. Trump had not discussed his views regarding US troop strength in South Korea, much less military exercises, with Defence Secretary Mattis, who was conspicuously absent from the summit.

Wedge issues

US secretary of state Pompeo discovered the extent of the differences between Washington and Pyongyang when he went to Pyongyang four weeks after the Singapore summit on a mission that left the United States grasping for leverage in its dealings with both Koreas. Beyond pro forma statements, the Americans had to get along with their South Korean ally while South Korean Leaders talked about the need to "consult closely" with North Korea as well as the United States. The North Koreans deepened the wedge between South Korea and the US despite a ritualistic show of unity between Pompeo and the foreign ministers of South Korea and Japan after the debacle of his talks with North Korea's chief negotiator Kim Yong-chol, vice chairman of the Workers' Party under Chairman Kim Jong-un.

A spokesman for Moon promised that the South would "closely consult with the US and North Korea for the complete denuclearisation of the Korean

Peninsula and the establishment of peace". That statement cast the United States and North Korea as equals after North Korea's foreign ministry pilloried the Americans for their "unilateral and gangster-like demand for denuclearisation just calling for CVID, declaration and verification" while ignoring calls for a "peace regime" and a "declaration on the end of the [Korean] war". Pompeo, in his first comment on the North's statement, said that if the "requests" made at his talks in Pyongyang were "'gangster-like,' then the world is a gangster, because there was a unanimous decision at the United Nations Security Council about what needs to be achieved".[15] There was, however, no real unanimity among allies as they awaited the next treacherous step.

North Korean demands for an end-of-war declaration drove a wedge between the US and South Korean policymakers. "The declaration of the end of war", said North Korea, would be "the first process of defusing tension and establishing a lasting peace mechanism on the Korean peninsula, and at the same the primary factor in building confidence between the DPRK and the US".[16] The Americans, however, viewed North Korean pressure for a peace treaty in place of the Korean War armistice as a ploy to end the US-South Korean alliance and as a means to end the US troop deployment in South Korea.

Kim Yong-chol handed Pompeo a letter in which "Chairman Kim expressed his expectation and conviction that good personal relations forged with President Trump and his sentiments of good faith ... would be further consolidated through future dialogues ...". Trump himself had "suggested adopting a new way to resolve the issues of bilateral relations and the denuclearisation of the Korean peninsula". The statement was almost sentimental about Trump: "We still cherish our confidence in President Trump".[17]

The fourth and last point of the Trump-Kim statement entailed the return of some of the remains of Americans missing in the Korean War along with the search for more. Trump announced that remains of 200 soldiers had already been returned, but that statement was not only premature but hyperbolic. After Pompeo persuaded the North Koreans to talk at Panmunjom about transfer of remains, they were ready to transfer 50 to 55 sets at the new Kalma Airport near the port of Wonsan in south eastern North Korea on July 27, 65th anniversary of the armistice.

"Today's actions represent a significant first step to recommence the repatriation of remains from North Korea", said the White House, "and to resume field operations in North Korea to search for the estimated 5,300 Americans who have not yet returned home".[18] The North Koreans, of course, were sure to charge outrageous "expenses" for searching for remains, as they had done in joint operations for 11 years until 2005 when President George W. Bush, fearful for the security of Americans, halted the gambit.

At Panmunjom, where US and North Korean soldiers had been staring across the line at each other 24 hours a day, there was euphoria in the air at a ceremony that I attended in Freedom House, the imposing building on the south side of the Joint Security Area. No high-ranking officers from the United States, South Korea, and the 16 countries that had participated in the war breathed a word about "denuclearisation". There was no suggestion that the North Koreans might want to wring further concessions while hoarding many more remains of those who had died in combat or perhaps had been prisoners whom the North had avoided releasing in the prisoner exchange after the signing of the 1953 truce.

Major General Shin Sang-bum, senior South Korean member of the UN Command, acknowledging the role of soldiers who had "come from thousands of miles away" to defend South Korea, said it was "our solemn wish today to keep the peace", for which UN forces had "set the conditions". He studiously avoided mentioning Trump, Kim Jong-un, or Moon as he credited the North-South summit on April 27 and the US-North Korean summit of June 12 with having made possible "a permanent peace to be established in this time of change". In a comment fraught with political overtones, he reminded the assemblage that "institutions must adjust themselves". In that spirit, he pleaded for "unrelenting support, so the seed of peace planted on April 27 may flourish and bear fruit".[19]

Another summit?

Prospects of a second Trump-Kim summit loomed as the last best hope to jump-start the stalled "complete denuclearisation" process even as North and South Korean emissaries were arranging a third summit between Kim and Moon – a possible prelude to Kim and Trump meeting again. North Korea made increasingly clear that it was not going to do away with its nuclear programme unless or until the United States agreed on a "declaration" formally ending the Korean War; the need for a second Trump-Kim summit assumed urgency.

The North's party newspaper *Rodong Sinmun* was emphatic that a peace declaration was "the demand of our time", "the first process" in guaranteeing security.[20] Moon said that he, too, would like to see such a declaration by the end of 2018, and Kim invited him to Pyongyang for their third inter-Korean summit.

The Americans were wary of any agreement that might lead to withdrawal of US troops, but what about a second Trump-Kim summit? One immediate problem would be full disclosure of North Korea's inventory of nukes and missiles and the facilities for making them. US intelligence agencies estimated that the North Koreans had produced anywhere between 20 and 80 warheads and were building a powerful second plutonium reactor at their main nuclear complex at Yongbyon. They also had hidden facilities for making warheads with highly enriched uranium. An inventory, as Pompeo had been demanding since Singapore, was crucial.

A legion of sceptics observed that Trump had little to show for all the hype. Joseph Nye, a distinguished analyst with a long record of writing on the issue, noted that Trump, for all his posturing, fits into "a long tradition of American presidents who have been taken to the cleaners". The North Koreans, he observed, had "lied to us consistently for nearly 30 years".[21]

The earnest hope of the State Department was agreement on a "timeline" for North Korea to get rid of its nukes and missiles and shut down the facilities for making them. Kim Yong-chol, having been hosted by Pompeo in New York,

Washington, and Pyongyang, had spurned his attempts to get a date-by-date schedule for a climb-down from the pinnacle the North Koreans had reached as the world's ninth nuclear weapons power.

In fact, the United States and North Korea had not reached a viable agreement since the Geneva framework at the height of their first real nuclear crisis in 1994. The North under terms of the Geneva framework had shut down its Yongbyon reactor under inspection by the International Atomic Energy Agency (IAEA), but the deal broke down in 2002 after the North was revealed to be developing a separate programme for making nukes with highly enriched uranium.

Work on twin nuclear-energy power stations, to be built under the terms of the Geneva agreement with huge infusions of South Korean and Japanese funds, ground to a halt. The United States stopped shipping heavy oil, also as agreed in Geneva, to fulfil the North's energy needs until the reactors went on line. North Korea retaliated by expelling IAEA inspectors at the end of 2002 and resumed fabricating warheads at Yongbyon. It also withdrew from the Nuclear Non-Proliferation Treaty, setting the course that led to six nuclear tests from October 2006 to September 2017.

In an atmosphere of renewed and pervasive mutual suspicion, Trump agreed it would be good to see Kim again. The North saw Trump as the key to peace, while Bolton harboured the view that Kim might still give up his nukes and missiles. In one burst of optimism, Bolton portrayed Trump as "giving Kim Jong-un a master class in how to hold a door open for somebody".[22] Trump, in a letter to Kim, suggested that Pompeo go back to Pyongyang, which he had already visited three times.

US policy on North Korea was in flux while the White House and the State Department puzzled over what Trump might do next. The new US ambassador to South Korea, Harry Harris, had a message for Korean journalists: "One of the things that hasn't happened is the demonstrable moves towards denuclearisation before we can entertain something like the end-of-war declaration", he said. "We need to see the move, and I haven't seen that yet".[23] Those remarks caused a tempest in diplomatic tea cups. Neither Pompeo nor Bolton knew in advance that Harris would be talking to the media.

Splitting the alliance

North Korea artfully deepened the wedge between the United States and South Korea with a letter relayed to Pompeo by the North's UN mission in which Kim Yong-chol said the US had to agree to a "peace declaration" before the North would get rid of its nuclear warheads or the facilities for making them. As a result, Trump in late August cancelled what would have been Pompeo's fourth mission to Pyongyang. At the same time, North Korea's state media made clear that Moon needed to intensify pressure on Trump.[24]

General Vincent Brooks, commander of US Forces Korea as well as the UN Command, in answer to a question that I asked him at the Seoul Foreign Correspondents' Club in August, said that such a declaration "has to be understood in advance" and "there are elements we have not worked out" – presumably including the future of the UN Command.[25] Many South Koreans believed Trump's ability to resolve the nuclear standoff was waning. As for Kim Jong-un, his strategy all along had been to deepen differences between Seoul and Washington.

As Moon prepared for his third summit with Kim in September 2018, this time in Pyongyang, Kim projected the image of a congenial Leader. "People don't bother about Kim very much", said Jang Sung-un, an office worker. "It's Trump and the Americans the media worry about".[26] Kim's munificence offensive was enhanced by another round of reunions in August bringing together families divided by the Korean War – the first such gathering in nearly three years and the 21st since regular get-togethers were agreed on in Pyongyang in June 2000 by Kim Jong-il and Kim Dae-Jung, the architect of the "Sunshine policy" of reconciliation with the North.

The reunions would all be held in the tourist zone of Mount Kumkang above the North-South line on the east coast. Typically, several hundred South and North Koreans got to spend three days and two evenings with one another. Those who participated, a tiny fraction of the 57,000 South Koreans still alive more than 65 years after the war, returned home full of praise for Kim's approval of the reunions, seen as another step on the way to North-South reconciliation.

The president of the South Korean Red Cross, Park Kyung-seo, responsible for organising the South Koreans, said that the reunions were "90 per cent for humanitarian principles" while "indirectly moved by political dynamism". Park hoped that Moon and his North Korean counterpart would agree on another round regardless of "political circumstances".[27] Moon, meeting Kim again two weeks later, hoped to persuade him of the need for a second summit with Trump even though Kim Yong-chol's letter to Pompeo made it clear that the North Korean position was immutable.

At the same time, North Korean commentaries attacked the United States for "double-dealing attitudes" and "hatching a criminal plot to unleash a war against the DPRK".[28] The North's state media avoided singling out Trump for criticism, but the rhetoric had South Korean Leaders wondering if the goodwill generated in Singapore in June was dissipating. Moon faced rising pressure from the North to ask the United States to make significant concessions, doing away with sanctions imposed by the United States and the United Nations.

"Nothing will work", said Kim Kisam, a former analyst with the South's National Intelligence Service, now living in the United States. "The North Koreans think the South Koreans are nothing to them. They think they have already defeated the South Koreans".[29]

A dispute between the United States and South Korea over the South's plans for opening a liaison office in the Kaesong Industrial Complex inside North Korea near Panmunjom deepened differences between the United States and South Korea. The complex was shut down in 2016 by Moon's conservative predecessor, Park Geun-hye, whose impeachment as president by the National Assembly in December 2016 during the Candlelight Revolution was confirmed by a court decision in March 2017. Park remained in prison (she was eventually convicted in April 2018 on abuse of power and corruption charges) while Moon rode to victory in a special election in May 2017 with 41 per cent of the vote.

US officials, sensitive to Moon's popularity, did not want to confront him and his advisers over allocation of funds needed to open and maintain such an office in violation of sanctions. Instead, they played up the historic US-South Korean alliance as though nothing could go wrong. "This alliance is more than a partnership or friendship", Ambassador Harris told a gathering in Seoul. "It's a camaraderie that has lasted for generations and will continue for generations to come. I look forward to bolstering our alliance, the lynchpin of our security in Asia".[30]

Such words, however, rang hollow in an atmosphere of pervasive doubts about the relationship. "It is political games that they are playing", said Signe Poulsen, Korean representative of the UN Office of High Commissioner for Human Rights. North-South family reunions "are something tragic... a bargaining tool when it should never be".[31] In the great game of North-South relations, General Brooks, winding up 28 months in Korea, sought "to understand why North Korea is doing what it's doing".[32]

Another Moon-Kim summit

No sooner had Moon returned on September 20, 2018, from his third summit with Kim than Trump concluded that Kim had "agreed to allow nuclear inspections, subject to final negotiations ..." Actually, Kim and Moon had said in their "Pyongyang joint declaration" that the North had "expressed its willingness to continue taking additional steps, such as the permanent shutdown of the Yongbyon nuclear facility" where an aging five-megawatt reactor produced plutonium for warheads, including six detonated in underground tests beginning in October 2006. There was one catch: the United States had to "take corresponding measures ...".[33]

Trump's ecstasy over "inspections" reflected Kim's pledge to allow inspectors to watch the dismantling of a facility for testing the engines of long-range missiles in the village of Tongchang-ri close to the Chinese border on the west coast. Trump said Kim had agreed to do all that "in the presence of international experts" but seemed unaware of the North's call for the United States to take "steps" in tandem. The North's idea of "corresponding measures" implied US acquiescence to a "peace declaration", the precursor to a treaty.

Kim made clear that he was sticking to his guns, that is, his nukes and missiles, on the second day of a three-day mission that ended with the South Korean president and his entourage of about 200 ministers, aides, journalists, and the chieftains of a dozen of the South's industrial empires watching "mass games" enacted by thousands of performers in a display of North Korean economic and military prowess.

The spectacle, from the time Moon and his wife alighted at Pyongyang's gleaming new airport to hugs and smiles by Kim and wife against a backdrop of goose-stepping soldiers and cheering throngs, did not inspire confidence that a solid peace was at hand. In the third meeting between Moon and Kim, their first in the North Korean capital, it was clear that Kim was not about to give up his precious nukes and the missiles for firing them at distant targets. Instead, a South Korean pool report quoted Kim carefully saying "regional conditions stabilised and a more advanced outcome is expected".

Trump's aides and South Korean conservatives dreaded another Trump meeting with Kim for a summit in which he might make more concessions while joining Kim in a "peace declaration". Trump fuelled these fears by his response to what the White House had called "a very warm, very positive letter" from Kim that exuded Kim's confidence in his ability to win over the US president after failing with Pompeo. Trump had said that sanctions had to remain in place until North Korea began dismantling its nuclear stockpile and the facilities for making them, but he also said he would follow Moon's lead.[34]

Kim showed his eagerness to showcase North Korea's economic rather than military prowess in a parade in Pyongyang on September 9, 2018, the 70th anniversary of the founding of the DPRK, where no long-range missiles were on display. The sense was that Kim, besides aiming to bring Trump into line, also wanted to demonstrate his peaceful intentions to China's President Xi Jinping, on whom the North depended for almost all its oil and many other necessities. China still made a show of enforcing UN sanctions but countenanced numerous violations, including trade by private entrepreneurs.

Trump seemed thrilled by Kim's seeming forbearance. "Thank you to Chairman Kim", he exulted in a tweet after Kim requested a second summit. "We will both prove everyone wrong! There is nothing like good dialogue from two people that like each other!"[35] Trump's joy over "a big and very positive statement from North Korea" confirmed an earlier tweet in which he had said "Thank you to Chairman Kim" for having proclaimed "'unwavering faith in President Trump".[36]

No one expected North Korean "denuclearisation" to gain speed as Pompeo, on his fourth mission to Pyongyang, pleaded with Kim Jong-un to show he was getting rid of the arsenal that he was holding as a club over the United States.[37]

Obstacles to summitry

The improbability of any substantive progress became clear when South Korean foreign minister Kang Kyung-wha suggested that the United States give up its demand that North Korea reveal the whereabouts of its stockpiles of nuclear weapons and facilities. Instead, why not settle for the North shutting down its main complex at Yongbyon? Daniel Russel, who had served as assistant secretary of state during some of the toughest moments of the North Korean standoff, scoffed at letting "North Korea set the agenda and come up with half-baked measures" only "to demand concessions".[38]

The Americans persisted in wanting to know where the North Koreans were manufacturing all their nukes and missiles, where they were storing them, and what they had besides that old five-megawatt reactor at Yongbyon, which was now ready for the scrapheap. Kang believed that all the Americans had to do was to get the North Koreans to close the Yongbyon complex for an end-of-war "peace declaration" or peace treaty.

Russel, vice president of the Asia Society, believed it would be a mistake to take the bait. "A peace declaration or end-of-war declaration is at best a diversion from the real issue of denuclearisation", he said at a symposium held in Washington by the Institute for Corean [sic] American Studies (ICAS). "More likely", he added, it would mean the end of the mission of US forces to defend the South.[39]

In fact, Pompeo and the American team faced two major problems. First, Kang's boss, President Moon, was committed to getting the parties to the 1953 truce – North Korea, the United States, and China – to agree to what the Americans viewed as a phony end-of-war declaration. Second, nobody knew what Trump might do. Could Pompeo shrug off Kang's proposal and get something going when he saw Kim Jong-un in September 2018 or would he just go there for "party planning", as Russel put it, for a second Trump-Kim summit?

One has to go back to the first Trump-Kim séance in Singapore in June 2018 to grasp how unpredictably Trump could behave in his quest to get along with a Leader with whom he "fell in love".[40] Nobody in the Pentagon, the State Department, or the National Security Council had known that Trump would agree to cancel the joint US-South Korea military exercises when he met Kim. Nor was anyone prepared for Trump calling such war games "provocative" – a word from the North Korean lexicon.

Whatever understanding Pompeo had hoped to extract on his fourth mission to the North Korean capital, he could not forget that Trump might choose to make a dramatic gesture, maybe even that "peace declaration", against the advice of his closest aides, including hawkish National Security Adviser John Bolton. Moon and his aides, who were excited about an historic bid to bring about good relations between South and North, could not understand why South Korean conservatives, not to mention American military and diplomatic experts, were sceptical.

"We have a chance to heal the pain of inter-Korean division and cast away our perpetual fear of war", Kim Eui-kyeom, a media aide at the Blue House, had said earlier. "But it's also true", he added, "that this moment could be described as a candle in the wind" – a reminder of the danger of betraying the reforms promised in the Candlelight Revolution.[41]

Since the Singapore summit, the absolutist CVID no longer dominated the conversation. The controversial compromise and concessions that Moon and Kang espoused raised endless issues about verification of dismantling the Yongbyon complex. Who would confirm its dismantlement? And could inspectors return periodically to make sure it was still shut down? Those questions clearly needed answering.

North Korea's stubborn refusal to list all its missile and nuclear facilities intensified doubts about whether any deal had a chance. "The North Koreans have consistently played a game", said Larry Niksch after years studying North Korea at the Congressional Research Service. "We have never gotten into what is beyond Yongbyon". The question was "how could we get them to get into negotiations outside Yongbyon into the rest of North Korea". Evans Revere, a former senior diplomat at the State Department and the US embassy in Seoul, agreed. "We'd be fools to take this offer", he said of Kang's call for a step-by-step process. "The goal of North Korea is to undermine the validity and the viability of the US-Republic of Korea alliance and the rationale for the US military presence". The proposal "plays into their hands".[42]

Falling "in love"

Always there was Trump, whose mind seemed as difficult to fathom as that of Kim Jong-un. Having threatened to inflict "fire and fury" on North Korea in 2017 if the North fired a long-range missile at the U.S., he now cited those "beautiful letters … great letters" that Kim had written as the two "fell in love".[43]

At the UN General Assembly in September 2018, a year after denouncing Kim in the same forum as "rocket man", Trump said that sanctions would remain in place until North Korea gave up its nukes and missiles.[44] In fact, the US and North Korea were following two-track policies in which Trump and Kim wooed each other with kind words and flattery while the US stuck to its demands for an end to North Korea's nuclear programme and the North said it would do nothing without "corresponding measures", including an end of sanctions.

It was far from clear, however, where or how or even whether the two tracks would converge, much less achieve their goals. Kim at this stage seemed to harbour more distrust for Pompeo than for Bolton, despite having hosted Pompeo at a lavish luncheon in Pyongyang as recently as October 2018. Humiliated by Trump's walkout from the meeting in Hanoi on February 28, 2019, Kim held Pompeo, not Bolton, responsible for the debacle.

Kwon Jong-gun, director-general for American affairs at the North's Foreign Ministry, in words carried in English by KCNA, said he was "afraid, if Pompeo engages in the talks again, the table will be lousy once again and the talks will become entangled". If talks with the United States were to resume, said Kwon, "I wish our dialogue counterpart would be not Pompeo but other [sic] person who is more careful and mature in communicating with us". Kim, signalling that he was ready to return to testing missiles, and possibly warheads, pointedly witnessed the firing of a new tactical weapon – though probably not a missile.[45]

As if to show he had other friends to turn to, Kim in April 2019 played the Russian card, meeting President Vladimir Putin in Vladivostok for their first summit. In more than three hours of conversation, Putin said that they had discussed "what should be done to improve the situation"; and Kim said, they had "a very fruitful exchange" about ways to achieve "a peaceful settlement".[46] Before returning to Moscow, Putin called for "international security guarantees" for the North in which Russia would participate. "It's unlikely that any agreements between two countries will be enough", he said, suggesting a revival of the dormant six-party talks that included China, Russia, Japan and the two Koreas, as well as the United States.[47]

Trump said he would be glad to see Kim for a third summit but insisted he still give up his nuclear programme. Some analysts believed that Trump, first by threatening North Korea and then by pursuing a diplomatic tack, might be getting somewhere. "First you soften them, then you deal with them", said David Ignatius, *The Washington Post* columnist and author, explaining Trump's foreign policy modus operandi in a lecture at Princeton University in October 2018. "We begin to see what a new deal would look like. ... The outlines are beginning to emerge".[48] The outlines, however, were blurred. By flattering Kim, Trump believed that Kim would have to come to terms while Kim, pursuing a similar strategy, played on Trump's ego in order to wring concessions without "denuclearisation".

Both played the role in their rendezvous on the North-South line at Panmunjom. The overriding sense was that the meeting, an extended photo-op, represented the aspiration if not the inspiration for a lasting deal. "It is very symbolic", said Joseph Yun, the former US envoy to North Korea, on duty as global affairs analyst for CNN at Imjin Gak, a park and amusement area south of the DMZ. "At a minimum the meeting has to kick off a major process, and if it doesn't, I will be very disappointed".[49] Yun's successor, Stephen Biegun, was with Trump as he talked of setting up "new teams" to discuss a real deal.

Whatever happened, for Trump the meeting with Kim in the DMZ was a moment of glory, a success that he could always claim even if the North never came to terms on denuclearisation. "That was very quick notice, and I want to thank you", he told Kim after shaking hands. "We met and we liked each other from day one, and that was very important".[50]

As for the failure to come to terms with Kim, Trump found a scapegoat in National Security Adviser Bolton, whom he dismissed on September 10, 2019. "We were set back very badly", he said, "when John Bolton talked about the Libyan model", in which the late Libyan Leader Muammar Gaddafi had given up his nascent nuclear programme in 2003 without ever making a warhead.[51] The great flaw in the Libyan example, as North Koreans noted, was that NATO-backed rebels deposed and killed Gaddafi eight years later.[52] North Korea, though, still had to contend with Pompeo, whom the North's foreign minister Ri Yong-ho dubbed the "poisonous plant of American diplomacy".[53] Trump might see Kim as a friend to meet again, but the inescapable sense was that North Korea would remain nuclear-armed in defiance of promises of economic blessings and an end to sanctions as rewards for giving up its nuclear programme.

Notes

1 "Remarks by President Trump Before a Briefing on the Opioid Crisis", The White House, August 8, 2017, at www.whitehouse.gov/briefings-statements/remarks-president-trump-briefing-opioid-crisis/ (accessed July 2, 2019).
2 Donald Kirk, "Trump Becomes First Sitting American President to Step into North Korea—A Win for Kim Jong Un", *The Daily Beast*, June 30, 2019, at https://news.yahoo.com/donald-trump-becomes-first-sitting-141036110.html (accessed July 2, 2019). The author witnessed the proceedings as broadcast on CNN, BBC and South Korean networks.

3 Ibid.
4 The author witnessed the press conference as carried on large screens at the International Press Centre set up in Hanoi for the occasion.
5 Ibid.
6 Anna Fifield and Ashley Parker, "North Korea's Kim Jong Un Invites South Korea's President to Pyongyang", *The Washington Post*, February 10, 2018, at www.washingtonpost.com/world/north-koreas-kim-jong-un-has-invited-south-koreas-moon-jae-in-to-pyongyang/2018/02/10/d7db9dde-0ddd-11e8-998c-96deb18cca19_story.html?utm_term=.390451be8e9a (accessed July 2, 2019).
7 Alex Ward, "Mike Pence Sat Just Feet Away from Kim Jong Un's Sister at the Olympics Opening Ceremony", *Vox*, February 9, 2018, at www.vox.com/2018/2/9/16994596/pence-olympics-kim-north-korea-opening-ceremony (accessed July 2, 2019).
8 Rick Noack and Joyce Lee, "The Historic Kim-Moon Meeting as It Unfolded April 27", *The Washington Post*, April 27, 2018, at www.washingtonpost.com/news/worldviews/wp/2018/04/27/the-historic-kim-moon-meeting-as-it-unfolded/?utm_term=.927d9020b525 (accessed July 2, 2019).
9 "Joint Statement of President Donald J. Trump of the United States of America and Chairman Kim Jong Un of the Democratic People's Republic of Korea at the Singapore Summit", The White House, June 12, 2018, at www.whitehouse.gov/briefings-statements/joint-statement-president-donald-j-trump-united-states-america-chairman-kim-jong-un-democratic-peoples-republic-korea-singapore-summit/ (accessed July 2, 2019).
10 Ibid.
11 "Trump and Kim sign Document to Conclude Summit, but What Did It Say?" Associated Press, June 12, 2018, at www.pbs.org/newshour/world/trump-and-kim-sign-document-to-conclude-summit-but-what-did-it-say (accessed July 2, 2019).
12 "Joint Statement …", No. 9.
13 Steve Holland et al., "Trump in Surprise Summit Move Says He Will Halt Korea War Games", Reuters, June 12, 2018, at https://uk.reuters.com/article/us-northkorea-usa/trump-in-surprise-summit-move-says-he-will-halt-korea-war-games-idUSKBN1J821H (accessed July 8, 2019).
14 Donald Kirk, "Forget Nukes. Will Kim Jong Un Pull Back His Big Guns?" *The Daily Beast*, June 18, 2018, at www.thedailybeast.com/forget-nukes-will-kim-jong-un-pull-back-his-big-guns (accessed July 8, 2019).
15 "Pompeo Rebuts N., Korea's 'Gangster' Claim, Vows Continued Sanctions", Yonhap, July 8, 2018, at https://en.yna.co.kr/view/AEN20180708002553315 (accessed July 8, 2019).
16 "FM Spokesman on DPRK-US High-level Talks", *Pyongyang Times*, July 7, 2018, at www.pyongyangtimes.com.kp/?bbs=27058 (accessed July 8, 2019); Steve Holland et al., No. 13; Donald Kirk, No. 14.
17 Ibid.
18 "Statement from the Press Secretary on the Repatriation of Remains from North Korea", The White House, July 26, 2018, at www.whitehouse.gov/briefings-statements/statement-press-secretary-repatriation-remains-north-korea/ (accessed July 2, 2019).
19 Donald Kirk, "North Korea's Plan for a Peace to End All Peace," *The Daily Beast*, July 27, 2018, at www.thedailybeast.com/north-koreas-plan-for-a-peace-to-end-all-peace?ref=scroll (accessed July 2, 2019).
20 "DPRK urges US to Agree to Declare End to Korean War", CGTN, August 9, 2018, at https://news.cgtn.com/news/3d3d514f32597a4d79457a6333566d54/share_p.html (accessed July 2, 2019).
21 David E. Sanger and William J. Broad, "Once 'No Longer a Nuclear Threat,' North Korea Now in Standoff with US", *The New York Times*, August 10, 2018, at www.nytimes.com/2018/08/10/us/politics/north-korea-denuclearize-peace-treaty.html, (accessed July 2, 2019).

22 "Fox News Sunday with Chris Wallace", The Internet Archive, August 5, 2018, at https://archive.org/details/KTVU_20180805_170000_Fox_News_Sunday_With_Chris_Wallace (accessed July 2, 2019).
23 Lim Min-hyuk, "U.S. Ambassador Urges Caution in Ending Korean War", *The Chosun Ilbo*, August 3, 2018, at http://english.chosun.com/site/data/html_dir/2018/08/03/2018080301326.html (accessed July 2, 2019).
24 Josh Rogin, "Why Trump Canceled Pompeo's Trip to North Korea", *The Washington Post*, August 27, 2018, at www.washingtonpost.com/news/josh-rogin/wp/2018/08/27/why-trump-cancelled-pompeos-trip-to-north-korea/?utm_term=.e87cdb3939f2 (accessed July 2, 2019).
25 Author's notes, General Brooks spoke at the Seoul Foreign Correspondents' Club on August 22, 2018.
26 Author's notes, interview, August 22, 2018.
27 Interview with the author, Sokcho, August 20, 2018.
28 "North Korea Newspaper Blasts 'Double-dealing' U.S. after Pompeo's Trip Canceled", Reuters, August 26, 2018, at www.reuters.com/article/us-northkorea-usa/north-korea-newspaper-blasts-double-dealing-u-s-after-pompeos-trip-canceled-idUSKCN1LB0BY (accessed July 2, 2019).
29 Interview with the author, August 27, 2018.
30 Author's notes, Diplomatic Roundtable, East West Center Association Conference, Lotte Hotel, Seoul, August 25, 2018.
31 Author's interview, No. 30.
32 Author's notes, No. 26.
33 "Pyongyang Joint Declaration of September 2018", Korea.net, September 19, 2018, at www.korea.net/Government/Current-Affairs/National-Affairs/view?subId=680 &affairId=750 &pageIndex = 1&articleId=3397 (accessed July 2, 2019). Also see, *The National Committee on North Korea* at www.ncnk.org/node/1633 (accessed September 15, 2019).
34 "WH: N. Korea Sent Trump 'Warm, Positive' Letter", Associated Press, September 10, 2018, at www.apnews.com/bec0b48feb8444848538cc96449beb79 (accessed July 2, 2019).
35 Donald J. Trump, Twitter Post, September 9, 2018, 8:31 a.m., at https://twitter.com/realdonaldtrump/status/1038812262549663744?lang=en (accessed July 2, 2019).
36 Donald J. Trump, Twitter Post, September 6, 2018, 3:58 a.m., at https://twitter.com/realdonaldtrump/status/1037656324010663937?lang=en (accessed July 2, 2019).
37 "Pompeo Cites Progress Made on North Korea Trip", Associated Press, October 7, 2018, at www.politico.com/story/2018/10/07/pompeo-north-korea-kim-880706 (accessed July 2, 2019).
38 Donald Kirk, "As Pompeo Heads for Pyongyang, the Big Question: Can Denuclearization Wait Forever?" *The Daily Beast*, October 5, 2018, at www.thedailybeast.com/as-pompeo-heads-for-pyongyang-the-big-question-can-denuclearization-wait-forever (accessed July 2, 2019).
39 Ibid.
40 Roberta Rampton, "'We Fell in Love:' Trump Swoons over Letters from North Korea's Kim", Reuters, September 30, 2018, at www.reuters.com/article/us-northkorea-usa-trump/we-fell-in-love-trump-swoons-over-letters-from-north-koreas-kim-idUSKCN1MA03Q (accessed July 2, 2019).
41 Jihyun Kim, "North Korea Reporting: Riddled with Errors, Even in Neighboring South Korea", *Korea Exposé*, July 10, 2018, at www.koreaexpose.com/north-korea-reporting-in-south-korea-riddled-with-errors-misreporting/ (accessed July 2, 2019).
42 Donald Kirk, No. 41.
43 Roberta Rampton, No. 43.
44 "Remarks by President Trump to the 73rd Session of the United Nations General Assembly, New York, NY", The White House, September 25, 2018, at www.whitehouse.

gov/briefings-statements/remarks-president-trump-73rd-session-united-nations-general-assembly-new-york-ny/ (accessed July 2, 2019).
45 Joyce Lee and David Brunnstrom, "North Korea Urges Trump to Drop Pompeo from Talks; U.S. Plays Down Weapons Test", Reuters, April 18, 2019, at www.reuters.com/article/us-northkorea-weapon/north-korea-urges-trump-to-drop-pompeo-from-talks-u-s-plays-down-weapons-test-idUSKCN1RT2KY (accessed July 2, 2019).
46 "Seoul Hopeful Putin-Kim Talks Will Help Peace", Associated Press, April 25, 2019, at www.apnews.com/e07d2b0208db4647ac84abbaff412c0f (accessed July 2, 2019).
47 Vladimir Soldatkin and Maria Vasilyeva, "Putin Says U.S. Guarantees Unlikely to Prompt North Korea to De-Nuclearize", Reuters, April 25, 2019, at www.reuters.com/article/us-northkorea-russia/putin-says-u-s-guarantees-unlikely-to-prompt-north-korea-to-de-nuclearize-idUSKCN1S02TP (accessed July 2, 2019).
48 Author's notes, David Ignatius, lecture, Princeton University, October 3, 2018.
49 Joseph Yun, in conversation with CNN anchor Jim Sciutto, Imjin Gak, South Korea; conversation monitored by the author, June 30, 2019.
50 "Remarks by President Trump, Chairman Kim Jong Un, and President Moon in Greeting at the Korean Demilitarized Zone", The White House, June 30, 2019, at www.whitehouse.gov/briefings-statements/remarks-president-trump-chairman-kim-jong-un-president-moon-greeting-korean-demilitarized-zone/ (accessed July 2, 2019).
51 Jeff Mason and David Brunnstrom, "Trump Says Bolton a 'Disaster' on North Korea, 'Out of Line' on Venezuela", https://www.reuters.com/article/us-usa-trump-bolton-firing/trump-says-bolton-a-disaster-on-north-korea-out-of-line-on-venezuela-idUSKCN1VW2B0/ (accessed January 2, 2020)
52 Minjung Kim and Donald Kirk, "What Differentiates Kim Jong-Il from Gaddafi: Problems of Nuclear Development Factor Analysis Methods and Proposal of Alternatives," Institute of Nuclear Materials Management, 58th annual meeting, 2017, at www.inmm.org/INMM/media/Archives/Annual%20Meeting%20Proceedings/2017/a460_1.pdf
53 Hyung-jin Kim, "North Korea Foreign Minister Calls Pompeo 'Poisonous Plant,'" Associated Press, August 23, 2019, at www.apnews.com/a059eac6b7c44463b6d8379ca19cfb09

2 China's relations with North Korea

Surmounting the "Great Wall"

Anurag Viswanath

In recent years, North Korea – long forlorn, isolated, and "international pariah" – has catapulted in popular imagination as a significant player in North-East Asia. In 2018–2019, the Democratic People's Republic of Korea (DPRK, henceforth North Korea) has seemingly been wooed by two of the largest economies and political powers in the world – the United States and China, powers which sit on opposite sides of the political spectrum. In June 2019, President Donald Trump became the first sitting US president to cross the demarcation line into North Korea. This historic breakthrough was preceded by yet another significant breakthrough when Chinese president Xi Jinping visited North Korea – the first in 14 years (since President Hu Jintao's visit in 2005). Ironically, 2019 marked 70 years of diplomatic relations between China and North Korea and 60 odd years of diplomatic stalemate between the United States and North Korea.[1]

President Trump and Chairman Kim's last-minute crossover across the demarcation line was orchestrated through an unconventional tool of diplomacy – President Trump's tweet, which indicated an interest and willingness to meet Chairman Kim. Just days earlier, President Xi had concluded a no less historic visit to North Korea where he pledged to "find a political solution to the Korean peninsula issue".[2] Both visits honed the importance of North Korea.

North Korea responded to Chinese and American overtures by walking the diplomatic tightrope. On the one hand, North Korea reaffirmed an "unchanging" and "invincible" friendship with China. On the other hand, with the United States, North Korea recognised the "great relationship" and articulated a willingness to "eliminate the unfortunate past and open a new future".[3] In the evolving political configurations, however, America is not the only key player, so also is China.

For China, Korea has been a critical neighbour since the Korean War (1950–1953). In 1950, Korea, united in history since 676 C.E.,[4] was divided along the 38th parallel into North Korea and the Republic of Korea (ROK, henceforth South Korea). The Korean War divided Korea into opposing camps, but without a formal conclusion. Instead, a Korean Armistice Agreement (1953) was the in-place ceasefire, which resulted in an uneasy truce. With "an even distribution of gains and losses",[5] there was no clear victor or loser. Alarmingly, it was a war that had not technically ended.

For China, which is geographically contiguous with North Korea (1,420 km of shared border), North Korea became the buffer between China and the United States/South Korea/Japan. In recent decades, the rise of China and collapse of the former Soviet Union only added to the complexity. Today, a nuclear North Korea is the separation and buffer between rising Chinese power and established American might, the de facto setting for the "first great power-war of the twenty first century".[6]

That Chinese strategic thinking has to factor in North Korea goes unsaid. While North Korea was initially a "Soviet satellite"[7] controlled by its "Soviet puppet masters", as Andrei Lankov noted, Chinese influence during the Korean War, and after, has consolidated China into North Korea's biggest benefactor, donor, and economic partner.

Yet, paradoxically for China, North Korea has been an unpredictable neighbour, one that tries China's patience. China-North Korea relations have gone from "special" to normal "state to state" in 2012.[8] China characterised North Korea's nuclear tests as *hanran* (flagrant).[9] Despite North Korea being the lesser economy, and ideologically bound to China by the Treaty of Friendship, Cooperation and Mutual Assistance, 1961, and by a secret pact on the shared boundary, 1963, North Korea has been, by virtue of its geography, akin to the "tail that has wagged the dog".

For China, North Korea has never been the "intrinsically valuable trading partner, model of communism or military ally".[10] China's relations with North Korea are complex and exacerbated by American presence and visibility, its "pivot" in Asia, and the backdrop of China-US trade war. For China, North Korea has been a "strategic shield" and a "strategic ally" – but with the onset of political and economic undercurrents and evolving political configurations, also a "strategic liability" and a "strategic dilemma". What complicate the China-North Korea relationship are China's economic entanglements in North-East Asia and the evolving situation where South Korea, Russia, China, and the United States have reached out to North Korea.

This chapter examines (1) the importance of North-East Asia and China's North-East Asian policy in the context of its neighbourhood policy; (2) the reason North Korea was, is, and shall remain a critical factor in China's strategic thinking; (3) equity and constraints in China-North-East Asia relations; and (4) China's "strategic dilemma". The chapter concludes by discussing why a solution remains elusive despite progress in the face of divergent goalposts of the stakeholders – US demand for complete denuclearisation of North Korea, China's "freeze for freeze" initiative, North Korea's understanding of denuclearisation, South Korea's push for the denuclearisation of North Korea and reunification, and the Japanese intention of stopping North Korea's short-range missiles and support for its denuclearisation.

Significance of North-East Asia

North-East Asia is a unique configuration of powers, its geostrategic importance writ in stone. This is where great powers (Russia, Japan, the United States, and

China), rising power (China), and nuclear powers (Russia, China, and de facto North Korea) intersect. This is precisely why the grand junction is vulnerable and polarised. In the 19th and 20th centuries, North-East Asia was riven with rivalry and war between Japan and China (1895), as well as Russia and Japan (1905). This was followed by the Japanese colonisation of Korea, which was followed by the Korean War.

Unified Korea occupied a central position, as it was lodged between three geographical/cultural areas: China, Russia, and Japan. It was described as a "shrimp among whales" yet exhibited the paradox of "isolation from and engagement with the world".[11] Since the Korean War, the United States, despite not being an Asian power, has been a primary stakeholder, "pivot", and de facto "balancer" in Asia. The current imbroglio is traced back "to the colonial history of Korea and Korean anti-Japanese resistance, as well as the post-war partition of Korea (one-sidedly) by the Allied Forces".[12] The Koreas were divided up along the 38th parallel by two young (American) officers under great pressure, who used a *National Geographic* map for reference.[13]

The two Koreas stand separated by the Demilitarized Zone (DMZ), which is roughly 4 km wide and 250 km long. Because of the political impasse, the train from Dorasan Station (South Korea) to Gaesong (Kaesong, North Korea) has been unable to navigate the short distance. Seoul is only 55 km away from the North Korean border. Seoul, home to a fifth of South Korea's population, lives in the constant shadow of nuclear North Korea. The DMZ itself, described as "the scariest place on earth", is fortified with landmines, military bunkers with the North's largest artillery force of 13,000 systems and 2,300 multiple rocket launchers,[14] and is "a monument to a stalemate"[15] in the region.

Seen from the North Korean perspective, 28,500 American troops – the largest contingent of US forces – are based across 83 sites in South Korea, apart from 15 military bases that include one naval, two air force, and 12 army bases.[16] About 40,000 to 60,000 US personnel are based in Japan in 112 bases (the majority in Okinawa), with the Seventh Fleet, the largest among the US navy's deployed forces, headquartered in Japan.[17] *Camp Humphreys* at Pyeongtaek (60 km south of Seoul) is the largest American base in Asia and the largest overseas military base. The base, the size of central Washington, is where American soldiers "eat Popeye's chicken and drink from Arby's cups"[18] in a distant land. The base is slated to grow by another 40,000 troops by 2022, buoyed by America's 1953 Mutual Defence Treaty with South Korea.[19]

China and North-East Asia

In terms of security, North-East Asia is of great strategic significance to China. For China, North-East Asia is where the Great Wall – built with the intent of keeping invaders out – begins (at its border with North Korea at Dandong). Historically, this was the troubled frontier through which invaders came. The only non-Han dynasties of China have been the Mongols in the 13th century (1271–1368) and the Manchus in the 17th–20th centuries (1644–1911). Both invaded through the North-East corridor.[20] In the 20th century, China fought two wars here – the Korean War (1950–1953) and another with the Soviet Union (1969).

In the last decades, China has expressed an interest in maintaining political stability on its margins and with its neighbours, articulated as "peaceful rise". With China's rise, it has abandoned "biding its time" (*taoguang yanghui*) and embraced a more "go-out" (*zou chuqu*) foreign policy, a shift from what diplomat and ex-president of China Foreign Affairs University Wu Jianmin calls a "responsive diplomacy" (*fanying shi waijiao*) to "pro-active diplomacy" (*zhudong shi waijiao*).[21] According to David Shambaugh, following the Asian Financial Crisis (1997) and "Peace and Development Debate" (1999), China stepped up its "neighbourhood policy" (*zhoubian waijiao*), a shift from its earlier passive policy. This has entailed "a sustained period of proactive and regional diplomacy under the rubric of 'establish good neighbourliness, make neighbours prosperous, and make them feel secure' (*mulin, fulin, anlin*)".[22] In the 2000s, the focus on its periphery resulted in stabilisation of the neighbourhood.

As the world's second largest economy, China actively engaged with the vibrant economies of South Korea, Japan, America, and Taiwan, but North Korea continues to be subsidised. As the second most important power, China has to balance its responsibilities as a socialist power and its new global responsibilities. Samuel Kim observes that China's approach is determined by three main concerns – views North Korea as an integral part of its external security environment and seeks stability at the geostrategic crossroads of North-East Asia; economic engagement in the Peninsula to check and counter American influence or Japanese hegemony; and a Korea "divided or united" that poses no challenge of any kind to the legitimacy of the People's Republic of China (PRC) as a socialist state and a multinational empire.[23] Economic interests further complicate the picture, not least with the friendly but fractious China-North Korea relations.

China-North Korea relations

North Korea as a strategic shield

North Korea is positioned at what Victor Cha calls "the heart of the most vibrant economic region of the world". As Cha notes, "It has the globe's second largest economy on its border (China), the third largest across the seas (Japan), and the fifteenth largest economy (South Korea) contiguous to it, with which it shares a common language".[24] Seen from a strategic perspective, North Korea constitutes a "strategic shield". Its proximity, the shared borders with China, and the fact that that it keeps the US military presence at bay make it a coveted natural ally. Though North Korea is one-eightieth the size of China, with a fraction of China's population (25 million versus 1.4 billion) the relationship has been described as a "lips and teeth" relationship (*chunchi guanxi*), where one (lips) cannot exist without the other (teeth).

Even so, the China-North Korea relationship is quite complex. It has been said that China regards North Korea as a reflection of its former self: China circa 1970, with Seagull and Songchonggang bicycles, Vinalon shirts and food coupons.[25]

As an immediate neighbour,[26] North Korea is easily accessible (railway, river crossings, and bridges) across a border separated by the Yalu and Tumen rivers, and Mountain Paektu (*Changbai* in Chinese). The North Korean city of Sinuiju is easily visible from a high-rise in Dandong (Liaoning province, China), as they are only a mile across the Sino-Korean Friendship bridge over the Yalu river.

Dandong is the key point for China's trade, aid, and oil with North Korea. Dandong is also a living symbol of Sino-Korean friendship, where the Memorial of the War to Resist America and Aid Korea (1993) stands. Political instability and nuclear crisis in North Korea will have far-reaching implications on China (refugees, possibility of earthquakes, nuclear accident), unlike America, which is a stakeholder but very far away in terms of geography.

China-North Korea: strategic allies with historical and ideological ties

China's involvement in the Korean War (which famously claimed Mao Zedong's son Mao Anying) and China and North Korea's shared socialist ideology make them strategic allies. According to Li Nan, "Not only did Mao transfer 40,000 PLA [People's Liberation Army] officers to the newly established Korean People's Army (KPA) but also intervention via Chinese People's Volunteers Army (PVA) following post-Inchon landing debacle saved Kim's regime".[27] China's PVAs withdrew in 1957,[28] whereas American troops continued their presence in South Korea.

In addition to supporting China during the War, several leaders of North Korea's Workers Party, including founding father Kim Il-sung and his successor, Kim Jong-il, studied in China. In fact, North Korea shadowed China's socialist experience in Kim's speech of 1955, "On Eliminating Dogmatism and Formalism and Establishing *Juche* in Ideological Work". *Juche* (self-reliance), *juche–sasang* (*juche* ideology), and *juche seong* (*juche-ness*, or the state of independence)[29] have mirrored China's socialist goals. In response to the withdrawal of China's PVA came the *seoungun cheongch'i* or *seoungun sasang* (military first) principle.[30]

North Korea also followed China's "Great Leap Forward" (GLF) with "*Chollima Undong*" (Flying Horse Movement, 1958) with the promise of a triple revolution in technology, culture, and ideology, and a slogan reminiscent of China's GLF: "Let us dash forward at the speed of *Chollima*".[31] In the 1960s, China began to provide military aid to North Korea. Though China's "Cultural Revolution" (1966–1976) threw the relations off-balance, they were restored in the 1970s. Li Nan has noted that during the early 1970s, the Chinese-built shipyard could produce four Type-33 (Romeo Class) submarines a year for North Korea, which still accounts for about 20 such North Korean submarines operational today. The 30-km-long oil pipeline built from Dandong to Sinuiju which fulfils 80 per cent of North Korea's needs was also built during this time. North Korea's trade with China rose from 88.3 per cent in 2012 to 89.1 per cent in 2013, and to about 90 per cent in 2014.[32] China is North Korea's most important trade partner and accounted for 86.4 per cent and 91.4 per cent of its exports and imports in 2017, respectively, followed by India, Russia, and Pakistan.[33]

Is North Korea a strategic liability for China?

Nonetheless, China's relationship with North Korea is far from smooth and has been "ad hoc",[34] as You Ji terms it. In fact, observers have noted that the "lips to teeth" relationship is overstated and more likely "propagandistic pablum",[35] more "myth, than fact".[36] As a socialist partner, China has expressed its reservations about North Korea's dynastic succession and the leader's greatness (*suryong*) and purported "mystical Mangyongdae family origins".[37] Kim Il-sung was at the helm for 44 years, followed by his son Kim Jong-il (1994–2011) for 17 years and grandson, Kim Jong-un, who has been at the helm for eight years. This is unlike China, where succession has been quasi-institutionalised.

Despite China's reform push in 1978, North Korea has resisted economic reforms. In theory, North Korea has proclaimed *byungjin* (simultaneous development of military and economy, in 2016). But in practice, North Korea has been reluctant to embrace the Chinese model of development. Kim Jong-il described China's market economy as the "fishing rod of temptation".[38] Thus, reforms in North Korea have had an erratic trajectory. In 2002, North Korea established the Sinuiju Special Administrative Region (SAR), Kaesong Industrial Complex (KIC), and the Mount Kumgang Tourist Zone. Kim Jong-il visited several successful reform complexes and facilities in China (Dalian, Tianjin, 2010–2011), but nothing came of it. In 2011, Chinese reports highlighted the risks to investment, lack of transparency, and economic problems in North Korea. Reports suggest that Chinese investment has mainly been concentrated in mining and shipping. But there have been problems. In 2012, China's Xiyang Group, which had invested $38 million, ended up losing $55.3 million as it was expelled without reason.[39] Jaewoo Choo opines that failed economic cooperation has been a key element in the breakdown in relations. North Korea's execution of Kim Jong-un's uncle, Jang Song-thaek, in 2013, the main "go-between" and power broker between China and North Korea, was a further dampener.

North Korea as a nuclear neighbour

North Korea conducted its first nuclear test in 2006, apparently made possible by the proliferation network run by Pakistani nuclear physicist A.Q. Khan, from whom they acquired "centrifuges to enrich uranium", and companies in Ukraine, which gave them "access to high-performance liquid-propellant rocket engines".[40] In 2012, North Korea constitutionally declared itself to be a nuclear weapons state and passed the Nuclear Weapons State Law in 2013. Since then North Korea, which is not a party to the Missile Technology Control Regime (MTCR), has been responsible for proliferation. Besides Libya, "other customers of North Korean missiles or missile technology include Pakistan, Iran, Egypt, Syria, and Vietnam".[41]

The reality is that China, not the United States, sits next to a nuclear North Korea, which has conducted six nuclear tests, with many of its nuclear facilities along the Sino-North Korean border. The last nuclear test has been equated to a hydrogen bomb with "at least 100 kilotons" yield.[42] In 2017, both the Hwasong-14 and Hwasong-15 missile tests demonstrated their ability to go beyond Japan and reach American soil. China's worry is that North Korea's nuclear weapons development could trigger a regional nuclear arms race involving Japan, Taiwan, and South Korea, threatening China's comparative advantage.[43] Several other experts, notably Li Nan, opine that Japan and South Korea (not Taiwan) may jump into the nuclear arms race. In fact, China may have confirmed its worst fears with the gradual American shift from conventional deterrence to nuclear deterrence. Japan is also seeking to revise and amend its pacifist post-war constitution. South Korea has deployed Terminal High Altitude Area Defence (THAAD) in Sangju (North Gyeongsang province) – these developments have implications on China's security.

China's economic entanglements in North-East Asia

Equity

A rising China cannot ignore the South Korean economic success story. Unlike China, whose Gini-coefficient shows a growing gap, South Korea has achieved growth with equity. In China's economic calculus, South Korea carries more weight than North Korea. China cannot afford to ignore Japan either. As has been said, both China and Japan graze in the same grassland.[44] Japan-China trade increased from a billion dollars in 1972 to $312 billion in 2014. China is Japan's largest trading partner, and Japan is China's third largest trading partner. As Ming Wan notes, for a decade during 1993–2004, Japan was China's largest trading partner.

Scott Synder notes that the economic component of China's relationship with South Korea is underscored by Dale Copeland's "theory of trade expectations", which argues that economic cooperation induces interdependence. Trade between China and South Korea has grown at double-digit rates for over 15 years, from $2.56 billion in 1990 to over $100 billion in 2005. In 2004, China surpassed the United States as South Korea's largest trading partner and is now South Korea's largest bilateral partner. By 2006, South Korea had set up more than 30,000 enterprises with an accumulated investment of $35 billion, and 2007 marked the celebration of the Korea-Chinese Friendship Year.[45] It is estimated that of the nearly $500 billion goods exported by South Korea, around $125 billion were sent to China (a quarter of its exports), of which three-quarters was accounted for by the processing trade (assembled and exported to a third country).[46] The technology gap between the two has been narrowing[47] – where a Samsung phone is as good as a Huawei.

China-South Korea signed the China-South Korea Free Trade Agreement (CKFTA) on June 1, 2015. Fifty per cent of South Korea's incoming 17 million tourists in 2016 were from China.[48] The development of four China-Korea industrial parks in Yantai, Yancheng, and Huizhou in China and Saemangeum Development in South Korea have been incorporated into the FTA.[49] But China's increasing competitiveness has given rise to debates in South Korea on the demerits of economic engagement. Allegations of China "hollowing out" the South Korean economy by the influx of cheap goods from China and issues relating to technology leaks, espionage, and intellectual theft have plagued the relations. In a recent case (2018), Samsung accused two companies (names not disclosed) for selling its bendable screen technology to a Chinese rival.[50] Following THAAD deployment (operational 2017), South Korea's Lotte Group closed 100 odd stores in China. Cosmetic sales and group tours to China faltered, and sales of Hyundai and KIA Motors dropped.

But despite the political downturn, South Korean exports to China witnessed high, double-digit growth of 12 per cent in 2017.[51] In Japan, China is considered key for growth as "net exports (to China) contributed exactly one-third of Japan's economic growth since the beginning of 2017".[52]

Implications

Since the cementing of China's economic ties with South Korea, there have been shifts in China's "one-Korea" (pro-Pyongyang) policy. As Samuel King explains, China has moved from a "one-Korea *de-jure*" to a "two-Koreas *de-facto*" policy to finally, a two-Koreas "*de-facto* and *de-jure*" policy. In response to South Korea's *Nordpolitik* (Northern Diplomacy) in 1992, China also sought diplomatic leverage to make South Korea terminate its relationship with Taiwan.[53] This was a departure from China's own policy, where "one plus one" (China plus Taiwan) is one, but "one plus one" (North Korea and South Korea) is two.[54] In fact, China and South Korea have upgraded relations from a "cooperative partnership" to a "comprehensive cooperative partnership" in 2003.

Constraints – China's versus others' interests

The picture in North-East Asia is mixed. A zero-sum game with one clear winner would jeopardise the status quo on the Peninsula. Despite political differences, the major stakeholders and economies are intertwined as economic partners. But economic cooperation aside, realpolitik dictates that while all the stakeholders sleep on the North-East Asian bed, all have "different dreams", because of differing security perceptions and national interests.

China and South Korea are significant economic partners and yet have considerable differences. The same applies to China's relationship with Japan. China feels the security risk of the THAAD (in South Korea) as the radar capability goes beyond North Korea. The Army/Navy Transportable Radar Surveillance (AN/TPY-2) with a detection range of 1,500 km–2,000 km is capable of detecting most of China's strategic missiles targeting the United States.[55] Li Nan suggests that China's missile activities on land and at sea in northern and eastern China are vulnerable, given the radar's ability to collect data, such as on China's missile tests and missile, including where warheads and decoys are released. In December 2017, President Moon Jae-in met President Xi Jinping in Beijing and discussed China's "Three Oppositions" (3 No's) to THAAD. These included: China's opposition to additional deployment of THAAD batteries, no to Korea's prospective participation in the US-led missile defence system in North-East Asia, and no strengthening of US-Korea-Japan military relations. South Korea has acquiesced to the Chinese demands.

As much as China is the rising power, Japan is the old sentinel of Asia. China-Japan relations have faltered because of territorial disputes over the *Senkaku* Islands (*Diaoyu* in Chinese, Pinnacle in English), in the maritime zone surrounding *Okinotorishima,* and on the maritime boundary between Japan and China in the East China Sea.[56] As Asia's old guard, Japan's role and relationship with North Korea is also critical in terms of how it perceives and negotiates the situation; its response in case of a humanitarian crisis; the Non-combatant Evacuation Operations (NEOs) for Japanese nationals in the Peninsula; and the logistics support for American forces and reunification costs (reunification of Korea).[57]

Japan continues to struggle with the historical baggage of its colonisation of Korea (1910–1945) when Korea was integrated under the *naisenittai* (making Japan and Korea [into] one body).[58] The issues of comfort women and discrimination against Korean workers, citizens, and residents in Japan (*Zainichi Koreans*) persist to this day. Japan faces the threat of North Korean intrusions into Japanese waters and missiles that fly over Hokkaido. "J-Alert" – the Japanese emergency warning systems – are now a well-honed response to North Korean threats.

The critical issue for Japan-North Korea is that of the abductees. North Korea has been behind the kidnappings of Japanese civilians. Kim Jong-il admitted to the kidnappings during Japanese prime minister Junichiro Koizumi's visit to Pyongyang in 2002. Thirteen Japanese had been kidnapped by "elements of a special agency of a state", of which five were living in North Korea and eight were dead.[59] The dead include the tragic case of the young school girl Yokota Megumi, who was kidnapped from Niigata (she committed suicide in 1993 in North Korea).

Japan's White Paper on Defence (2018) has justified the budget request of the Ministry of Defence of ¥5.3 trillion in April 2019. Prime Minister Shinzo Abe, who won a third term in 2018, has also sought to amend the "no-war" clause of Article 9 in its post-war pacifist constitution (which has not been amended in the 72 years of its history).[60] The constitutional revision seeks to clarify and formalise the legal status of the Self Defence Forces (SDF, the de facto Japanese military). The re-militarisation of Japan will dramatically impact North-East Asia.

China's strategic community and North Korea

Unlike China-South Korea and China-Japan relations, which are underpinned by economics, China-North Korea relations are underpinned by subsidy. Part of China's strategic community as well as public intellectuals *(gongzhi)* view North Korea as an economic and strategic burden – an unspoken "pay for your buffer" rationale of a (de facto) nuclear power that makes it a "strategic liability".[61] China spearheaded the Six-Party Talks (2003–2009) when North Korea pulled out of the Nuclear Non-Proliferation Treaty in 2003. By 2009, the Talks had failed.

In 2012, China stated that its relationship with North Korea was a "normal state to state one". In 2012, 29 Chinese fishermen were kidnapped by North Korea, and in 2013, a Chinese fishing boat hijacked for a ransom.[62] These actions were seen as signals of Pyongyang's displeasure about China's policies, including Beijing's blunt criticism of North Korea's satellite launch, its warnings against a third nuclear test, and possibly, even China's suspension of the repatriation of North Korean defectors.[63] In fact, China's strategic community is divided over North Korea. "Traditionalists" in China, that is, the Communist Party of China (CPC), and the PLA want to maintain the North Korean "buffer zone" for realpolitik and ideological reasons. But "strategists" in the Ministry of Foreign Affairs (MFA) and academia want a more "normal relationship" with North Korea, because of the high costs of maintaining an unpredictable neighbour.[64]

But China's abandoning of North Korea would be tantamount to China giving a big gift to the United States and South Korea, "*song dali*".[65] Yoichi Funabashi[66] argues that China should be able to have economic leverage over North Korea, but the patron is a likely hostage to North Korea's ambivalence, recalcitrance, and shifting stances, locked in a "mutual hostage relationship".[67] You Ji opines that China has to "re-adjust its approach constantly".[68] On the other hand, South Korea faces an "entrapment dilemma" in which it "cannot afford to isolate China even as it remains allied with the United States".[69]

China's strategic dilemma

Unpredictable relations with North Korea and the evolving political situation pose a strategic dilemma for China. China's economic entanglements with North-East Asian neighbours also posit a dilemma, as China's economic interests do not match its security interests.

In the evolving situation, China, which has been a critical player with respect to North Korea since 1950, was sidelined in the thaw between the United States, South Korea, and North Korea in 2018.

During 2012–2017, while there were six summits and two visits by President Xi and President Park (of South Korea), no meetings took place between Chairman Kim and President Xi. But since March 2018, four meetings have materialised between China and North Korea. In 2019, President Xi visited Pyongyang (the first in 14 years), where he was greeted by children singing a song laden with symbolism: "I love you China". The China-North Korea 1961 Treaty is to expire in 2021.

Progress in North-East Asia

Some of the dramatic changes in North-East Asia have taken place because President Trump has made nuclear diplomacy with North Korea his "signature foreign policy project", a move that the American media views as one of President Trump's "biggest potential legacies".[70] The first President Trump-Chairman Kim summit took place in Singapore (2018), followed by the second summit at

Hanoi (2019). The first summit ended on a positive note and a joint statement committing to "establish new US-D.P.R.K. relations, lasting and stable peace regime on the Korean Peninsula, complete de-nuclearisation and US recovering POW/MIA [prisoner of war/missing in action] remains".[71] The second summit ended abruptly with neither a statement or a document nor an agreement. North Korea indicated that it was ready to dismantle the ageing Yongbyon nuclear complex in lieu of sanction relief but kept mum about undeclared nuclear facilities. The United States remained sceptical about North Korea's nuclear arsenal, continued uranium production, warheads, and missiles.[72] But after months of stalled relations, in a dramatic move, President Trump reversed the stall, crossing the demarcation line into North Korea. But relations continue to "yo-yo", with the diplomatic thaw giving way to tensions. The stall led to President Trump asking the national security adviser John Bolton to step down in September 2019.[73]

North Korea has opened up diplomatic channels with America, China, Russia, Japan, and Korea. There have been three inter-Korean meets in 2018 (April, May, and September). The first in Panmunjom (April 2018) concluded with the "Panmunjom Declaration for Peace, Prosperity and Unification of the Korean Peninsula". President Moon Jae-in visited North Korea in September 2018. Relations have improved, but progress remains tardy.

The anticipated economic reset between North and South Korea has yet to take place. The Kaesong Industrial Complex, with more than 100 participating South Korean companies, has stalled, and so has the East Asian Railway Community (EARC),[74] which seeks to link the six North-East Asian countries (the two Koreas, China, Mongolia, Japan, Russia) with US participation. North Korea continues to reel under sanctions and economic contraction, the worst in 30 years. It is also in the midst of a severe "hunger crisis", with 10 million North Koreans at risk and a food deficit estimated at 1.36 million metric tonnes.[75]

Conclusion

A combination of geographical determinism, history, politics, and economics has made North-East Asia a complex security riddle. North-East Asia is characterised by a dramatic asymmetry of power, nuclear weapons, and economic interdependence as well as by divergent goalposts of the stakeholders. It would be naïve to view economic interdependence as a sufficient condition for peace.[76] It is also premature to gauge the success of President Trump's diplomacy or even of President Xi's diplomacy. In practical terms, "maximum pressure" on North Korea continues with sanctions intact.

A solution remains elusive because a zero-sum game with a clear winner would upset the status quo. China, as Li Nan writes, seeks to "avoid war and chaos" (*buzhan, buluan*) and achieve "non-nuclearization" (*buhe*, denuclearisation) in the Peninsula. President Xi's visit to North Korea (2019) articulated the optimism of an "inevitable trend" towards a political settlement. The US demands are denuclearisation and suspension of long-range missiles. Japan seeks American friendship and North Korea's suspension of short-range missiles, which impact its security; resolution of the abductee issue alongside amendment of the Japanese Constitution; trade with China; and denuclearisation. South Korea wants the US security umbrella, trade with China, resumption of trade with North Korea, and steps towards denuclearisation.

The opposite scenario is equally interesting. China's nightmare would be North Korea biting the American economic bait. For China, the "buffer" would then be lost. Japan's militarisation and going nuclear, a possibility that has risen with the re-election of Shinzo Abe's win in the national elections (July 2019), with the Liberal Democratic Party (LDP) winning a majority of seats in the upper house (but short of the "supermajority" required to amend the Constitution), posits a formidable challenge. Though Abe is short of the "supermajority" required to amend the Constitution, the issue is likely to remain alive. For the United States, a likely nightmare would be the challenge to the US "pivot". There is little doubt that a trilateral combine of North Korea, China, and Russia would pose a huge challenge to the US "pivot".

For South Korea, despite the optimism of being one race (*minjok*) and unification, a "three-pronged defense system" is being developed to meet North Korean missile threat.[77] That the economic costs of sudden collapse or of unification would be high and that the success of unification depends on Japanese cooperation is recognised. South Korea and Japan have yet to shed historical animosity. In fact, the issue of Korean forced labour during Japanese colonisation remains an unresolved issue. Since July 2019, this issue led to an escalation of trade war between Japan and South Korea, with South Korea calling off talks to join the Japan-led Comprehensive and Progressive Trans-Pacific Partnership. For Japan, a North Korea-US deal that includes long-range missiles and omits short-range missiles and the Japanese abductees would be a matter of concern.

Further, China supports "double freeze" (also referred to as "freeze-for-freeze" or "suspension for suspension") and denuclearisation, where North Korea would freeze its nuclear activities in exchange for the cessation of joint military exercises by the United States and South Korea. As for North Korea and the United States, there is no common understanding, as Park Hahnkyu indicates,[78] on what Complete, Verifiable, Irreversible, Denuclearisation (CVID) means. North Korea views the CVID as the removal of the US nuclear umbrella in the Peninsula, the same position it has taken since 1992 when the two Koreas signed the Joint Declaration on the Denuclearisation of the Korean Peninsula that seeks a "reciprocal, phased and step-by-step approach" to the issue.

North Korea's position was spelt out in the statement issued on July 6, 2016, where it made demands that included full disclosure of US nuclear weapons (in South Korea), US assurance that it would not bring nuclear strike capability to South Korea, and the declaration of the withdrawal of US troops which hold the right to use nuclear weapons from South Korea.[79] North Korea seeks denuclearisation of the Korean Peninsula, including removal of the US nuclear umbrella over South Korea, whereas the United States interprets denuclearisation as denuclearisation of North Korea. Washington's expectations are visibly different, seeking "rapid and complete denuclearisation".

The mechanism through which denuclearisation is sought to be achieved is also conceived differently. China and Russia back engagement through the Six-Party Talks; the US seeks to achieve this through "maximum pressure", which has so far not worked. North Korea views the possession of nuclear weapons as critical for regime stability and for deterrence of what has been termed North Korea's "siege mentality".[80] Yang Xiyu opines that North Korea takes the "Libya example as a major lesson",[81] rationalising that had Gaddafi not given up the country's nuclear weapons, the United States and its allies would not have attacked them. Bong-Guen Jun has indicated that in the last 25 years, there have been seven "vicious cycles"[82] of nuclear crises, agreements, and collapse which have created distrust between the United States and North Korea. The blockade of North Korean exports of iron ore, seafood, and textiles and the closure of inter-Korean projects such as the Kaesong Industrial Complex and Mount Kumgang (tourism) tours have not helped. The US seizure of the cargo ship *Wise Honest*, in May 2019, further strained relations.

In May 2019, North Korea resumed testing short-range missiles, the first time after 2017. In July 2019, weeks after the goodwill visit by President Xi and meeting with President Trump, North Korea tested short-range missiles from Wonsan to protest an impending military exercise between the United States and South Korea.

North Korea is a "weak actor" but a defiant one, resisting and manipulating the powerful – what Charles Armstrong calls the "tyranny of the weak", "dealing with the outside world to its maximum advantage".[83]

In the Peninsula, all factors are known. Relations are improving, and each stakeholder seeks to leverage its relationship with North Korea (and vice versa). However, the outcome so far remains an unknown: Collapse, unification, Six-Party Talks, US truce with North Korea, or North Korean integration with China's economy and continued Chinese security assurance? All stakeholders walk a fine line between war and peace. Peace, denuclearisation, and status quo in North-East Asia are desirable goals – but in the face of the evolving situation, the magic formula eludes China, as it does the other stakeholders.

Notes

1 "I Love You China: North Korea Woos Xi in Lavish State Visit; Kim Says North Korea-China Ties Invincible", *The Straits Times*, June 21, 2019, at www.straitstimes.com/asia/east-asia/xi-and-kim-agree-to-have-close-and-strategic-ties-reports-north-korean-media/ (accessed July 23, 2019).
2 Natasha Turak, "Trump Becomes First US Sitting President in History to Cross Border into North Korea", CNBC, June 30, 2019, at www.cnbc.com/2019/06/30/rtrs-190630-trump-kim-quotes-dmz-eu.html (accessed July 24, 2019).
3 "Trump in North Korea: KCNA Hails 'Amazing Visit'", BBC, July 1, 2019, at www.bbc.com/news/world-asia-48821790 (accessed July 24, 2019).
4 This needs some qualification; as Michael J. Seth explains, 676–935 C.E. is the period called United Silla, but the Silla did not control the northern third of the modern boundaries of Korea. Michael J. Seth, *A Concise History of Korea: From the Neolithic Period through the Nineteenth Century*, Rowman & Littlefield, Oxford, 2006, p. 49.

5 Stanley Sandler, *The Korean War: No Victors, No Vanquished*, Routledge, London, 2003, p. 264.
6 Caitlin Talmadge, "Beijing's Nuclear Option: Why a U.S.–China War Could Spiral out of Control", *Foreign Affairs*, 97 (6), November/December 2018, p. 46.
7 Andrei Lankov, *From Stalin to Kim Il Sung: The Formation of North Korea 1945–1960*, Rutgers University Press, New Jersey, 2002, p. 194.
8 Scott Synder, *China's Rise and the Two Koreas: Politics, Economics, Security*, Lynne Rienner, Colorado, 2009, p. 9.
9 Heungkyu Kim, "The Sino-North Korean Relationship at the Crossroads", in Haksoon Paik & Seong-Chang Cheong (eds.), *North Korea in Distress: Confronting Domestic and External Challenges*, Sejong Institute, Seongnam, 2008, p. 170.
10 Victor Cha, *The Impossible State: North Korea, Past and Future*, Harper Collins, New York, 2012, p. 318.
11 Adrian Buzo, *The Making of Modern Korea*, Routledge, Abingdon, 2007, pp. 2–12.
12 Sonia Ryang (ed.), *North Korea: Toward a Greater Understanding*, Lexington Books, Lanham, 2009, p. 11.
13 Suk-Young Kim, *DMZ Crossing: Performing the Emotional Citizenship Along the Korean Border*, Columbia University Press, New York, 2014, p. 5.
14 Victor Cha, No. 10, p. 219.
15 Suk-Young Kim, No. 13, p. 7.
16 Gu Guoliang, "China's Policy Toward the DPRK's Nuclear and Missile Programs", in Carla Freeman (ed.), *China and North Korea: Strategic and Policy Perspectives from a Changing China*, Palgrave Macmillan, New York, 2015, p. 169.
17 Oliver Holmes, "What Is the US Military's Presence near North Korea", *The Guardian*, August 9, 2017, at www.theguardian.com/us-news/2017/aug/09/what-is-the-us-militarys-presence-in-south-east-asia (accessed December 1, 2018); Christine Kim, "South Korea Says It Wants U.S. Troops to Stay Regardless of Any Treaty with North Korea", Reuters, May 2, 2018, at www.reuters.com/article/us-usa-southkorea-northkorea/south-korea-says-it-wants-us-troops-to-stay-regardless-of-any-treaty-with-north-korea-idUSKBN1I305J (accessed November 25 and December 1, 2018).
18 Joseph Hincks, "Inside Camp Humphreys, South Korea: America's Largest Overseas Military Base", *Time*, July 12, 2018, at http://time.com/5324575/us-camp-humphreys-south-korea-largest-military-base/ (accessed June 18, 2019).
19 Jon Letman, "USAG Humphreys: The Story Behind America's Biggest Overseas Base", *The Diplomat*, November 6, 2017, at https://thediplomat.com/2017/11/camp-humphreys-the-story-behind-americas-biggest-overseas-base/ (accessed November 25 and December 1, 2018).
20 Pamela Crossley and Richard M. Eaton, "Conquest, Rulership, and the State", in Sheldon Pollock and Benjamin Elman (eds.), *What China and India Once Were: The Pasts that May Shape the Global Future*, Penguin Random House, Gurgaon, 2018, pp. 63–91.
21 Zhiqun Zhu, "China's Warming Relations with South Korea and Australia", in Mingjiang Li (ed.), *Soft Power: China's Emerging Strategy in International Politics*, Lexington Books, Plymouth, 2009, p. 187.
22 David Shambaugh, "Coping with a Conflicted China", in David Shambaugh (ed.), *The China Reader: Rising Power*, Oxford University Press, New York, 2016, p. 362.
23 Samuel S. Kim, "China and the Future of the Korean Peninsula", in Tsuneo Akaha (ed.), *The Future of North Korea*, Routledge, London, 2002, p. 113.
24 Victor Cha, No. 10, p. 7.
25 Paul French explains, *Juche* is underpinned by self-sustainability and self-defence (*chawi*). The latter positions the military as the primary social grouping above the working class and peasantry. As for *Juche* year, Sweeny explains that *Juche* Year Zero starts on April 15, Anno Domini 1912 – the date on which Kim Il-sung was born. Paul French, *North Korea: The Paranoid Peninsula – A Modern History*, Zed Books, London,

1988, pp. 18, 38. John Sweeny, *North Korea Undercover: Inside the World's Most Secret State*, Bantam Press, London, 2013, p. 98.
26 China has a huge Korean community in the Yanbian Korean Autonomous Prefecture (Jilin province), where 40 per cent (of the 2 million population) are Koreans who migrated into China in the late 17th century. Besides, Korean is the official language. Tumen, a city in Yanbian, is connected to Namyang in North Korea across the Tumen River bridge, at http://arabic.china.org.cn/english/travel/53647.htm (accessed September 11 2019).
27 Li Nan, "China's Evolving Policy Towards North Korea: From Strategic Asset to Liability", *East Asian Policy*, 9 (4), October–December 2017, p. 17.
28 See, Cheng Xiaohe, "Evolution of Lips and Teeth Relationship: China-North Korea Relations in the 1960s", in Carla P. Freeman (ed.), No. 16, p. 121.
29 Charles K. Armstrong, "Socialism, Sovereignty and the North Korean Exception", in Sonia Ryang (ed.), No. 12, pp. 41–53.
30 See, Gavan McCormack, "North Korea and the Birth Pangs of a New Northeast Asian Order", in Sonia Ryang (ed.), No. 12, pp. 23–41; Sonia Ryang, "North Korea: Going Beyond Security and Enemy Rhetoric", in Sonia Ryang (ed.), No. 12, pp. 1–23; Li Yongchun, "North Korea's Guiding Ideology and Its Impact", in Carla P. Freeman (ed.), No. 16, pp. 226–231.
31 Han Shik Park and Kyung Ae Park, *Asian Studies Monograph Series*, Asian Research Service, Hong Kong, 1990, pp. 63, 67, 111.
32 Sung Chull Kim, "North Korea's Search for a Breakthrough", *East Asian Policy*, 7 (1), January–March 2015, p. 156.
33 Min-Hua Chiang, "North Korea's Economic Prospect after Trump-Kim Summit", *East Asian Institute Background Brief No. 1389*, September 20, 2018, p. 11.
34 You Ji, "Dealing with the North Korea Dilemma: China's Strategic Choices", *No. 239*, S Rajarathnam School of International Studies, Singapore, June 21, 2011, p. 32.
35 David Shambaugh, "China and the Korean Peninsula: Playing for the Long Term", *Washington Quarterly*, 26 (2), 2003, pp. 43–56, cited in Robert Kelly "China's Interests in Korean Unification: How Much Longer Is the 'Buffer' Worth It?" *The Korean Journal of Security Affairs*, 19 (2), December 2014, pp. 4–21.
36 You Ji, No. 33, p. 3.
37 Jin Zhe, "Hereditary Succession and the DPRK Leadership", in Carla P. Freeman (ed.), No. 16, pp. 241–247.
38 Paul French, No. 25, p. 157.
39 North Korea committed to turning the former into a processing trade area and to the "One Bridge, Two Islands" development, where the New Yalu Bridge would be built with Chinese collaboration. In addition, MoUs were signed granting Chinese access to ports (North Hamkyung, Ranjin), construction of railways and highways linking Chungjin, Namyang and Tuman, and Rajin and Hunchun. Jaewoo Choo, "Breakdown in China-North Korea Relations: Caused Not by the Third Nuclear Test but by Failed Economic Cooperation", *The Korean Journal of Security Affairs*, 21 (1), June 2016, pp. 42–49.
40 Scott D. Sagan, "Armed and Dangerous: When Dictators Get the Bomb", *Foreign Affairs*, 97 (6), November/December 2018, p. 38.
41 Bertil Lintner, *Great Leader, Dear Leader: Demystifying North Korea Under the Kim Regime*, Silkworm, Chiang Mai, Thailand, 2005; Stephan Haggard and Marcus Noland, *Famine in North Korea: Markets, Aid and Reform*, Columbia University Press, New York, 2007, p. 247.
42 As assessed by Air Force General John Hyten, chief of US Strategic Command. See, Kim Sung Chull, The North Korean Nuclear Crisis in 2017: New Challenges and Risks, *East Asian Policy*, 10 (1), January/March 2018, pp. 135–136.
43 Han S. Park, "North Korea as a U.S.-China Flashpoint", *Korea Review*, II (2), November 2012, p. 21.

44 Ming Wan, *Understanding Japan-China Relations: Theories and Issues*, World Scientific, Singapore, 2016, p. 189.
45 Zhiqun Zhu, No 21, pp. 188–191.
46 Kylie Ferrier, "Just How Dependent South Korea on Trade with China"? Korea Economic Institute of America, at http://keia.org/just-how-dependent-south-korea-trade-china/ (accessed December 2, 2018).
47 Jae Ho Chung and Jiyoon Kim, "Is South Korea in China's Orbit? Assessing Seoul's Perceptions and Policies", *Asia Policy*, 21, January 1, 2016, pp. 134–135.
48 "Chinese Tourists Returning to South Korea after Missile Cools", *South China Morning Post*, May 2, 2018, at www.scmp.com/news/china/diplomacy-defence/article/214 4327/chinese-tourists-returning-south-korea-after-missile (accessed December 3, 2018).
49 Lye Liang Fook and Chen Juan, "China-South Korean Relations: Terminal High Altitude Area Defence System Deployment and Implications for Bilateral Ties", *East Asian Policy*, 9 (4), October–December 2017, p. 32.
50 Sam Kim, "South Korea Charges 11 with Selling Samsung Technology to China", November 29, 2018, at www.bloomberg.com/news/articles/2018-11-29/south-korea-charges-11-with-selling-samsung-technology-to-china (accessed December 2, 2018).
51 Lye Liang Fook and Chen Juan, No. 48, p. 39.
52 Michael Ivanovitch, "Japan's Trade with China Is Booming, but Irreconcilable Differences Persist", CNBC, September 2, 2018, at www.cnbc.com/2018/09/03/china-japan-trade-booms-despite-irreconcilable-differences—commentary.html (accessed June 18, 2019).
53 Scott Synder, No. 8, pp. 31–37.
54 Samuel S. Kim, No. 23, pp. 113–114.
55 Wu Riqiang, "South Korea's THAAD: Impact on China's Nuclear Deterrent", *RSIS*, July 27, 2016, at www.rsis.edu.sg/rsis-publication/rsis/co16192-south-koreas-thaad-impact-on-chinas-nuclear-deterrent/#.XAOu-C2B365 (accessed June 18, 2019).
56 Michael Hahn, "The Legal Aspects of Japan's Territorial and Maritime Disputes with Neighbouring States", in Thomas J. Schoenbaum (ed.), *Peace in Northeast Asia: Resolving Japan's Territorial and Maritime Disputes with China, Korea and the Russian Federation*, Edward Elgar, Cheltenham, 2008, pp. 26, 27, 42.
57 Jonathan D. Pollack and Ching Min Lee, *Preparing for Korean Unification: Scenarios & Implications*, RAND, Santa Monica, 1999, p. 13.
58 Sonia Ryang (ed.), *Koreans in Japan, Critical Voices from the Margin*, Routledge, London, 2000, pp. 2, 5.
59 Tessa Morris Suzuki, *Exodus to North Korea: Shadows from Japan's Cold War*, Rowman & Littlefield, Maryland, 2007, pp. 9, 12, 22.
60 Anurag Viswanath, "Japan-North Korea Relations Remain in a Freeze – Shinzo Abe Seeks an Evolution of the Yoshida Doctrine", *Financial Express*, October 13, 2018, at www.financialexpress.com/opinion/japan-north-korea-relations-remain-in-a-freeze-shinzo-abe-seeks-an-evolution-of-yoshida-doctrine/1347518/ (accessed May 10, 2019).
61 Li Nan, No. 27, p. 19.
62 Zhu Feng and Nathan Beaucamp Mustafaga indicate that four schools of thought contend in China – Nationalists, Realists, Internationalists, and Liberalists, each rationalising China's policy towards North Korea. According to them, Nationalists still understand China-North Korea relationship in terms of both historical memory and its criticality as buffer; Realists "maintain that Pyongyang is still a strategic asset, so Beijing must protect the DPRK …(and) regard the regimes nuclear program as a failure of Chinese policy linked to excessively close ties to the United States"; Internationalists focus that China's globalist reputation is taking a beating because of North Korean provocations and last of all; Liberalists "reject North Korea's value to

China, either as a strategic buffer or for any other strategic purpose". Instead, they seek a China-focus on the people of North Korea. Zhu Feng and Nathan Beauchamp Mustafaga, "North Korea's Security Implications for China", in Carla Freeman (ed.), No. 16, pp. 41–49.
63 Bonnie S. Glaser and Brittany Billingsley, "China-North Korean Ties in the Wake of the Death of Kim Jong Il", *Korea Review*, II (2), November 2012.
64 You Ji, No. 33, pp. 10–15.
65 Li Nan, No. 26, p. 23.
66 Scott Synder, No. 8, p. 131.
67 Ellen Kim and Victor Cha, "Between a Rock and a Hard Place: South Korea's Strategic Dilemmas with China and the United States", *Asia Policy*, 21, January 2016, p. 111.
68 You Ji, No. 33, pp. 10, 32.
69 Ellen Kim and Victor Cha, No. 66, p. 112.
70 Jane Perlez and Mark Landler, "Xi Jinping Will Make First Visit to North Korea ahead of Meeting with Trump", *The New York Times*, June 17, 2019, at www.nytimes.com/2019/06/17/world/asia/xi-jinping-north-korea.html (accessed June 23, 2019).
71 "Joint Statement of President Donald J. Trump of the United States of America and Chairman Kim Jong Un of the Democratic People's Republic of Korea at the Singapore Summit", The White House, June 12, 2018, at www.whitehouse.gov/briefings-statements/joint-statement-president-donald-j-trump-united-states-america-chairman-kim-jong-un-democratic-peoples-republic-korea-singapore-summit/ (accessed May 15, 2019).
72 David Sanger and Edward Wong, "How the Trump-Kim Summit Failed: Big Threats, Big Egos, Bad Bets", *The New York Times*, March 2, 2019, at www.nytimes.com/2019/03/02/world/asia/trump-kim-jong-un-summit.html (accessed May 15, 2019).
73 Demetri Sevastopulo and Aime Williams, "Trump Fires Bolton after Tensions on Iran and North Korea Boil Over, *Financial Times*, September 11, 2019, at www.ft.com/content/5b881f18-d3e4-11e9-8367-807ebd53ab77 (accessed September 11, 2019).
74 Lankov explains Hyundai Kumgang Mountain tourism project is also in stasis. The project stemmed from South Korean government's "Sunshine Policy" 1998–2008 and was to be operational but like the KIC and EARC is languishing. Andrei Lankov, "Holiday in North Korea: Lessons from Mount Kumgang", NK News, May 19, 2019, at www.nknews.org/2019/05/holiday-in-north-korea-lessons-from-mount-kumgang/ (accessed September 11, 2019). Also see Anurag Viswanath, "Hanoi Summit: Will the Economic Hook Open the Diplomatic Window?" *Financial Express*, March 9, 2019, at www.financialexpress.com/opinion/hanoi-summit-will-the-economic-hook-open-the-diplomatic-window/1510049/ (accessed May 15, 2019).
75 "North Korean Families Facing Deep Hunger Crisis After Worst Harvest in Ten Years, U.N. Assessment Shows", UN News, May 3, 2019, at https://news.un.org/en/story/2019/05/1037831 (accessed May 15, 2019).
76 Ming Wan, No. 43, p. 16.
77 According to Seung-chan Boo, the three elements are the Kill Chain pre-emptive attack system, the Korea Air and Missile Defence System (KAMD), and the Korea Massive Punishment and Retaliation Plan (KMPR) (p. 39). Seung-chan Boo, North Korea's Nuclear Reality, South Korea's Arms Anxiety. *Global Asia*, 13 (1), March 20, 2018, p. 39, at www.globalasia.org/v13no1/cover/north-koreas-nuclear-reality-south-koreas-arms-anxiety_seung-chan-boo (accessed September 11, 2019).
78 Park Hahnkyu "Trust but Verify: Donald Trump, Kim Jong Un and a Denuclearising North Korea after the Singapore Summit", *East Asian Policy*, 10 (3), July/September 2018, p. 10.
79 Robert Carlin, "North Korea Said It's Willing to Talk Denuclearization (But No One Noticed)", *The Diplomat*, July 13, 2016, cited in Tae-Hwan Kwak, "Inter-Korean

Relations: From Nuclear Confrontation to Peaceful Coexistence", *The Korean Journal of Security Affairs*, 23 (1), June 2018, p. 26. According to Tae-Hwan Kwak, North Korea's demand for a declaration on the withdrawal, but not immediate withdrawal, is a changed policy stance. Also see, Robert Carlin, "DPRK Repeats Stance on Denuclearization", 38 North, December 21, 2018, at www.38north.org/2018/12/rcarlin122118/ (accessed July 24, 2019).
80 Tae-Hwan Kwak, Ibid., p. 25.
81 Yang Xiyu, "China's Role and Its Dilemmas in the Six Party Talks", in Carla P. Freeman (ed.), No. 16, pp. 185–188.
82 Bong-Geun Jun, "Enough Failure Use Strategic Diplomacy to Denuclearize North Korea", *Global Asia*, 11 (4), Winter 2016, p. 22.
83 Charles K. Armstrong, *Tyranny of The Weak, North Korea and The World, 1950–1992*, Cornell University Press, Ithaca, 2013, pp. 3–4, 291–293.

3 Japan's security pledge in the Korean Peninsula

Kohtaro Ito

Inter-Korea reconciliation versus Japan's scepticism

The situation on the Korean Peninsula has moved rapidly towards reconciliation since the North Korean chairman of the State Affairs Commission Kim Jong-un announced, during his 2019 New Year's Day address, the North's participation in the 2018 Pyeongchang Winter Olympic Games. Consequently, the South Korean administration of Moon Jae-in, too, has held three summit meetings – in April, May, and September 2018 – with the objective of building a peace regime on the Korean Peninsula. It is significant that this thrust towards reconciliation has been achieved despite North Korea not revealing a concrete path to denuclearisation and South Korea's aggressive attitude towards the North, about which the South has often been cautioned by the United States.

In contrast to the positive changes in the inter-Korean relationship, Japan's perception of North Korea as a serious threat has remained consistent. Underlying Japanese concerns about North Korea's denuclearisation talks, in particular, is the deep-rooted distrust of North Korea since the first nuclear crisis in the 1990s. Therefore, Japan has been sceptical about peace on the Korean Peninsula. According to some experts, the situation on the Korean Peninsula was in a flux even after the decision to hold the US-North Korea summit meeting had been taken. Retired vice admiral of the Japan Maritime Self-Defence Force (JMSDF) Yoji Koda claimed that the United States recognised the threat to Japan and that Japan should prepare for the worst.[1]

At the US-North Korea summit meeting in Singapore on June 12, 2018, both countries agreed to denuclearise and improve bilateral relations. It is necessary to note that Complete, Verifiable and Irreversible Denuclearisation (CVID) was not included in the joint statement of the summit talks, deepening the scepticism about North Korea's denuclearisation. Japan's prime minister Shinzo Abe, however, has not changed his position on seeking CVID of North Korea. Meanwhile, at a press conference on June 22, Japan's chief cabinet secretary Yoshihide Suga spoke about temporarily stopping the missile protection training drills scheduled nationwide, considering the positive mood following the US-North Korea summit meeting.[2] On June 28, 2018, the Japanese government downgraded the alert level of the JMSDF's Aegis destroyers against a possible North Korean missile launch.[3] The Terminal-Phase Ballistic Missile Defence (BMD) Patriot Advanced Capability (PAC)-3 systems deployed in Hokkaido, Chugoku, and Shikoku regions were also withdrawn on July 30.

Nonetheless, the Japanese response to the inter-Korean summit held in Pyongyang on September 18 and 19 was more cautious compared to that of South Korea. Apart from *Asahi Shimbun*,[4] Japan's major newspaper editorials after the summit were of the opinion that the future of the denuclearisation talks was uncertain.[5] Each of them emphasised that inter-Korean cooperation would be possible only after North Korea was completely denuclearised. That tone was dominated by the opinion that neither the left nor the right prioritised the "denuclearisation of North Korea at first".[6]

Moreover, regarding the country's stand on North Korea's denuclearisation, many Japanese experts think that Japan cannot help but maintain a neutral attitude due to its non-involvement strategy in the Korean Peninsula to date. But it is likely that the US and Chinese confrontation will intensify, and a great game among major powers would commence. Therefore, the experts also agree that Japan's strategy for the future must take into consideration such likely scenarios as well.

In this context, the remarks of the president of the National Graduate Institute for Policy Studies (GRIPS) Akihiko Tanaka are representative of the views held by most Japanese experts. According to him, Japan does not have the means to influence the situation on the Korean Peninsula at this time. He further states:

> It is important that the international community continues to be interested in the North Korean problem, maintaining, or possibly intensifying, sanctions in case the negotiation fails. Or if denuclearisation progresses and peace comes, we need to prepare for that, too. While strengthening the Japan-US alliance, Japan should further improve the ballistic missile defence. However, rather than making conventional efforts to enhance the ability of the JSDF, including its counter-attacking ability, we must be more imaginative, especially if denuclearisation progresses, considering the promise of the Japan-North Korea Pyongyang Declaration. Unfortunately, discussions in Japan are not progressing as to what kind of blueprints we should draw.[7]

In Japan, there were concerns about the threat posed by the situation on the Korean Peninsula until the spring of 2018. These became less pronounced by the summer of 2018 once the negotiations on the denuclearisation of North Korea started. However, the security dilemma in North-East Asia has further deepened, and each country is struggling to address the military build-up. Therefore, depending on any agreement on North Korea's denuclearisation, the declaration ending the Korean War (1950–1953) and the signing of a peace treaty may lead to a big change in the security architecture of the region that is vital for Japan, including the dismantlement of the United Nations Command (UNC) and the reduction or withdrawal of the United States Forces Korea (USFK). There is a possibility of such an agreement. At the same time, it is fully conceivable that the denuclearisation talks between the United States and North Korea will not be successful, and the military tension that prevailed in 2017 may recur.

The question, therefore, arises: how would Japan respond to these two developments? At first glance, it seems that Japan's hedging strategy may allow it to prepare for contingencies, at least in the near future.

Preparing for contingencies

Improving the ballistic missile defence capability of Japan

In the security architecture of the Korean Peninsula, the spotlight is on the United States and South Korea, which are at the forefront in the Demilitarised Zone (DMZ), as compared to North Korea and China. Japan's position has been one of support to the United States and South Korea, and it has indirectly contributed to regional security through defensive military power. Japan has avoided taking the initiative on the security structure and active engagement. In any case, there seems a social consensus about the present role of Japan in the Korean Peninsula because of the negative heritage of its colonial past.

At the same time, Japan has enjoyed a strategic advantage because South Korea acts as a buffer on the Korean Peninsula. Moreover, Japan has enhanced its military power under the Japan-US alliance regime. This has enabled the JSDF to build up its defence capabilities with express speed under the principle of exclusive defence, achieve national security, and invest in economic development with the minimum necessary defence burden. In this context, some conservatives in Japan have emphasised the importance of South Korea as an anti-communist breakwater and suggested that Japan should engage more actively with the country. On the other hand, a sense of caution against "involvement in the Korean Peninsula contingency" is also strong and widely shared.[8]

Looking back, following the first nuclear crisis in the 1990s, Japan became a target for North Korea in the Korean Peninsula security structure when it developed the *Nodong*, a single-stage and mobile liquid propellant medium-range ballistic missile. Following the continued development of nuclear and ballistic missiles by North Korea, Japan began to deploy a variety of defensive equipment, with the ability to detect, intercept, and share information. (In a way, the main reason to improve Japan's defence capability has been to strengthen missile defence against the North Korean threat.)

Thus far, only six countries in the world (the United States, Japan, South Korea, Australia, Spain, and Norway) have the Aegis destroyers that play a central role in this missile defence system. Most of these are concentrated in countries in the Asia-Pacific. In addition, the power of the PAC-3 missile interception system was upgraded first in Japan and later in other countries. Not only is the Transportable Radar Surveillance (TPY)-2 (i.e. X-band radar) for detecting ballistic missiles for the US military located in Shariki, Aomori Prefecture, and Kyogamisaki, Kyoto Prefecture, in Japan, but the location of Japan's unique J/FPS-5 ground-based warning control radars is well distributed across the four Japan Air Self-Defence Force (JASDF) bases.[9] Thus, Japan has high-level missile detection capabilities and a front-line ballistic missile defence against North Korea. Further, these assets have improved Japan's relationship with the US military, which regularly utilised JASDF's capabilities in the face of the repeated military provocation by North Korea until November 29, 2017, when North Korea last launched an inter-continental ballistic missile, *Hwasong-15*. Moreover, the improved exchange of information with friendly nations (within the context of its alliance with the United States), supported by the Act on the Protection of Specially Designated Secrets established in December 2013, has helped bolster Japan's intelligence capacity, too.

Furthermore, in December 2017, the Japanese government decided to deploy the Aegis-Ashore system at two domestic sites. Moreover, once the Standard Missile (SM)-3 Block IIA anti-short- and intermediate-range ballistic missiles, which are being jointly developed in Japan and the United States, are installed aboard the existing Japan-US Aegis destroyers, they will cover almost the entire land area of Japan. Cruise missiles and bombers can also be targeted by SM-6 anti-air and anti-surface interceptor missiles launched by the Aegis-Ashore system. It is clear that these are not targeting North Korea, which has no cruise missiles and bombers supported by powerful airpower, but China.[10]

Further, in October 2018, the 38th Air Defence Artillery Brigade Headquarters of the US Army were established within the US Army Sagami General Depot in Sagamihara City, Kanagawa Prefecture. In addition to the three missile defence units of the US Army in Japan, a Terminal High Altitude Area Defence (THAAD) missile unit in Guam is also under the command of the same headquarters.[11] The creation of these new military assets and the command system of the US Army is expected to not only improve the ballistic missile defence capability of Japan and the United States but also reduce the burden on maritime forces, centring on the Aegis destroyers of the JMSDF. From the point of view of the Japan-US alliance, it is hypothesised that Japan will become a more important strategic base for the US military, thus strengthening the alliance and its deterrence power.

In terms of the legal system, the passing of the Legislation for Peace and Security in 2015, which allows the JSDF to operate around the Korean Peninsula in support of the US military, marked a significant milestone. In wartime and in peacetime, in addition to providing bases for the US military for moving into the Korean Peninsula, the JSDF is also allowed to use force to protect the weapons of the United States and other allies. Indeed, in May 2017 the JMSDF's *Izumo* (DDH-183) and *Sazanami* (DD-113) were for the first time charged with defending the US Navy cargo ship *Richard E. Byrd* (T-AKE-4). It is obvious that these new actions are necessary for protecting Japan and South Korea.

Changing the consciousness of Japanese citizens

For many people in Japan, North Korea's nuclear and ballistic missile development that has been going on since the 1990s was an external matter. This is because the missile impact points were off the coast of Japan, such as in the Sea of Japan, except for the *Gwangmyeongseong-1* on August 31, 1998, and the *Gwangmyeongseong-2* on April 5, 2009, which passed over mainland Japan. And so, it did not seem like a familiar threat. However, since 2016, the threat has increased significantly, as North Korea's missiles have flown closer to the mainland of Japan. On March 17, 2017, the Japanese government organised the first resident evacuation drill, due to the threat from the ballistic missiles, in Oga City, Akita Prefecture. The government has also ensured improvement in the citizen protection system; emergency messages can now be delivered to the media outlets as well as individual mobile phones through an emergency information network system (EM-net) and the national instantaneous warning system (J-ALERT).

On September 15, 2017, a mobile intermediate-range ballistic missile, *Hwasong-12*, launched by North Korea flew over Japan. Warnings were issued in the morning, at around 7 a.m., and the TV programmes were interrupted all at once by a screen that conveyed the missile alert. The threat also temporarily halted the railroads in the East Japan area.

When ballistic missiles loaded with nuclear weapons were actually tested, the simulation that calculated the expected damage attracted considerable social interest. Several discussions relating to damage estimate, economic impact, and Business Continuity Planning (BCP) were also held.

In addition to dealing with the threat of ballistic missiles, the concern of Japanese private companies in the second half of 2017 was how to evacuate officials and their families from South Korea in case of a Korean Peninsula emergency. The Japanese government took counter-measures in the spring of 2017, dispatched government officials to South Korea, and conducted a field survey.[12] However, the South Korean opposition to the execution of Non-combatant Evacuation Operations (NEOs) in its territory and waters is a concern. Moreover, in the event of an NEO in its territory, South Korea wants the USFK to become the primary actor instead of the JSDF.

In 2018, the growing hope of reconciliation between North and South Korea and the US-North Korea summit in Singapore came as a welcome relief for Japan. Resident evacuation drills from ballistic missiles were cancelled. However, the problem of evacuating Japanese residents in Korea remains a concern, particularly if there is another emergency in the Korean Peninsula in the near future (at this point, it is unclear whether discussions regarding an NEO in South Korea are still taking place within the government).

The threat consciousness among Japanese citizens has been fostered not only by the tensions on the Korean Peninsula but also by the expanding Chinese military power. In particular, the threats to the south-western region of Japan are particularly acute, in view of the interplay between Japanese and Chinese coast guards on the Senkaku Islands after the 2000s and the rapid increase in the scrambles against Chinese military planes flying into Japan's Air Defence Identification Zone (JADIZ). These military threats from North Korea and China help the Abe administration towards building a national defence build-up. To this effect, the Legislation for Peace and Security enacted in 2015 almost overcame the problem of collective self-defence, which was an issue for many years. Additionally, with regard to equipment, it has become possible to introduce light aircraft carriers and Joint Air-to-Surface Standoff Missiles (JASSM) and to create amphibious units, which were considered taboos as they deviated from the established exclusive defence framework.

In the latest National Defence Programme Guidelines of December 2018, it was decided that a professional maritime transport unit would be established in the Japan Ground Self-Defence Force (JGSDF) to improve the projection capacity of the land forces to the remote islands. In December 2018, the Japan Ministry of Defence announced its decision to increase its procurement of F-35s from 42 to 147 aircraft. Among these newly acquired aircraft, 42 were to be replaced with fighter aircraft with Short Take-off and Vertical-landing (STOVL) functions.[13] As a result, it was decided to acquire the F-35B, and a new powerful military asset was created by converting the Izumo-class helicopter destroyers into aircraft carriers. The *Izumo* has been the centre of strategic communications of the JSDF since it was commissioned in March 2015: for example, its three-month-long deployment from May 1 to August 9, 2017 to the South China Sea and the Indian Ocean, including goodwill visits to Singapore, Cam Ranh Bay, Subic, Chennai, and Colombo, and multilateral exercises, such as Pacific Partnership 2017 and Malabar 2017. It performs multilateral functions and is at the forefront of the India-Pacific strategy.[14]

The JGSDF is working hard to move the military force to the south-west and switch to manoeuvrable troops for island defence and recapture operations. To begin with, a Coast Observation Unit was created on Yonaguni-jima in the Nansei Islands in March 2016 (an area that did not have any land forces, except on the main island of Okinawa). Furthermore, security forces, ground-to-air missile units, and ground-to-ship missile units were stationed on Amami-Oshima and Miyako-jima in March 2019. The Japanese Ministry of Defence began the construction of a garrison with similar units in Ishigaki-jima. Additionally, in March 2018, the first full-scale Amphibious Rapid Deployment Brigade (ARDB) was launched in Sasebo City, Nagasaki Prefecture. The stationing of a landing force on the opposite shore of the Korean Peninsula across the Tsushima Strait could not have been imagined ten years ago. Although the training between the US Marine Corps (USMC) and the Republic of Korea Marine Corps (ROKMC) has been suspended because of the denuclearisation talks with North Korea, the JGSDF's ARDB unit participated in "KAMANDAG 2", the joint exercise between the USMC and Armed Forces of the Philippines, and "Blue Chromite", the first landing exercise with the USMC in October 2016 in Tanegashima, Kagoshima Prefecture. According to a report in the *Sankei Shimbun*, by the end of March 2019, Japan will train to deploy its ARDB unit in the East China Sea using transportation ships of the JMSDF.[15]

Emerging possibility of US disengagement

Fluctuation of the US-South Korea alliance and strengthening functions of the UNC

From 2016 to 2018, actions that heralded huge changes in the security architecture inside and outside of the Korean Peninsula became obvious. Former South Korean president Park Geun-hye faced a significant political scandal in the latter half of 2016, resulting in the first presidential impeachment in the constitutional history of South Korea. In May 2017, with the presidency of Moon Jae-in, a progressive government took office for the first time in nine years. On the future Korean Peninsula policy, President Moon Jae-in clarified his stance that South Korea was willing to enter into a dialogue with North in order to ease tensions. In terms of its relationship with the United States, South Korea is gearing to implement the transfer of the wartime Operational Control (OPCON) from the USFK to Seoul, which had been indefinitely postponed by the Park Geun-hye administration.

Further, the future of the US-South Korea alliance has become uncertain. For the first time, a lieutenant general of the Canadian Army, rather than a US Army general, was appointed deputy commander of the UNC in May 2018. There is also a rise in the number of army officers from Canada and Australia among the UN staff. Also, it is said that 100 Australian troops and 60 New Zealand troops participated in the US-Korea joint military exercise in 2016.[16]

In light of this trend, Japan also increased its presence by taking advantage of its position as a backward support base of the UN military, on the basis of Article 5 of the position agreement, which was signed in June 1954. There are seven US military bases in Japan (Camp Zama, US Fleet Activities Yokosuka, Commander Fleet Activities Sasebo, Yokota Air Base, Kadena Air Base, Marine Corps Air Station Futenma, and White Beach Naval Base), which it has also been allowed to use. Some maritime patrol aircraft of the UN Forces countries deployed in the Kadena Air Base, such as the Royal Australian Air Force (RAAF), have patrolled the waters around the East China Sea, to monitor the secret "ship-to-ship cargo transfer" on the high seas, which would allow North Korea to escape UN Security Council sanctions.[17] Japan has been strengthening regional security by incorporating UNC member states, including European countries such as the United Kingdom and France, into a security apparatus for North-East Asia, including the Korean Peninsula. It goes without saying that these will be an effective deterrent against North Korea, but its deterrent effect on China is also an expected consequence.

In addition to the framework of the UN Forces, Prime Minister Abe released the Free and Open Indo-Pacific Strategy (FOIPS) in August 2016 for the United States, India, and Australia. It seeks diplomacy and security cooperation with these four countries (the Quad). In addition to multilateral military exercises – Japan-US-Australia and Japan-US-India – Japan has also supported capacity building for South-East Asian countries. The latest National Defence Programme Guidelines reflect the trend of strengthening cooperation with major countries in the Asia Pacific, including Australia, India, and the United States, and describe the order as "Australia, India, Southeast Asian countries".[18]

On the diplomatic side, Japan was also a participant at the foreign ministerial conference in Canada in January 2018, in addition to the delegations from the UNC sending states, including South Korea. China and Russia did not participate in the meeting, and the Chinese Foreign Ministry spokesperson at a regular press conference said:

> As initiators of the meeting, the US and Canada co-hosted the meeting under the banner of the so-called UN Command sending states. That is Cold War mentality pure and simple, and will only drive a wedge among the international community and undermine the concerted efforts to seek proper settlement of the Korean Peninsula nuclear issue.[19]

Regarding diplomacy with North Korea, high-level talks between Japan and North Korea were held to negotiate the return of Japanese people abducted by North Korea. Reportedly, the director of Cabinet Intelligence Shigeru Kitamura (one of Prime Minister Abe's aides) had confidential contact with high-ranking North Korean officials twice: in July 2018 (in Vietnam) and October 2018 (in Mongolia).[20] In the opinion poll released by the *Yomiuri Shimbun* on October 4, 2018, the percentage of Japanese people who wanted "Japan-North Korea summit meeting should be held earlier" rose from 38 to 50 per cent.[21] The Abe administration aims to respond to both pressure and dialogue from North Korea while monitoring the direction of the denuclearisation talks with North Korea and the trend of domestic public opinion.

According to reports and expert forecasts in Japanese and foreign media immediately after the US-North Korea talks in June of 2018, North Korea will be denuclearised only in the framework of the following four countries: North and South Korea, the United States, and China. Some analysts predicted that Japan would be in isolation with regard to the negotiation talks on North Korea's denuclearisation, implying that the changes in the Korean Peninsula as a whole would be decided without Japan's involvement. However, the Japanese government has never intended a closer involvement, keeping a constant distance while maintaining pressure on North Korea to denuclearise. Nonetheless, the Japan-US alliance has become more significant than ever, as the relationship between the United States and China continues to deteriorate because of trade friction. Furthermore, Japanese financial capital within the Peninsula is now even more important, with regard to providing economic support to North Korea after denuclearisation.

Japan fearing the return of the Acheson line

In the National Security Strategy (NSS), Japan's top strategic document formulated by the Abe administration in 2013, the Korean Peninsula is referred to as the "North Korea issue". It lays down the Japanese government's response to North Korea's nuclear and missile development.[22] However, it does not contain strategic documents regarding either how the security architecture of the Korean Peninsula affects Japan or how Japan intends to deal with the Peninsula over the medium and long term.

Nonetheless, it provides a glimpse into a part of the Japanese government's current perception of the Korean Peninsula strategy. After the US-North Korea summit meeting on June 12, 2018, the Japanese government was stirred into action by a series of sudden developments relating to the United States and North Korea. Ahead of the US-North Korea summit meeting, the Abe administration sent the Secretary General of National Security Secretariat Shotaro Yachi to Singapore to gather information about the outcome of the meeting. According to the news release, the Japanese side was apparently told from the US side that the topic of the US forces in South Korea would not touched upon, which would have reassured Japan.[23] However, at the press conference after the summit talks, US president Donald J. Trump announced the cancellation of joint US-South Korea military exercises, which surprised Japanese government officials. Many experts described this as one of the significant concessions to North Korea at this stage of the talks, that is, the suspension of deployment of strategic assets, such as long-range bombers like B-1 and B-52 and Strategic Submarine Ballistic Nuclear (SSBN). Reportedly, the plan was "to gradually reduce the scale of exercises at the final stage of denuclearisation". On June 18, the suspension of the US-South Korea joint military exercise "Ulchi-Freedom Guardian (UFG)" was officially announced. Furthermore, immediately after the second US-North Korea summit in Hanoi in February 2019, the US and South Korean governments decided to end the joint military exercises "Key Resolve (KR)" and "Foal Eagle (FE)", too. Subsequently, they decided to scrap all three major joint exercises, including UFG and, instead, hold them in a modified, downscaled form.

Japanese experts do not deny the change in the security environment in the Korean Peninsula. Specifically, there is a concern that the reduction or withdrawal of the USFK troops from South Korea will be decided either by the United States alone or by the United States and South Korea together, without Japan's involvement. Furthermore, Japan is reluctant to consider the Tsushima Strait as Japan's new defence line, which is reminiscent of the Acheson line (which is said to have triggered the Korean War), by losing South Korea as a buffer zone between the United States and China.[24] It is less certain whether the relationship between the United States and its allies in the Indo-Pacific region after 2019 will develop further, as the US defence secretary James Mattis, who valued strategic relationships with allies, resigned on January 1, 2019.

From a short-term perspective, it is expected that not only the US military's ability to respond quickly but also the ability of South Korean forces to play a part in the joint force will be affected following the cancellation of the US-South Korea joint military exercises. From the perspective of deterrence against China and the rapid change in Japan's security architecture in the North-East Asian region, time may be approaching for Japan to proactively speak to the United States and South Korea regarding the future US military presence in this region.

Challenges in Japan-South Korea ties

After the visit of South Korean president Lee Myung-bak to Takeshima in August 2012, the relationship between Japan and South Korea, which had been one of conflict because of historical issues, improved. Further, the statement on the "Comfort Women" issue by foreign ministers of Japan and South Korea at the joint press conference on December 28, 2015, removed one of the major barriers to better relations between the two countries.[25] Security cooperation between the two countries, which had been suspended, resumed, mainly in terms of exchanges between the defence officials of the two countries. During the Kumamoto earthquake that occurred in April 2016, two South Korean Air Force C-130 transport aircraft flew to Kumamoto airport with assistance and provided disaster support to Japan.[26] This was a positive event that symbolised the developing security cooperation between Japan and South Korea.

After the conclusion of the General Security of Military Information Agreement (GSOMIA) in November 2016, the cooperation mechanism for military information between Japan and South Korea was completed, and the framework for a more multi-layered Japan-South Korea security cooperation was created. It goes without saying that this framework had a positive influence on security cooperation between Japan, the United States, and South Korea. The South Korean Navy's Aegis destroyer *Sejong the Great* (DD-991) participated in the United States and Japan's joint naval ballistic missile warning exercise, "Pacific Dragon 2016", in June 2016, for the first time.[27] Since then, a total of six ballistic missile launch detection drills have been undertaken by the navies of Japan, the United States, and South Korea. Although exercises with weapons cannot be conducted, security cooperation among the three countries has been steadily strengthened.

However, every time there has been a military provocation by North Korea, Japan, the United States, and South Korea have made appeals for "strengthening tri-country cooperation", but it is hard to say whether the three countries share a vision or plan for how far, specifically, this security cooperation can advance in the future. Notably, the three counties have not overcome their differences in recognising cooperation, and that gap has gradually become apparent.

Furthermore, the Japanese government must be wary of not only North Korea and China but also the South Korean defence build-up, even though it has not revealed an official response to the build-up. Following consultations with the United States in 2017, the warhead weight limit of South Korean ballistic missiles was relaxed altogether.[28] This will increase not only the North Korean threat but also the destructive power of the ballistic missiles themselves for the Japanese Islands in their range. In addition, South Korea is supposed to independently develop Submarine-Launched Ballistic Missiles (SLBMs), slated for completion in 2020.[29] On September 14, 2018, President Moon attended the launch ceremony held for South Korea's first 3,000-ton class submarine, *Dosan Ahn Chang Ho* (SS-083), which will be equipped with SLBMs.[30] According to a report in *Hankook Ilbo* on March 16, 2018, the Moon administration is aiming to develop a variant of the French Navy's Barracuda-class (5,300 tons) nuclear submarine to counter the threat of North Korean SLBMs. On the other hand, South Korea also has reservations regarding Japan's defence build-up.

As a nation that shares the values of the Indo-Pacific Strategy, such as rule of law and freedom of navigation, Japan wanted South Korea to become a partner.

However, on October 31, 2017, South Korea made a "three no's agreement" – no additional THAAD deployment, no participation in the United States' missile defence network, and no establishment of a trilateral military alliance with the United States and Japan – with China to dispel China's security concerns. Thus, South Korea seems keen on building diplomatic relations with Japan and the United States while distancing itself from the Indo-Pacific Strategy that Japan and the United States are focussing on. The New Southern policy, which the Moon administration regards as one of its most important diplomatic initiatives, is focussed on developing economic relations between South-East Asian countries and India, but cooperation in the security field has yet to be seen.

Further, the importance of South Korea is decreasing in Japan's strategic framework. Japan's latest National Defence Programme Guidelines give a country-specific description under "Active Promotion of Security Cooperation", and South Korea is described as the fourth partner after Australia, India, and South-East Asian countries.[31] Given what was first described in the "National Defence Programme Guidelines for FY 2014 and Beyond",[32] it is clear that South Korea's importance in the Abe administration's security cooperation policy has declined.

Conclusion

The confrontation between Japan and China in the Senkaku Islands after the 2000s and the repeated military provocations by North Korea until 2017 fostered awareness regarding the security threat to Japan. As a response to the growing regional insecurity, since 2013, Prime Minister Abe has been making special efforts on Japan's security policy, including the establishment of the National Security Council (NSC) and the National Security Secretariat and the adoption of the NSS. The Abe administration also changed to restrictively interpret Article 9 of the Constitution so that Japan can exercise the right to collective self-defence. Moreover, important laws and policies, such as restricted exercise of self-defence rights, were enacted in 2014; the peace and security legislation was formulated in 2015; and the Japan-US Defence Cooperation Guidelines were revised in 2015. Thus, the clear and present threat to Japanese citizens was acknowledged, mainly on account of the rising threat from China.

The Abe administration took advantage of the international political situation to strengthen the security set-up. The greater the military provocation by North Korea, the more Japan could increase troop operations and multilateral exercises under the new system. There is no change in shifting to the south-western defence and remote island defence for deterrence against China and the strategic communication in peacetime. However, the tensions arising from the situation on the Korean Peninsula have strengthened not only Japan's military relations with the United States and Australia but also its formerly weak military relations with other countries, such as the United Kingdom, Canada, and France. These options have become an important strategic asset for advancing Japan's Indo-Pacific strategy.

Japan's Korean Peninsula strategy will be a deterrent for not only North Korea but also China because of strengthened cooperation between Japan, the United States, and South Korea while letting South Korea function as a buffer between China and North Korea. Until 2017, when the military tension between the United States and North Korea was at its peak, the strategy was rather significant to all concerned.

Following the Japan-South Korea agreement in December 2015, the security cooperation between Japan, the United States, and South Korea was strengthened as Japan expected, thus increasing the pressure on North Korea. However, because of fluctuations in the domestic politics in South Korea, a new friction is developing between Japan and South Korea, but the interaction between military personnel is continuing and the GSOMIA is being automatically renewed every year. (Notably, as the relationship between Japan and South Korea has drastically deteriorated since the fall of 2018, the relationship between the militaries has also begun to be affected.) Moreover, the security cooperation between Japan and South Korea is likely to remain stagnant in the future.

Japan fears that the reduction or withdrawal of the USFK will be decided only by the United States alone or by the United States and South Korea. Japan, the United States, and South Korea are under pressure to rebuild their security strategy in preparation for the sudden structural change in the US-South Korea alliance. However, it is apparent that Japanese policy cannot keep pace with the rapidly changing situation on the Korean Peninsula, as well as of the world. In the first half of 2018, before the National Defence Programme Guidelines, issued every five years, were revised, a number of experts called for the revision of the NSS.[33] In fact, the Abe administration reportedly showed signs of wanting to revise the NSS five years ahead of schedule in December 2017.[34] However, since a new Defence Programme Guidelines were formulated without a revision of the NSS, the move was criticised.[35] The most important issue for the Abe administration's 2019 diplomatic and security policy is to formulate a new NSS, after studying North Korea's denuclearisation negotiation process.

It is also necessary to formulate a medium- to long-term strategy that looks more than a decade ahead. As Narushige Michishita, professor at GRIPS, points out, "Japan should recognize that the era of trivialising the problem of the Korean Peninsula as the problem of North Korea was over".[36] Thus, from the perspective of Japan's national interest, it is necessary to have a clearer strategic goal and flexibility with regard to understanding the situation on the Korean Peninsula, including not only North Korea but South Korea, and how to secure it.

Notes

1 Yoji Koda, "Taiwa no saki ni aru Beichō shōtotsu saiaku no shinario kara se wo mukeruna" [Do Not Turn Away from the Worst Scenario of the US-North Korea Conflict], *Wedge*, Tokyo, March 20, 2018, p. 15 (in Japanese).
2 "*Seihu Misairu Hinankunren wo chushi seishiki happyo*" [Abandoning Missile Evacuation Drills: Official Announcement], Mainichi Shimbun, June 22, 2018 (in Japanese), at https://mainichi.jp/articles/20180623/k00/00m/010/084000c (accessed December 22, 2018).

3 "*Kitachosen misairu keikai wo kanwa. Nihonseihu, jyoji tenkai wo kaijyo*" [Relaxing North Korean Missile Alert; Japanese Government Cancels Military Deployment at All Times], *Asahi Shimbun*, July 1, 2018 (in Japanese), at www.asahi.com/articles/ASL6Z423YL6ZULZU001.html (accessed December 12, 2018).
4 Editorial, *Asahi Shimbun*, September 20, 2018 (in Japanese).
5 Editorials in *Nihon Keizai Shimbun*, *Tokyo Shimbun*, *Yomiuri Shimbun* and *Sankei Shimbun*, September 20, 2018 (in Japanese).
6 Kohtaro Ito, "*'Botong gugga'leul jihyanghaneun han-il-yang-gug*" [Japan and South Korea Aiming for a Normal Country], Policy Brief No. 45, Ilmin International Research Institute, Korea University, October 15, 2018, p. 2 (in Korean).
7 Akihiko Tanaka, Yuji Miyamoto and Lee Jong-won, "*Rendō suru Higashiajia no samitto gaikō*" [Interlocking East Asia Summit Diplomacy], *Diplomacy*, Tokyo, May 31, 2018, p. 23 (in Japanese).
8 Tadashi Kimiya, "Nihon no anzen hoshō to Chōsenhantō" [Japan's National Security and Korea Peninsula], in Tadashi Kimiya (ed.), *Chōsenhantō to higashiajia* [Korea Peninsula and East Asia], Iwanami Shoten, Tokyo, 2015, pp. 80–81 (in Japanese).
9 "*Kitachōsen no misairu wo miharu senrigan kikkō moyō no Gamerarēdā FPS5*" [A Clairvoyant Watching North Korean Missiles 'Gamera Radar' FPS5], *Sankei Shimbun*, June 3, 2017 (in Japanese), at www.sankei.com/premium/news/170603/prm1706030017-n2.html (accessed December 20, 2018).
10 Koji Inoue, "*Rikujō-gata ījisu no chōsho wa '12-ri de ugokaseru koto' rokkīdo mātin tantō fuku shachō, hikkusu-shi ni kiku*" [The Advantage of Land-based Aegis Is Being Able to Move with 12 People. Asking Mr. Hicks Vice President for Lockheed Martin], *Nikkei Business Online*, February 26, 2018 (in Japanese), at https://business.nikkeibp.co.jp/atcl/report/15/110879/021400783/ (accessed December 26, 2018).
11 "*Beigun, Sagamihara ni misairu bōei no shin shirei-bu THAAD mo shiki e*" [US Military Founded a New Headquarters for Missile Defence in Sagamihara; also Commands THAAD], *Asahi Shimbun*, October 31, 2018 (in Japanese), at www.asahi.com/articles/ASLB04FS1LB0ULOB00Y.html (accessed December 23, 2018).
12 "*Zaikan hōjin hogo, sonae isogu seifu, taihi-sho wo kakuho*" [Protecting Japanese People in South Korea, the Government Preparing Quickly, Secured Evacuation Area], *Nihon Keizai Shimbun*, September 5, 2017 (in Japanese), at www.nikkei.com/article/DGXKASFS04H8K_04092017PP8000/?n_cid=DSPRM2946&waad=cCtk5cBF&gclid=EAIaIQobChMI5MXS8vTB3wIVTaSWCh27nAY_EAEYAiAAEgIQ4_D_BwE (accessed December 12, 2018).
13 "*F-35A no shutoku-sū no henkō ni tsuite*" [About Changing the Number of Acquisitions of F-35A], National Security Council, Ministry of Defence, December 18, 2018 (in Japanese), at www.mod.go.jp/j/approach/agenda/guideline/2019/pdf/f35a.pdf (accessed December 27, 2018).
14 See Ministry of Defence, at www.mod.go.jp/msdf/izumo-sazanami/en/index.html (accessed December 27, 2018) and Embassy of Japan in India (in Japanese) at www.in.emb-japan.go.jp/itpr_ja/00_000438.html (accessed September 14, 2019).
15 "*Rikuji suiriku kidō-dan, Senkaku shūhen ni tenkai ritō dakkan butai, nendonai ni mo*" [The GSDF's Amphibious Rapid Deployment Brigade Unit being Deployed Around the Senkaku Islands Area Within This Fiscal Year], *Sankei Shimbun*, August 6, 2018 (in Japanese), at www.sankei.com/politics/news/180806/plt1808060004-n1.html (accessed December 2, 2018).
16 "*Yuensa busalyeong-gwan-e kaenada jangseong naejeong*" [UNC Nominating a Canadian General as a Deputy Commander], *Chosun Ilbo*, May 19, 2018 (in Korean), at http://news.chosun.com/site/data/html_dir/2018/05/19/2018051900205.html (accessed December 20, 2018).
17 "Monitoring and Surveillance Activities by Partner Countries Against Illicit Maritime Activities Including Ship-to-ship Transfers", Ministry of Foreign Affairs, April 28, 2018, at www.mofa.go.jp/press/release/press4e_002017.html (accessed December 2, 2018).

18 *"Heisei 31-nendo ikō ni kakaru bōei keikaku no taikō ni tsuite"* [National Defence Programme Guidelines for FY 2019 and Beyond], Ministry of Defence, December 18, 2018, pp. 14–15 (in Japanese), at www.mod.go.jp/j/approach/agenda/guideline/2019/pdf/20181218.pdf (accessed December 27, 2018).

19 *"Gaikō-bu, Amerika Ka no `Kokuren-gun'-mei no kaigō kaisai wa reisen shikō"* [Ministry of Foreign Affairs; The Meeting of 'UN Forces' Held by US and Canada Holds Cold War Thought], People's Network, (Japanese version), January 19, 2018, at http://japanese.china.org.cn/politics/txt/2018-01/19/content_50246762.htm (accessed December 20, 2018); "Foreign Ministry Spokesperson Lu Kang's Regular Press Conference on January 17, 2018", Ministry of Foreign Affairs, People's Republic of China, at http://tl.chineseembassy.org/eng/fyrth/t1526532.htm (accessed August 6, 2019).

20 *"Nitchō jōhō tōkyoku ga gokuhi sesshoku"* [Intelligence Authorities Are in Confidential Contact], *Kyodo News*, October 19, 2018 (in Japanese), at https://this.kiji.is/425748769616282721?c=39546741839462401 (accessed December 27, 2018).

21 *"Nitchōkaidan `hayaku' 50-pāsento ni jōshō, shinchō-ha to gyakuten"* [Japan-North Korea Top Summit; Rising to 50% 'as Soon as Possible.' Reversing from Cautious], *Yomiuri Shimbun*, October 4, 2018 (in Japanese), at www.yomiuri.co.jp/feature/TO000302/20181004-OYT1T50043.html (accessed December 27, 2018).

22 "National Security Strategy", National Security Council, December 17, 2013 (in Japanese), Cabinet Secretariat, at www.cas.go.jp/jp/siryou/131217anzenhoshou/nss-e.pdf (accessed December 1, 2018).

23 *"Anpo, kenen fukameru Nihon `beikan enshū chūshi' sōtei-gai, shin'i wa"* [Security, Japan Deepening Concern "Abortion of US-South Korean Exercise" Unexpected, Real Intention Is?], *Asahi Shimbun*, June 13, 2018 (in Japanese), at www.asahi.com/articles/DA3S13539119.html?iref=pc_ss_date (accessed December 12, 2018).

24 See, for instance, Koji Murata, *"Zaikanbeigun tettai no akumu `toranpu o daini no kātā ni shite wa naranai'"* [The Nightmare of Withdrawing USFK; President Trump Should Not Be the Second President Carter], *WEB Voice*, December 7, 2018 (in Japanese), at https://shuchi.php.co.jp/voice/detail/5833 (accessed December 12, 2018).

25 "Announcement by Foreign Ministers of Japan and the Republic of Korea at the Joint Press Occasion", Ministry of Foreign Affairs, Japan, December 28, 2015 at www.mofa.go.jp/a_o/na/kr/page4e_000364.html (accessed December 27, 2018).

26 "Assistance from the Republic of Korea in Response to the Kumamoto Earthquake", Ministry of Foreign Affairs, Japan, April 27, 2016, at www.mofa.go.jp/mofaj/a_o/na/kr/page3_001673.html (accessed December 27, 2018).

27 "Trilateral Pacific Dragon Ballistic Missile Defence Exercise Concludes", June 27, 2016, US Navy, at www.cpf.navy.mil/news.aspx/130035 (accessed December 27, 2018).

28 *"Kankoku misairu dantō jūryō seigen wo teppai kokubō-ryoku kyōka, Amerika to gōi"* [South Korea, Eliminating Missile Warhead Weight Restriction and Strengthening Defence Capability. Agreement with the United States], *Mainichi Shimbun*, September 5, 2017 (in Japanese), at https://mainichi.jp/articles/20170905/k00/00e/030/246000c (accessed December 27, 2018).

29 *"Hangughyeong SLBM imi gaebal jung...4nyeon dwi siljeonbaechi"* [South Korean Type SLBM Is Already Under Development... Four Years Later Deployment], *Joongang Ilbo*, May 27, 2016 (in Korean), at https://news.joins.com/article/20085844 (accessed December 27, 2018).

30 *"Gugnae cheos 3,000t-geub jamsuham... baejeon-yeog sajeong-gwon SLBM tabjae ganeung"* [The First 3,000-Ton Class Submarine. The Whole North Korea Is within Range. It Is Possible to Install SLBM], *Donga Ilbo*, September 15, 2018 (in Korean), at http://news.donga.com/home/3/all/20180915/92010775/1 (accessed December 27, 2018).

31 *"Heisei 31-nendo ikō ni kakaru bōei keikaku no taikō ni tsuite"*, No. 18, p. 15.

32 "National Defense Program Guidelines for FY 2014 and Beyond", Ministry of Defence, Japan, December 17, 2013, p. 10, at www.mod.go.jp/j/approach/agenda/guideline/2014/pdf/20131217_e2.pdf (accessed December 27, 2018).

33 See, for instance, Masashi Nishihara, Ryoichi Oriki, Akihiko Tanaka and Hideshi Tokuchi, "Policy Recommendations on Japan's National Security Strategy and Defense Policies", Research Institute for Peace and Security, July 23, 2018, at www.rips.or.jp/jp/wp-content/uploads/2018/07/RIPS-15-Policy-Recommendationfor-print.pdf (accessed December 27, 2018).
34 "*Kokka anzen hoshō senryaku, rainen kaitei e kita jōsei kinpaku-ka, bōei taikō maedaoshi ni tomonai kentō chakushu*" [National Security Strategy, Next Year's Revision, Situation Tense in the North, Analysis in Advance of the Defence Outline], *Sankei Shimbun*, December 7, 2017 (in Japanese), at www.sankei.com/politics/news/171207/plt1712070005-n1.html (accessed December 27, 2018).
35 See, for instance, Yuki Tatsumi, "Abe 'chōki seiken' wa naze 'anpo bijon' wo surū shita no ka" [Why Did Abe 'Long-Term Administration' Thru 'Security Vision'], *Newsweek* (Japanese version), October 15, 2018, at www.newsweekjapan.jp/stories/world/2018/10/post-11103.php (accessed December 2, 2018).
36 Narushige Michishita, "*Gekidō suru Higashiajia no anpo kankyō*" [Turbulent East Asian Security Environment. Japan's Four Scenarios], *Chuo-Koron*, October 2018, pp. 66–73 (in Japanese).

4 The twists and turns of Russia's relations with North Korea

Georgy Bulychev and Valeriia Gorbacheva

Russia remains one of the four key players in the Korean Peninsula – the USSR in fact established the Democratic People's Republic of Korea (DPRK) after the World War II and supported it throughout the Cold War – although after the dissolution of the Soviet Union in 1991, Moscow's influence has certainly dwindled. In the three post-Soviet decades, Russia-North Korea relations experienced ups and downs, in keeping with policy changes. These trends were not always correctly interpreted in other countries, even in Russia itself. Expertise on North Korea remains sharply divided, on the basis of ideology. Many Western specialists (e.g. Victor Cha, Bruce Klinger, Nicholas Eberstadt, and Stephen Haggard) and a number of Russian scholars (e.g. Alexey Arbatov, Vasily Micheev, Georgy Kunadze, and Alexander Lukin) discount the influence of Russia in Korean affairs or see it as mostly negative. At the same time, a number of Russian scholars (e.g. Valery Denisov, Oleg Davydov, Yuri Vanin, Anatoly Torkunov, Alexander Vorontsov, Alexander Zhebin, and Konstantin Asmolov) emphasise the importance of Russia-North Korea relations and Russia's role in the Korean Peninsula, sometimes echoing North Korean views. However, most of the practising politicians and experts take a balanced line; both are critical of the North Korean regime and its actions and attitude but, at the same time, acknowledge the legitimate interests of the North Korean state in accordance with the basic norms and principles of international relations and the strategic interests of Russia. This chapter traces Russia-North Korea relations in seven phases – from 1991 until now.

First period: 1991–1996

The Russian Federation's political line towards North Korea in the early 1990s was prompted by the challenges faced by democratic Russia in the aftermath of the collapse of the USSR.

This transition was preceded by the reality that USSR gave up its basic foreign policy principles following *"perestroika"* and the "new thinking" in the 1980s, which Kim Il-Sung did not support and warned of a possible rift in bilateral relations because of the new priorities in Gorbachev's policy. The North Korean leader did not hide his thoughts in this regard.[1] He understood that the USSR was focussed on the normalising of relations with the West and other capitalist countries in the Asia-Pacific region, including South Korea. Improvement in USSR-South Korea relations before and after the 1988 Summer Olympics in Seoul made North Korea realise that it had to prepare for the worst in spite of Soviet assurances that Moscow would not establish diplomatic relations with the South. But this promise was soon broken in 1990, when the USSR was still in existence.

It is now widely known that North Korean leaders decided to bolster its nuclear programme in the second half of the 1980s[2] as a security guarantee, in case the USSR reneged from its obligations as an ally. The economic aid and ties with USSR dried up.

In 1990, the USSR Committee for State Security (KGB) reported the suspected creation of a nuclear device prototype by the North to the USSR Communist Party Central Committee.[3] But no political reaction followed, as the USSR foreign policy system started to collapse.

North Korean propaganda branded the changes in the USSR a betrayal of socialism and predicted negative outcomes. In September 1990, North Korean fears panned out. Two months after the meeting between Mikhail Gorbachev and South Korean leader Roh Tae-woo in San Francisco, Eduard Shevardnadze visited Pyongyang to inform Kim Il-sung about Moscow's decision to establish diplomatic relations with Seoul. The North Korean leader refused to meet with the Russian delegation, and the then North Korean foreign minister, Kim Yong-nam, threatened Eduard Shevardnadze with several negative consequences, including a veiled threat to build nuclear weapons.[4] However, Moscow did not take this threat seriously.

A new era in bilateral relations began after the USSR collapsed in 1991. The relationship worsened during the Boris Yeltsin administration, which did not even offer official condolences to Pyongyang on the death of the Great Leader Kim Il-sung in 1994. The president's entourage and new leaders of the foreign policy establishments did not even accept the advice of Russian experts on Korea and believed that North Korean regime would collapse in the same manner as the communist countries of Eastern Europe.

Russia joined hands with South Korea and pressed the North to abandon its nuclear programme. Russia also coordinated with the United States to put pressure on the DPRK. Washington even asked Moscow to install spy equipment in its embassy in Pyongyang (the request was denied).[5] Russia also refused to let the terminally ill ex-East German leader Erich Honecker emigrate to the DPRK. Russia was pressured by South Korea and the West to accept North Korean defectors and to close the so-called "labour camps" – forestry enterprises where North Korean guest workers toiled.

In the mid-1990s, South Korea increased pressure on Russia to unilaterally withdraw from the Treaty of Friendship, Cooperation and Mutual Assistance with the North. However, North Korea did not rely on the so-called "Alliance treaty" any more, describing it "an empty shell". So, it did not contribute much to the deterioration of relations and instead only created resentment in Pyongyang towards Russian diplomats, who they said were "dancing to the tune of the

South" (especially after allegations that a Russian diplomat worked for South Korean intelligence, in the second half of 1990s).[6]

In March 1994, Russia suggested a six-party conference to solve the North Korean nuclear problem, but it was ignored by the other parties.[7] In October 1994, North Korea signed the Agreed Framework with the United States and strengthened its position in the international arena, which reduced its need for Russia's political support.

Thus, the first period of democratic Russia's transition marked the worst period in the whole history of bilateral relations since the creation of the DPRK, and Russia was seen as an unfriendly country if not hostile. Thereafter, Moscow's influence on North Korea reduced drastically. By the mid-1990s, the crisis in Russian foreign policy vis-à-vis the strategically important area in Russia's Eastern frontier became obvious.

Second period: 1996–2002

Russia had to improve relations with North Korea and "stand on both legs on the Korean Peninsula".[8] As early as in 1996, normal dialogue between the two countries was resumed at all levels, especially after Yevgeny Primakov replaced pro-American Andrey Kozyrev as the foreign minister.

In January 1996, Yevgeny Primakov set out the vision of a "multipolar" world to challenge what he described as the "unipolar" system dominated by the United States. This shift in Russian foreign policy contributed to significant positive changes in its bilateral relations with North Korea, as Russia was getting closer to North Korean view of the world and that of its arch-enemy – the United States. The DPRK again began describing Russia as a "friendly nation" and expressed its willingness to strengthen the bilateral relations in spite of different ideological systems.

At the same time, the North Korean foreign policy itself went through important transformations following the progress in the relations with the United States during Bill Clinton's administration, Kim Dae-jung's administration in South Korea, and the unprecedented economic crisis in the North.

Negotiations on a new treaty were held at the end of Boris Yeltsin's era and the beginning of Vladimir Putin's presidency, when national interest became the priority of new Russian foreign policy. The Foreign Policy Concept of the Russian Federation stressed Russia's adherence to a "multi-polar world",[9] which did not contradict North Korea's political goals and aspirations and provided room for cooperation on international arena. The DPRK sought to strengthen its position in its talks with the United States and appreciated Russian support.

The visit of Igor Ivanov, then Russian foreign minister, to Pyongyang in February 2000 – the first in a decade after Eduard Shevardnadze's visit – marked a watershed in bilateral relations.[10] If the previous visit symbolised the end of the era of Soviet internationalism, this one indicated a new level of relations.

A new intergovernmental Treaty on Friendship, Good-Neighbourliness and Cooperation was signed in Pyongyang on February 9, 2000, and became the formal basis of bilateral relations. Both countries declared their determination to respect the aims and principles of the Charter of the United Nations (UN) and the generally recognised norms of international law, and to strive for peace and security in North-East Asia and in the whole region. As a result of frank and intimate talks in April 2000 between Russian and North Korean diplomats, in May, the Russian president was invited by Kim Jong-il to visit North Korea, a first in its history.

Vladimir Putin's visit to Pyongyang in July 2000[11] – the first visit by a Russian leader (and the first visit of an acting president of one of the G8 countries) to the North – was also one of his first trips as the president of Russia, providing him with a personal understanding of the Korean situation. The trip was marked by many firsts, including the Pyongyang Declaration, the first international document (not counting the declaration with the South) signed by North Korean leader Kim Jong-il on July 19, 2000.[12] North Koreans regard this document as a basic one regulating bilateral relations, as they considered the main motive for Russia's insistence (prompted by South Korea and the West) on the drafting of the bilateral treaty. Unlike the 2000 Russia-DPRK Treaty, the Pyongyang Declaration was signed when Russia realised the importance of taking a balanced line on the Korean Peninsula.

The return visit of Kim Jong-il (his epic railroad journey throughout Russia in 2001, which resembled Kim Il-sung's railroad trip in 1984) received tremendous publicity, mostly negative in Russia. Kim Jong-il visited Russia the next year, too, in an attempt to start regular summit diplomacy (he said during the first visit that he hoped to visit Russia about a dozen times before he died). These visits had a positive effect on not only the bilateral relations but also North Korean attempts to get out of isolation. It was the first time a North Korean leader came to a post-communist country and saw its experience of reforms.

On August 4, 2001, the two leaders signed the Moscow declaration, in which the North acknowledged the necessity of better relations with the South, the United States, and Japan, and reiterated a freeze on missile tests and its commitment to settle all disputes through dialogue.

During 2001–2003, the bilateral relations were almost at the highest level of trust in their history, at least after their deterioration in the 1950s, which saw several political controversies between the two countries.

Third period: 2003–2008

These efforts were ruined by the uranium crisis of 2002 triggered by the inclusion of North Korea by US president into an "axis of evil",[13] which was tantamount to its withdrawal from the Agreed Framework. It soon became a dead letter.[14] Then South Korean president Kim Dae-jung's suggestion to President Bush in 2002 that a liberal line towards the North should be taken was rejected, so Pyongyang decided that it should not waste efforts in improving relations with Seoul but should directly talk with the United States – so any support from Russia, formerly the rivalling superpower to the United States, would be useful.

Thus, cordial Russia-North Korea relations allowed Russia to play a proactive role during the 2002–2003 crisis. Moscow, as early as in November 2002, floated the idea of a "package deal" – peace and security guarantees to North Korea in exchange for giving up its nuclear weapons. In January 2003,[15] Kim Jong-il said that about 60 per cent of Russia's suggestions could be accepted, and they in fact provided the basis for the Six-Party Talks in August 2003.

In spite of the fact that Moscow was the initiator of the Six-Party Talks process, the United States tried to prevent Russia from participating in the talks. China was also lukewarm – seeing, despite the recent improvement in Russia-China relations, the Korean issue as their own area of responsibility (along with the United States). The little-known and unpublicised fact is that it was only thanks to Kim Jong-il's insistence on Moscow's participation that the Russian diplomats took their place at the negotiation table (and Japan was included as a counterbalance).[16] Thus the positive attitude of Putin was repaid in kind.

At the same time, on-the-ground Russia-North Korea bilateral relations cooled down in spite of the dialogue at the highest level through secure channels because of the negative attitude of the foreign policy establishment towards North Korean "provocations". Nevertheless, agreements on economic cooperation were steadily implemented. The issue of settlement of North Korean debt owed to Russia started to be discussed, although the Russian financial negotiators were reluctant to give any concessions. In 2008, a joint venture, "RasonConTrans", was set up for the reconstruction of the Rajin-Khasan railway section, a part of the trans-Korean railway, as a pilot project. Gazprom and the North agreed on the main characteristics of a gas pipeline and planned to start the feasibility studies. The two countries also discussed electric power transmission lines. However, in 2008, the global financial crisis' negative consequences resulting in deteriorating economic situation and uncertainty of political atmosphere in Russia, where a transition of power from Vladimir Putin to Dmitry Medvedev was underway, were not conducive for cooperation. Moreover, the Six-Party Talks failed, Lee Myong-bak's conservative government in the Republic of Korea (ROK) was hostile to the DPRK, and hostilities on the Korean Peninsula were renewed. Seoul was also concerned about the future of the regime of Kim Jong-il, who suffered a stroke in August 2008, and there was no scheme for hereditary transition of power.

Fourth period: 2008–2011

During the more pro-Western Dmitry Medvedev's presidency (2008–2012), Kremlin's attitude towards the North was ambivalent, so the period 2008–2011 saw a certain stagnation in bilateral ties. Medvedev's political establishment, especially its pro-Western wing, did not want to be associated with such a notorious regime. Its provocations became an additional irritant in the complicated relations between Moscow and the West. Kremlin did not see any point in spoiling its relations with the United States or South Korea because of North Korea. South Korean president Lee Myong–bak, who met Medvedev several times, declared his desire for a "strategic partnership". Kremlin did not question, at least publicly, Cheong Wa Dae's concept of unification and Seoul's version of the sinking of the *"Cheonan"* corvette in 2010, putting blame on the North while criticising North Korean provocations, including the artillery attack on Yeonpyeong Island and the development of its nuclear and missile programmes.

Russian position on many issues, including the North Korean missile test in April 2009, created problems in its relations with the North. In April 2009, Kim Jong-il refused to meet with the visiting Russian foreign minister and later, in November 2009, with the Federation Council speaker.

However, there was no alternative for Russia but to maintain stable relations with the North to prevent hostilities on the Korean Peninsula. North Koreans were also troubled by the situation – and at the end of his term, President Dmitry Medvedev agreed to meet with Kim Jong-il. They met in August 2011 in Ulan-Ude.[17] This was the last foreign tour of the North Korean leader. Important agreements were reached during the meeting, including the possibility of North Korea's return to the Six-Party Talks and the construction of a gas pipeline from Russia to the ROK through North Korean territory.

South Korea and the United States did not support these initiatives and blocked the idea to resume talks by imposing unacceptable preconditions, such as concrete steps on Pyongyang's part, to demonstrate a genuine commitment to Complete, Verifiable, and Irreversible Denuclearisation (CVID) – "that meant a declaratory statement plus some additional actions or measures that have not been disclosed".[18] Russia's need for improving relations with Pyongyang in the face of the brewing confrontation with the West became obvious to many forward-looking experts.

Fifth period: 2011–2014

Kim Jong-il's death in December 2011 initially did not change the Russian approach to the Korean Peninsula significantly. In contrast to their South Korean and Western colleagues, Russian experts have never doubted the new leader's capability to retain power. Some of them expected that the young leader's attempts to introduce changes and revive the struggling North Korean economy would result in a sound policy. The "Leap Day Deal" of February 29, 2012, which stipulated that the United States and North Korea should normalise relations and resume talks on denuclearisation, raised their hopes.

However, North Korean Unha-3 rocket launching to put a satellite into orbit in April 2012, in defiance of the protests of the international community, including Russia, shattered these expectations. Russia felt betrayed, and the Western and South Korean partners did their best to amplify this feeling. Russian politicians even called the North Korean counterparts "cheats and swindlers, playing scams with the world".[19] Ultimately, with some reservations, Russia approved the UN sanctions imposed on the DPRK. As a result, Russia-North Korea relations were marked by mistrust during the first years of Kim Jong-un's rule.

At the same time, Russia has never stopped trying to persuade North Korea to refrain from provocation and to re-engage in a constructive dialogue. Russia also continued to resolve some pending issues in bilateral relations, including the lingering problem of North Korea's debt, which was considered as a stumbling block for further development in economic ties. As a result of the talks in 2010–2012, the two countries agreed to write off 90 per cent of the debt and to reinvest the remaining 10 per cent as part of a debt-for-aid plan to develop energy, health care, and educational projects in North Korea.[20] Russia also offered food aid to North Korea through direct supplies and channels of the World Food Programme.

However, these controversial attempts to balance engagement and pressure on North Korea – in a follow-up of the Western policy – resulted in weakening Russia's position on the Korean Peninsula. In fact, the UN sanctions were agreed upon between China and the United States. The North Korean nuclear test on February 12, 2013, created a new crisis in bilateral relations, as the DPRK's behaviour was regarded as

> incompatible with generally accepted norms of international community and deserves denunciation and an adequate reaction of international community. We regret that they did not listen to us, considering many decades of good neighbourly relations that connect us to this country.[21]

Pyongyang was dissatisfied with Russia's inability to understand its "struggle for survival" and considered it a betrayal. The new generation of North Korean elite, who had no direct knowledge of the country like their predecessors, came to the conclusion that Russia did not pay enough attention to the Korean Peninsula and was hypocritical in its Korean policy. However, the DPRK, rightly anticipating a deterioration of relations between Russia and the West, made gestures to show its readiness for closer ties with Russia. Despite the Russian officials ignoring the anniversary of the end of the Korean War in July 2013, the North Korean show *Arirang* included the slogan "Russia-Korean friendship from generation to generation". The unexpected visit of Kim Yong-nam, the North's ceremonial head of state, to the opening ceremony of the Winter Olympics in Sochi in February 2014, where he met Vladimir Putin, could be considered as another North Korean attempt to improve relations with Russia.

Sixth period: 2014–2017

The "crusade" against Russia started by the West in the wake of Ukrainian crisis and takeover of Crimea changed the whole calculus. The period after 2014 was marked by better understanding between Russia and North Korea in spite of missile and nuclear tests by the latter. The change could be explained by two factors: attempts to put Russia in international isolation after the Ukrainian crisis and Kim Jong-un's attempts to become more independent of China by using the "Russian card".[22]

Russian politicians believed that the cooling of China-North Korea relations after the Jang Song Thaek incident gave Russian diplomacy a chance to build closer relations with the North Korean elite. Xi Jinping's hegemonistic and authoritative course and generational change in China affected relations with the North. The end of 2014–2015 was marked by a considerable rise in the number of contacts, especially in the economic sphere. High-level North Korean officials, including Choe Ryong-hae, Kim Jong-un's close aide and the party's vice chairman; Ri Su-yong, then foreign affairs minister; parliament members; and economic delegations visited Russia. The Russian deputy prime minister Yury Trutnev and Minister Alexander Galushka visited North Korea several times.

The two sides restated their goal to increase the annual direct turnover to a billion dollars by 2020[23] (while indirect trade operations amounted to roughly $900 million), establish a Russia-North Korea Trading House to enable electronic payments, and open accounts in the banks of the two countries.

This resulted in a new model of cooperation between the two countries — Russian investments and supplies in exchange for access to North Korean natural resources. The countries reached a deal by which Russia was to improve North Korea's railway network in return for access to the North's mineral resources. The project (known as "Pobeda") was funded by a product-sharing agreement. The Sever Group started to supply coal to the Kim Chaek Iron and Steel Complex in exchange for pig iron. The same scheme was discussed for Russian electricity supply to North Korean Rason, Chondin, Tancheon, and the Wonsan tourism cluster. Russia and North Korea also agreed on cooperation in free economic zones and the construction of a road bridge. The year 2015 was designated the year of friendship, and numerous events were held. North Korea even offered military cooperation, but the Russian response was muted.

However, at that time Moscow failed to bring Kim Jong-un out of diplomatic isolation; at first, Kim was eager to accept Vladimir Putin's invitation to visit Moscow on the occasion of 70th anniversary of victory in May 2015, but then he changed his plans (either following the "advice not to go" from the jealous Chinese "elder brother" or domestic difficulties due to a purge in military).

The growing turbulence in the world following President Trump's election; instability in the Western camp, including the European Union (EU) and the G-7; the rising tensions between the "sole superpower" and emerging centres of power, including China; and unprecedented hostility towards Russia, in fact, pushed Russia and North Korea closer to each other.

However, initially as the hostilities on the Korean Peninsula rose in 2017, Russian position was ambivalent and mostly influenced by its interest in improving the relations with the incoming Trump administration. Therefore, Russia in fact backed up the US policy of "maximum pressure" and relinquished all the decision-making on Korean issues to China and the United States (partly because of being engrossed in the much more important Syrian and Ukrainian issues). Moscow also reluctantly followed Beijing in sanctioning and isolating North Korea for its numerous nuclear and missile tests.

Seventh period: 2017–2019

Despite the initial irritation with North Korean provocations, military rhetoric, and the crisis in 2016–early 2017, which brought the region to the brink of war, Russia later started to take note of North Korea's position as well as legitimate interests and the concerns of all parties involved and insisted on a diplomatic settlement. President Putin denounced the sanctions and pressure policy against North Korea on many occasions. For example, in September 2017, he said that it was quite absurd to include Russia along with the DPRK in the sanctions list and then ask Russia to participate in the sanctions. "They would rather eat grass than abandon nuclear programme unless they feel safe", he added. He also said that any sanctions against the North are useless and ineffective.[24]

Russia stressed political and diplomatic methods to defuse the crisis. In July 2017, Russia and China put forward the idea of a "double freeze" that had been proposed by the North in 2015 but ignored by the United States, in spite of its potential to stop North Korea's missile and nuclear programmes.[25] According to the Russia-China proposal, North Korea should voluntarily announce a moratorium on the testing of nuclear explosive devices and ballistic missile tests, and the United States and South Korea should, accordingly, refrain from large-scale joint exercises. The three parties involved should begin simultaneously. During the negotiating process, all parties concerned would push for a peace and security mechanism to normalise relations between the countries.

In fact, this plan was much closer to the North Korean vision of a "step-by-step" and "action for action" approach than the United States and ROK's unconditional CVID and "Big deal" concept. North Korean diplomatic outreach at the beginning of 2018, including an active dialogue with the South in fact reflected the idea of the "first stage" of the initiative – a freeze of nuclear and missile tests in exchange for the US-South Korea halt of military drills.[26]

In 2016–2017, Russia and North Korea had to put almost all economic projects on hold, and the volume of bilateral trade – both direct (from only $84 million in 2015 to $77 million in 2016)[27] and indirect via third countries, amounting to hundreds of millions of dollars – declined. Big Russian companies feared to cooperate with the North because of concerns of secondary Western sanctions.[28]

In March 2018, the eighth session of the Intergovernmental Commission on Cooperation in Trade, Economy, Science and Technology[29] in Pyongyang agreed on trade issues against the background of sanctions and measures to support bilateral projects, including the Rajin-Hasan project, and new initiatives, as well as the request to ease visa requirements for Russian citizens to boost tourism, were discussed, too.

As time passed, Russia became more sceptical about sanctions, which are used to suffocate the North Korean regime. Resolutions 2270, 2321, 2356, 2371, 2375, and 2397 were forced through the UN Security Council in 2016 and 2017, with only marginal Russian involvement. President Vladimir Putin had to agree to them because of his foreign policy advisers' insistence.

Russia was especially concerned with limits to petroleum product exports and the requirement to expel all North Korean workers who play a significant role in the Russian Far East, within two years. US pressure in this issue clearly irritated Russia. On November 30, 2017, Sergey Lavrov reiterated Russia's position on the issue: sanction pressure had reached its limit, and all resolutions did not only impose sanctions but also required the resumption of the political process and talks. He stressed that this requirement was completely ignored by the United States.[30] In December 2019 Russia together the China, recognizing "the necessity ... to ensure the welfare, inherent dignity, and rights of people in the DPRK, and reaffirming that the measures previously introduced by the UN Security Council are not intended to have adverse humanitarian consequences for the civilian population of the DPRK" on 16 December, 2019 introduced a draft resolution to the UN Security council. The suggested measures included, inter alia, to "exempt the inter-Korean rail and road cooperation projects from existing UN sanctions" and temporary lifting of the import prohibition provision for "the specific items and corresponding HS Codes of certain industrial machinery and transportation vehicles which are used for infrastructure construction and cannot be diverted to the DPRK's nuclear and ballistic missile programmes, and certain items in the humanitarian and livelihood field is not applicable to the specific items and corresponding HS Codes. However the declaration was not adopted and put in to a back-burner.

The only project Russia managed to protect from sanctions in 2017 was the Rajin-Hasan coal transit; however, Russia-based coal exporters with foreign ownership declined to continue shipments, which paralysed the activities of the operating company JV "RasonConTrans" in 2018 after record results (more than 2 million tons of coal was shipped in transit in 2017).[31]

Russia was caught off guard by the fast-moving sequence of events that followed Kim Jong-un's proposal for dialogue with the ROK and the United States (January 1, 2018). While the Russian Foreign Ministry procrastinated, the events developed in a flash-like manner, pushing Russia to the sidelines. It was only in April 2018, after Kim Jong-un's visit to China and the announcement of the North-South and DPRK-US summit plans, that North Korean foreign minister Ri Yong-ho went to Moscow for talks with his Russian counterpart Sergey Lavrov.

The Russian foreign minister visited Pyongyang on May 31, 2018, when he met North Korea's leader Kim Jong-un. The visit of Russian Senate speaker Valentina Matvienko in September 2018 was important for better policy coordination between the two countries. Kim confirmed the importance of Russia for settling the Korean nuclear issue and said that the approaches of the two countries towards the settlement of the Korean Peninsula's nuclear issue "were similar" while confirming its commitment to the reunification of the two Koreas.

Russia was also concerned because despite the historic US-North Korea summit on June 12 in Singapore and consequent summits and exchanges, Washington continued to insist that North Korea should first take the irreversible steps, to dismantle its nuclear facilities, and promised to fulfil its side of the bargain only after that.

The Putin-Kim summit in April 2019 restored Russia's position in the resolution of the Korean issue and outlined a scenario where negotiations would become more realistic, even in a multilateral format. However, the Russian president said that a resolution would only be possible if the negotiations between the United States and North Korea made progress. Putin also restated the need for providing international security guarantees for North Korea, in case of denuclearisation. However, speaking at the press conference, Putin was very cautious in his predictions about the development of the diplomatic process between the United States and the DPRK.

Thus, hopes of economic breakthroughs have gone unfulfilled. Only the theoretical possibility of creating a railway transit bridge and an oil and gas pipeline remain. Beside, these will require huge investments for the modernisation of the railway structure of the DPRK. Putin expressed scepticism about the possible role of South Korea in trilateral projects, citing the oblique term "shortage of sovereignty" (meaning that the United States would never permit this).[32]

The issues of cooperation in other areas were discussed in June 2019 during a meeting of the two countries' Co-Chairmen of the Intergovernmental commission. The discussions showed, that the prospects of such projects as construction of automobile bridge across border river of Tumangan, as well as electronic trading venue, were dim.[33] Against this background, what are the challenges as well as the future role of Russia in the Korea Peninsula?

First, Russia wants to maintain normal bilateral relations with Pyongyang and does not want to allow sanctions to spoil the spirit of good-neighbourliness. Second, Russia would promote denuclearisation, but only in a form that would be suitable for maintaining security. Russia would under no circumstance allow the use of military force to make Pyongyang abandon its nuclear programme or change the North Korean regime (effectively wiping out the North Korean state from the political map). Third, Russia is interested in multilateral cooperation with the DPRK's participation in North East Asia and in a collective security mechanism.

In all, Russia hopes that the ongoing diplomatic process between the DPRK and ROK, as well as the DPRK-US détente, brings about a decisive change in the mood on the Korean Peninsula and helps resolve the problems of security in a comprehensive manner by political means. Russia is prepared to be a part of the multi-party process to provide a system of guarantees for a new peace and security arrangement in North East Asia.

Notes

1 A. Panin and V. Altov, *Severnaya Koreya. Epoha Kim Chen Ira na zakate* (North Korea: The End of Kim Jong Il's era), Olma-Press, Moscow, 2004.
2 George D. Toloraya, "Russia and the Issues of the Korean Peninsula", *MGIMO Review of International Relations*, 4 (37), 2014, pp. 82–91.
3 "DPRK Nuclear Program: How It All Started?"-RIA, February 9, 2007, at https://ria.ru/20070209/60461507.html (accessed September 12, 2019).

4 Georgiy Boulychyov and Alexandre Vorontsov, "North Korea – An Experiment in Nuclear Proliferation", in A. Arbatov (ed.), *At the Nuclear Threshold. The Lessons of North Korean and Iranian Crises for the Non-proliferation of Nuclear Weapons*, Rosspan, Moscow, 2007, pp. 16–33, at http://carnegieendowment.org/files/12398nuclear_threshold_russian.pdf (accessed July 21, 2019).
5 Interviews with former Russian officials.
6 Russian Official Charged in South Korean Spy Scandal, Monitor, 4 (135), July 15, 1998, at https://jamestown.org/program/russian-official-charged-in-south-korean-spy-scandal/ (accessed on September 13, 2019).
7 George D. Toloraya, No. 2, p. 89.
8 Ibid.
9 Minister of Foreign Affairs of the Russian Federation Igor Ivanov on an Official Visit to the DPRK, Ministry of Foreign Affairs of Russia, Moscow, February 10, 2000, at www.mid.ru/ru/maps/kp/-/asset_publisher/VJy7Ig5QaAII/content/id/607264 (accessed May 13, 2019).
10 Ibid.
11 "Russia-DPRK Joint Declaration", Kremlin, Moscow, July 19, 2000, at http://kremlin.ru/supplement/3183 (accessed May 18, 2019).
12 Ibid.
13 "Text of President Bush's 2002 State of the Union Address", *The Washington Post*, January 29, 2002, at www.washingtonpost.com/wp-srv/onpolitics/transcripts/sou012902.htm (accessed July 7, 2019).
14 Stephen Zunes, "Deconstructing George W. Bush: A Critical Analysis of the 2002 State of the Union Address", Foreign Policy in Focus, January 31, 2002, at http://fpif.org/deconstructing_george_w_bush_a_critical_analysis_of_the_2002_state_of_the_union_address/ (accessed July 22, 2019).
15 Alexander Yakovenko, "The Official Spokesman of Russia's Ministry of Foreign Affairs, Answers a Russian/Foreign Media Question About a Package Solution to the Korean Problem", The Ministry of Foreign Affairs of the Russian Federation, January 12, 2003, at www.mid.ru/en/foreign_policy/news/-/asset_publisher/cKNonkJE02Bw/content/id/536594 (accessed June 16, 2019).
16 Interviews with former Russian officials.
17 "Meeting with Chairman of the National Defence Committee of the Democratic People's Republic of Korea Kim Jong Il", Kremlin, Moscow, August 24, 2011, at http://en.kremlin.ru/events/president/news/12421 (accessed June 7, 2019).
18 "North Korea: Beyond the Six Party Talks", Asia Report No. 269, International Crisis Group, June 16, 2015, p. 7, at www.refworld.org/pdfid/557fe26c4.pdf (accessed June 20, 2019).
19 Alexander Vorontsov and Georgy Toloraya, "Military Alert on the Korean Peninsula: Time for Some Conclusions", Carnegie Moscow Center, May 2014, pp. 1–44, at http://carnegieendowment.org/files/CP_Korea_web_Eng.pdf (accessed July 13, 2019).
20 "Joint Statement of President Donald J. Trump of the United States of America and Chairman Kim Jong Un of the Democratic People's Republic of Korea at the Singapore Summit", The White House, June 12, 2018, at www.whitehouse.gov/briefings-statements/joint-statement-president-donald-j-trump-united-states-america-chairman-kim-jong-un-democratic-peoples-republic-korea-singapore-summit/ (accessed July 23, 2019).
21 "Comment by the Information and Press Department on the Situation around DPRK", Ministry of Foreign Affairs of Russia, 2013, at www.mid.ru/foreign_policy/news/-/asset_publisher/cKNonkJE02Bw/content/id/115682 (accessed June 17, 2019).
22 Alexander Vorontsov and Georgy Toloraya, No. 19, p. 227.

23 7th session of the Russia-DPRK Intergovernmental Commission, Ministry for the Development of the Russian Far East, 2015, at https://minvr.ru/press-center/news/1454/ (accessed June 15, 2019).
24 "US Comes to Russia with 'Absurd' Request for More Sanctions Against North Korea", *Sputnik*, September 11, 2017, at https://sputniknews.com/asia/201709111057286851-north-korea-russia-us-sanctions/ (accessed June 15, 2019).
25 "Joint Statement by the Russian and Chinese Foreign Ministries on the Korean Peninsula's Problems", Ministry of Foreign Affairs of Russia, July 4, 2017, at www.mid.ru/en/foreign_policy/news/-/asset_publisher/cKNonkJE02Bw/content/id/2807662 (accessed May 13, 2019).
26 "Russia Has Urged US to Take Steps to Slow down Military Activities Around Korean Peninsula", TASS, April 21, 2018, at http://tass.com/politics/1001100 (accessed June 30, 2019).
27 "Dynamics of Russia's Foreign Trade with North Korea from 2010 to 2017", Russian Foreign Trade, 2018, at http://en.russian-trade.com/reports-and-reviews/2018-07/dynamics-of-russian-trade-with-north-korea-from-2010-to-2017/ (accessed June 2, 2019).
28 "Russia Mulls Response to U.S. Sanctions over North Korea: Ifax", Reuters, August 16, 2018, at www.reuters.com/article/us-usa-northkorea-sanctions-russia/russia-mulls-response-to-u-s-sanctions-over-north-korea-ifax-idUSKBN1L10T8 (accessed June 12, 2019).
29 8th session of the Russia-DPRK Intergovernmental Commission, Ministry for the Development of the Russian Far East, 2018, at https://minvr.ru/press-center/news/14170/ (accessed July 11, 2019).
30 Andrew Osborn, "Russia Accuses U.S. of Trying to Provoke North Korean Leader 'to Fly off Handle'", Reuters, November 30, 2017, at www.reuters.com/article/us-northkorea-missiles-russia-usa/russia-accuses-u-s-of-trying-to-provoke-north-korean-leader-to-fly-off-handle-idUSKBN1DU115 (accessed June 30, 2019).
31 http://rasoncontrans.com/en/company.html
32 "Press Conference After Meeting Between Vladimir Putin and Kim Jong-un", RIA Novosti, April 25, 2019, at https://ria.ru/20190425/1553029975.html (accessed June 15, 2019).
33 http://rasoncontrans.com/press-center/item/120-20190606.html

Part II
Contending perspectives

5 Denuclearisation and peace regime on the Korean Peninsula

Perspectives of the two Koreas

Jina Kim

Introduction

North Korea pushed ahead with its long-range missile launch on April 13, 2012, in violation of its February 29, 2012, agreement with the United States. After a third nuclear test on February 12, 2013, North Korea declared its permanent status as a nuclear weapons state on March 9, adopting a policy of the parallel development of nuclear weapons and the economy (*Byungjin* Policy) on March 31. North Korea enacted a law on April 1 to affirm its status as a so-called self-reliant nuclear power. At the seventh Workers' Party Congress in May 2016, North Korea reaffirmed its commitment to the *Byungjin* Policy. Despite strong opposition from the international community, the North demonstrated its will to enhance its nuclear deterrence capabilities by conducting additional 17 missile tests in 2017. The prevailing view at the end of 2017 was that North Korea had no intention of denuclearising.[1] Hence, North Korea's decision to attend the Pyeongchang Winter Olympics in South Korea after a year of unprecedented tensions came as a surprise for many in the international community. The leaders of the two Koreas met three times in 2018 and had a very brief encounter at the Joint Security Area in June 2019 as ties warmed between Seoul and Pyongyang.

At the first inter-Korean summit meeting in the Demilitarized Zone (DMZ) separating the Democratic People's Republic of Korea (DPRK) and Republic of Korea (ROK) on April 27, 2018, the two Koreas confirmed that their goal was to make the Korean Peninsula nuclear weapons free, thus setting the direction for further talks. At the first-ever US-DPRK summit meeting in Singapore on June 12, US president Donald Trump and the North Korean leader Kim Jong-un signed a document asserting that the United States would provide security guarantees to North Korea in exchange for the North's unwavering commitment to the complete denuclearisation of the Korean Peninsula. More specific measures, including the permanent dismantlement of the Yongbyon nuclear facility, were discussed at the September 19 inter-Korean summit in Pyongyang.[2] The second US-DPRK summit in Hanoi on February 27–28, 2019, ended without a joint statement, although each side claimed that the meeting was very productive.[3] President Moon later paid a working visit to Washington in April 2019, to discuss how to revive the diplomatic process between the United States and North Korea.

Details such as deadlines, the scope, and verification methods for the implementation of denuclearisation of the North have yet to be agreed upon. Achieving a consensus on a denuclearisation road map is impossible because political, technological, and diplomatic issues all have to be considered together. In the past, denuclearisation was a bilateral issue between the United States and North Korea. The current situation is a multi-party game as South Korea became involved early on, as a facilitator of the talks. South Korea's involvement is unavoidable owing to the interconnectedness of three issues – inter-Korean exchanges and cooperation, denuclearisation, and military confidence building measures (CBMs). Military CBMs are a guarantor for sustainable progress in socio-economic cooperation and exchanges. However, without denuclearisation, confidence building would be limited.

Denuclearisation will lead to the lifting of sanctions and the green lighting of these programmes on the Korean Peninsula. Facilitating mutual exchanges and cooperation is one of the ways to incentivise North Korea to remain committed to the talks on denuclearisation. However, the actors involved seem to have different priorities with regard to the sequence of activities they wish to pursue in exchange for the trade-offs and their timelines.

It is significant that the United States and North Korea have once again embarked on talks that had been stalled for about ten years: in 2009, the Six-Party Talks involving China, the United States, North and South Korea, Japan, and Russia were stalled as the negotiating parties failed to narrow their differences, regarding the verification and procedures for denuclearisation. Moreover, the four pillars of the Singapore agreement between President Trump and Chairman Kim Jong-un included not only the process of denuclearisation but also the furthering of diplomatic relations between the United States and North Korea, and the establishment of a lasting and stable peace regime on the Korean Peninsula. Some argue that this is merely a reaffirmation of the 2005 joint statement following the fourth round of the Six-Party Talks. However, the six parties at the time agreed to discuss the peace regime at a "separate forum" and as a major agenda item. It is also worth noting that the 2005 joint statement called upon the parties to "negotiate" peace arrangements, while this time it was the United States and North Korea that agreed to "build" a peace regime on the Korean Peninsula. Nonetheless, there is uncertainty about how to get the ball rolling.

President Trump continues to emphasise that his relationship with Chairman Kim is very good, and that he is in no rush.[4] Given that the US government has specified the scale and level of denuclearisation required and the conditions for the lifting of sanctions on many occasions, North Korea's demand for the partial lifting of sanctions in exchange for the opening up of the Yongbyon nuclear complex only leads to confusion. There is a view that Pyongyang had no intention of accepting Washington's terms of negotiation and miscalculated that it was President Trump's personal agenda to forge just any deal with North Korea.

The current situation gives rise to the following questions: What are the prospects that the talks on denuclearisation will continue? What is the outlook for denuclearisation and the establishment of a permanent peace regime on the Korean Peninsula?

This chapter explains the stands of the two Koreas on denuclearisation, the attendant dilemmas that are difficult to tackle, and the likely challenges facing the international community.

Four hypotheses

It was in late 2017 that North Korea began making its diplomatic overtures. There are four hypotheses with regard to its decision to re-commence the denuclearisation talks (also see Table 5.1):

1. The first hypothesis is that North Korea is no longer able to cope with international sanctions. If this is true, then North Korea is pursuing the short-term agenda of the lifting of sanctions. The US "secondary boycott" must have been a major concern for North Korea. Negotiations allowed North Korea to improve its relations with China, which is its number one trading partner. However, it is not likely that the United States will lift sanctions unless the North takes practical, concrete measures towards denuclearisation. North Korea could just muddle through without actually engaging in talks because of the many loopholes in the current North Korean sanctions regime. However, before the talks with the United States and South Korea, North Korea declared that it was shifting its focus to the economy. The leadership in Pyongyang asked the North Koreans to endure the tough times until the country became strong and prosperous. Their logic was that North

Table 5.1 North Korea's intentions and related hypotheses[5]

Hypothesis	1	2	3	4
Road map milestone	Intermediate (alleviation/lifting of sanctions)	Early (confirm stance)	Intermediate (freeze plus)	Final (denuclearization)
Background	Strengthened sanctions	Changes in the ROK/US govt.	Confidence in nuclear deterrence	Political decision
Precondition	Lifting must be possible before the actual denuclearisation	Backlash after summit must be small	Changes in denuclearisation principles and reaching a compromise must be possible	A momentum of lengthy negotiations must be sustained
Risk	Medium (weakening of cooperation in international sanctions against the DPRK)	High (provides legitimacy in seeking non-diplomatic options)	High (acknowledged as a nuclear weapons state)	Low
Uncertainty	Providing the DPRK breathing room	Enter into a prolonged stalemate	US-DPRK compromise and ROK interests do not match	Changes in political schedule, defection

Korea can focus on its economic development once it has stabilised the security environment by developing nuclear weapons. North Korea would declare the denuclearisation talks a success once the obstacles hindering the recovery of its economy had been removed.[6]

2   Second, it is possible that North Korea wants to simply deescalate the situation following multiple missile tests in 2017, expecting that others would seek an alternative path other than military confrontation between Pyongyang and Washington. It is not the first time that North Korea has proposed talks for the peaceful settlement of the situation on the Korean Peninsula. However, the international community has always responded cautiously because North Korea, repeatedly in the past, sought a declaration ending the Korean War; the dismantling of the UN Command (UNC); the withdrawal of US Forces in Korea (USFK); and a peace treaty that included the whole package. In August 2013, North Korea held an unofficial 1.5 track meeting with the United States, where Vice Foreign Minister Ahn Myung-hoon reiterated North Korea's stance that the agenda should include the easing of military tensions and the establishment of a peace regime and a nuclear-free world.[7] In July 2016, the North Korean government spokesperson demanded disclosure of all US nuclear assets in the South and verification of bases where nuclear weapons are stored, an assurance that the United States would not bring strategic assets into the Korean Peninsula, a security guarantee of no nuclear weapons use against North Korea, and the withdrawal of the USFK.[8] It became a routine practice that North Korea lays out difficult negotiation conditions to accept, and if the negotiations fails, it pours blame on the other side. It is possible that North Korea would repeat the same argument to change the equilibrium on the Korean peninsula, which met rejection from the United States and South Korea in the past. However, North Koreans may expect that the leadership change in Washington and Seoul, with President Trump and President Moon assuming office, can produce a different outcome.

3   Third, North Korea is confident that the negotiations will have a favourable outcome. Throughout 2017, North Korea showed off its deterrence capabilities by demonstrating its ability to develop Intercontinental Ballistic Missiles (ICBMs) and by ratcheting up its rhetoric against the US threat of "fire and fury". In his 2018 New Year's Day address to the nation, Chairman Kim stressed that the entire US mainland is within the range of North Korea's nuclear weapons, and hence the United States would never attack North Korea.[9] At the same time, his remarks were very calculated, avoiding any unnecessarily harsh rhetoric. In the same address, he also signalled his willingness to talk with South Korea in order to improve inter-Korean relations, suggesting that a peaceful dialogue was the only way to de-escalate the tensions on the Korean Peninsula. And it is possible that North Korea can achieve a sort of compromise in the long run. Undoubtedly, Complete, Verifiable and Irreversible Denuclearisation (CVID) is extremely difficult to achieve; and third-party inspection of its undeclared facilities has always

been a disputed point with the North. In such a scenario, North Korea may expect the international community to choose risk reduction rather than continuing endless debates on verification.

4   The fourth hypothesis is that North Korea wants to be recognised as a completely normal country through denuclearisation, which would be ideal. In this scenario, North Korea is likely to remain cooperative. In recent times, North Korea's attitude certainly appears slightly different compared to the past, as it has remained cautious in its rhetoric, showing its interest in keeping the momentum alive and not engaging in provocative or threatening actions. It emphasised, for example, sustainable development through economic and technological cooperation at the inter-Korean dialogue in 2018 and sought investment in infrastructure such as roads and railways, rather than a one-sided, one-time assistance.[10] Chairman Kim insisted that the national efforts should be concentrated on boosting North Korea's economy in his New Year's speech on January 1, 2019, and his plan of "Total Construction of North Korean Economy" was again emphasized at the Supreme People's Assembly in March 2019. This is indicative of North Korea's long-term plan.

Whatever the reasons that drew North Korea to the negotiating table, it is clearly in North Korea's interests to continue the dialogue process. However, North Korea's proposal for denuclearisation talks in 2018 came with preconditions, that is, "as long as the military threats against North Korea are resolved and the security of the North Korean regime is guaranteed". At the same time, North Korea wants "a dialogue in which each party can discuss and resolve issues of mutual interest on equal ground".[11] And now as bilateral talks between the United States and North Korea have been stalled post the Hanoi summit, concerns are being raised that Washington and Pyongyang have reached a deadlock. We should note that the past negotiations failed not because of an absence of interest in dialogue but because of conflicting priorities, dilemmas, and mistrust. Against this backdrop, we should explore the variables that are likely to be in play throughout the talks with the North.

North Korea's perspective

Definition and scope of denuclearisation

The international community has been using the term "denuclearisation of the North" to imply the termination of North Korea's nuclear programme. Many experts in South Korea still prefer to use this term to emphasise that North Korea's nuclear programme is the subject of denuclearisation. On the other hand, North Korea has been consistent in making a distinction between "denuclearisation of North Korea (*Chosun*)" and "denuclearisation of the Korean Peninsula (*Chosun Bando*)". North Korea argues that denuclearisation of the North alone violates its sovereignty and seeks to dismantle its socialist system by negating its nuclear deterrence ability.[12] Therefore, it rejects any unilateral action to dismantle its nuclear programme, saying, "What the US wants is not the denuclearisation of the Korean Peninsula but the Americanisation of the Korean Peninsula".[13] In this light, one should note that this time North Korea agreed to negotiate on the condition that there must be no threat to its security and the Kim regime would not be threatened. Whereas, the Trump administration is pressurising North Korea to agree to an all-inclusive deal – dismantlement of its weapons of mass destruction (WMDs) and its ballistic missile programmes. The biggest concern is that the dismantling of its WMD – nuclear, biological, and chemical weapons – programme increases North Korea's sensitivity to the change in military balance on the Korean Peninsula.

It is also not clear whether all parties concerned share a common definition of the phrase the "denuclearisation of the Korean Peninsula". According to North Korea, "denuclearisation of the Korean Peninsula" means no nuclear assets on or around the Korean Peninsula: "If the US truly wants to denuclearise the Korean Peninsula, it should immediately withdraw US troops and all forms of weapons including nuclear weapons deployed in South Korea".[14] In July 2017, North Korea issued a statement reiterating, "The denuclearisation we claim includes the abolition of the nuclear weapons in the South and denuclearisation around the Korean Peninsula".[15]

From the North Korean perspective, the denuclearisation of the Korean Peninsula means establishing a Nuclear Weapons Free Zone (NWFZ) on the Korean Peninsula and its vicinity. North Korea introduced the term "Zone of Peace" into its discourse in the 1950s.[16] It continued to seek the withdrawal of the USFK and denuclearisation of South Korea after the United States reiterated its commitment to providing a nuclear umbrella to South Korea and began the *Team Spirit* US-South Korea joint military exercises around 1975–1976.[17] At the Sixth Workers' Party of Korea (WPK) Congress Meeting in October 1980, Kim Il-sung proposed turning the Korean Peninsula into an everlasting zone of peace and an NWFZ by prohibiting the production, introduction, and use of nuclear weapons.[18] NWFZ, by definition, is a region in which countries commit themselves not to manufacture, acquire, test, or possess nuclear weapons.[19] It has always been the case that parties to the NWFZ call upon nuclear weapons states not to use or threaten to use nuclear weapons against nuclear weapons states. One should note that North Korea's proposal to establish a zone of peace on the Korean Peninsula entails a Washington declaration of the non-use of nuclear weapons against the North. Thus, how to navigate the space between these two interests – that is, agreeing to the demand for a legally binding negative security assurance and reserving the right to use nuclear weapons in case of unforeseen events – is an issue for the US-South Korea alliance.

Facing a deadlock in their denuclearisation talks, the United States and North Korea both seem to be refusing to make any concessions. North Korea seeks to address the issues between the two sides in light of terminating US hostility, arguing that its nuclear armament was inevitable due to the antagonistic nature of their relations. One should note that for North Korea, ending "hostile acts" means ending pressure in the military, diplomatic, economic, and social domains. North Korea's so-called "central link theory" dictates that the other problems will resolve themselves once this key issue has been resolved.[20] When offering talks with the United States after a series of missile launches between May and September in 2019, the Ministry of Foreign Affairs in Pyongyang stressed that Washington should come to the negotiating table with acceptable new proposals.[21] In this regard, North Korea is likely to seize this opportunity to continue the dialogue process until it can resolve all of the other problems by playing the nuclear card. If the North Koreans are playing a game of chess, they may not bring the "denuclearisation queen" into play before they have advanced their bishops and pawns to safeguard their interests, that is, the suspension of ROK-US military exercises, lifting of economic sanctions, normalisation of diplomatic relations, and so on.

Sequence of action

Given the lack of trust between the two sides, each hopes that the other will take the initiative to take measures to build trust first. Undoubtedly, there is disagreement on the sequence of actions preferred by each side, but we should also be aware of what the leadership in Pyongyang communicates to its domestic audience. At the US-DPRK summit in Singapore, President Trump and Chairman Kim confirmed that mutual trust can facilitate denuclearisation.[22] North Korea seems to take this statement to mean that mutual trust-building measures are likely to proceed ahead of denuclearisation, or at least simultaneously. Right after the Singapore summit, North Korea's Foreign Ministry spokesperson stated that the two sides agreed on the principle of taking simultaneous and step-by-step measures for achieving denuclearisation.[23] He also said that North Korea would take the next step if the United States took the first step towards building trust. However, US secretary Pompeo said, "North Korea will first have to fulfil its commitment to denuclearise".[24] North Korea complains that it has already given up too much, while the United States argues that North Korea has done nothing regarding denuclearisation. Moreover, North Korea continues to argue that its demand for the removal of nuclear weapons from the Korean Peninsula is irreversible, while the removal of a nuclear threat to the North Korean regime is reversible.

One should also note that North Korea cannot take any unilateral action beyond what has already been decided upon. On April 20, 2018, North Korea decided on its future actions during the third plenary session of the seventh Central Committee of the WPK, a key body in the North.[25] The meeting declared that economic development was now a priority for North Korea and that North Korea no longer needed any nuclear or ICBM tests, so, the nuclear test site now had no purpose.[26] As far as fulfilling its own commitment to shut down the test sites, North Korea has already taken the necessary steps before holding talks with the United States and South Korea. That is, North Korea has decided to show restraint with regard to its "future" nuclear weapons development programme. Hence, additional steps, such as opening up the test sites for verification of North

Korea's past nuclear weapons programme, would be up for a deal. The strategic shift is aimed at building its image as a responsible nuclear weapons state, receiving enhanced support from China and Russia for seeking diplomatic solutions, and pressuring the United States to take further steps in response. By doing so, North Korea has created the conditions for striking a deal.

At the same time, the leadership in Pyongyang has political capital at stake. Chairman Kim has to prove that the strategic shift from developing nuclear capabilities to revitalising the economy was the right direction for the North. It should be noted that Chairman Kim's visits and on-site instructions in 2018 focussed on the economic activities. He made 37 trips that were economy related, while he visited a military base just once between January and mid-December 2018.[27] His frequent trips to industrial sites and economic zones near North Korea's border with China were also aimed at rallying support at home for his economic drive. North Korea's focus on economic development continued in 2019, and Chairman Kim gave a lengthy speech on economic development at a plenary meeting of the WPK Central Committee on April 10. In June 2018, an end-of-war declaration seemed to take centre stage in talks, but North Korea remained silent on this issue in the months following the September 2018 inter-Korean summit. Rather, North Korea raised the issue of lifting sanctions in exchange for its phased denuclearisation. The reality is that Pyongyang had a different trade-off in mind when the leadership made the strategic shift in advance, that is, the revitalisation of the economy.

The question is whether the North will return to its past practice of provocation actions. Since the North's offer to negotiate a conditions-based denuclearisation was not well-received in the past, there has been a cycle of peace overtures, warning signals, policy shifts, and provocations. Before the third nuclear test in February 2013, North Korea had warned that the agreement made at the Six-Party Talks would be annulled. Then, it vowed to take steps to expand and strengthen its nuclear-deterrent capability at home and abroad. In June 2015, North Korea's Defence Committee issued a special statement suggesting talks in exchange of the cancellation of the Ulchi-Freedom Guardian (UFG), repeating its request for a "freeze-for-freeze" course of action. When this proposal was rejected by the United States, North Korea warned in July that it would launch missiles if its sovereignty was threatened. The regime also declared that it had entered the final phase of satellite development in September. North Korea conducted its fourth nuclear test in January 2016 and simultaneously proposed halting nuclear tests and starting talks on a peace treaty. In order to attract international attention and support for such demands, North Korea warned that its response to the ROK-US alliance would be a pre-emptive offensive. Whenever North Korea makes a proposal for talks, it is accompanied by demands for parallel and simultaneous action.

However, it is too early to assume that North Korea will again back away from the negotiation table, repeating the past pattern of peace overtures and provocations (see Figure 5.1). The frequency with which denuclearisation is being mentioned by the regime has also increased, unlike in the past when North Korea took a

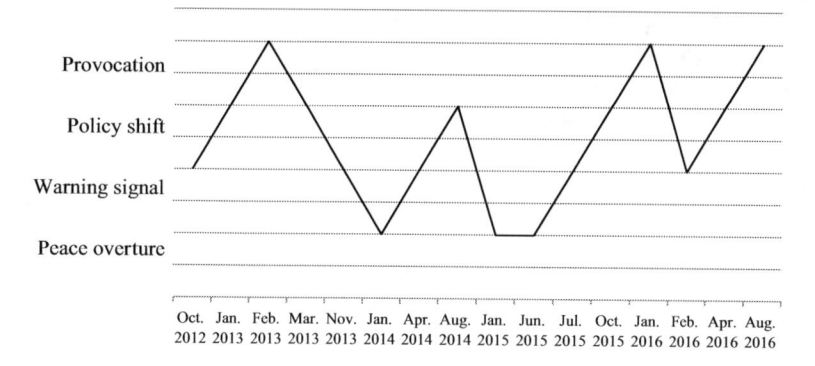

Figure 5.1 North Korea's pattern of behaviour.

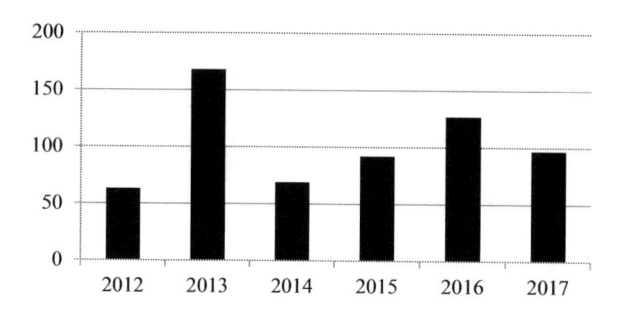

Figure 5.2 References to denuclearisation.
Source: Rodong Shinmun.

tough stance on its nuclear weapons development. It should be noted that the term "denuclearisation" makes an appearance in the *Rodong Shinmun*, the official newspaper of the Central Committee of the WPK, at critical times, as was the case particularly in 2013 and 2016 when North Korea conducted nuclear tests (see Figure 5.2).

South Korea's perspective

Three key documents

South Korea's concept of denuclearisation is based on the 1992 Joint Declaration on the Korean Peninsula. On November 8, 1991, President Roh Tae-woo made a declaration regarding the denuclearisation of the Korean Peninsula and the establishment of peace on the Peninsula. This was a pre-emptive move by the South Korean government to halt the construction of a nuclear reprocessing facility in North Korea.[28] In January 1992, the two Koreas agreed that they would not test, manufacture, produce, receive, possess, store, distribute, or use nuclear weapons.[29] It was also agreed that the South and the North would use nuclear energy only for peaceful purposes and would not operate nuclear reprocessing facilities or uranium enrichment facilities. In order to verify the denuclearisation of the Korean Peninsula, the South and the North discussed mutual inspection through the Inter-Korean Nuclear Control Joint Commission. However, at this time, the two sides did not address issues such as the withdrawal of US troops, removal of the US nuclear umbrella, or the guarantee of neighbouring countries to ensure the Korean Peninsula would remain free from nuclear threats.

In 1994, when the United States and North Korea reached an agreement to finalise the overall resolution of the nuclear issue on the Korean Peninsula, South Korea welcomed the US-DPRK Agreed Framework. It should be noted that the key objective of this agreement was to achieve peace and security on a nuclear-free Korean Peninsula. This key document reaffirmed the denuclearisation of the Korean Peninsula, calling on the United States to make a formal assurance to the North on the non-use of nuclear weapons by the United States and for North Korea to take steps to implement the Inter-Korean Joint Declaration on the Denuclearisation of the Korean Peninsula.[30] As practical steps towards these goals, the agreement specified actions such as a freeze on North Korea's nuclear activities, supporting the provision of light water reactors to North Korea and heavy oil for energy losses caused by the freezing of nuclear activities, and normalising political and economic relations between North Korea and the United States. As an executive member of the Korean Peninsula Energy Development Organisation (KEDO), South Korea contributed funding for the light water reactor with a commitment to pay for up to 70 per cent of the project.[31] It used the multilateral forum as a vehicle to engage in a dialogue with the North in order to reduce tensions on the Korean Peninsula during the mid-1990s.

As a member of the Six-Party Talks, South Korea endorsed the joint statement of the fourth round of the Six-Party Talks on September 19, 2005. The joint statement reaffirmed the peaceful and verifiable denuclearisation of the Korean Peninsula.[32] Again, it was highlighted that the 1992 Joint Declaration of the Denuclearisation of the Korean Peninsula should be followed and implemented. South Korea reaffirmed its commitment not to receive or deploy nuclear weapons, in accordance with the 1992 Joint Declaration, and called for joint efforts for a lasting peace regime on the Korean Peninsula. What was agreed to by the six parties included total abandonment of all nuclear weapons by North Korea, a return to the treaty for the non-proliferation of nuclear weapons (NPT) and the International Atomic Energy Agency (IAEA), a US negative security assurance confirming that it had no intention to attack or invade the North with nuclear or conventional weapons, and efforts to promote economic cooperation and normalise diplomatic relations. This shows that the basic idea presented and endorsed by all parties concerned has been consistent.

The same holds true for South Korea's policy for the improvement of inter-Korean relations. The fact that the ROK government's policies towards North Korea are not event-driven but consistent is often overlooked. South Korea's position on denuclearisation has been very clear: it does not accept a nuclear-armed DPRK and prefers a peaceful resolution and a comprehensive, step-by-step approach based on the principle of action for action. This is not entirely new for an international audience. The ROK Foreign Ministry initiated the so-called "Korea formula" in 2014 and continued to explore the possibilities and conditions for holding a multilateral dialogue in 2015. The difference is that, in the past, South Korea was not a major actor in denuclearisation negotiations. However, South Korea under the Moon Jae-in government seeks to facilitate talks between the United States and North Korea.

Principles and action plans

When President Moon Jae-in vowed in his inauguration speech that he would try to persuade North Korea to resolve the nuclear issue, many commented that "the liberal government is set to change policy on North Korea".[33] There seems to be a tendency to think that any so-called "liberal government" seeks proactive engagement with the North. However, a conservative government held 24 inter-Korean dialogues in 2013, mostly on economic cooperation. This number is higher than that in 2006, when there was an inter-Korean summit. It was in 2013 that North Korea conducted its third nuclear test. This shows that efforts to enhance inter-Korean exchanges and cooperation are always in accordance with South Korea's grand strategy. The Moon Jae-in government views that the establishment of a peace regime is a long-term process. It is believed that reconciliation and confidence building during this process can naturally create a peaceful environment in which further talks on denuclearisation and the peace process can take place.

The Moon government is pursuing four policy objectives (see Table 5.2): first, a gradual, comprehensive approach, in which a "freeze" of North Korea's nuclear weapons programme can be the first step. This is a small step but a feasible option that does not evoke much resistance from North Korea. Second, South Korea is pursuing inter-Korean dialogue to establish a peace regime on the Korean Peninsula while holding simultaneous talks on denuclearisation, because history shows that inter-Korean talks cannot make progress without talks between the United States and North Korea. Third, South Korea is seeking to institutionalise practices for the sustainable implementation of an agreement. This is an effort

Table 5.2 Policy objectives of the Moon Jae-in government

	Policy objectives	Action plan
1	Gradual, comprehensive approach	Freeze and then denuclearise
2	Simultaneously pursue inter-Korean dialogue and nuclear talks	Play a facilitating role
3	Ensure sustainability of agreement	Institutionalise practices
4	Mutually beneficial cooperation	Shape conditions for peaceful unification

to ensure the continuity of South Korea's policy towards North Korea, which is often affected by changes in the political climate. Fourth, South Korea seeks mutually beneficial cooperation with the North.

Under the overarching goal of a "Korean Peninsula of Peace and Prosperity", the Moon government initiated national policies that were implemented by the ministries of national defence, foreign affairs, and national unification (see Figure 5.3).[34] It should be noted that the South Korean government seeks inter-Korean reconciliation and denuclearisation on the basis of strong security and responsible defence. This is because "sustainability" of peace cannot be guaranteed only by diplomacy. It should also be noted that after the Hanoi summit ended without an agreement between the United States and the DPRK, President Moon proposed a long-term "New Korean Peninsula Initiative" on March 1, 2019. He reaffirmed his wish to establish a permanent peace regime on the basis of a close ROK-US coordination and a settlement in the US-DPRK talks.[35] The purpose of his address was to provide a blueprint for the coming century by pursuing inter-Korean reconciliation, developing sustainable economic cooperation, and establishing a new order of peace and cooperation in North-East Asia. He emphasised that winning a settlement concerning practical and institutional measures for a complete termination of hostile relations on the Korean Peninsula is key to achieve these goals. Indeed, it is not the first time that South Korea has proposed a new system that assures peaceful coexistence of the two Koreas. But all such efforts seem to get overshadowed by political events and misunderstandings regarding South Korea's approach to denuclearisation and peace arrangements.

One concern is that efforts to relieve the dire situation in North Korea may reduce the international community's negotiating power on the issue of denuclearisation. Humanitarian aid for North Korea ground nearly to a halt in 2018, as the United States stepped up the enforcement of sanctions.[36] In addition, the United States continues to tighten sanctions as part of its maximum-pressure campaign and refuses to grant special permission to aid workers to travel to North Korea.[37] In a situation where financial sanctions have shut down most relief groups operating in North Korea, South Korea's relief and assistance activities have drawn

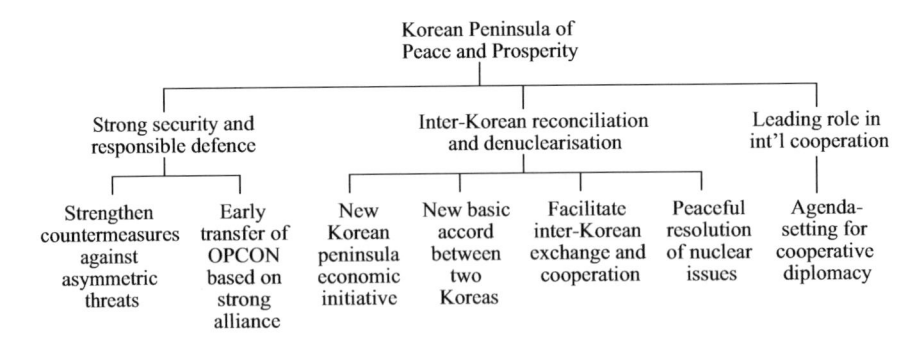

Figure 5.3 National policy initiatives of the Moon Jae-in government.

more attention than before. However, South Korea is not at the frontline of providing aid to the North. The South Korean government announced that it would donate $8 million to the North through international organisations in 2017, but it delayed the implementation of the plan due to strained inter-Korean relations.[38] Under the Lee and Park governments, South Korea allowed humanitarian assistance by non-governmental organisations (NGOs) and increased contribution to international aid projects as well. There were some fluctuations in the amount of aid given to UN agencies in the past, but it was almost US$20 million in 2009, US$12 million in 2013, US$13 million in 2014, and US$10 million in 2015.[39]

One of South Korea's key national agendas is the "New Korean Peninsula Economic Plan". However, in 2017, South Korea had consultations with companies that could be potential participants in inter-Korean economic cooperation, held seminar meetings to enhance understanding of the North-South single market, and designed communication systems and electric facilities. The agenda for "reshaping inter-Korean relations" has pursued a realistic goal of restoring inter-Korean communication channels, in order to begin talks. This is because under the tough sanctions, most financial transactions with North Korea are blocked, and efforts to facilitate inter-Korean exchanges and cooperation cannot make much progress. In principle, South Korea's position is to implement UN sanctions while continuing talks. The South Korean government has been seeking to discuss pending issues, such as humanitarian issues and the easing of military tensions, but has been adjusting the pace when it comes to improving inter-Korean relations.

Challenges ahead

We should try and understand the intrinsic difficulties in getting North Korea to denuclearise. Changing the narrative about the utility of nuclear weapons is not easy. Changing the security paradigm that relies on deterrence is also not likely. Therefore, South Korea will need to make strategic decisions regarding multiple challenges.

First, progress in inter-Korean relations can only be limited, without a grand bargain between the United States and North Korea. Indeed, various projects to improve inter-Korean relations are being explored, but efforts to denuclearise have failed to keep pace. South Korea may seek to conclude a basic inter-Korean accord as an alternative to signing a peace treaty, in order to continue the peace-building initiatives. However, this inevitably brings up the issue of redefining relations between the North and the South and a review of the defence posture. It is possible that debates on the role of the ROK-US alliance will continue. Resolving the disagreements between the two allies will be a challenge. Many have already expressed concerns about the possibility that North Korea's overture aims at exploiting a gap between Washington and Seoul.[40]

Second, one should note that the implementation of conventional disarmament before denuclearisation is an impediment to nuclear talks. The two Koreas agreed to set up a high-level consultative body to discuss conventional arms control and disarmament. However, the prospect of weakening conventional forces via disarmament motivates North Korea to rely even more on its nuclear capabilities. After denuclearisation, it will be difficult for North Korea to implement conventional disarmament. And after giving up the nuclear component of its military power, North Korea will worry about the change in military balance on the Korean Peninsula vis-à-vis South Korea. There are two ways to resolve this issue: North Korea can choose to rely on building conventional weapons with asymmetric capabilities, or South Korea can make extensive changes in its military posture to alleviate North Korea's concerns about its decreasing military capabilities.[41] However, this is not a decision that South Korea can make unilaterally without consulting with its ally.

Third, it is possible that a continually increasing engagement of the United States with North Korea for denuclearization will make other contentious issues between the two countries as a major agenda item that complicates denuclearization talks. What North Korea condemns as hostile policies of the United States includes not only the US military presence on the Korean Peninsula but also the imposition of sanctions, demands for human rights improvements, and the free flow of information into the North.[42] On the US side, many people in Washington are critical of meeting with the leadership in Pyongyang, which is notorious for its human rights abuse, and it is argued that the US government cannot keep avoiding talks on other issues, such as cyber threat, illegal trafficking, money laundering, and so on.[43] However, if these issues are raised in the negotiations, it is likely that North Korea will describe these attempts as interference in its domestic affairs.

Fourth, there is no consensus on the scope of change and acceptable regional ramifications. South Korea downplays a "peace declaration" as a symbolic gesture, while the United States worries that it will spark debates on the role of the UNC and the USFK. Further, this will widen the split between conservatives and liberals in South Korea. It will also send some confusing messages to the outside world. As talks on an end-of-war declaration continue, the role of the UNC could be the first issue that is discussed. The ROK understands that the UNC should continue until it is replaced by an effective alternative mechanism as agreed between the two allies at the Security Consultative Meeting.[44] In terms of the de facto significance of the UNC for peacekeeping and crisis management, one can argue that until unification, the UNC needs to monitor the DMZ and promote CBMs. However, North Korea has tried many times to dissolve the UNC, demanding the withdrawal of all foreign troops. The US forces in Korea are there under the mutual defence treaty between the United States and South Korea.[45] Therefore, even if the Korean Armistice Treaty is changed into a peace treaty, it will not have any legal implication for the status of the USFK. However, as part of the effort to remove the legacy of the Korean War, discussions on the role of the USFK are likely to emerge. Several alliance issues, including the transfer of operational control to South Korea, contributions to US-led global missions and out-of-area operations, and the scope of trilateral (US-South Korea-Japan) military cooperation, among others, could also be discussed.

Fifth, without verifying other suspicious activities, we cannot "freeze" North Korea's nuclear programme. We can only slow down the speed of its nuclear arming. Bringing North Korea into the nuclear non-proliferation regime and putting nuclear safeguards in place would be a desirable end state. This would contribute to the efforts to formally commence Fissile Material Cut-off Treaty (FMCT) and the Treaty on the Prohibition of Nuclear Weapons (TPNW). However, this means that North Korea would be granted rights guaranteed by the NPT regime that include the right to a civilian nuclear programme. There can be disputes over to what extent the international community should control North Korea's potential nuclear weapons capability. Questions may arise, such as how to make sure that North Korea's research and development efforts serve only peaceful purposes, how to manage all the people involved in the WMD programme in a way not to generate proliferation concerns, how to encourage all the concerned parties to accept a highly binding mechanism, and how to increase the cost of noncompliance with an agreement once reached.

Lastly, as talks between the United States and North Korea have stalled, frustrations over the delays in the lifting of sanctions are likely to make the North reassess the subjective utility of the negotiations on denuclearisation. North Korea, in cooperation with China and Russia, is emphasising the need to ease sanctions during its talks with the United States. However, Washington is sticking to its position of sanctions against North Korea until fully verifiable denuclearisation has been achieved.[46] Further, US unilateral sanctions against North Korea have been imposed not only because of nuclear proliferation but for a variety of reasons, including cyber threats, human rights abuse, and money laundering.[47] Even if the related sanctions are lifted due to denuclearisation, the other grounds for sanctions will remain intact, and it is difficult to expect that there will be accompanying changes in the framework. If North Korea does not get much foreign investment, it may not return to the negotiating table. This is likely to have a negative impact on the talks on denuclearisation.

There are underlying differences between Seoul and Washington regarding the utility of sanctions. South Korea argues that sanctions are a tool to bring North Korea to the negotiating table, whereas the United States believes that only sanctions can keep North Korea at the negotiating table. It has not yet been fully discussed under what conditions the sanctions could be partially lifted. There are concerns in Washington that granting sanctions exemptions in the absence of significant progress in denuclearisation can undermine the overall sanctions regime, and similar views were presented when people discussed setting up an inter-Korean liaison office in the North Korean border city of Kaesong. South Korea argued that transferring power supplies to cross-border facilities would not go against the sanctions.[48] South Korea cannot seek an exemption from the UN every time it seeks to engage in civil exchanges and economic cooperation. Besides, proving that the North Korean leadership is not the main recipient of those supplies to the North will be a burden on the South Korean government.

Conclusion

Despite the risks and uncertainties, the current efforts towards denuclearisation can be assessed positively at three levels. First, they have provided a momentum for bettering inter-Korean relations. Denuclearisation, inter-Korean exchanges and cooperation, and building military trust are all interconnected. Military CBMs to support inter-Korean exchanges remain unresolved despite the numerous agreements and declarations. The denuclearisation agreement of 2018 is an opportunity to promote better inter-Korean relations, which, in turn, could restore momentum to the negotiations.

Second, it is important to continue talks for the sake of crisis management on the Korean Peninsula. The diplomatic option of resolving the North Korean nuclear issue will continue to be pursued unless there is an official declaration of the failure of the denuclearisation talks. No one can deny that the crisis levels on the Korean Peninsula have dropped significantly, compared to the situation in 2017, when there was a high possibility of military clashes between North Korea and the United States. In this regard, South Korea's role as an honest broker becomes more significant than before. Appeasement must continue lest North Korea lose its will to talk, while dispelling any unnecessary misapprehension that South Korea values inter-Korean relations above anything else.

Third, the diplomatic engagement with the North for the institutionalisation of cooperation on Korean issues should continue. It will further the working-level talks on a peace arrangement. High-level exchanges enable the opening up of many communication channels. They reduce unnecessary misunderstanding through information sharing, increase the predictability of mutual interest and expected behaviour, and ultimately have a spillover effect on cooperation in other fields. Efforts to implement the bilateral agreement on building a new relationship and a stable peace regime on the Korean Peninsula will continue to drive expectations for positive interactions.

The prerequisites for nuclear disarmament are trust among states and the capacity to deal with spoilers. Regarding the first prerequisite, we should note that nuclear disarmament is a confidence-building process that can transform the traditional security mindset. Multilateral cooperation among states needs redirect approaches that are currently based on the highly calculated moves of individual states to hedge against uncertainties in the future. Currently, countries in North-East Asia are not ready to embrace the notion of cooperative security. Mini-lateral channels such as the ROK-China-Japan Trilateral Cooperation Secretariat (TCS) and the US-ROK-Japan Defence Trilateral Talks (DTT) will play a central role in changing the environment through agenda-setting, institutional design, public awareness, and transformation of traditional thinking about the security paradigm.

Regarding the second prerequisite, one should note that a nuclear-weapons-free Korean Peninsula would require not only the elimination of nuclear weapons by the North but also strengthening of national capacity to deal with proliferation concerns. Hence, export controls and capacity building to monitor dual-use items and technology should form part of the discussion on the North Korea issues. Questions as to how to ensure a sustainable peace when North Korea renounces its nuclear arsenals, as well as how to keep political commitment and public interest in the long run, will remain. These require a holistic approach for establishing institutionalised practices within an agreed framework, information-sharing to detect any breakout, and arrangements to take collective counter-actions to prevent deception or defection.

Notes

1 Victor Cha and Katrin Fraser Katz, "The Right Way to Coerce North Korea", *Foreign Affairs*, April 1, 2018.
2 Pyongyang Joint Declaration at the Fifth Inter-Korean Summit, September 19, 2018.
3 "Donald Trump and Kim Jon Un Leave Vietnam Without a Deal", *The Economist*, February 28, 2019.
4 "Remarks by President Trump and President Moon Jae-in of the Republic of Korea Before Bilateral Meeting", The White House, April 11, 2019, at www.whitehouse.gov/briefings-statements/remarks-president-trump-president-moon-jae-republic-korea-bilateral-meeting/ (accessed August 9, 2019).
5 Jina Kim, "Issues Regarding North Korean Denuclearization Roadmap with a Focus on Implications from the Iran Nuclear Deal", *Korean Journal of Defense Analysis*, 30 (2), June 2018, pp. 171–193.
6 In June 2013, the DPRK argued that its status as a nuclear–weapons state will only be temporary.
7 Su Ho Yim, "Where Does the Nuclear Issue Go?" *Tongil Hankuk*, 358, October 2013, pp. 20–21.
8 "Statement by the DPRK Government Spokesperson," *Rodong Shinmun*, July 7, 2016.
9 "Kim Jong Un's 2018 New Year's Address", National Committee on North Korea (NCNK), January 1, 2018, at www.ncnk.org/node/1427 (accessed August 9, 2019).
10 Interview with the Bureau of Exchange and Cooperation, Ministry of National Unification, June 2018.
11 Right after the Singapore summit, North Korea said, "President Trump has expressed his intention to lift the sanctions as the relationship improves … If the U.S. takes steps to improve relations first, North Korea can take the next step."
12 Jeon Jong-ho, "The Demand for an Unfair Denuclearization of the North", *Rodong Shinmun*, March 31, 2015.
13 "Policy Errors Lead to Ruin", *Rodong Shinmun*, November 28, 2016.
14 Lee Hyun-do, "The Policy of Antagonizing North Korea Cannot Escape Destruction", *Rodong Shinmun*, October 23, 2013; "The Provocative Absurdity of Pushing the North-South Relationship to the Brink of Collapse Will Never be Tolerated", *Rodong Shinmun*, July 19, 2015; "We Condemn the Hysterical Madness of the US", Korean Central News Agency, July 5, 2016; Un Jong-chul, "We Need to Withdraw the US Invasion Force from the South", *Rodong Shinmun*, June 22, 2016.
15 Statement by DPRK Government Spokesperson, *Rodong Shinmun*, July 7, 2017.
16 Koo Gab-woo, "A Prototype Discourse in North Korea, 1947–1964", *Modern North Korean Studies*, 17 (1) 2014, pp. 230–231.
17 Kim Jin-chel, "Study on North Korea's Denuclearized Zone Argument", *Security Studies*, 17, 1987, p. 144.
18 North Korean Workers' Party, the Sixth Convention Central Committee Report, *Rodong Shinmun*, October 11, 1980.
19 Arms Control Association, Nuclear Weapon Free Zone at a Glance, at www.armscontrol.org/factsheets/nwfz (accessed September 11, 2019).

20 *Understanding North Korea: Totalitarian Dictatorship, Highly Centralized Economies, Grand Socialist Family*, Institute for Unification Education, Ministry of Unification, Seoul, South Korea, 2015, p. 44.
21 "North Korea launches two projectiles, hours after nuclear talks offer", *The Guardian*, September 10, 2019.
22 Statement by the DPRK Foreign Ministry Spokesperson, June 13, 2018; Statement by DPRK Foreign Ministry Spokesperson, July 7, 2018.
23 "Statement by the DPRK Foreign Ministry Spokesperson," *Rodong Shinmun*, July 7, 2018.
24 Remarks by Michael R. Pompeo at the Japan-U.S.-ROK joint press conference, July 8, 2018.
25 Sung-eun Lee, "Kim Calls an Unusual Party Meeting", *Joongang Daily*, April 21, 2018.
26 Lee Je-hun, "Economic Development Becomes a Priority for North Korea", *Hankyoreh*, April 23, 2018.
27 As of December 15, 2018, among his 115 appearances, 12 were for military, 37 for economy, 25 for diplomacy, and 25 for political events.
28 "Roh Declares Nuclear-Free South Korea", *Korea Herald*, November 9, 1991, p. 1.
29 Joint Declaration of the Denuclearization of the Korean Peninsula, January 20, 1992.
30 Agreed Framework Between the United States of America and the Democratic People's Republic of Korea, October 21, 1994.
31 Annual Reports, KEDO, at www.kedo.org/annual_reports.asp (accessed December 1, 2018).
32 Joint Declaration of the Fourth Round of the Six-Party Talks, September 19, 2005.
33 Justin McCurry, "South Korea Set to Change Policy on North as Liberal Wins Election", *The Guardian*, May 9, 2017.
34 "Five-year Plan of Moon Jae-in Government and 100 National Agenda", *Policy Briefing*, July, 19, 2017, at korea.kr/archive/expDocView.do?docId=37595 (accessed November 2, 2018).
35 Address by President Moon Jae-in on 100th March First Independence Movement Day, *The ROK Cheongwadae Briefings*, March 1, 2019.
36 Hyonhee Shin, "As Food Crisis Threatens, Humanitarian Aid for North Korea Grinds to a Halt", Reuters, August 21, 2018.
37 Edward Wong, "US Bars American Aid Groups from Traveling to North Korea", *The New York Times*, October 17, 2018.
38 Christine Kim, "South Korea Approves $8 Million Aid to North Korea, Timing to be Decided Later", Reuters, September 21, 2017.
39 Dae Woo Lee et al., *Current Status of Humanitarian Aid to North Korea and Future Challenges*, Hyundai Research Institute, Seoul, South Korea, 2018; National Index, at www.index.go.kr/ (accessed December 3, 2018).
40 Cho Sang-Hun and David Sanger, "Kim Jong-un's Overture Could Drive a Wedge Between South Korea and the US", *The New York Times*, January 1, 2018.
41 In September, a new weapon system was displayed during a military parade in commemoration of the 70th anniversary of the founding of the DPRK. "North Korea to Hold Military Parade to Mark 70th Anniversary", Voice of America, September 8, 2018.
42 *North Korea Sanctions Program*, Office of Foreign Assets Control, Washington, US Department of the Treasury, 2016.
43 Laignee Barron, "A Lot of People Have Done Bad Things, President Trump Downplays North Korea's Human Rights Abuses", *Time*, June 14, 2018.
44 Joint Communique of the US-ROK Security Consultative Meeting, November 7, 1978.
45 The Korean War Armistice Agreement, July 27, 1953, Article 1, paras. 4–5; Article 2, para. 25 (i).

46 Roberta Rampton, "Pompeo Says North Korea Deal May Take Some Time, Sanctions to Remain", Reuters, July 19, 2018; "Pompeo Sanctions Enforcement Key to N. Korean Denuclearisation", Voice of America, September 14, 2018.
47 "Democratic People's Republic of Korea Sanctions", US Department of State, at www.state.gov/e/eb/tfs/spi/northkorea (accessed September 29, 2018).
48 Yeo Jun-suk, "Kaesong Office Plan Sparks Worries over Sanctions Violation", *The Korea Herald*, August 21, 2018.

6 Korean Peninsula and the evolving Sino-US strategic stability in the Indo-Pacific

Kuyoun Chung

Introduction

North Korea's nuclear programme has continued to be the Trump administration's foreign policy priority without any realistic chance of denuclearisation in the near term. While President Moon Jae-in of South Korea, President Donald Trump of the United States, and Kim Jong-un of North Korea have held a series of summits since April 2018, denuclearisation negotiation has been stalled. Such a deadlock is, however, likely to continue unless the United States and North Korea can negotiate a compromise on their unwavering positions: North Korea's intention of preserving its nuclear capabilities and the United States' position that "Final, fully verified denuclearisation (FFVD)" should be the goal of the negotiations. However, the fact that North Korea has not participated in any working-level meeting with the United States over the issue of denuclearisation has made the United States sceptical of the North's sincerity.

In retrospect, it was indeed a risk for the United States to hold a summit with the North. The progressive South Korean government of President Moon Jae-in expected that peace-building efforts on the peninsula, rather than economic sanctions and pressure, would catalyse the denuclearisation negotiations as it reduces the North's threat perception. Indeed, the North's threat perception has been remarkably heightened since the late 2017 when the United States spoke of a "bloody nose" by conducting a limited strike on a missile launch site in the North to show US resolve and induce the North to back away from pursuing its nuclear programme. From the beginning of 2018, North Korea suddenly attempted to revitalise the inter-Korean relationship and seek a rapprochement with the United States. While President Trump himself half-doubted the sincerity of this gesture, he agreed to meet Kim Jong-un. While the United States and North Korea could not agree on any specific road map for denuclearisation in their first summit, both countries were at least able to maintain the top-down diplomatic track throughout the year.

Meanwhile, the US-North Korea diplomatic track seems to have weakened China's traditional role as moderator in the denuclearisation negotiations and reduced its diplomatic influence on both Koreas. However, Kim Jong-un's multiple visits to Beijing before the North-South Korea summit and the US-North

Korea summit were enough to appease China, and allow it to sustain its influence on both Koreas. Besides, President Trump's unexpected decision to pause the US-Republic of Korea (ROK) joint military exercises after the first US-North Korea summit re-confirmed China's proposal for denuclearisation, "suspension for suspension". As a result, China's leverage on the peninsula vis-à-vis the United States was reinforced, making the regional balance of power unfavourable for the United States amid escalating Sino-US strategic competition.

Indeed, President Trump himself adds an element of uncertainty into the prospect of denuclearisation and the maintenance of regional order in the Indo-Pacific. He has frequently shown an inclination towards isolationism and advocated American retreat and retrenchment from the global stage. Northeast Asia has not been an exception. At the first US-North Korea Summit in Singapore on June 12, 2018, President Trump revealed his attitude towards retreat from Northeast Asia, arguing that "North Korea is not the US neighbourhood", and unilaterally suspended the US-ROK joint military exercises, which have for long served to maintain US-ROK military readiness and regional deterrence. What is worse, President Trump's personal desire for retrenchment in the region coincides with the North's demand that the United States should withdraw its forces, strategic assets, and extended deterrence out of the Peninsula. This would make US allies question the US commitment to defend the region as well as the existing security architecture as a whole. While the US Congress and foreign policy establishments in Washington DC still prefer to maintain American liberal order in the region and even passed the Asia Reassurance Initiative Act of 2018 (S. 2736) in December 31, 2018, it is uncertain as to who will control foreign policy agenda in a divided government following the 2018 midterm election.

Altogether, while the prospect of actual denuclearisation remains uncertain, the US retrenchment, in tandem with South Korea's strategy of pushing détente on the Korean peninsula, is unlikely to counter China's growing assertiveness in the region. China indeed has gradually increased the size and sophistication of its nuclear forces to maintain a survivable arsenal in the case of a potential conflict with the United States. Not only has China enhanced its domestic capability to enrich uranium, which could be easily utilised to produce fuel for nuclear warhead; it has also deployed missiles to penetrate US missile defences.[1] Therefore, negotiations relating to the North's denuclearisation are likely to affect the security environment in the Indo-Pacific, especially during times of escalating strategic competition.

This chapter investigates how the strategic environment in the Indo-Pacific is likely to evolve in the course of North Korea's denuclearisation. First of all, this inquiry is premised on the understanding that escalation of the Sino-US strategic competition will also affect the strategic environment in which North Korea's denuclearisation is negotiated. Furthermore, any end state of the denuclearisation on the Korean Peninsula is expected to be marked by a shift in the strategic interests of regional powers in the Indo-Pacific. It will influence not only the concept of regional strategic stability but also the extended deterrence that has long sustained US strategic dominance in the region. Therefore, it is necessary to discuss strategic aspects of the current denuclearisation negotiations and how they will impact the Sino-US strategic competition that will define the security environment in a foreseeable future.

In other words, this chapter discusses how the denuclearisation of North Korea would affect the regional powers' understanding of strategic stability in the region and how it will affect the Sino-US power asymmetry in the broader Indo-Pacific region. It not only discusses how North Korea's siege mentality and corresponding strategic goals shape its denuclearisation strategy but also explores how the denuclearisation process might affect the US deterrence structure in the Indo-Pacific.

Progress on denuclearisation negotiation

North Korea's siege mentality and evolving strategic goals

North Korea's denuclearisation strategy reflects the latest strategic guidelines of the Worker's Party of Korea (WPK). For decades, North Korea's strategic guidelines evolved from its National Defence-Economic Development *Byungjin* strategy (1966), *Songun* (military first)-Economic Development Strategy (2003), Economy-Nuclear Development *Byungjin* strategy (2013) to the latest Socialist Economic Development strategy (2018). With the Economy-Nuclear Development *Byungjin* strategy, the Kim Jong-un regime pursued the parallel development of both the economy and its nuclear programme but prioritised the nuclear sector. The Kim Jong-un regime then coupled its nuclear deterrent with economic development in the expectation that as the North completes its nuclear development, it will reallocate its budget from nuclear development to economic development. The nuclear programme was therefore seen as a shield which would protect the North from external threats, while they continued to develop their economy.

The North Korean regime's threat perception stems from a siege mentality. Siege mentality is the feeling in a country that the rest of the world has highly negative intentions towards it.[2] Thus, according to North Korea, its domestic and international difficulties mostly stem from the hostile policies of the United States and its allies. North Korea's response to international sanctions is an example of how the isolated leadership in Pyongyang views itself as a nation under siege. For instance, following the last round of the United Nations (UN) Security Council sanctions imposed on North Korea for conducting its fifth nuclear test in September 2016, Ja Song Nam, the UN ambassador of the Democratic People's Republic of Korea (DPRK), defended his country's efforts to strengthen its nuclear deterrence against the ceaseless hostile moves by the United States. In a letter to the UN Security Council, Ambassador Ja stated that "the US has intention of political suffocation and system collapse of the Kim Jong-un government" and alleged that following the 2012 death of North Korean leader Kim Jung-il, the United States began to openly plot the overthrow of the government in Pyongyang. A memorandum of the North Korean Foreign Ministry provides an extensive list of alleged US military provocations. These include: (1) increasing the number of US troops participating in joint military exercises with South Korea from 3,500 in 2013 to 27,000 in 2016; (2) deployment of nuclear-powered aircraft carriers and submarines as well as nuclear strategic bombers in the region; (3) practising pre-emptive strike exercises, simulating taking control of the North's nuclear facilities; and (4) deploying the US Terminal High Altitude Area Defence (THAAD) system in South Korea. While the United States and its allies argue that they are taking these stronger conventional measures to counter the increasing North Korean nuclear threats represented by multiple nuclear tests and missiles launches, these arguments have been interpreted by the North as offensive.[3]

Origins of North Korea's siege mentality, particularly with regard to the United States and its allies in the region, date back to Japanese colonisation in the early 20th century and the Korean War in 1950. It is deeply embedded in its anxieties regarding the potential revival of Japanese militarism and the possible subversive contingency plan that might be adopted by the United States.[4] During the Korean War, Kim Il-sung's intention to unify the Korean Peninsula was indeed frustrated by US and the UN intervention, which even pushed the North to the edge of regime collapse. Since then, the United States has been considered to be the biggest threat to the North and it has repeatedly evoked dismal experiences of the Korean War for the North Korean people, to emphasise the imperative to take a stand against the hostile acts of the United States. Such antagonistic historical memories relating to the United States and Japan even serve to justify the constant war mobilisation and war readiness inside the North. Condemnation and contempt for the United States and its allies have been all pervasive in North Korean politics, literature, arts, media, and education.[5] Even after the end of the Cold War, North Korea's siege mentality did not dissipate. Drawing lessons from Iraq and Libya, North Korea learned that authoritarian dictators who had forgone weapons of mass destruction in exchange for an economic incentive did not survive long. Muammar Gaddafi of Libya, for instance, was killed because of civil unrest within his own country.

Of course, the United States is not the only reason for this siege mentality. Asymmetric alliances between North Korea, China, and the Soviet Union during the Cold War have also strengthened the siege mentality. As a junior partner in the alliance, North Korea had struggled with political and economic interference, albeit with the two socialist countries consolidating a regime in the northern part of the Korean Peninsula.[6]

As the North saw itself plagued by external threats, the regime fostered strong fears of an imminent threat from outside to justify its control over its citizens, the massive expenditure on the military, and the continuing unchallenged rule of the Kim family. Moreover, North Korea portrays nuclear weapons as the most effective tool to counter the external threat from the United States and its allies.[7] Furthermore, nuclear weapons serve to preserve the existing Kim Jong-un regime in North Korea.

However, this allegedly defensive motivation for maintaining a nuclear programme could be tested soon. Theoretically, North Korea's strategic goals range from regime survival at the minimum and reunification of Korean Peninsula on its terms at the maximum, while the debate continues on whether North Korea's strategic goals can be moderated in between.[8] Moderation implies that the North would pursue economic reform, cut military spending, and improve relations with perceived adversaries, especially with the United States and its allies, instead of pursuing unification of the Peninsula on its terms. Why the North would choose such a policy of moderation remains a matter for debate among scholars. Those who argue that North Korea will opt for moderation emphasise its siege mentality and insist that North Korean leaders have been gradually liberalising the economy, while the struggle between the "traditional military" faction and "economic reformers" within the leadership continues.[9] From this perspective, North Korea is unlikely to pursue its aggressive strategic goal, that is, invade South Korea and complete the reunification of the Peninsula. Instead, it desires peaceful coexistence with the South.[10] On the other hand, there are those who argue that recently adopted reforms are simply an ad hoc adjustment to ensure regime survival. Furthermore, as the Kim Jung-un regime keeps indoctrinating its people with its resolve to unify the Korean Peninsula, it is less likely to publicly moderate its strategic goals as such gesture will incur audience cost, weaken the legitimacy of the regime, and destabilise the regime security.[11] For instance, when North Korea successfully launched the *Hwasung-14* Intercontinental Ballistic Missile (ICBM), the North Korean leader spoke of "the final victory", which indicates reunification of two Koreas.

Between strategic goals of regime survival and reunification, there are many other alternatives: North Korea might use its nukes as leverage to normalise relations with the United States and Japan,[12] might deter any response to its own low-level provocation around the Korean peninsula,[13] and might weaken the US alliances with South Korea and Japan.[14]

The problem is, regardless of their specific goals, the pace of its nuclear weapons and ballistic missiles programme might allow North Korea to move beyond any debate on moderation and achieve all of these objectives. In other words, the completion of its nuclear programme can enable the North to achieve a capability beyond minimal deterrence. North Korea now might figure that its nuclear weapons programme can enable it to take more risks and coerce its non-nuclear neighbours. Nuclear weapons could not only allow the North to deter the United States but also decouple the United States from its allies, weakening the US commitment of extended deterrence for them. Another possibility is that North Korea will provoke small-scale low-intensity conflicts around the Peninsula, as often suggested by the stability-instability theory.[15]

Of course, such reasoning might even lead to the speculation that new nuclear powers with non-survivable arsenals might have preventive-strike motivation. However, it needs more theoretical specifications.[16] Failing to specify how often one can identify preventive-strike motivation ex ante, however, their effect on non-survivable arsenal would be unfalsifiable and is hard to apply to the case of North Korea.[17] Instead, new nuclear powers are more likely to learn that there are limits to nuclear coercion, and nuclear weapons are not good for strategic aggrandisement.[18]

Strategic aspects of denuclearisation

North Korea seems to have developed its own denuclearisation road map. But why North Korea recently has deviated from its Economy-Nuclear Development *Byungjin* strategy and switched to the Socialist Economic Development strategy remains less clear. However, during the third plenary meeting of the seventh Central Committee of the WPK on April 20, 2018, Kim Jong-un declared that developing nuclear capability was completed, which makes the strategic environment more favourable for the Korean revolution.[19] Such a remark indicates that North Korea proactively accepted the denuclearisation, as it believes it would at least allow the North to be on a more equal footing vis-à-vis the United States.

As the North accepted the international request to denuclearise, it seems that the frame of security-security trade-off has been accepted by both the United States and the North. The security-security trade-off refers to an exchange in which the US concerns over the North's nuclear weapons are traded off against the North's security concerns relating to a potential US strike, which was suggested as a framework for denuclearising North Korea. In fact, the North has laid down the following conditions in return for denuclearisation: first, withdrawal of the US nuclear arsenal from the South (although the United States has currently no such arsenal on the Peninsula); second, suspension of the US-ROK joint military exercises on the Peninsula; third, renunciation of any nuclear and conventional attack against the North; and fourth, conclusion of a peace treaty and diplomatic normalisation. All of these conditions seek to address the siege mentality by strengthening national security rather than seeking economic compensation from the international community.

In the past, the frame of security-economy trade-off was proposed by the South and the United States, wherein US concerns over the North's nuclear weapons are traded off against the North's need to develop its economy. That is, the United States, South Korea, and international community financially compensate for the North's denuclearisation. However, the North wouldn't accept this suggestion by saying that the North does not "beg for help" from the United States and other international actors. Nonetheless, as the US sanctions against the North have got more stringent, the North is demanding relief, arguing that such sanctions are part of the US hostile policies that only strengthen its siege mentality. In fact, North Korea has in the past suggested that if the United States were to suspend its hostile policies in a number of domains, the North would resume talks with the United States and negotiate denuclearisation. North Korea pointed out that the very absence of diplomatic relations between the United States and North Korea is evidence that United States has been hostile to the North. In the security domain, North Korea argues that joint military exercises and strategic assets targeting the North along with the economic sanctions are also part of the hostile policy.

North Korea's denuclearisation road map has a phased approach in which both the United States and North Korea take simultaneous steps leading to the ultimate outcome: denuclearisation and the end of the US hostile policy towards the North. Three steps of denuclearisation and the corresponding measures that the US needs to take in order to compensate for denuclearisation have been suggested. The first step of denuclearisation eliminates the so-called "nuclear capability of the future", which includes measures such as the demolition of nuclear test and missile engine test sites that could be used to scale up its nuclear capability. The latest demolition of *Punggye-ri* test site on May 24, 2018, said to be an irreversible measure, corresponds to the first step of denuclearisation. The second step of denuclearisation eliminates "nuclear capability of the present", which includes the shutting down and verifying of fissile material-producing facilities. The final step of denuclearisation would provide lists of nuclear materials, nuclear warheads, intercontinental missiles, and relevant production facilities and allow them to be inspected, thus eliminating the "nuclear capability of the past".

In return for the first step of denuclearisation, North Korea demands suspension of the US-ROK joint military exercises, an end-of-war declaration, and the opening of a liaison office between the United States and the North. For the second step of denuclearisation, North Korea demands sanctions relief. For the third step, the North demands the conclusion of a peace treaty, complete lifting of sanctions and diplomatic normalisation at the ambassadorial level.

In a nutshell, North Korea's denuclearisation road map seeks first to build a trust with the United States before taking any serious denuclearisation measures. And it seems parallel to the argument of siege mentality that North's threat perception that it is beset by the United States. However, regardless of the existence of siege mentality, through such a denuclearisation road map, North Korea is asking the United States to readjust its deterrence structure in the Indo-Pacific region. Disagreement over the scope of denuclearisation clearly highlights the dilemma, because for the United States denuclearisation implies that the North rids itself of its nuclear arsenal, while the North's definition implies the denuclearisation of the entire Korean Peninsula, which includes readjusting the US extended deterrence structure across the Indo-Pacific. In this context, the United States and North Korea must first reach an agreement over the definition and regional scope of denuclearisation, which, however, appears to be unlikely.

What is clear is that despite periodic statements of North Korea's alleged readiness to abandon its nuclear weapons, North Korea prefers to remain a nuclear power in the near term and leverage this to make the most of the denuclearisation negotiations. Meanwhile, neither maximum pressure, including economic sanctions and threat of use of force, nor engagement, such as delivering economic benefits, would incentivise the North to give up nuclear weapons easily. One viable option then could be a compromise – freezing nuclear development and allowing the North to keep a limited number of nuclear weapons. This option, however, would be unacceptable to the United States, which oversees the global architecture of non-proliferation. Furthermore, such an option would inevitably strengthen the current deterrence structure in the Indo-Pacific, which would create more tensions vis-à-vis China and Russia, triggering even more conflicts and crises in the foreseeable future.

Deterrence architecture in times of power competition

Evolving concept of strategic stability and extended deterrence

The deterrence structure of the United States in the Indo-Pacific has been based on the US perception of strategic stability in the region. While many definitions of strategic stability have been used by scholars, including military doctrine and defence planning,[20] strategic stability has been defined as a "characteristic of deterrence based on mutually assured destruction".[21] During the Cold War, the relationship between the United States and the Soviet Union was stable as long as both knew that each could respond in a devastating way to a nuclear attack by the other. The idea of strategic stability was officially reflected in the preamble of the Antiballistic Missile Treaty of 1972 as the following: "Effective measures to limit anti-ballistic missile system would be a substantial factor in curbing the race in strategic offensive arms and would lead to a decrease in the risk of outbreak of war involving nuclear weapons".[22] To reach the state of strategic stability, relations between nuclear powers need to meet the following three conditions: (1) need to minimise the incentive for one side to conduct a first strike, (2) need to reduce the incentive for competition in the development and deployment of nuclear forces, and (3) need to provide a predictability and transparency during an escalating period of tension or crises. Failure to ensure strategic stability could result in a new form of nuclear competition and arms race, which can be detrimental to their own endeavour to maintain nuclear non-proliferation regime and ensure the international community's willingness to cooperate on issues of proliferation. While this concept lost its salience in the aftermath of the Cold War, it has gradually emerged in a different strategic environment in the Indo-Pacific. Leaders of current nuclear states – the United States, France, Great Britain, Russia, and China – are now shaping different strategic interests in an increasingly tense multipolar nuclear environment, adopting new technologies that could alter the traditional ways of maintaining strategic stability.

One of the core issues behind this adjustment is political. During the Cold War, the relationship between the United States and the Soviet Union, which was representatively maintained by strategic stability, was hostile in nature. Mistrust and suspicion prevailed between the two countries. However, Presidents Obama and Medvedev advocated a new policy by committing themselves to the building of new strategic relations based on mutual trust, openness, predictability, and cooperation. While this is not a complete departure from the Cold War concept of strategic stability, it has been argued that the goal of cooperative relationship could be more mutually beneficial than the Cold War concept of strategic stability, which rests on a broader economic, technological, and political background of two countries in the post-Cold War. As such, as the relationship between nuclear powers is evolving over time, the attributes of strategic stability are also changing.

Second, emerging technologies are complicating the maintaining of strategic stability.[23] Such technological innovations are blurring the conceptual distinction of what constitutes strategic capability, which only used to be about the nuclear weapons in the past. Non-nuclear weapons and technologies are now capable of destroying nuclear forces, their command and control systems, and civilian nuclear infrastructure. For instance, strategic non-nuclear weapons, including cyber warfare, precision or long-range conventional and hypersonic weapons, missile defence, and space and counter-space systems, are now part of the new deterrence tools.[24] These weapons have the potential to impact the status quo of strategic stability because of their non-traditional capabilities by striking an adversary's nuclear forces or nuclear command, control, and communications system or to blunt an attack without resorting to the use of nuclear weapon. The *US National Security Strategy* report of 2018 also admits these possibilities, saying that "deterrence today is significantly more complex to achieve than during the Cold War" and arguing that the proliferation of non-nuclear weapons and technologies may allow regional adversaries to attempt strategic attacks against the United States without resorting to nuclear weapons.[25]

Third, in view of these technological innovations, it is being debated whether limited use of nuclear weapons would be more credible than the traditional threat of massive retaliation with nuclear weapons. More diversified nuclear and non-nuclear capabilities make it difficult for nuclear powers to identify the weapon that could trigger a crisis with the potential for nuclear escalation. Besides, the ambiguities arising from an integration of nuclear and conventional systems are creating more uncertainties. Consequently, the *US Nuclear Posture Review* of 2018 emphasises the importance of a more flexible and tailored nuclear deterrent, such as a low-yield nuclear option.[26] By doing so, the United States can deter limited nuclear use by potential adversaries by matching their escalatory potential with a variety of limited use weapons. However, this situation might lower the threshold for nuclear use by providing more limited or proportional nuclear options.

In short, these three issues are actually compelling current nuclear states to enhance their nuclear capability and missile defences in addition to their conventional force structures. Furthermore, when it comes to the United States, its alliance commitments have led it to pursue the diversification of the US nuclear arsenal and conventional military capabilities such as long-range US precision strike capabilities.

Such issues pose fresh challenges for the United States in providing extended deterrence in the Indo-Pacific region as well. In a nutshell, extended deterrence is a promise to protect an ally from attack. With this promise, the United States sends a signal of deterrence to the potential attacker that it will respond to an attack on an ally and even strike pre-emptively if a threat is imminent. For an ally, this is a signal of assurance that it will be protected. During the Cold War, extended deterrence was rather simple, as it was based on the US-Soviet nuclear standoff and the balance of terror. With the end of the Cold War, the United States indeed brought home all of the tactical nuclear weapons deployed in

Northeast Asia. Instead, the United States retained the extended deterrence in its declaratory policy and maintains dialogues with its allies – South Korea and Japan. The Extended Deterrence Dialogue (EDD) between the United States and Japan and the Extended Deterrence Policy Committee (EDPC) between the United States and South Korea are mechanisms through which the United States can certify its policy transparency, coordinate, identify potential future decisions on this issue, and help South Korea and Japan to become more familiar with the US military capabilities committed to their defence.[27]

Failure to provide extended deterrence to allies is expected to not only embolden challengers to revise the status quo of the regional order but also raise concern among allies about the credibility of the US extended deterrence. Together with strategic stability, extended deterrence is essential for the US effort to consolidate the international nuclear order and to have a practical road map to achieve the long-term goal of nuclear elimination, as suggested by the *Nuclear Posture Review of 2010* published during the Obama administration.

However, the US extended deterrence in the Indo-Pacific, which contains full spectrum of strategic assets with nuclear and conventional capabilities, is facing some challenges. The changing security landscape, the Sino-US power competition in particular, gives US extended deterrence and strategic stability a renewed importance in a foreseeable future.

Regional deterrence architecture amid US-China strategic competition

The US-China nuclear relationship is substantially different from the US-Soviet Union nuclear relationship. First, China is neither an ally nor an adversary, which makes it different from the Soviet Union during the Cold War. Since the beginning of the diplomatic normalisation in the early 1970s, the United States has pursued an engagement strategy towards China, hedging between cooperation and competition. However, as the power parity between US and Chinese power has increased, strategic competition has become more salient. In particular, as China's Anti-Access and Area-Denial (A2AD) strategy increasingly impedes US maritime access and operations in the western-Pacific region, which is one of the critical elements of its extended deterrence, it poses a challenge to the United States in maintaining deterrence architecture in the region.

Furthermore, China is continuously modernising its nuclear weapon and delivery systems, increasing the survivability of its second-strike capability. However, it does not have numerical parity in terms of nuclear forces vis-à-vis the United States. While China owns fewer deliverable ICBMs that can reach the United States, it is diversifying its force posture to include mobile ICBMs, multiple independent re-entry vehicles, and ballistic missiles nuclear submarines. Besides, the integration of nuclear weapons and conventional forces are challenging the existing strategic balance in the Indo-Pacific.[28] With this development, China now says that it has achieved qualitative nuclear parity vis-à-vis the United States, such that both are capable of inflicting unacceptable damage on the other, which makes mutually assured destruction a certainty.[29] The United States has not yet explicitly accepted mutual vulnerability as the basis of strategic stability with China, as it did with the Soviet Union.

But China argues that the US acceptance of strategic stability vis-à-vis China would ease its concerns and lead it to moderate its nuclear modernisation programme. However, the United States neither supports nor opposes such request, which is partly due to Japan, one of the closest US allies. Japan strongly insists that the United States should not accept mutual vulnerability as the basis of strategic stability with China, because this would send China a signal that the United States would be agreed to be deterred in a future crisis and thus would not be expected by China to defend its interests or its allies in Asia.[30] In short, such an acquiescence would be a signal of appeasement for China and embolden it to the extent that it would change the regional status quo, under its own nuclear umbrella.

When it comes to extended deterrence, Chinese view has also changed. In the past, China did not oppose the US military presence in East Asia, as it could contain Japanese militarism. However, China now worries that US extended deterrence might weaken China's second-strike capability, which is why it is asking the United States to adopt the no-first-use principle. From the Chinese perspective, the extended deterrence would embolden US allies in this region and allow them to engage in provocative actions, as demonstrated in the case of Senkaku Islands dispute. However, the United States would certainly reject the idea of no-first-use as it would decouple the United States from its allies.

In a nutshell, the basic position of the United States is that any US-China agreement on strategic stability would jeopardise the credibility of the extended deterrence in the Indo-Pacific. Therefore, US deterrence on the Korean Peninsula gets more complicated as the North Korea's nuclear programme becomes more sophisticated. Components of US extended deterrence, which include conventional forces and missile defence networks that focus on North Korea, are perceived as threatening Chinese interests, thereby conflating the US-China strategic equilibrium.[31] Besides, the allied countermeasure around the Korean Peninsula could stimulate Chinese response even further.

To a certain degree, North Korea seems to be an obstacle to strategic stability between the US and China. The major issue between two countries is that both are not sure whether North Korea would accept the norms of a nuclear taboo, which inevitably forces the United States and its allies in the Northeast Asia to strengthen extended deterrence.[32] Again, such measures that strengthen extended deterrence, such as missile defence, new strike capability, and cybersecurity, are expected to weaken the survivability of the China's second-strike capability.

As a result, even though the Chinese leadership acknowledges and understands that the US extended deterrence over the Northeast Asia targets North Korea's nuclear programme, China cannot but modernise its nuclear capability and delivery system and innovate its cyber and space-based weapons, to offset the US dominance.

The 2018 *Nuclear Poster Review Report* is significant as it demonstrates the Trump administration's assessment of the strategic environment and pre-emptive responses to such challenges as the United States faces. In spite of many criticisms, there is both continuity and change in terms of the Obama administration's nuclear strategy. What has changed from the previous nuclear strategy is that it tips the balance between sustaining US efforts for arms control and maintaining an effective nuclear arsenal, which would signal a new arms race and consequently cause global instability. While the Trump administration made it clear that the United States will not use or threaten to use nuclear weapons against non-nuclear states, the 2018 *Nuclear Posture Review Report* makes mention of a wide range of non-nuclear scenarios in which the United States can make conduct the first use of a nuclear weapon.

Given that both China and the United States are on the slippery slope of a security dilemma, a certain endgame of North Korea's denuclearisation can push both countries to the edge. While North Korea might expect that its nuclear weapons make it equal to the United States with regard to negotiating denuclearisation, the United States would reject any assumption of mutual vulnerability as the basis of building a strategic relationship with the North. Particularly because North Korea violates international treaties, weakens the global non-proliferation regime, threatens its neighbours with nuclear coercion, and destabilises the regional status quo.[33]

Furthermore, as long as the North appeases China and uses it as leverage against the United States in the denuclearisation negotiations, the United States cannot but take a tough stance against China. Such measures include tightening economic sanctions, strengthening extended deterrence, and forging a multilateral security cooperation as in the case of Quadrilateral Security Dialogue. This would in return create a hostile environment around the denuclearisation negotiations, as the "hostile policies" of the United States that North Korea used to criticise.

Uncertainty, however, also stems from President Trump. It remains debatable whether he is sincerely willing to continue the denuclearisation negotiations with the North and whether he would maintain the current deterrence architecture in the Indo-Pacific, with the commitment to its allies that has been sustained for decades. While the United States would not easily readjust its deterrence architecture as demanded by the North, uncertainty around President Trump's stance on the denuclearisation negotiation, in addition to his preference for American retreat and retrenchment, could jeopardise the regional security architecture and deterrence structure.

Implications for the Korean Peninsula

This chapter briefly discusses the current status of North Korea's denuclearisation negotiation and how it would affect the Sino-US strategic competition, and, at the same time, how such competition would generate an inhospitable environment in which the United States and North Korea continue to negotiate.

As the ultimate endgame of denuclearisation for North Korea is substantially different from that of the United States, it not only renders the possibility of successful denuclearisation negotiations remote but also creates an unfavourable balance of power situation for the United States to maintain the momentum of the negotiations. Such conceptual gap left the United States with few options but to counter Chinese assertiveness in the region, while making strategic competition even more intense.

Uncertainty of the President Trump's personal preference over American retrenchment and retreat from Northeast Asian allies – Japan and South Korea – is another critical element that would determine the fate of denuclearisation negotiation. If President Trump was to cut a deal with the North that involved reducing the US military presence around the Korean Peninsula, in return for the North's interim denuclearisation, it would render South Korea and Japan vulnerable to Chinese assertiveness in the region, not to mention the North's potential provocation, on the basis of its remaining nuclear capability.

Ultimately, it boils down to whether President Trump would like to maintain a regional order that has been successful for decades and strengthen the existing security architecture in the wider region of the Indo-Pacific. The liberal internationalist order that emphasised the rule of law, including nonproliferation, human rights, and democracy, is being weakened under President Trump. Although the advent of a divided government in the United States after the 2018 midterm election makes it difficult to predict who will control the foreign policy agenda during the remaining term of President Trump, strategic uncertainty in the Indo-Pacific and the struggles of US allies in the Indo-Pacific to manage strategic hedging amid a power transition in the region would persist. This would make the denuclearisation of the North unlikely in the immediate future.

Notes

1 Matthew Kroenig, "Approaching Critical Mass: Asia's Multipolar Nuclear Future", *NBR Special Report* # 58, National Bureau for Asian Research, June 2016.
2 Daniel Bar-Tal and Dikla Antebi, "Beliefs About Negative Intentions of the World: A Study of the Israeli Siege Mentality", *Political Psychology*, 23 (4), 1992, pp. 633–645.
3 Brian Padden, "Sanctions Reinforce North Korea Siege Mentality", Voice of America, December 19, 2016, at www.voanews.com/sanctions-reinforce-north-korea-siege-mentality/3641712.html (accessed May 29, 2019).
4 Kenneth Quinones, "Juche's Role in North Korea's Foreign Policy," in Tae Hwan Kwak and Seung-Ho Joo (eds.), *North Korea's Foreign Policy Under Kim Jong-Il: New Perspectives*, Ashgate Publishing Company, Burlington, 2009, pp. 15–38.
5 Bomi Kim, "Siege Mentality of North Korea: Socio-Political Analyses on Foreign Policies of Kim Jong Un Regime", A Paper Presented at the Annual Conference of Korean Association of International Studies, 2014.
6 Barry Gill, "North Korea and the Crisis of Socialism: The Historical Ironies of National Division", *Third World Quarterly*, 13 (1), 1992, pp. 107–130.
7 *Military and Security Developments Involving the Democratic People's Republic of Korea: Report to Congress*, Office of the Secretary of Defense, 2017.

8 Andrew Scobell, "North Korea's Strategic Intentions", Strategic Studies Institute, 2005.
9 Selig Harrison, *Korean Endgame*, Princeton University Press, Princeton, 2001; Victor Cha and David Kang, *Nuclear North Korea: A Debate About Engagement Strategies*, Columbia University Press, New York, 2003.
10 Bruce Cummings, *North Korea: Another Country*, The New Press, New York, 2004.
11 Kongdan Oh and Ralph C. Hassig, *North Korea Through the Looking Glass*, Brookings Institution Press, Washington, DC, 2000; Stephen Bradner, "North Korea's Strategy", in Henry D. Sokoloski (ed.), *Planning for a Peaceful Korea*, Strategic Studies Institute, US Army War College, Carlisle, 2001.
12 "Statement of DPRK Foreign Ministry Spokesman", Ministry of Foreign Affairs of the DPRK, December 24, 2017; "Press Release of DPRK Mission on Sanction", KCNA, November 5, 2017.
13 "Nuclear Force of DPRK Is Powerful Weapon for Defending Peace", *Rodong Sinmum*, February 23, 2018.
14 "Rodong Sinmum Hails Successful Test-Fire of Hwasung-15", KCNA, November 30, 2017.
15 Glenn Snyder, "The Security Dilemma in Alliance Politics", *World Politics*, 36 (4), July 1984, pp. 461–495; Robert Jervis, *The Illogic of American Nuclear Strategy*, Cornell University Press, Ithaca, 1984.
16 Michael Horowitz, "Nuclear Power and Militarized Conflict: Is There a Link?" in Adam N. Stulberg and Matthew Fuhrman (eds.), *The Nuclear Renaissance and International Security*, Stanford University Press, Stanford, 2013, pp. 288–312.
17 Michael D. Cohen, "How Nuclear Proliferation Causes Conflict: The Case for Optimistic Pessimism", *The Nonproliferation Review*, 23 (3–4), 2016, pp. 425–442.
18 Erik Gartzke, "Nuclear Proliferation Dynamics and Conventional Conflict", 2010, at http://dss.ucsd.edu/~egartzke/papers/nuketime_05032010.pdf (accessed May 29, 2019); James Lindsay and Ray Takeyh, "After Iran Gets Bomb: Containment and Its Complications", *Foreign Affairs*, 89, March-April 2010, pp. 33–50.
19 *DPRK Report on the Third Plenary Meeting of the Seventy Central Committee 2018*, The National Committee on North Korea, at www.ncnk.org/resources/publications/dprk_report_third_plenary_meeting_of_seventh_central_committee_of_wpk.pdf (accessed May 30, 2019).
20 Elbridge A. Colby and Michael S. Gerson (eds.), *Strategic Stability: Contending Interpretations*, Strategic Studies Institute and US Army War College Press, Carlisle, 2013.
21 John D. Steinbruner, "National Security and the Concept of Strategic Stability", *Journal of Conflict Resolution*, 22 (3), 1978, pp. 411–428.
22 "Treaty Between the United States of America and the Union of Soviet Socialist Republics on the Limitation of Anti-Ballistic Missile Systems", US Department of State, May 26, 1972.
23 Robert E. Berls, Jr., Leon Rats and Brian Rose, "Rising Nuclear Dangers: Diverging Views of Strategic Stability", NTI paper, October 2018.
24 Robert A. Manning, "The Future of US Extended deterrence in Asia to 2025", Atlantic Council, Brent Scowcroft Center on International Security, 2014.
25 *National Security Strategy of the United States 2018*, The White House, December 2017.
26 *Nuclear Posture Review 2018*, US Department of Defence, February 2018.
27 Brad Roberts, "Extended Deterrence and Strategic Stability in Northeast Asia", Universite Paris, Pantheon Sorbonne, Paris, France, March 9, 2015.
28 Linton Brooks and Mira Rapp-Hooper, "Extended Deterrence, Assurance and Reassurance in the Pacific During the Second Nuclear Ages", in Ashley J. Tellis, Abraham M. Denmark, and Travis Tanner (eds.), *Strategic Asia 2013–2014: Asia in the Second Nuclear Age*, National Bureau of Asian Research, Washington DC, 2013.
29 Joseph F. Pilat and Nathan E. Busch (eds.), *Routledge Handbook of Nuclear Proliferation and Policy*, Routledge, London, 2015, p. 54.

30 Brad Roberts, No. 27.
31 Robert A. Manning, No. 24, p. 6.
32 James L. Schoff and Li Bin, "A Precarious Triangle: US-China Strategic Stability and Japan", Carnegie Endowment for International Peace Report, November 2017, p. 9.
33 Thomas Henriksen, *America and the Rogue States*, Palgrave MacMillan, New York, 2012.

7 DPRK's proliferation activities and the denuclearisation talks

Security in the Indo-Pacific and beyond

Lami Kim

Introduction

The Democratic People's Republic of Korea (DPRK, aka North Korea) became a de facto nuclear weapons state in 2006 when it conducted its first nuclear test. It has since acquired sophisticated missile capabilities, which were demonstrated by its successful intercontinental ballistic missile (ICBM) tests in 2017. North Korea claims it can now deliver its nuclear warheads to any targets in the world.

According to academic theories that explain the factors enabling nuclear proliferation, North Korea is an unlikely country to succeed in acquiring nuclear weapons. Statistical analyses have suggested that economic capability is a key factor – economically prosperous countries are significantly more likely to acquire nuclear weapons, all else being equal. International status is another important factor. Global and regional power status increases the likelihood of acquiring nuclear weapons.[1] North Korea is one of the most impoverished countries in the world with a per capita income of merely $1,300 in 2016, according to the Bank of Korea.[2] It lacks even basic infrastructure and suffers from a chronic energy shortage. Without nuclear weapons, North Korea is neither a power to be reckoned with internationally, nor regionally. Nonetheless, it has successfully acquired nuclear weapons and their delivery vehicles.

How could this impoverished and backward country develop sophisticated nuclear and missile capabilities? The answer to this lies in the external assistance from both state and non-state actors. Assistance from the Soviet Union in the 1960s contributed to the DPRK's reprocessing capabilities. The DPRK's enrichment programme also received considerable support from Pakistan's Abdul Qadeer Khan (also known as A.Q. Khan) network. Without such external assistance, it would have been harder, and taken much longer, for the DPRK to build such sophisticated weaponry.

Now that North Korea has acquired the capability to provide sensitive nuclear materials, equipment, technologies, and know-how to other actors, it has become one of the key proliferators of these capabilities. Although the proliferation of nuclear weapons and missiles entails serious repercussions, North Korea is making these bold moves to generate much-needed foreign currency. Facing dire economic

122 *Lami Kim*

hardship, North Korea has engaged in various types of illicit activities from drug trafficking and money laundering to nuclear and missile sales. Moving forward, if the ongoing denuclearisation negotiations fail, international sanctions will likely be heightened, further exacerbating the already impoverished North Korean economy. In that event, North Korea would have a greater incentive to engage in the risky yet highly lucrative nuclear and missile smuggling business, raising concerns that belligerent countries or terrorist groups may acquire destructive weapons from the DPRK. This potentiality is one more reason that a successful North Korean denuclearisation process would benefit the Indo-Asia Pacific region and beyond.

This chapter first illustrates how foreign assistance has aided in the DPRK's development of nuclear and missile capabilities, and how the DPRK now is a proliferator of such capabilities to other countries, including nuclear aspirants in volatile areas, such as the Middle East and South Asia. It then discusses, from a global non-proliferation perspective, the implications of the failure of the ongoing denuclearisation negotiations.

At the outset, I acknowledge the difficulties inherent in verifying some of the information in this chapter, due to the challenges of tracking North Korea's highly clandestine proliferation activities. Also, I do not claim to provide a comprehensive analysis of these activities. It took a long time for national intelligence agencies to understand the nature and the scope of A.Q. Khan's proliferation network, as well as the respective nuclear programmes in Libya and Syria.[3] The DPRK case is a tougher one, as it is one of the most isolated and mysterious countries in the world. Despite such limitations, the DPRK's illicit proliferation activities are of grave importance and thus should be studied while remaining mindful of errors.

How illicit proliferation activities helped the DPRK's nuclear and missile programmes

DPRK's nuclear weapons programme

The DPRK started pursuing its nuclear weapons programme in the 1950s, having experienced nuclear threats during the 1950–1953 Korean War. In December 1952, Pyongyang established the Atomic Energy Research Institute, but no progress was made, as it lacked the technical capacity and had difficulties in acquiring foreign assistance. As the development of nuclear weapons requires sophisticated technologies to produce nuclear fissile materials, namely uranium enrichment or plutonium reprocessing, most nuclear weapons countries have received external support in some ways. The DPRK tried to obtain assistance from the Soviet Union, its key ally, which acquired nuclear weapons in 1949. Although the Soviet Union refused to help the DPRK build nuclear bombs, it provided civil nuclear assistance under the 1959 agreement on the peaceful use of nuclear energy. The Soviets trained North Korean scientists and technicians and provided extensive assistance to the DPRK in building the Yongbyon Nuclear Research Centre and a small research reactor, which advanced North Korea's nuclear technology.[4]

Based on the know-how acquired from the Soviet Union as well as open source information, Pyongyang built a gas-graphite reactor modelled after the United Kingdom's Calder Hall reactor. The construction of the first reactor of this type, the Yongbyon 5MWe, began in 1979 and was completed by 1986.[5] This type of reactor suited the DPRK, as it produces plutonium moderating natural uranium with graphite, both of which are abundant in the DPRK, without requiring heavy water, which it lacked.[6] Using this reactor, the North Koreans began producing plutonium in the late 1980s. When the International Atomic Energy Agency (IAEA) inspected the Yongbyon site in 1992, it discovered that several kilograms of plutonium had been diverted in violation of the IAEA safeguards, which heightened tension between the United States and the DPRK and had the potential of bringing war back to the Korean Peninsula.

Having averted a military clash, Pyongyang and Washington signed the Agreed Framework in 1994, in which the former promised to freeze and eventually dismantle its plutonium reprocessing programme in return for the latter's provision of oil, two light water reactors, sanctions relief, security assurance, and eventual normalisation of diplomatic relations.[7] The DPRK initially halted the reprocessing facility under IAEA supervision and removing spent fuel rods from the country. However, difficulties in securing funding amid strong opposition from the US Congress caused a delay in the construction of the light water reactors and repeated postponements of the delivery of US oil.

Against this backdrop, North Korea began to seek assistance for uranium enrichment using centrifuges as an alternative route to nuclear weapons. When the DPRK began its pursuit of enrichment is unclear. The Central Intelligence Agency (CIA) assessed that such efforts began in the early 2000s,[8] while Walter Clemens, a political scientist at Boston University, suggests that it started in earnest in the 1990s.[9] As its plutonium facilities were under stringent inspection (also, these facilities could easily be monitored from the air), North Korea pursued the enrichment track using centrifuges, which were not discernible from afar.[10]

The main contributor to the DPRK's enrichment programme was the A.Q. Khan Network. Abdul Qadeer Khan played an essential role in Pakistan's development of nuclear weapons using centrifuge technology he acquired while working at Urenco, a European nuclear fuel company.[11] He served as the head of the Khan Research Laboratory, Pakistan's enrichment programme based in Kuhuta, from 1975 to 2001. During his tenure, Khan sold gas-centrifuge technology that could be used for uranium enrichment to a number of states, including North Korea, Iran, and Libya.[12] Khan allegedly transferred blueprints and components for gas centrifuges to North Korea along with potential supplier lists. Former Pakistani president Pervez Musharraf acknowledged that the A.Q. Khan network provided centrifuges to the DPRK in 2000 along with "a flow meter, some special oils for centrifuges, and coaching on centrifuge technology including visits to top-secret centrifuge plants".[13] It is unclear whether the Pakistani government directly supported or at least condoned the Khan network's trade with the DPRK, although several Pakistani officials were involved.

In addition, the DPRK acquired large quantities of high-strength aluminium, another key ingredient for centrifuges, from Russia and the United Kingdom in 2002–2003. According to Clemens, "[A] simple tally of the amounts and types of equipment and material sought by North Korea suggested plans to develop a 5,000-centrifuge-strong enrichment capacity".[14] By the time Siegfried Hecker, a leading nuclear expert, visited North Korea in 2010, the DPRK had acquired some 2,000 centrifuges.[15]

With such external assistance combined with indigenous technological breakthroughs, the DPRK has now acquired nuclear bombs. Since its first nuclear test in October 2006, North Korea has conducted five more nuclear tests. The latest and the sixth nuclear test conducted in 2017 was estimated at somewhere between 50 kilotons (kt) and 250 kt, which suggests that North Korea has acquired nuclear warheads that are far more destructive than the atomic bombs dropped on Hiroshima and Nagasaki, which were approximately 13 kt and 23 kt, respectively.[16] Pyongyang claimed that the bomb tested in 2017 was a hydrogen bomb,[17] a weapon that derives its energy from nuclear fusion, which is far more powerful than the atomic bomb, which relies on nuclear fission.

DPRK's missile programme

The DPRK's missile programme, too, was made possible by foreign technology. In the 1970s, the DPRK purchased Soviet-supplied short-range missiles (Scud-B missiles) from Egypt and reverse-engineered them to make its earliest missiles.[18] By the mid-1980s, the DPRK had developed its variant of the Scud-B missile system, the *Hwasong-5* (with a range of 300 km), and in the early 1990s its variant of the Russian Scud-C, the *Hwasong-6* (500 km).[19] In the 1990s, North Korea also developed the *Rodong-1* (1,300 km), a medium-range missile upgraded from the *Hwasong-6*. The *Rodong-1* likely incorporated design features of the Russian R-21 Submarine-Launched Ballistic Missile (SLBM) and the R-5 theatre ballistic missiles. Allegedly, Russian and Chinese scientists aided in the development of the *Rodong*. After the end of the Cold War, the DPRK attempted to acquire missile technology from former Soviet scientists who had lost their lifelines at home and thus were incentivised to sell their knowledge. In the early 1990s, the North Koreans acquired the SS-N-6 system, an SLBM also called the R-27, from the Russians. The Russian government denied any affiliation with individuals who had sold the missile system to the DPRK. Using advanced propellants from this missile, the DPRK developed the *Musudan*, an intermediate-range ballistic missile (2,500–4,000 km).[20] The *Taepodong* (4,000–10,000 km), a longer-range missile that the DPRK tested in the 2000s and the 2010s, derived from the *Rodong*.[21] In August 2016, North Korea conducted its first successful SLBM test, which travelled about 480 km towards Japan.[22] Dual-use technologies procured from the international marketplace contributed to the advancement of the DPRK's missile programme. Debris from the Unha-3 satellite launches in 2012 and 2016 included dual-use items, such as electronic components from China, Switzerland, the United Kingdom, South Korea, and the United States.[23]

The DPRK's ICBM programme, reportedly based on procurement of key components from abroad, made significant progress in 2017. After a series of failures possibly caused by American efforts to sabotage the DPRK's missile programmes, in 2017 the DPRK successfully tested the *Hwasong-14*, a type of ICBM that has a range greater than 5,400 km, and the *Hwasong-15*, which has an estimated range of around 12,000 km. US defence secretary James Mattis assessed that these tests demonstrated the DPRK's capability to hit "everywhere in the world basically".[24] It should be noted, however, that it is uncertain whether the DPRK has acquired re-entry technology, which protects a nuclear warhead from the intense heat and vibrations generated when a missile re-enters earth's atmosphere. Western missile experts assessed that some key components of the DPRK's ICBMs were of Soviet design. Rocket engines used in these missiles, for example, were reportedly smuggled from Yuzhmash, a Ukrainian factory in Dnipro, according to American intelligence agencies. The state-owned factory that remained Russia's primary missile producer after Ukraine's independence had been a target of DPRK espionage for some time, which was illustrated by the 2011 arrest of two North Korean spies for attempting to steal missile secrets from the factory. Reportedly, North Korea successfully acquired missile technology from the factory after the removal of pro-Russian President Viktor Yanukovych in 2014. Having lost Russia, its primary buyer, illicit smuggling became highly attractive for the factory's scientists and engineers. If true, this illicit smuggling explains the sudden successes of North Korea's ICMB tests in 2017.[25]

DPRK as a nuclear and missile supplier

With the advancement of the DPRK's nuclear and missile capabilities, it has transformed from a recipient to a supplier of nuclear and missile assistance. Illicit nuclear and missile smuggling is a lucrative business given the scarcity of supply and the high risk involved, and so has been a source of much-needed hard currency for the DPRK's impoverished economy.

The DPRK's economy drastically declined in the 1990s due to the loss of financial assistance from the Soviet Union, combined with natural disasters. The ration system, on which people had relied for food and essential goods, collapsed, which led to a severe famine, also known as the "Arduous March," that killed more than one million people. Its pursuit of nuclear and missile capabilities has invited economic sanctions, thereby exacerbating the country's economic problems. According to the Bank of Korea based in Seoul, North Korea's economy was merely 2 per cent of South Korea's in 2016.[26]

Against this backdrop, the DPRK has been engaged in exporting minerals, such as gold bullion and coal, and in the illicit trafficking of narcotics, arms, counterfeit currency, and cigarettes in pursuit of hard currency.[27] According to a 2012 Korea Trade-Investment Promotion Agency report, the North Korean regime had earned about a billion dollars per year through illicit activities. The Kim regime's slush fund accumulated in this way has been used to distribute luxury goods, such as Mercedes cars and Omega gold watches, to the elites, in order to ensure their acquiescence to his hereditary succession, as well as to finance its nuclear and missiles development.

Illicit arms sales constitute a major source of income. For decades, North Korea has sold conventional arms, particularly cheap Cold-War era weapons, to countries in volatile regions, such as the Middle East, North Africa, and South Asia. For instance, the DPRK sold M-46 field guns to Myanmar in the late 1990s. In 2003, North Korean technicians, who were believed to be helping Myanmar equip their vessels with surface-to-surface missiles, were spotted at a Myanmar navy base. In 2008, the DPRK provided Myanmar with artillery pieces and truck-mounted 240 mm multiple launch rocket systems. In addition, some evidence suggests that the DPRK has helped Myanmar dig tunnels and build underground defence facilities. The DPRK, in return, is believed to have been paid in food. The military cooperation seems to have continued even after Myanmar normalised relations with the West in 2010.[28] Recently, the DPRK has increased its arms trade with Egypt, as the United States, its key ally, cut military aid. In 2016, the US authorities seized a North Korean ship, *Jie Shun*, carrying 30,000 rocket-propelled grenades en route to Egypt.[29] According to a March 2018 *New York Times* report, Egypt allowed North Korean diplomats to use the North Korean embassy in Cairo as a base for their arms sales in the region. According to the report, North Korean diplomats under sanctions due to their involvement in proliferation activities have been based in Cairo and continued to work with Sudan's state-controlled defence industry.[30] The DPRK's weapons sales are in violation of United Nations (UN) Security Council sanctions.[31]

The DPRK's weapons trade goes beyond conventional weapons. Victor Cha, a renowned Korea expert who served as the director of Asian Affairs for George W. Bush's National Security Council, said, "[n]o country has been more consistent in its willingness to sell its weapon systems to other bad actors [than North Korea]", and "Pyongyang would do the same with its nuclear and ballistic missile capabilities".[32] Indeed, there is considerable reportage concerning North Korea's engagement in nuclear and missile trades with nuclear aspirants, in particular Iran, Syria, and Pakistan.

North Korea has contributed to Iran's nuclear programme by providing nuclear materials, technology, and personnel. During the 1980–1988 Iran-Iraq War, for example, North Korea sold Iran conventional weapons worth a billion dollars, in addition to providing training and military assistance.[33] Since then, North Korea has contributed to Iran's conventional military capabilities by providing them with ground, naval, and other weaponry. The two countries built strong military cooperation in the early 1980s and began cooperating in the nuclear and missile fields in earnest in the early 2000s. As the A.Q. Khan network, which had provided Iran with nuclear materials, technologies, and scientific know-how, had been shut down, North Korea stepped in to fill the gap and provide assistance to Iran's fledgling nuclear weapons programme. Multiple media sources have reported that North Korean scientists and engineers were working in Iran's nuclear and missile facilities. It appears that the North Koreans secretly entered Iran via China and Russia and offered their assistance in various areas, including nuclear weapons design. In 2003, *Los Angeles Times* journalist Douglas Frantz wrote: "So many North Koreans are working on nuclear and missile projects in Iran that a resort on the Caspian coast is set aside for their exclusive use".[34] In 2011, European press reported that North Korea sold Iran a computer programme that would help Iran's nuclear weapons programme by simulating neutron flows. In February 2013, Mohsen Fakhrizadeh-Mahabadi, who is widely reported to be in charge of Iran's cooperation with North Korea on the production of highly enriched uranium, and other key Iranian nuclear experts, observed the DPRK's underground nuclear test. Political scientist Bruce Bethtol wrote:

> The evidence over a period that now spans well over a decade is clear. Whether it is assisting in the design and building of a nuclear warhead, providing computer software that will aid in building a nuclear weapon, building nuclear facilities that are capable of resisting bunker buster bombing attacks, or even providing yellow cake materials for Tehran's nuclear program, North Korea has been knee-deep in assisting Iran's nuclear program.[35]

In addition, North Korea helped Iran build ballistic missiles. In the 1980s, Pyongyang sold Iran Scud-Bs and Scud-Cs. Also, the DPRK has established missile facilities and assembled and manufactured missiles in Iran, so that Iran can develop the capability to produce missiles on its own. It is easier to evade international sanctions by transferring parts, technology, and personnel, as well as to help a recipient country assemble missiles, than to transfer entire missile systems. In 2003, the DPRK helped Iran build the *Shahab-3*, a version of the *Rodong*, in return for both hard currency and oil. In 2008, Iran tested the *Shahab-3*, and later, in 2015, it tested its upgraded version, the *Emad*. Additionally, the DPRK sold 18 units of the *Musudan* in 2005, on which Iran's *Shahab-4* was modelled. Tehran tested the *Shahab-4* in 2006 and the *Khorramsharh*, an upgraded version of the *Musudan*, in 2017. In 2015, Israeli media released imagery of a 27-metre-long Iranian missile system, the same size as the North Korean *Taepodong-1*, indicating that the Iranian system was a likely product of cooperation with North Koreans. Some evidence suggests that Iran and North Korea cooperate in the development of ICBMs, too. In 2013, *World Tribune* reported that US intelligence officials had unearthed a deal between Iran and North Korea, according to which Iran financed North Korea's ballistic missile programme in return for North Korea's provision of missile components, technology, and expertise.[36]

Syria is another recipient of the DPRK's proliferation activities. Both countries were once under Soviet influence and began their military cooperation in the 1960s. The DPRK supported Syria's military conflicts with Israel in the 1967 Six-Day War, the 1973 Yom Kippur War, and the 1982 Lebanon War by supplying conventional weapons, such as artillery, guns, tanks, and rocket launchers.

Since the end of the Cold War, the DPRK has allegedly sold the Syrians Scud missiles and built missile production facilities in Syria. As it did with Iran, North Korea transferred parts of missiles and helped assemble them in Syria in order to evade sanctions. In addition, North Korea is known to have been the principal architect of a secret Syrian nuclear reactor that Israel destroyed in an airstrike in 2007.[37] Former CIA director Michael Hayden argues that "[v]irtually every form of intelligence – imagery, signals, human source, you name it – " attested to the DPRK's involvement in Syria's nuclear programme and the evidence is "overwhelming".[38] One piece of evidence is that the Syrian reactor had the same design as the above-mentioned Yongbyon reactor.[39] It seems that this reactor was possibly built by trilateral cooperation among the DPRK, Syria, and Iran. According to Ali Reza Asghari, former deputy defence minister of Iran, Iran paid the DPRK up to $2 billion for the construction of the Syrian reactor. After the reactor was destroyed by the Israelis, about 45 tons of yellow cake, which had originally been transferred from the DPRK to Syria, was reportedly re-transferred to Iran through Turkey.[40] More recently, the DPRK has allegedly aided Syria's Assad regime since the Syrian Civil War broke out in 2011. A UN Panel of Experts reported that the DPRK transferred to Syria not only conventional arms between 2012 and 2017 but also components for chemical weapons in 2016 and that North Korean chemical technicians continue to work in Syria.[41] If true, then the DPRK is partially responsible for the Assad regime's chemical attacks.[42]

Pakistan is another recipient of the DPRK's missile assistance. The DPRK transferred the *Rodong* missile technology to Pakistan in the 1990s. Pakistan, at that time, was pursuing missiles that could reach Indian targets but had difficulties in securing the necessary foreign assistance, as it was increasingly isolated due to its nuclear ambitions as well as its ties with the Taliban. Under international pressure, even China, its close ally, refused to assist Pakistan in missile development. Pakistan thus turned to the DPRK. In 1998, Pakistan tested the *Ghauri-1* missile, which was modelled after the *Rodong*. North Korea also helped Pakistan with the launching and deployment of the missiles on Pakistani soil.[43]

Given its clandestine nature, it is impossible to ascertain the full extent of the DPRK's proliferation activities. It is probable that the customer list for the DPRK's arms, nuclear, and missile sales is far longer than is currently known. It has been suggested that Iraq, Libya, and Yemen have also received missile assistance from the DPRK[44] and that Nigeria has received a similar offer from Pyongyang.[45] In addition, the Institute for Science and International Security recently revealed that North Korea had distributed marketing brochures to potential customers, offering to sell nuclear-grade graphite, an internationally controlled material that can be used in nuclear reactors.[46]

In sum, the DPRK's nuclear and missile capabilities threaten peace and security on the Korean Peninsula and the surrounding region, but their ramifications go well beyond that, given Pyongyang's engagement in nuclear and missile trade in pursuit of hard currency.

Denuclearisation negotiations and DPRK's proliferation activities

If the DPRK denuclearises, its proliferation activities would likely stop. At the time of writing in May 2019, negotiations aimed at denuclearising the DPRK and establishing a peaceful regime on the Korean Peninsula were ongoing. In a dramatic turnaround after heightened fears of a military conflict on the Korean Peninsula, diplomatic engagement began with the Olympic détente in early 2018, which led to three inter-Korean summits and the first US-DPRK summit in June 2018 in Singapore. However, the second US-DPRK summit held in Hanoi in early March 2019 collapsed due to disagreements between the two sides over the appropriate timing and compensation for denuclearisation. While Pyongyang demands a gradual, phase-by-phase approach to denuclearisation and substantial sanctions relief during the process, Washington has an all-or-nothing approach that requires Pyongyang's complete denuclearisation before any rewards are offered. Whether the negotiations will lead to the DPRK's denuclearisation and peace on the Korean Peninsula remains to be seen, but amid the prolonged stalemate, pessimism that the talks will eventually unravel is increasingly gaining ground.

Implications of the failure of the ongoing negotiations will be significant, not only for both Koreas but also for peace and security in the Indo-Pacific region and the world at large. The failure of the denuclearisation diplomacy will likely lead to the return of tension on the Korean Peninsula. The DPRK launched short-range ballistic missiles twice, on May 4 and May 9, 2019, for the first time since 2017. These launches seem to be aimed at bringing the United States back to the negotiating table. President Trump played down the launches, saying, "They're short-range and I don't consider that a breach of trust at all".[47] However, one cannot rule out the possibility that the DPRK will test ICBMs in order to further provoke the United States and South Korea into granting concessions. Such tests could also lead to the mastery of re-entry technology required to launch nuclear attacks against the United States, thereby achieving nuclear deterrence vis-à-vis the United States. In that case, President Trump might again contemplate the "bloody-nose" option of surgical strikes on the DPRK's nuclear and missile facilities or return to his earlier threats to "totally destroy" the DPRK. Trump may well argue that all options except for military ones have been exhausted, an argument that may find less resistance in the international community in the aftermath of diplomatic failure.[48] Any military actions against the DPRK, however, not only would cause massive casualties in both Koreas, but also could aggravate the already thorny relations between China and the United States. Given China's military alliance with the DPRK, one cannot rule out the possibility that a conflict between the United States and China could erupt.[49] Therefore, successful denuclearisation negotiations between Washington and Pyongyang are critical for ensuring peace and security on the Korean Peninsula and the Indo-Pacific region.

Stakes are also high for global efforts to prevent nuclear proliferation. If diplomacy fails, sanctions would likely toughen, dealing a blow to the DPRK's already shaky economy. In order to survive, Pyongyang would be motivated to continue or even expand its proliferation activities. Such concerns are particularly relevant in light of the DPRK's economic hardships. As mentioned above, North Korea's economic situation has significantly deteriorated due to its pursuit of nuclear and missile capabilities. Since North Korea's first nuclear test in 2006, the UN Security Council has passed nine rounds of economic sanctions – banning export of coal, minerals, textiles, seafood, agricultural products, etc., as well as import of luxury goods; freezing assets of individuals involved in the DPRK's nuclear programme; and limiting oil and natural gas imports. In particular, the DPRK's numerous nuclear and missile tests in 2016 and 2017 prompted one of the harshest sanctions regimes in history. China's decision to join in the international efforts to impose economic sanctions on the DPRK in response to the missile tests in 2017 dealt a major blow to North Korea's economy.[50] UN sanctions, collectively, "target 90 per cent of North Korea's publicly reported export products".[51]

In addition to the multilateral sanctions, individual countries have imposed unilateral sanctions on North Korea. The US unilateral sanctions on North Korea are far more restrictive than UN sanctions. The US sanctions not only North Korean entities, but also those that provide the DPRK with support, such as Chinese and Russian firms and individuals, termed the "secondary boycott". In September 2017, President Trump toughened financial sanctions by authorising the Treasury Department to block any entities trading with North Korea from the US financial system. Treasury Secretary Steven Mnuchin said, "[f]oreign financial institutions are now on notice that, going forward, they can choose to do business with the United States or with North Korea, but not both".[52] South Korea limited its economic and cultural exchanges with North Korea after North Korea sank its naval ship, the *Cheonan*, in 2010, killing 46 sailors. In the wake of North Korea's 2016 missile test, then president Park Geun-hye closed the Kaesong Industrial Complex,[53] from which the DPRK earned more than $500 million per year.[54] Lastly, Japan has limited its commercial relations with North Korea over the latter's nuclear and missile provocations. In 2016, Japan froze North Korean assets and banned remittances of over $880 to North Korea. The European Union (EU) has passed economic restrictions, which include a cap on remittances to North Korea, a ban on exports of luxury goods, and a ban on EU investment in North Korea's economic sectors.[55]

As a result, the DPRK's economy contracted by 3.5 per cent in 2017 and 4.1 per cent in 2018.[56] In March 2018, a UN report estimated that about 10.3 million North Koreans, or 40 per cent of North Korea's population, were undernourished.[57] The situation has deteriorated over the course of 2018, as North Korea's exports decreased by 86.3 per cent and its imports by 31.2 per cent, from the previous year.[58] It is notable that the regime has not decreased imports at the same rate. This is presumably in order to minimize the effects of sanctions on the quality of life for its people, but must be leading to a drop in its foreign currency reserves. South Korean economists who recently studied North Korea's foreign currency reserves estimated that at this rate, North Korea will almost, if not completely, run out of foreign currency reserves by the end of 2020.[59]

Experts at the Asian Institute for Policy Studies, a South Korean think tank, warned of an imminent economic crisis in North Korea, pointing to the rapid deterioration of its economy and no sign of sanctions relief in the near future.[60] Severe economic hardships could undermine the legitimacy of the Kim regime and lead to political instability.

Dwindling hard currency could also lead to a coup. Up to this point, the Kim regime has distributed luxury goods to North Korean elites in order to buy their loyalty. However, the funds Kim Jong-un inherited from his father were already halved by 2014 according to Radio Free Asia,[61] and recent economic sanctions have continued to contract the regime's slush fund. Hence, disbursement of luxury gifts will grow increasingly difficult, potentially jeopardising the elites' support and the regime's own survival. Against this backdrop, lucrative nuclear and missile proliferation activities could prove to be highly tempting for the Kim regime, particularly if it fears regime collapse.

If the ongoing denuclearisation negotiations lead to a successful agreement, they would translate into sanctions relief, and North Korea would likely drop its proliferation activities. Although such activities provide considerable economic benefits, under any future agreement, detection would result in a return to the harsh sanctions the DPRK has striven hard to escape. Moreover, full-scale economic development by integrating with the global economy would provide larger economic gains than illicit proliferation activities. However, if the negotiations fail and the prospects of sanctions relief fade, the Kim regime would actively seek to trade its nuclear and missile capabilities for desperately needed hard currency, which is critical for Kim Jong-un's hold on power. Alternatively, the DPRK could barter its nuclear and missile assistance for oil, food, and other goods that it needs.

The DPRK's proliferation activities pose serious threats to international peace and security. Potentially, the DPRK could increase provision of weapons of mass destruction (WMD), including nuclear weapons, to other countries. For example, the DPRK would be the most likely supplier if the Syrian regime of Bashar Assad tries to acquire the nuclear option. The DPRK is also likely to continue to assist Iran in its nuclear and ballistic missile programmes, as the Iran deal has unravelled. Such assistance to Syria and Iran makes it likely that non-state actors in the Middle East, namely Hamas and Hezbollah, could also access WMD. Further, one cannot rule out the possibility of the DPRK transferring nuclear or radiological materials to terrorist organisations, which could use those materials to detonate dirty bombs or radiological dispersal devices that could contaminate large areas, sowing panic and causing extraordinary financial losses. There are already reports that terrorist organisations have attempted to collect nuclear materials for the purpose of making dirty bombs.[62] Though not highly probable, Pyongyang could aid terrorist organisations in its desperate need for hard currency and essential goods, if its survival was at stake.

The DPRK's nuclear and missile issues are of grave importance, not only for peace and security on the Korean Peninsula and the Indo-Pacific region, but also for international security. The successful resolution of these issues is critical for international efforts to prevent proliferation of nuclear weapons and missiles to other regions, too. This aspect of the ongoing denuclearisation diplomacy has largely been ignored and should be taken into consideration as the negotiations continue.

Notes

1 Dong-Joon Jo and Erik Gartzke, "Determinants of Nuclear Weapons Proliferation", *Journal of Conflict Resolution*, 51 (1), 2007, pp. 175–179.
2 Han Gwang-deok, "North Korea's GDP Grew 3.9% in 2016, with $1,300 Per Capita Income", *Hankyoreh*, July 23, 2017, at http://english.hani.co.kr/arti/english_edition/e_northkorea/803901.html (accessed November 15, 2018).
3 Greogory L. Schulte, "Stopping Proliferation Before It Starts – How to Prevent the Next Nuclear Wave", *Foreign Affairs*, 89, 2010, at www.foreignaffairs.com/articles/2010-07-01/stopping-proliferation-it-starts (accessed November 20, 2018).
4 "North Korea", Nuclear Threat Initiative, October 2018, at www.nti.org/learn/countries/north-korea/nuclear (accessed April 30, 2019).
5 "Yongbyon 5MWe Reactor", Nuclear Threat Initiative, July 19, 2018, at www.nti.org/learn/facilities/766 (accessed November 15, 2018).
6 Nicholas L. Miller and Vipin Narang, "North Korea Defied the Theoretical Odds: What Can We Learn from Its Successful Nuclearization?" *Texas National Security Review*, 1 (2), 2018, at https://tnsr.org/2018/02/north-korea-defied-theoretical-odds-can-learn-successful-nuclearization/#_ftn3 (accessed September 30, 2018).
7 "The U.S.-North Korean Agreed Framework at a Glance", Arms Control Association, July 2018, at www.armscontrol.org/factsheets/agreedframework (accessed May 15, 2019).
8 Mark Fitzpatrick, *Nuclear Black Markets: Pakistan, AQ Khan and the Rise of Proliferation Networks: A Net Assessment*, International Institute for Strategic Studies, London, 2007, pp. 55–56.
9 Walter C. Clemens Jr., *North Korea and the World: Human Rights, Arms Control, and Strategies for Negotiation*, University Press of Kentucky, Lexington, 2016, pp. 106–107.
10 Catherine Collins and Douglas Frantz, "The Long Shadow of A.Q. Khan: How One Scientist Helped the World Go Nuclear", *Foreign Affairs*, January 31, 2018, at www.foreignaffairs.com/articles/north-korea/2018-01-31/long-shadow-aq-khan (accessed December 1, 2018); Siegfried S. Hecker, "What We Really Know About North Korea's Nuclear Weapons: And What We Don't Yet Know for Sure", *Foreign Affairs*, December 4, 2017, at www.foreignaffairs.com/articles/north-korea/2017-12-04/what-we-really-know-about-north-koreas-nuclear-weapons (accessed December 15, 2018).
11 After India's 1974 nuclear test, Khan, who was at the time working at a Urenco's Almelo plant based in the Netherlands as a metallurgist, secretly stole centrifuge designs and a list of potential nuclear suppliers, which contributed to Pakistan's two centrifuge models, P-1 and P-2. See: Chaim Braun and Christopher F. Chyba, "Proliferation Rings: New Challenges to the Nuclear Non-proliferation Regime", *International Security*, 29 (2), 2004, p. 13.
12 In 2004, Khan confessed on live television that he had illegally proliferated nuclear technology to North Korea and other countries, including Iran and Libya, though he retracted this statement later. See: Catherine Collins and Douglas Frantz, No. 10; Joshua Pollack and George Perkovich, "The A.Q. Khan Network and Its Fourth Customer", Carnegie Endowment for International Peace, January 23, 2012, at https://carnegieendowment.org/2012/01/23/a.q.-khan-network-and-its-fourth-customer-event-3505 (accessed November 25, 2018).

13 Quoted in Mary Beth Nikitin, "North Korea's Nuclear Weapons: Technical Issues," *Congressional Research Service*, December 16, 2009, p. 7.
14 Walter Clemens Jr., No. 9, pp. 107.
15 Siegfried S. Hecker, "What I Found in North Korea", *Foreign Affairs*, December 9, 2010, at www.foreignaffairs.com/articles/northeast-asia/2010-12-09/what-i-found-north-korea (accessed October 15, 2018).
16 James Griffiths and Angela Dewan, "What Is a Hydrogen Bomb and Can North Korea Deliver One?" *CNN*, September 22, 2017, http://edition.cnn.com/2017/09/03/asia/hydrogen-bomb-north-korea-explainer/index.html (accessed September 15, 2018); Bonnie Berkowitz and Aaron Steckelberg, "North Korea Tested Another Nuke. How Big Was It?" *Washington Post*, September 14, 2017, www.washingtonpost.com/graphics/2017/world/north-korea-nuclear-yield/?utm_term=.6815af72661d (accessed September 15, 2018); and John Malik, "The Yields of the Hiroshima and Nagasaki Nuclear Explosions", Los Alamos National Laboratory, September 1985, at http://atomicarchive.com/Docs/pdfs/00313791.pdf (accessed December 15, 2018).
17 Jack Kim and Ju-min Park, "Possible Two-stage Hydrogen Bomb Seen 'Game Changer' for North Korea", Reuters, September 3, 2017, at www.reuters.com/article/us-northkorea-missiles-thermonuclear-ana/possible-two-stage-hydrogen-bomb-seen-game-changer-for-north-korea-idUSKCN1BE0PT (accessed March 1, 2018).
18 Joby Warrick and Julie Vitkovskaya, "North Korea's Nuclear Weapons: What You Need to Know", *The Washington Post*, March 9, 2018, at www.washingtonpost.com/news/worldviews/wp/2018/03/06/5-things-to-know-about-north-koreas-nuclear-weapons/?noredirect=on&utm_term=.5294a20a0544 (accessed October 4, 2018).
19 "Hwasong-5 ('Scud B' Variant)", *Missile Threat*, Missile Defense Project, Center for Strategic and International Studies, August 8, 2016 (last modified June 15, 2018), at https://missilethreat.csis.org/missile/hwasong-5/ (accessed December 15, 2018); "Hwasong-6 ('Scud C' Variant)", *Missile Threat*, Missile Defense Project, Center for Strategic and International Studies, August 8, 2016 (last modified June 15, 2018), at https://missilethreat.csis.org/missile/hwasong-6/ (accessed December 15, 2018).
20 "Musudan (BM-25)", *Missile Threat*, Missile Defense Project, Center for Strategic and International Studies, August 8, 2016 (last modified June 15, 2018), at https://missilethreat.csis.org/missile/musudan (accessed April 9, 2019).
21 "Taepodong-2 (Unha-3)", *Missile Threat*, Missile Defense Project, Center for Strategic and International Studies, August 8, 2016 (last modified June 15, 2018), at https://missilethreat.csis.org/missile/taepodong-2/ (accessed April 9, 2019).
22 Anna Fifield, "North Korea Hails 'Greatest Success' of Submarine-Launched Ballistic Missile", *The Washington Post*, August 25, 2016, at www.washingtonpost.com/world/north-korea-hails-greatest-success-of-submarine-launched-ballistic-missile/2016/08/25/6a7b9160-35ef-4d7c-a411-8ecdcc376fa5_story.html (accessed September 30, 2018).
23 UN Security Council, "Report of the Panel of Experts Established Pursuant to Resolution 1874 (2009)", S/2014/147, March 6, 2014, pp. 22–23.
24 Zachary Cohen, Ryan Browne, Nicole Gaouette and Taehoon Lee, "New Missile Test Shows North Korea Capable of Hitting All of US Mainland", *CNN*, November 30, 2017, at www.cnn.com/2017/11/28/politics/north-korea-missile-launch/index.html (accessed November 9, 2018).
25 William J. Broad and David E. Sanger, "North Korea's Missile Success Is Linked to Ukrainian Plant, Investigators Say", *The New York Times*, August 14, 2017, at www.nytimes.com/2017/08/14/world/asia/north-korea-missiles-ukraine-factory.html (accessed December 11, 2018); Simon Shuster, "How North Korea Built a Nuclear Arsenal on the Ashes of the Soviet Union", *Time*, February 1, 2018, at http://time.com/5128398/the-missile-factory/ (accessed December 11, 2018).

26 According to the Bank of Korea, North Korea's nominal Gross National Income in 2016 was approximately ₩ 36.4 trillion, 2.2 per cent of that of South Korea, which was estimated to be ₩ 1,639.1 trillion. "North Korea's GDP Grew 3.9% in 2016, with $1,300 Per Capita Income", *Hankyoreh*, July 23, 2017, at http://english.hani.co.kr/arti/english_edition/e_northkorea/803901.html (accessed December 20, 2018).
27 Mark Fitzpatrick, No. 8, pp. 56–57; see also, Sheena Chestnut, "Illicit Activity and Proliferation: North Korean Smuggling Networks", *International Security*, 32 (1), 2007, pp. 80–111.
28 Bertil Lintner, "North Korea, Myanmar in a Sanctions-Busting Embrace", *Asia Times*, February 8, 2018, at www.asiatimes.com/2018/02/article/north-korea-myanmar-sanctions-busting-embrace/ (accessed December 20, 2018).
29 Emma Chanlett-Avery, Mark E. Manyin, Mary Beth D. Nikitin, Caitlin Elizabeth Campbell, and Wil Mackey, "North Korea: U.S. Relations, Nuclear Diplomacy, and Internal Situation", *Congressional Research Service*, July 27, 2018, p. 24, at https://fas.org/sgp/crs/nuke/R41259.pdf (accessed December 20, 2018).
30 Declan Walsh, "Need a North Korean Missile? Call the Cairo Embassy", *The New York Times*, March 3, 2018, at www.nytimes.com/2018/03/03/world/middleeast/egypt-north-korea-sanctions-arms-dealing.html (accessed November 30, 2018).
31 UN Security Council Resolutions 1718, 1987 and 2087 prohibit the DPRK's all weapons sales.
32 Joby Warrick, "Suspicious Factory Underscores Challenges Verifying North Korea's Nuclear Promises", *The Washington Post*, April 21, 2018, at www.washingtonpost.com/world/national-security/suspicious-factory-underscores-challenge-of-verifying-north-koreas-nuclear-promises/2018/04/21/fad9764c-457d-11e8-8569-26fda6b404c7_story.html?utm_term=.fe57dccd8f8d (accessed December 1, 2018).
33 Bruce E. Bechtol, Jr., "North Korea's Illicit Weapons Trade", *Foreign Affairs*, June 6, 2018, at www.foreignaffairs.com/articles/north-korea/2018-06-06/north-koreas-illegal-weapons-trade (accessed March 3, 2019).
34 Quoted in Bruch E. Bechtol, Jr., *North Korean Military Proliferation in the Middle East and Africa: Enabling Violence and Instability*, University Press of Kentucky, Lexington, 2018, p. 82. Similarly, in 2011, a South Korean media outlet quoted a diplomat as saying: "Hundreds of North Korean scientists and engineers are working at about 10 nuclear and missile facilities in Iran, including Natanz … They are apparently rotated every six months." For details, see: "'Hundreds of N. Koreans' Working in Iran Nuke Facilities", *Chosun Ilbo*, November 14, 2011, at http://english.chosun.com/site/data/html_dir/2011/11/14/2011111400526.html (accessed March 16, 2019).
35 Quoted in Bruch E. Bechtol, No. 34, p. 86.
36 Ibid., p. 91.
37 Joby Warrick, No. 31.
38 Bruce E. Bechtol, Jr., No. 34, p. 83.
39 David E. Sanger, "Bush Administration Releases Images to Bolster Its Claims About Syrian Reactor", *The New York Times*, April 25, 2008, at www.nytimes.com/2008/04/25/world/middleeast/25korea.html (accessed May 11, 2019).
40 Bruce E. Bechtol, Jr., No. 34, p. 84.
41 See "Note by the President of the Security Council", UN Security Council, March 5, 2018 (S/2018/171), at www.un.org/ga/search/view_doc.asp?symbol=S/2018/171 (accessed May 12, 2019).
42 The UN and the Organisation for the Prohibition of Chemical Weapons accused the Syrian Government of using chemical weapons on multiple occasions since the Syrian Civil War broke out. See, "Timeline of Syrian Chemical Weapons Activity, 2012–2018", Arms Control Association, November 2018, at www.armscontrol.org/factsheets/Timeline-of-Syrian-Chemical-Weapons-Activity (accessed May 5, 2019). See also, Jay Solomon, "Trump's North Korea Talks Need to Address Syrian and

Iranian Proliferation", *Washington Institute for Near East Policy*, March 22, 2018, at www.washingtoninstitute.org/policy-analysis/view/trumps-north-korea-talks-need-to-address-syrian-and-iranian-proliferation (accessed May 13, 2019).
43 Samuel Ramani, "The Long History of the Pakistan-North Korea Nexus", *The Diplomat*, August 30, 2016, at https://thediplomat.com/2016/08/the-long-history-of-the-pakistan-north-korea-nexus (accessed May 3, 2019); Bruch E. Bechtol, Jr., No. 34, pp. 82–83.
44 Joseph Cirincione, Jon B. Wolfsthal and Miriam Rajkumar, *Deadly Arsenals: Nuclear, Biological and Chemical Threats*, Carnegie Endowment for International Peace, Washington, 2002, pp. 250–251.
45 Nicholas Kralev, "North Korea Offers Nigeria Missile Deal", *Washington Times*, January 29, 2004.
46 David Albright, "Chongsu Nuclear-Grade Graphite Production Plant? North Korea May Be Proliferating Controlled Nuclear Goods", Institute for Science and International Security, April 20, 2018, at http://isis-online.org/uploads/isis-reports/documents/Chongsu_April_20_2018_Final.pdf (accessed May 3, 2019).
47 "Trump Says North Korea's Recent Missile Launches Not Breach of Trust – Politico", *Reuters*, May 10, 2019, at https://af.reuters.com/article/worldNews/idAFKCN1SH005 (accessed May 10, 2019).
48 For this reason, James Acton argued the risk of a military clash between the United States and the DPRK heightened with the beginning of the denuclearisation negotiations in June 2018. See, James Action, Twitter Post, October 16, 2018, at https://twitter.com/james_acton32/status/1052202785486368769 (accessed May 5, 2019).
49 Pursuant to the 1961 Sino-North Korean Treaty of Friendship, Cooperation and Mutual Assistance, the two countries have agreed to defend each other in case either nation is attacked. However, it should be noted that the alliance has been weakened in recent history, which makes it questionable whether China would come to the DPRK's aid if the United States attacks the DPRK. See, Eleanor Albert, "The China-North Korea Relationship", Council for Foreign Relations, March 13, 2019, at www.cfr.org/backgrounder/china-north-korea-relationship (accessed May 9, 2019).
50 China accounted for over 90 per cent of North Korea's overall trade since 2014. See, "2017 북한 대외무역 동향" [2017 North Korean Trade Trend], Korea Trade-Investment Promotion Agency, July 18, 2018, at http://news.kotra.or.kr/user/globalBbs/kotranews/11/globalBbsDataView.do?setIdx=249&dataIdx=168031 (accessed May 7, 2019).
51 Eleanor Albert, "What to Know About the Sanctions on North Korea", Council on Foreign Relations, January 3, 2018, at www.cfr.org/backgrounder/what-know-about-sanctions-north-korea (accessed May 7, 2019). For more information on UN sanctions on North Korea, see James L. Schoff and Feng Lin, "Making Sense of UN Sanctions on North Korea", Carnegie Endowment for International Peace, at https://carnegieendowment.org/publications/interactive/north-korea-sanctions (accessed December 20, 2018).
52 "Remarks by Secretary Mnuchin on President Trump's Executive Order on North Korea", Delivered at UN General Assembly Press Briefing, US Department of the Treasury Press Center, September 21, 2017, at www.treasury.gov/press-center/press-releases/Pages/sm0162.aspx (accessed December 15, 2018); Emma Chanlett-Avery et al., No. 29, pp. 6–8.
53 Justin McCurry, "Seoul Shuts Down Joint North-South Korea Industrial Complex", *Guardian*, February 10, 2016, at www.theguardian.com/world/2016/feb/10/seoul-shuts-down-joint-north-south-korea-industrial-complex-kaesong (accessed May 7, 2019).
54 More than 100 South Korean companies participated in the industrial complex employing over 50,000 North Korean workers and generating around 20–30 per cent of North Korea's estimated total exports at its peak in 2014 and 2015. Emma

Chanlett-Avery, Mark E. Manyin, Mary Beth D. Nikitin, Caitlin Elizabeth Campbell, and Wil Mackey, "North Korea: U.S. Relations, Nuclear Diplomacy, and Internal Situation", *Congressional Research Service*, July 27, 2018, p. 15 (endnote 35), https://fas.org/sgp/crs/nuke/R41259.pdf (accessed September 17, 2019).
55 Eleanor Albert, No. 51.
56 Lee Kwan Kyo, "Gross Domestic Product Estimates for North Korea in 2018," *Bank of Korea*, July 26, 2019, https://www.bok.or.kr/eng/bbs/E0000634/view.do?nttId=10053001&menuNo=400069 (accessed September 20, 2019).
57 "DPRK Needs and Priorities Plan 2018", United Nations in the Democratic People's Republic of Korea, March 2018, at http://kp.one.un.org/content/dam/unct/dprk/docs/unct_kp_NP2018.pdf (accessed November 1, 2018).
58 "2018년 북한 대외 무역규모 전년 대비 절반 수준으로 축소[North Korean Trade Balance Halved in 2018]," *Korea Trade-Investment Promotion Agency*, July 19, 2019, at www.kotra.or.kr/kh/about/KHKICP020M.html?ARTICLE_ID=3019858&RowCountPerPage=10&Page=1&SEARCH_TYPE=SJCN&SEARCH_VALUE=&MENU_CD=F0138&TOP_MENU_CD=F0104&LEFT_MENU_CD=F0138&PARENT_MENU_CD=F0117 (accessed September 20, 2019).
59 장형수 [Zang Hyoung-soo] and 김석진 [Kim Suk-jin], "북한의 외화수급 및 외화보유액 추정과, 북·미 비핵화 협상에 대한 시사점" [Estimation of the Balance of Foreign Exchange and Foreign Exchange Reserves of the Kim Jong-Un Regime and Implications for North Korea-US Denuclearization Negotiations," 현대북한연구 *[Review of North Korean Studies]*, 22(1), 2019, pp. 37–38.
60 이용수 [Lee Yong-soo] and 김지섭 [Kim Ji-seop], "국제제재 길어지며... '북한경제, 예상보다 빨리 한계 상황 도달'" [With Prolonged International Sanctions...North Korean Economy Reaching Its Limits Earlier than Expected], 조선일보 [*Chosun Ilbo*], December 20, 2018, at http://news.chosun.com/site/data/html_dir/2018/12/20/2018122000331.html?utm_source=naver&utm_medium=original&utm_campaign=news (accessed May 3, 2019).
61 Joonho Kim, "Kim Jong Un Slush Fund 'Running out' as North Korea Tests Weapons Despite Sanctions", Radio Free Asia, January 25, 2018, at www.rfa.org/english/news/korea/fund-01252018143318.html; May 3, 2019. 박희석 [Park Hee-seok], "김정은, 김정일이 물려준 '범죄자금 40억 달러' 거의 썼다는 주장 나와... 핵·미사일 개발과 사치·향락에 탕진" [Kim Jong-un Said to Have Nearly Exhausted $4 Billion Slush Fund Inherited from Kim Jong-il On Nuclear and Missile Tests and Luxury Goods], 월간조선 [*Monthly Chosun*], January 27, 2018, at http://monthly.chosun.com/client/mdaily/daily_view.asp?Idx=2761&Newsnumb=2018012761 (accessed November 10, 2018).
62 Patrick Malone and R. Jeffrey Smith, "The Islamic State's Plot to Build a Radioactive 'Dirty Bomb'", *Foreign Policy*, February 29, 2016, at https://foreignpolicy.com/2016/02/29/the-islamic-states-plot-to-build-a-radioactive-dirty-bomb (accessed May 3, 2019).

8 Russia and the two Koreas
Archana Upadhyay

Introduction

Geographically, economically, politically, and strategically, the Korean Peninsula has always been of vital importance to Russia. Throughout the 20th century, under successive regimes, Korea had been the focus of Russia's attention and foreign policy initiatives. In the aftermath of the collapse of the Soviet Union in December 1991, the Russian Federation emerged as the legal successor of the Soviet Union in North-East Asia and one of the major foreign policy challenges for Russia was to deal with the vexed legacy of the Cold War period on the Korean Peninsula. Resetting ties with the two Koreas in the fast changing global strategic environment, thus, became a key foreign policy objective for New Russia.

The history of Russia's engagement with the Korean Peninsula is fairly long. Therefore, in recognition of this historical reality, in 2004, Russia and both the Koreas celebrated two prominent anniversaries: the 140th anniversary of the beginning of Korean resettlement in Russia and the 120th anniversary of the establishment of bilateral relations between the Russian empire and Korea under the Chosun dynasty. However, despite the historical linkages, Russia's relationship with the Peninsula has largely been complex and often marred with uncertainties. The base line of Russia's modern Korean policy is the perception that both the Democratic People's Republic of Korea (DPRK) and the Republic of Korea (ROK) are independent states and ought to be treated as such. This new approach towards the Peninsula coincided with the advent of Mikhail Gorbachev in 1985 and his declaration to reconstruct Soviet foreign policy through his "new thinking" in foreign policy that called for the transformation of international relations from confrontation to cooperation.[1] A realistic assessment of Soviet policy towards Korea thus began to take shape.

The recognition that developments in the Korean Peninsula were proving to be a major obstacle to superpower cooperation in the region, and beyond, played no small role in the renewed assessment of the Korean situation. In the changed scenario, South Korea came to be viewed as a potential economic partner capable of making significant contribution to the economic development of Russia, particularly of the Russian Far East.[2] This changed perception of the ROK was a marked departure from the prevailing Soviet view of South Korea being nothing but a "satellite" of the United States. It was also recognised that South Korea could have its own independent foreign policy interests that may not necessarily always correspond to the interests of the United States. Thus, on the eve of the disintegration of the Soviet Union, South Korea came to be viewed as a potential donor and a business partner. On the other hand, North Korea, though a "socialist partner", was seen more as an obstacle in pursuit of the goals of the "new thinking" so passionately espoused by Gorbachev.

It is against the background of the far-reaching historical changes, initiated during the Gorbachev years and carried forward by the leadership of post-Soviet Russia, that the resetting of Russia's relationship with the two Koreas started taking concrete shape. This chapter attempts at understanding the "Korea factor" in the overall foreign policy strategy of the Russian Federation. Russia's position on some of the key issues dominating the strategic landscape of the Korean Peninsula has also been discussed and evaluated.

Korea in Russia's foreign policy strategy

Gorbachev's legacy continued to inspire the foreign policy strategy of New Russia, and in the summer of 1992, the Russian Foreign Ministry openly advocated seeking a balanced policy towards the Korean Peninsula, clearly implying two sets of independent relations. The key drivers for this changed approach were primarily security and economic considerations.[3] With the advent of Vladimir Putin in 2000, the changed approach got further reinforced through a number of policy documents confirming the pursuit of a strategy of open, multidirectional, and balanced relations in regard to the two Koreas.[4] It is noteworthy that these changes did not happen in a vacuum, but were the consequence of far reaching developments that took place inside Russia and in its immediate and extended neighbourhood including the Korean Peninsula.[5] The driving force of this new foreign policy approach was the belief that Russia's geopolitical position, as the largest Eurasian power, imposed on it the responsibility of guaranteeing both global and regional security. This clearly presupposed the pursuit of complimentary foreign policy objectives in bilateral and multilateral arrangements with the primary goal of securing a prominent role for Russia in an increasingly multipolar world.[6] Towards this end, the Asia-Pacific region has been identified as a very important region where Russia aims at achieving *three critical* objectives: securing the country's eastern borders, maximising the potential for economic cooperation with the Asia-Pacific countries, and enhancing the living standards of Russia's eastern communities in its Far Eastern region. As Russia's domestic and external interests are intertwined in North-East Asia, it becomes imperative for Russia to engage with other prominent actors in the region and also strive for a settlement on the Korean Peninsula through the cooperative endeavour of all stakeholders.[7]

Russian foreign policy on the Korean Peninsula has been primarily driven by a combination of security and economic concerns, with the following as key goals: (1) reducing tensions and ease military confrontations between the ROK and the DPRK, (2) preventing the spread of Weapons of Mass Destruction (WMD) on the Peninsula, (3) preventing ecological and humanitarian disaster on Russian soil in the eventuality of a military confrontation, (4) activating the Korean factor in favour of Russia's economic development, (5) restoring Russian influence on the Peninsula and strengthening its position in North-East Asia as a whole, and (6) ensuring the security of Russia's Far East regions.[8] These objectives necessitated urgent steps to contain the drift in the Russia-North Korean relations, which had become evident in the aftermath of the collapse of the Soviet Union. The pro-West thrust of Russian foreign policy during the Yeltsin years had severely impacted and derailed Russia's traditional ties with North Korea.[9]

Simultaneously, it also meant forging greater engagement with the ROK. Through a number of high-profile visits, the prospects of regional economic cooperation between the two countries were explored. Russia hoped that its ties with Seoul would speed up the economic revival of its entire Far Eastern region, and, in return, the ROK hoped to find inlets to the rest of Russia as well as the Central Asian States. Russia also hoped to become a reliable intermediary between the two Koreas and, towards this end, advocated trilateral cooperation combining Russian technologies, North Korean workers, and South Korean investments. The restoration of the inter-Korean railway and its link with the Trans-Siberian Railroad (TSR) found great traction as an alternative transportation route that would tremendously cut down on cost and time while shipping goods from the region to Europe.

Russia's "Turn to the East" policy and the two Koreas

Russia's "Turn to the East" policy is broadly understood as a foreign policy strategy aimed at focussing on the Asia-Pacific trajectory of its external policy for expanding its economic and political influence in the Asia-Pacific region.[10] This policy, significantly, exhibits a great deal of compatibility with the "New Northern Policy" of the current Moon Jae-in administration[11] that seeks to create a stable and peaceful Korean Peninsula by addressing the issues of economic connectivity in the region. What is particularly noteworthy of both foreign policy initiatives is the acknowledgement of the importance of the North Korean participation for the success of any such endeavours. Broadly, both these policy pronouncements have two overarching goals: the first is to promote economic cooperation in a variety of relevant fields among the countries of the region, and the second is to mitigate military tensions on the Korean Peninsula.[12] What is particularly noteworthy is the fact that both Russia and the ROK are united in their understanding of the idea of the "promotion of the security by means of development".[13] This idea is very much in conformity with the accepted narrative in international relations that propounds the political and security benefits of economic integration programmes.[14]

From the Russian perspective, a stable Korean Peninsula is key to Russia's security interests in the Asia-Pacific region. Hence, Russia's key security goal in the Peninsula is the prevention of any direct military confrontation between the two Koreas or any other kind of military conflict resulting from the intervention of a third party or on account of overconcentration of armed forces on the Peninsula. Such a prospect has serious potential to destabilise the security of Russia's Far East by triggering an arms race in the region.[15] Russia also believes that given its status as a great power and a permanent member of the United National Security Council (UNSC), it has a role to play in the developments on the Peninsula. This is imperative for Russia's own developmental needs, particularly in regard to the development of its neglected Far Eastern region.[16] It is noteworthy that in the 2008 strategy for economic development, titled *On the Concept of the Long-Term Socio-Economic Development of the Russian Federation in the Period up to 2020*, South Korea has been identified as a potential partner assisting Russia in boosting the economic development of its Far East.[17] It is against this broad strategic context that the idea of "nine bridges" of cooperation between Russia and the ROK, as enunciated in the "New Northern Policy" of the Moon administration, assumes significance. The "nine bridges" entail cooperation in sectors such as agriculture, fisheries, natural gas, rail transportation, and ship building, and the establishment of the Northern Sea Route.[18]

One of the most critical areas of cooperation between Russia and the ROK is the energy sector. This becomes particularly significant in the context of the symbiotic attraction between the energy-rich Russia and the energy-hungry South Korea. Having continuous access to energy sources, particularly gas, is crucial for South Korea's sustained economic development. The oil and natural gas sectors have been the driving force behind Russia's economic growth in recent years, and one of the principle challenges for Russia has been to enhance its export revenues through the expansion of its oil and natural gas exports.[19] Most of Russia's oil and gas resources are ideally located to serve the Pacific Rim markets. It is estimated that out of the total energy resources in North-East Asia, close to 84 per cent of hydrocarbons and 62 per cent of solid fuel are concentrated in the Far Eastern part of Russia.[20] The vast oil and gas reserves, coupled with the growing energy demands of countries across the border, namely China, Japan, and South Korea, offer immense possibilities for forging enduring energy security partnerships between Russia and these countries.[21] Given the instability in the Middle East, Russia offers a cost-effective alternative energy supply source to the countries in the region.[22] However, lack of pipeline infrastructure and a true ice-free port in the Russian Far East has proved to be a major bottleneck in the exploration and the marketing of these resources. Improved rail infrastructure and expansion of pipeline network to deliver low-cost oil from East Siberia and Sakhalin Island to South Korean and Japanese markets offer immense trade potential. Creation of an "energy and natural gas resource belt" extending across the Korean Peninsula's East Sea coastline into Russia is an important component of the ROK's "New Northern Policy".[23] Apparently, in the larger scheme of things, Russia is uniquely positioned to act as a bridge between the Korean Peninsula and other Asian markets.

The "North Korean Factor" in Russia's outreach to the Korean Peninsula

There is increasing recognition both in Russia and in the ROK that the success of Russia's "turn to the East" policy and the ROK's "New Northern Policy" is heavily dependent on the DPRK.[24] Given the absence of direct geographic connection between Russia and the ROK, the centrality of North Korea for the fructification of any Korea-centric outreach clearly stands out. Russians have been candid enough to acknowledge that "the road to Seoul lies through Pyongyang".[25] This is very significant in two senses: Figuratively, this implies that for effective engagement with the ROK, Russia must be seen to be an influential player in the Peninsula, capable of placing constructive pressure on North Korea. Improved ties with Russia, it is expected, would make the DPRK somewhat flexible in its dealings with the ROK and also with the outside world. In the literal sense, it is a given that any overland rail, road, or pipeline connectivity with the South would have to go through North Korean territory. Such connectivity would connect not only Russia to South Korea but also South Korea to Europe through Russia. The prospects of a rail line connecting the TSR to South Korean markets offer an attractive alternative to maritime shipping through the circuitous Indian Ocean shipping lanes. This overland route will not only offer freedom from the constant threat of sea piracy but will also be two to three times shorter than the maritime route. The ice-free North Korean port of Najin offers opportunities to Russia for year-round trade with Japan and South Korea; hence, it figures prominently in the larger scheme of cooperative partnership between Russia and the two Koreas.[26]

It is significant that in 2000, Russia and the DPRK replaced the Soviet-era 1961 treaty with the conclusion of a new treaty of Friendship and Cooperation. This new treaty provides the basis for normal state-to-state ties between the Russian Federation and North Korea. The signing of this treaty was followed by an official visit by President Putin in July 2000 to the DPRK – the first-ever visit by a Russian or Soviet leader to North Korea. This visit inaugurated a new chapter in Russia-DPRK ties, with both sides agreeing to promote exchanges in commercial, economic, scientific, and technological fields. Russia also declared its interest to become a principal mediator between both Koreas and enthusiastically championed three-way economic projects, especially the modernisation and utilisation of the inter-Korean railway connecting it with the Russian Far East and the TSR.[27] Moreover, Putin's landmark visit served the purpose of sending an unambiguous message about Russia's intention to seek its own area of influence in North-East Asia by influencing the trajectory of political and military events in the Peninsula while simultaneously engaging with other powers in the economic sphere. A return visit by Kim Il-sung to Russia in August 2001 further solidified and improved the bilateral ties. These high-profile visits, it was hoped, would ensure a role for Russia in influencing the North Korean national security policies, including its nuclear policy.[28] More recently, North Korea declared 2015 as the "Year of Friendship" with the Russian Federation. The year saw the creation of the North Korea-Russia Business Council through the sustained efforts of the Ministry of Far Eastern Development.[29]

Despite the clear convergence of interests between Russia and South Korea at a variety of levels, their shared vision of promoting peace through commerce is not without challenges given the unpredictable security dynamics in the Korean Peninsula. However, both Russia and South Korea have reached out to the DPRK and have mooted the idea of trilateral economic cooperation in several sectors. This, it is hoped, would create the material conditions for the easing of tensions on the Peninsula.

The "Korean question" and Russia's approach

The Korean Peninsula is one of the few theatres in Asia where the world's major powers are directly involved. Russia has well-entrenched interests in North East Asia, and over the past two decades, Russia's policy has been to enhance its presence and role in the Peninsula, more so after a period of dwindling leverage in the 1990s. With the "turn to the East" policy taking centre stage in Russia's foreign policy strategy, the "Korean question" has acquired renewed significance. The key questions are: what are Russia's core interests in the Korean Peninsula? What is Russia's position on some of the key issues dominating the strategic landscape of the Korean Peninsula, notably the Korean security crisis, originating primarily out of the nuclear and missile programme of the DRPK? What is Russia's position on the unification of the two Koreas? What kind of future does Russia envisage for the DRPK?

Russia's core interests in the Korean Peninsula are primarily rooted in the prevention of any large-scale conflict or militarisation of the region that may result in any kind of shift in the geopolitical balance in Asia. The presence of the US "strategic assets" in the region is also a cause of concern, as it has the potential to trigger an arms race embracing other actors in the neighbourhood. Therefore, Russia believes that any solution to the "Korean question" should be sought within a multi-party diplomatic process, reflective of the interests of all parties concerned.[30] In this regard, it is Russia's considered view that any settlement of the Korean issue should be through the process of mutual concessions and compromise more so on account of the breakdown of the Six-Party Talks.[31] Russia's position on some of the pertinent issues in regard to the "Korean question" – notably *denuclearisation, unification,* and *economic sanctions* – has had a clear bearing on shaping the international discourse around the complexities on the Korean Peninsula.

Denuclearisation

The latest version of the Russian Foreign Policy Concept outlines denuclearisation as one of the key objectives of Russian foreign and diplomatic efforts on the Korean Peninsula. Paragraph 89 of the document states that "Russia has always championed a non-nuclear status for the Korean Peninsula and will support its denuclearisation in every possible way, believing that this objective can be attained through the Six-party Talks".[32] However, Russia believes that the "all options" approach of the United States to curtail the North Korean missile and nuclear programmes will not work, and the only effective way to address the challenge would be through political-diplomatic tools. The US demand for "Complete, Verifiable and Irreversible Denuclearisation (CVID)" as prerequisite for any lasting solution in the Peninsula is unworkable, as it is unlikely that North Korea will be willing to give up its nuclear weapons. Given the fate of Iraq's Saddam Hussein and Libya's Muammar Gaddafi, possession of nuclear weapons offers safeguards to the DRPK against any possible US military intervention.[33] Further, Russia does not view the nuclear issue as being solely North Korea specific but sees it as a "nuclear problem of the Korean Peninsula".[34] This, in other words, would mean the inclusion of the South Korean territory in any deal on the nuclear issue. The denuclearisation of the entire peninsula would mean the irreversible removal of the US nuclear arsenals, bombers, and submarines on the Peninsula. It would also mean the removal of the US nuclear umbrella guarantees for South Korea.

In the absence of an effective military cooperation treaty with Russia, North Korea primarily has to rely on its own forces. The 2000 treaty between Russia and North Korea, which was signed to update the 1961 North Korea-Soviet Treaty of Friendship, Cooperation and Mutual Assistance, has no clause on military cooperation. Though Russia officially continues to oppose the DRPK's nuclear status on the basis of the interpretation of the Treaty on the Non-Proliferation of Nuclear Weapons (NPT), it claims to understand the North Korean motives of holding on to the WMD. Russia also holds the view that the DPRK nuclear programme is not solely about national pride. There are legitimate economic considerations that drive the programme. Given the limited natural resources possessed by North Korea, nuclear energy offers the only accessible and effective energy source for the country.[35]

A stable North Korea, more than a non-nuclear North Korea, is in Russia's interests as it guarantees the stability of its eastern borders. Any attempt at forceful regime change will result in massive troop deployment in the entire region, resulting in unpredictable security consequences. Flow of refugees into the Russian territory is an eventuality that Russia is most concerned about.[36] Nuclear weapons, from the Russian perspective, guarantee the security of the North Korean regime and thereby ensures stability in the region. For Russia, a viable solution to the Korean nuclear crisis, therefore, needs to take into account the greater regional security environment of North-East Asia.

Korean unification

In regard to the Korean unification, Russia is supportive of the idea as long as it is the outcome of a process free of outside interference and results in the creation of a unified peaceful and prosperous Korea. A unified Korea dependent on any foreign power, be it the United States or China, would be counter to Russian interests, and Russia would not favour any such move. Russia believes that any unification according to formulas proposed from outside may result in the creation of a powerful pro-American state on the borders of both Russia and China. Overall, the Russian position towards the unification of Korea remains passive. Preservation of the status quo in the Korean Peninsula for as long as possible suits Russia's interests. Though Russia believes that peaceful unification of the North and the South through gradual rapprochement and cooperation is feasible, it will take a while for a mutually acceptable ideological compromise formula to emerge for a joint Korea to become a reality. It would be in Russia's interest if a unified Korea chooses a policy and status of a neutral state. This would put to rest a number of security apprehensions. In the meantime, a practical approach would be to go beyond the bilateral format of economic engagement and focus on economic ventures that are trilateral in nature. Moscow has already invested in three very big trilateral projects, namely joining railways of the North and the South with the TSR and the building of gas and oil pipelines from Russia to South Korea across the territory of North Korea.

Sanctions

For its nuclear weapons and its ballistic missiles programme, North Korea has drawn international condemnation in the form of UN-sponsored economic and financial sanctions. These sanctions have been in place for more than a decade now, and in addition to the UN sanctions, the United States has also imposed its own unilateral sanctions on North Korea. It is noteworthy that, though the DPRK had ratified the NPT in 1985, it withdrew from it in 2003, citing US aggression as the main reason for pulling out of the treaty. Subsequently, it carried out its first nuclear test in 2006. North Korea's leadership regards the possession of nuclear weapons as the sole guarantee for its survival. The presence of US military bases and joint military exercises of the United States and its allies in its immediate neighbourhood are viewed as acts of extreme provocation and hostility. While the sanctions have severely impacted the North Korean economy, their effectiveness has been undermined due to lack of effective enforcement. Countries and businesses have found ways to circumvent sanctions, particularly the shipping and trading companies, fuel and the mineral resource exporters, and the overseas employers of North Korean nationals.[37]

Though Russia has been an essential partner in the UNSC deliberations to impose sanctions on North Korea over its nuclear and missiles tests, its unofficial policy towards sanctions differs from that of the United States. While for the United States, sanctions are legitimate tools of coercive diplomacy aimed at weakening the political foundations of a "rogue state", Russia believes that sanctions should remain as punitive measures only against specific violations of international law. Complete isolation of a country through economic targeting may not yield the desired result and may lead to further belligerence that may have disastrous consequences. There has been a general resistance by Russia to sanctions against the civilian industries of the DPRK, particularly the oil-related sanctions. Russian companies are known to have re-exported North Korean coal and trans-shipped oil and petroleum products to other countries, and North

Korean guest workers continue to be hired in construction projects in Siberia. At the UN, Russia has successfully worked with China to lessen the impact of the sanctions on North Korea.

The way ahead

The detente on the Korean Peninsula since the late 2017 has provided opportunities for Russia to craft a more elaborate triangular diplomacy with both China and the United States to promote a settlement on the Korean Peninsula in consonance with Russia's own interests in the region. To achieve this goal, it is necessary for Russia to maintain good working relations with the DPRK while seeking cooperation with the other major regional players. While disagreements remain over what ought to be the way forward to resolve the Korean problem, there is a clear view suggesting the adoption of a realistic approach to North Korea, implying a balanced mix of pressure in conjunction with effective diplomatic measures. Russia believes that a peaceful transformation of the DPRK is both desirable and achievable. All it calls for is an active engagement policy aimed at modifying the country's economic system through the introduction of market levers that would create spaces for autonomous economic decision-making. A gradual liberalisation of the state ideology within the unifying framework of nationalism would be the next logical step.[38]

Though the two high-profile summits between the US president Donald J. Trump and the North Korean leader Kim Jong-un in Singapore (June 2018) and Hanoi (February 2019) did not result in any tangible outcomes, yet they are indicative of a forward moment. So was the first-ever summit meeting between Putin and Kim in April 2019. For Russia, the summit provided an opportunity to emphasise upon its relevance in the resolution of the "Korean question". The importance of denuclearisation on the Korean Peninsula was reiterated, and Putin lent his support to North Korea's advocacy of a phased process of denuclearisation along with confidence-building measures with the United States. Russia believes that the sanctions cannot be an end in itself, and the collapse of the North Korean regime on account of internal contradictions does not seem likely any time soon. Hence, a multidimensional policy approach towards the "Korean question" in cooperation with China, the two Koreas, and the United States is the only way forward. A solution reflective of the interests of all the parties within a multiparty diplomatic process can prove to be meaningful and enduring.

Conclusion

In sum, economic interests and geographic proximity have combined to make the Korean Peninsula a crucial geopolitical, geo-economic, and geostrategic region for policymakers in Russia, and has thus largely shaped the contours of Russia's engagement with the two Koreas. So has the contemporary global strategic climate and Russia's desire to remain a relevant stakeholder in the region. The economic development of its Far East region; improving ties with South Korea; reinvigorating its old ties with North Korea, with an eye on playing a role in the geopolitical developments in the region; and getting a foothold into regional organisations that span across both North-East and South-East Asia have been Russia's clear foreign policy goals in regard to the Korean Peninsula. Russia is banking on its geographical location, UNSC membership, nuclear status, military prowess, and diplomatic experience to remain a relevant player in the region. Maintenance of the legitimacy of the non-proliferation regime is also Russia's policy goal and is clearly the cornerstone of its strategic position on nuclear issues. Its possible collapse, including the appearance of new nuclear states and actors, will be a severe blow to Russia's own political power, and therefore, Russia will never recognise the DPRK as a nuclear state. For Russia, the stability in the neighbourhood is of higher priority than the denuclearisation of the Korean Peninsula; therefore, it is keen to engage with all stakeholders on this vexed issue. Reduction of tensions and easing of sanctions would expand economic cooperation in East Asia, which clearly is in consonance with Russia's long-term interests in North-East Asia. Reeling under the impact of the anti-Russian economic sanctions, post the Ukrainian crisis in 2014, Russia seeks active political and economic engagement in North-East Asia. Russia's objective of emerging as an acknowledged major power in the Asia-Pacific region is entirely dependent on its ability to remain a full participant in the Korean peace process. The two Koreas are, thus, central to Russia's own stability and also its North-East Asia outreach.

Notes

1 The "New Political Thinking" was the doctrine put forth by the Soviet leader Mikhail Gorbachev in 1986 as a part of his reforms for the Soviet Union. Its key component was the de-ideologisation of international politics and the creation of system of mutual security based on the principle of interdependence of the world. It marked a major shift in the principles of Soviet foreign policy.
2 The development and modernisation of Siberia and the Far East are the key components of Russia's Asia-Pacific policy. The objective is to develop the local economy, diversify its exports from Europe to Asia, and utilise the potential of the region to enter into the Asia-Pacific market. The vast resources of the region – oil and natural gas, gold, diamond, copper, iron ore, and timber – have largely remained untapped due to lack of adequate investments. China, Japan, and South Korea have been identified as crucial partners.
3 Vasily V. Mikheev, "Russian Policy towards North Korea", *New Asia*, 7 (4), 2000, pp. 137–140.
4 "Foreign Policy Concept of the Russian Federation", June 12, 2000, pp. 4–16, at www.russianmission.eu/userfiles/file/foreign_policy_cocept_english.pdf (accessed July 20, 2019).
5 Inside Russia – the Chechen War and the rising tide of nationalism, in Russia's near aboard – North Atlantic Treaty Organisation (NATO) and European Union (EU) expansion plans and the creation of a national missile defence system, and on the Korean Peninsula – the idea of four-party talks on Korea (the two Koreas, the United States, and China) with the exclusion of Russia.
6 Evgeny Bazhanov, *Russia's Priorities in the Changing World*, Nauchnaia Kniga, Moscow, 2000, pp. 16–20.

7 Igor Ivanov, *Novaia Rossiiskaia diplomatiia* [New Russian Diplomacy], Olma-Press, Moscow, 2002, pp. 158–159.
8 Alexander Vorontsov, "Current Russia-North Korea Relations: Challenges and Achievements", Centre for Northeast Asian Policy Studies, Brookings Institution, 2007, at www.brookings.edu/fp/cnaps/papers/vorontsov2007.pdf.22 (accessed August 2, 2019).
9 In the early years of the post-Soviet period, Russia's foreign policy was largely influenced by pro-Western idealists, supporting the idea of market, self-determination, and integration with the Western capitalist system. Post-independence in 1991, the first Russian president Boris Yeltsin and his foreign minister Andrei Kozyrev maintained a strongly pro-American foreign policy stance. This phase continued till the dismissal of Kozyrev in 1996.
10 S. Fortescue, "Russia's Economic Prospects in the Asia Pacific Region", *Journal of Eurasian Studies*, 7 (1), 2016, pp. 49–59.
11 The "New Northern Policy" was unveiled by South Korean president Moon Jae-in the third Eastern Economic Forum in September 2017 in Vladivostok, Russia. It is a foreign policy strategy aimed at creating sustainable peace in the Korean Peninsula by improving South Korea's long-term economic prospects. The policy seeks to connect South Korea to the rest of Eurasia through the creation of western and eastern corridors running through North Korea into China and Russia.
12 Anthony V. Rinna, "Moscow's "Turn to the East" and Challenges to Russia-South Korea Economic Collaboration Under the New Northern Policy", *Journal of Eurasian Studies*, 10 (2), 2019, pp. 159–168.
13 V. Kozyrev, "Russia's New Global Vision and Security Policy in East Asia", in T. Akaha and A. Vassilieva (eds.), *Russia and East Asia*, Routledge, New York, 2014, pp. 41–65.
14 J. Lee and J.H. Pyun, "Does Trade Integration Contribute to Peace? *Review of Development Economics*, 20 (1), 2016, pp. 327–344.
15 Yong-Chool Ha and Beom-Shik Shin, *Russian Nonproliferation Policy and the Korean Peninsula*, Strategic Studies Institute, U.S. Army War College, Carlisle, 2006, p. 14.
16 Through a series of policy pronouncements and legislative initiatives, under the presidencies of Medvedev (2008–2012) and Putin (2000–2008, 2012–present), attempts have been made to make the Russian Far East the centre of large-scale development. In 2012, the Ministry of Far Eastern Development was created specifically for the development of Russia's Far Eastern region as well as facilitating cooperation with external partners.
17 Anthony V. Rinna, No. 12.
18 Office of the President of Russia, 2017, at http://en.kremlin.ru/events/president/news/page/84 (accessed July 22, 2019).
19 In 2007, Russia had the distinction of being the world's largest exporter of natural gas and the second largest exporter of oil. In recent times, claims have been made that it has surpassed Saudi Arabia in volume of oil exports, making it the largest producer of "Black Gold" in the world.
20 M. Potapov, "Energy Inter-Dependence in East Asia: Russia's Contribution to Energy/Gas Cooperation in East Asia", in Gennady Chufrin and Mark Hong (eds.), *Russia-ASEAN Relations – New Directions*, ISEAS Publishing, Singapore, 2007.
21 Estimates suggest that about two-thirds of the total natural gas supply of the world goes to North-East Asia, and by 2030, the region will account for 23 per cent of global demand. Steady economic growth, rising standards of living, and increasing urbanisation are all together expected to contribute to this demand. See Potapov 2007.
22 Currently, China, Japan, and Korea import 50, 70, and 80 per cent, respectively, of their oil requirements from the Middle East.
23 T. Kang, *The Eurasian Era and the New Northern Policy's Vision – China and Russia's Tasks for the Future of North-South Cooperation*, Hankyoreh Peace Research Institute, Seoul, 2018.

24 The strategic significance of North Korea for Russia is immense. Not only does Russia share a 12-mile border with the DPRK, but it is only through the territory of North Korea that Russia can have any kind of overland connectivity with South Korea, currently the 15th largest economy in the world.
25 Alexander Vorontsov, No. 8.
26 John W. Bauer, "Unlocking Russian Interests on the Korean Peninsula", *Parameters*, 39 (2), 2009, pp. 55–57, at https://ssi.armywarcollege.edu/pubs/parameters/Articles/09summer/bauer.pdf (accessed July1, 2019).
27 *Diplomaticheskii Vestnik*, 2000, pp. 62–63.
28 Yury Fokine and Evgen Bazhanov (eds.), *4ii Rossisko-koreiskie forum* [The Fourth Russian-Korean Forum], Nauchnya Kniga, Moscow, 2002, pp. 15–19.
29 Troyakova, T. (2016). Rol' rossiyskogo Dal'nego Vostoka v razvitii otnosheniy s KNDR [The role of the Russian Far East in developing relations with the DPRK]. Izvestiya Vostochnogo instituta [Eastern Institute Herald], 31, 2016, pp. 45–54.
30 Georgy Toloraya, "Korea: A Bone of Contention or a Chance for Cooperation? A View from Russia", *The Asian Forum: Special Forum*, February 19, 2019, at www.theasanforum.org/koreaa-bone-of-contention-or-a-chance-for-cooperation-a-view-from-russia/ (accessed August 5, 2019).
31 After North Korea's withdrawal from the NPT and its admission to having a clandestine nuclear programme, the Six-Party Talks were initiated in 2003 to restart negotiations in order to find a solution to the North Korean nuclear crisis. The six members included the United States, China, Russia, Japan, North Korea, and South Korea. The process was held intermittently, achieved a breakthrough in 2005, and in 2009 and 2013, the negotiations broke down over the DRPK's missile and nuclear tests, leading to harsh UN sanctions.
32 "Foreign Policy Concept of the Russian Federation", Ministry of Foreign Affairs of the Russian Federation, November 30, 2016, at www.mid.ru/en/foreign_policy/news/-/asset_publisher/cKNonkJE02Bw/content/id/2542248 (accessed July 25, 2019).
33 Alexander Gabuev, "Bad Cop, Mediator or Spoiler: Russia's Role on the Korean Peninsula", Carnegie Moscow Centre, April 24, 2019, at https://carnegie.ru/commentary/78976 (accessed June 25, 2019).
34 Georgy Toloraya, No. 30.
35 Alexander Vorontsov, No. 8.
36 Anastasia Barannikova, "What Russia Thinks About North Korea's Nuclear Weapons", *Bulletin of the Atomic Scientists*, April 24, 2019, at https://thebulletin.org/2019/04/what-russia-thinks-about-north-koreas-nuclear-weapons/ (accessed July 28, 2019).
37 Artyom Lukin and Lyudmila Zakharova, "Russia-North Korea Economic Ties: Is There More than Meets the Eye?" Report by the Foreign Policy Research Institute, 2017, pp. 1–16.
38 Alexander Vorontsov, No. 8, pp. 19–20.

9 Mongolia and the North-East Asian peace process

Alicia Campi

Introduction

One of the more important facilitators for talks concerning the peace process on the Korean Peninsula has been the country of Mongolia. For some observers, this has come as a surprise because Mongolia was never involved in the Six-Party Talks.[1] However, Mongolia has been active in promoting denuclearisation and peace building throughout the North-East Asian region for several decades and has sought participation in multilateral forums discussing Korean Peninsular issues. It has a record of acting as a non-judgmental active facilitator between the Democratic People's Republic of Korea (DPRK, aka North Korea) and other nations hostile to the Kim regime, such as Japan, South Korea, and the United States. Today, its diplomatic role has been recognised by the world community as constructive and perhaps even essential, if the roadblocks to progress are to be overcome.

Mongolia's Ministry of Foreign Affairs states that the goal of its Asian activism is "to strengthen its position in the Asian region, to intensify bilateral relationships with other regional countries, to engage to a dialogue on political, security and economic cooperation of the region and to participate in the regional integration processes."[2] It particularly seeks greater political and economic connections with North Korea, which emanates from the belief that both nations share the geo-spatial problem of being isolated from the greater Asian region that comes from their dependence on China and Russia, their two bordering superpower neighbours. Landlocked Mongolia's efforts to diversify its economy are linked to serving as a diplomatic bridge to North Korea, so that the two countries can become an alternative transit route to the Pacific. Mongolian foreign policy expert Migeddorj Batchimeg predicted, as early as the mid-2000s, that Mongolia would be increasingly interdependent on both governments on the Korean Peninsula, because of economic cooperation and cultural affinity.[3] This would strengthen its overall position in Asia, enhance its international reputation as a mediator nation, and secure its place in future regional political and economic integration while leveraging its "small nation" status in regional politics. At a 2014 forum examining "Mongolia's Diplomacy with the Two Koreas," former US ambassador to Mongolia Mark C. Minton observed that both nations have a very strong interest in having as much strategic leverage and breathing room as they can possibly design .... They want to have other partners. They want some traction in regional affairs and in global affairs that allows them to escape the rather vice-like dynamic of just existing and having diplomatic space between two powerful neighbors.[4]

For Pyongyang, strengthening ties with a non-nuclear Mongolia could bring in a measured economic modernisation and the benefit of Mongolia's experience in attracting donor assistance and foreign investment. Meanwhile, Seoul has come around to realising that Mongolia's multifaceted ties with the DPRK, which stem from its present non-threatening status and communist-era commonalities, can be useful in ways that direct Korea-to-Korea negotiations cannot.

Historical contacts between Mongolia and the DPRK

Mongolia became a satellite of the Soviet Union in 1924 but always retained its independence as a nation. After World War II, it became the second country to recognise the DPRK led by founder Kim Il-sung on October 15, 1948. While it did not commit soldiers in the Korean War, it provided food aid to the North (226,000 head of horses, cattle, sheep, goats; 5,000 tons of wheat; 120,000 pieces of clothing and shoes; 7,300 tons of meat; and other foodstuffs).[5] The Mongolian government provided refuge and education until 1959 for about 200 children of high-ranking DPRK leaders. After the armistice in 1953, Mongolia sent reconstruction assistance in the form of 10,000 horse "volunteers".[6] During the Cold War era, North Korea exported chemical products, window glass, rice, toothpaste, and knitwares to Mongolia, while it imported Mongolian leather and various animal by-products. Larger joint venture projects in synthetic fibres, coal mining, and iron manufacturing were discussed but never implemented.

Summit visits have been a significant part of the relationship. Kim Il-sung visited Mongolia in 1956 and 1988. Mongolian Premier Yumjaa Tsedenbal visited Pyongyang in 1956. In 1988, the two countries signed a legal assistance agreement for the development of civil society and a criminal justice legal framework. In 1998, a Mongolian-DPRK Interparliamentary Group was established, and the Speakers of both nations exchanged visits. However, with Mongolia's embrace of democracy in 1990, relations became increasingly strained and led to the closing of the DPRK embassy in 1999, following the state visit of South Korean president Kim Dae-jung to the Mongolian capital of Ulaanbaatar. Mongolian Prime Minister Nambar Enkhbayar reinvigorated the relationship by the signing of a Friendship Treaty in 2002 and making an official visit to the DPRK in December 2003. This led to the reopening of the North Korean embassy in August 2004. Mongolian President Natsag Bagabandi made a summit visit to Pyongyang in December 2005 and met with the DPRK leader Kim Jong-il, father of Kim Jong-un. Mongolian researchers say the purpose of Bagabandi's visit was to revitalise economic and political relations, but it is noteworthy that it took place just after the breakdown of the fifth round of the Six-Party Talks (November 9–11, 2005).

After the 2005 Enkhbayar summit, trade turnover did not increase but actually fell to only $40,000 annually because the Mongol side claimed there was little to buy.[7] There was greater cooperation in the agricultural sphere, as evidenced by Mongolian livestock experts working to develop massive stockbreeding grass zones by reclaiming the Sepho tableland in the DPRK's Kangwon province.[8] The North Koreans indicated they would welcome Mongolian investment and the opening of a Mongolian trade centre. They offered to let the Mongols utilise the deep-water port of Rajin-Songbon to provide sea access for Mongolian products, but the major obstacle to bilateral trade was regional rail interconnectivity.

After several years of little high-level contact, Presidential National Security and Foreign Policy Adviser Lundeg Purevsuren went to the DPRK in July 2013 to organise the state visit of Mongolian President Tsakia Elbegdorj to Pyongyang. Elbegdorj, a leader of Mongolia's democratic revolution and friendly towards the United States, sought to deepen connections with the DPRK regime through greater cooperation in trade, IT, and people-to-people exchanges. His four-day state visit in October 2013 particularly emphasised the long relationship between the two governments and celebrated the 65th anniversary of bilateral diplomatic relations and the 25th anniversary of DPRK founder Kim Il-sung's Ulaanbaatar visit. The Mongol leader pronounced that "Our two countries are good friends who didn't forsake each other in the times of need and desperation."[9] It was expected that he would be the first foreign head of state to meet Kim Jong-un, and the trip was promoted as symbolic of Mongolia as a "New Helsinki". In the end, the summit with Kim failed to materialise, but an undeterred Elbegdorj optimistically asserted that "Mongolia will cooperate with every country, including the Democratic People's Republic of Korea, for peace and stability in Northeast Asia."[10] He was the first head of state to visit the Panmunjom Demilitarised Zone and the first foreign leader to deliver a lecture at Kim Il Sung University, in which he controversially lauded the benefits of democracy.[11] Elbegdorj also addressed a Mongolia-DPRK business meeting and promised to expand bilateral economic ties: "We do see ample opportunities of cooperation in railways, air and auto-transport and sea-ports. ... Mongolia is interested in importing [a] highly qualified and organized workforce."[12] Not long after the President's trip, a memorandum of understanding (MOU) to set up a DPRK friendship joint company was signed,[13] while another MOU dealing with North Korean workers was agreed to by the DPRK's Ministry of Foreign Trade and Mongolia's Ministry of Labour.

Elbegdorj was interested in improving rail connectivity with partners such as North Korea and Russia to find trade alternatives to China. Progress was made in 2013 with the building of a Russian-gauge spur of the Trans-Siberian Railway from the Russian city of Khasan to the port of Rajin aka Nanjin in the Rason Special Economic Zone (RSEZ) (see Map 9.1). Mongolian exports to the zone, like the Russian ones, would pass through the Tumangang border rail facility[14] to eventually be shipped out of the port or via rail to the South Korean ports of Pohang and Busan. When Mongolia, in early 2015, tested moving 20,000 tons of

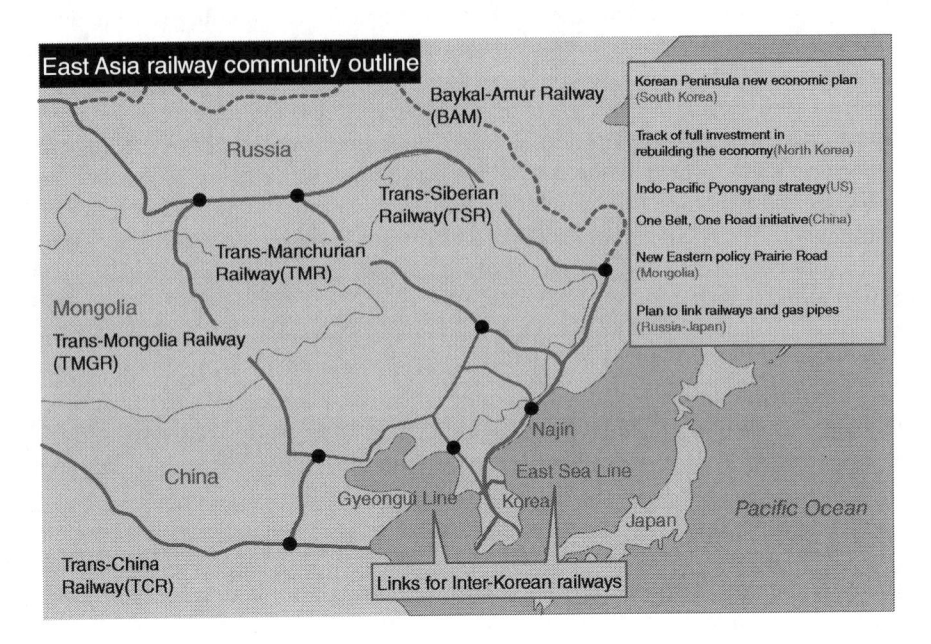

Map 9.1 East Asia Railway Community Initiative among China, Mongolia and Russia.
Source: http://english.hani.co.kr/arti/english_edition/e_northkorea/857919.html.

coal from its Sharyn Gol deposit to Rajin for delivery to South Korea,[15] Tugsuu Batbold, chairman of the Mongolian Railway Authority, said, "There are no technical problems with delivering coal to North Korea, and we are seeking ways to deliver coal through the trans-Siberian railway to Rajin."[16] He indicated that Mongolia was investigating how to deliver other metals, such as copper and gold, via this rail spur.

In June 2013, the Mongolian company HBOil JSC bought a 20 per cent share, valued at $10 million, in the state-owned DPRK company Korea Oil Exploration Corporation (KOEC) that operates the Sungri oil refinery in the RSEZ and is connected with the Russian railways system.[17] The deal was justified as a way for Mongolia, which has plentiful oil reserves but no oil refining capacity, to find a new source to refine its own crude oil for domestic use and reduce its dependence on Russia for petrol and diesel imports.[18] However, in January 2017, HBOil JSC withdrew from its joint venture in the DPRK because of the inclusion of KOEC on the international sanction list.[19] Despite the additional sanctions imposed by the world community on North Korea since early 2016, Mongolia has continued to move forward with trade cooperation. According to data released by Korea Trade-Investment Promotion Agency (KOTRA), bilateral trade since 2016 has increased by 43 per cent to reach $2.29 million, mainly due to Mongolian exports worth $1.92 million, which were up 55 per cent from 2016. During the same period, DPRK imports increased by 2.1 per cent to $370,000. Mongolian tobacco exports accounted for 92.2 per cent of this total.[20]

For over a decade, the DPRK sent thousands of construction and textile workers to Mongolia. Their salaries were paid in foreign currency to the DPRK government. The Mongols planned to use them to replace Chinese workers on mining and transport infrastructure projects,[21] but the pressure of international sanctions finally saw the end of this labour exchange in early 2018. Mongolia revealed that there were 20 North Korean joint ventures, including acupuncture and massage medical clinics, with the DPRK Health Ministry staff on five-year postings.[22] The present status of these enterprises is not clear. The actual numbers of North Korean workers have varied with time and reporting source. The original bilateral governmental agreement allowed up to 5,300 workers annually over five years,[23] although Chinese media reported that the number of North Koreans working in Mongolia had been dropping every year since peaking at 2,123 in 2013.[24] Other sources claimed that Mongolia issued work authorisations for 3,858 in 2015, 2,483 in 2016, and a total of 2,338 in 2017, and that over 1,200 North Koreans still were working until June 1, 2018.[25]

The two nations also have utilised sports, including international boxing matches in Ulaanbaatar, to strengthen relations. In 2013, Mongolia established an International Cooperation Fund which supported children's summer camps, basketball training, and other events with the DPRK to promote people-to-people exchanges. Mongolian humanitarian food aid to the DPRK has been channelled through international organisations, and the two countries have cooperated on physician exchanges. In recent years, there have been academic exchanges, North-East Asian mayoral forums, and women's parliamentary exchanges.

Mongolia, in a low-key manner, publicly has been opposing Pyongyang's nuclear weapons programme and quietly has provided temporary asylum for North Korean defectors coming through China. Starting in 2004, some South Korean civil society and religious groups offered to construct camps in Mongolia to house these refugees, but the Mongols refused permission. Mongolian Prime Minister Miyeegomb Enkhbold on a 2006 trip to China denied that there were plans to establish such refugee camps.[26] Yet, in that year, Stephen Noerper, a Mongolia specialist and head of the Institute of International Education's Scholar Relief Fund, estimated that 500 North Korean defectors were entering Mongolia each month.[27] Mongolia finally began to turn them away in June 2007, reportedly in response to North Korean pressure and a new South Korean policy to not welcome refugees coming via Mongolia and South-East Asia. There were media reports that South Korean president Lee Myung-bak supported the opening of Mongolian camps, but his successor Park Geun-hye did not endorse this policy. During the Elbegdorj era (2009–2017), the issue of North Korean refugees was downplayed overtly, although it was known that some of those who reached Mongolia were repatriated to South Korea.

Mongolian mediation initiatives for peace on the Korean Peninsula

During the 70 years of communism and in the first decades of its democratic era, Mongolia pursued a passive foreign economic policy that allowed its two neighbours, China and Russia, and the developed North-East Asian economies of Japan and South Korea in alliance with the remaining superpower, the United States, to dominate affairs on the Asian continent. Mongolian policymakers viewed the regional situation as delicate because North-South Korean issues could disrupt regional integration efforts and negatively affect long-term stability, while unresolved historical and territorial disputes among the nations continually roiled the region: "As an integral part of Northeast Asia, Mongolia prioritizes these regional concerns. It remains one of our top foreign policy objectives to not only develop and strengthen ties with our neighbors, but also to constructively contribute our share to the common well-being and security of the region."[28]

Mongolian interest in participating in regional security discussions dates back to the early 1980s, when it called for an all-Asian convention prohibiting the use of force to prevent conflicts. In the 1990s, it found that traditional bilateral political alliances with its two border neighbours and new bilateral trade and investment ties with Western and developed "Third Neighbours",[29] such as Japan, South Korea, European Community, and the United States, did not meet its need for diversified trade partners for its rich mineral resources and to break out of its landlocked situation in the eastern part of Eurasia. Disappointed with the results of its "Third Neighbour" strategy after waiting nearly 20 years for other nations to determine its economic development, Mongolia in the 21st century has undertaken a greater role in promoting its own vision of Eurasian regional connectivity. As a result, Mongolia has emerged as a rapidly growing mineral-based economy that increasingly is asserting its own voice in international and regional affairs, including Korean Peninsular security, expansion of northern corridor transit routes, border free trade zones, and nuclear non-proliferation. It has chosen both to work through existing mechanisms, such as United Nations (UN) multilateral organisations, Davos-organised economic summits, and Community of Democracies Governing Council, and, increasingly, to create its own institutional structures. Mongolia's activism in North-East Asia was explained by Mongolian Foreign Minister Luvsanvandan Bold: "What Mongolia can provide is leverage to improve the situation in the region and pursue the initiative for parties to share dialogue. We see a lot of room to be more active."[30]

American North-East Asian specialist Robert Bedeski termed Mongolia's policy towards the DPRK as "engagement" not containment.[31] Tsedendamba Batbayar, head of the foreign ministry's department of policy planning and policy analysis in 2015, stated that at the beginning of the new millennium, Mongolia "began to recognize its strategic potential in close relations with the DPRK."[32] He said that his nation strives to "be an honest broker" on the international scene and hopes that it can "open up new channels for dialogue" with North Korea.[33] This proactive approach first became evident when Mongolia served as a neutral venue for high-level talks on normalising Japan-DPRK relations back in September 2007 as part of the Six-Party Talks' framework. In 2000, it began to explore the idea of joining in the Six-Party Talks despite the lack of any positive feedback from the majority of its participants. In 2008, the Mongolian

Institute for Strategic Studies, which is associated with the Ministry of Defence and Mongolian intelligence agencies, hosted a conference on "Security Perspectives of Central and Northeast Asia: Ulaanbaatar as a New Helsinki," which was the catalyst for President Elbegdorj's Ulaanbaatar Dialogue on Northeast Asia Security (UBD) initiative a year later.

For Japan and the North Koreans, Mongolia has been a non-nuclear peace broker in the region through its productive hosting since November 2012 of DPRK-Japanese negotiations on longstanding abduction issues.[34] Arranging such meetings reflected Ulaanbaatar's contribution to regional stability in North-East Asia so it could play a role in deepening understanding and normalising DPRK-Japan relations. In March 2014, Ulaanbaatar hosted the first-ever reunion between the parents of one of the abductees, Megumi Yokota (who North Korea claims is dead), and her daughter, son-in-law, and child who live in North Korea. President Elbegdorj explained: "Japan, North Korea and other countries can come to discuss this issue on Mongolian soil. We would like to contribute to that. That is our only purpose."[35] Such mediation assistance continues today, as evidenced by the December 2018 visit to Tokyo of Mongolian Prime Minister Ukhnaa Khürelsükh, where this issue was raised by Japanese Prime Minister Shinzo Abe.

Mongolia has been touted as a host nation for DPRK-US summits, with former president Elbegdorj in October 2018 writing on Twitter: "Here is an offer: US President Trump and NK leader Kim meet in (Ulaanbaatar). Mongolia is the most suitable, neutral territory."[36] A week later, the current president Khaltmaa Battulga's chief of staff received DPRK ambassador O Sung Ho in Ulaanbaatar to discuss the proposal. Although Kim-Trump summits ultimately took place in Singapore and Vietnam, the possibility of an Ulaanbaatar summit meeting still is being seriously discussed.

The UBD Initiative

The premier activity initiated by Mongolia is its UBD, which was launched in 2013 with the objectives of defusing tension on the Korean Peninsula, enhancing North-East Asian security through open dialogue, and supporting the early resumption of the Six-Party Talks. The brainchild of President Elbegdorj, this new security dialogue mechanism illustrated Mongolia's larger ambition of acting not only as a third-party mediator in contentious issues based on its assertion of impartiality in any specific conflict, but also as an interested party in overall regional security. This initiative also was connected to the exclusion of Mongolia from the Six-Party Talks, which had broken down in 2008. Elbegdorj believed that the Korean situation and other North-East Asian regional disputes have festered for decades because the region lacks a functioning security dialogue mechanism. Altering this would "bring good influence to the world and especially open a new way of development for Mongolia."[37] Believing that its own interests would be best served when the regional security environment was stable, Mongolia was seeking to resolve disputes through dialogue and discussion. Yet, as a small power, it understood the necessity of not promoting the UBD as a replacement for, or in competition to, the Six-Party Talks but rather as an honest broker and vehicle for scholarly and research discussion to "open up new channels for dialogue" with North Korea.[38]

Mongolian officials had realised that they could not resolve the country's trade and foreign direct investment (FDI) imbalance that was heavily skewed towards China unless there was significant progress on building connectivity through North Korea to the Pacific. Believing that the lack of movement in the Six-Party Talks and Mongolia's continued exclusion from the process could not be overcome by further patience, Elbegdorj's decision to create the UBD was the culmination of years of failed Mongolian back-channel attempts to join the Six-Party dialogue and also an indication of DPRK support for Mongolian participation in regional discussions. There were concerns that Mongolia faced unique challenges in its role as a mediator, and its UBD might not be accepted by China, Russia, and the United States. Charles Krusekopf posited that if "Mongolia plays a more high-profile role with North Korea and multilateral actors, it will most likely be difficult to avoid some drama – posturing, rhetoric, and standoffs – emanating from various parties."[39] He credited Ulaanbaatar's willingness to pursue quiet diplomacy to gain Pyongyang's trust: "The value of Mongolia's role and activities for regional cooperation and peace stems from the fact that Ulaanbaatar does not assume airs or seek to dominate others."[40]

The UBD is organised along Track 1.5 and Track 2 channels, so as not to compete with the Six-Party Talks (Track 1).[41] Under this format, officials and politicians can meet with academics and talk about security issues under the Chatham House Rule.[42] The UBD's announced objective is to contribute to mutual understanding and greater confidence throughout Northeast Asia in order to achieve both "formal and practical security cooperation and consultation."[43] It is co-organised by the Mongolian Ministry of Foreign Affairs and Mongolia's Institute for Strategic Studies (ISS) with a focus on resolving or mitigating challenges to regional stability. The general fields selected for discussion are (1) traditional security issues, (2) non-traditional security issues, (3) energy connectivity, (4) environmental protection, and (5) infrastructural development.

The first UBD on June 17, 2014, included 35 representatives from Mongolia, Russia, China, Japan, DPRK, Republic of Korea (ROK), the United States, Germany, and the Netherlands. Discussion was focussed on North-East Asian security, reasons for the lack of a regional security mechanism, economic and environmental factors promoting regional cooperation, and ways to build trust and regional cooperation.[44] Parliamentarian Migeddorj Batchimeg opened the conference by remarking that Mongolia believed that there was no single formal mechanism for Korean Peninsula discussions and that the UBD could be a useful platform.[45] This first meeting saw a heated discussion on Asian historical disputes instead of on nuclear and militarisation issues on the Korean Peninsula, but the reaction of the Mongolian government was optimistic: the UBD "is not a single action, but a mechanism of trilateral or multilateral dialogues depending on the agenda."[46]

The second UBD conference took place on June 25–26, 2015. Although the number of participants was over 100 and included a representative from India, the North Koreans did not participate. The focus was on energy and transportation connectivity and traditional and non-traditional security trends and opportunities. Mongolian presenters acknowledged that neighbouring countries still questioned

> Mongolia's potential in this regard, so our efforts to play this role in the region must be more proactive. … Going forward, this engagement needs to be upgraded and expanded to continue to promote peace in the region and to impact the future of all countries in Northeast Asia.[47]

The third UBD was held on June 16–17, 2016, and focused on "Environmental Protection and Disaster Management in NEA." The DPRK Foreign Ministry sent a delegation headed by a director and a deputy from the Institute for American Studies. The DPRK representatives freely participated in the discussions.

The North Koreans, led by the foreign minister, participated in the fourth round of UBD, which was held on June 15–16, 2017, and was supported financially by the German Social Democratic Party-affiliated Friedrich Ebert Foundation. Despite the tensions caused by the imposition of new UN sanctions, ISS organiser Damba Ganbat maintained that the meeting was held because "Mongolia is in a unique position to act as an honest broker for peace and security in Northeast Asia, and Ulaanbaatar is the perfect place for a constructive dialogue between otherwise hostile countries."[48] He reminded participants that Mongolia was hosting other meetings at other venues in the hope that such efforts ultimately would lead to a collective architecture of peace and security in North-East Asia, comparable to the Organisation for Security and Cooperation (OSCE) in Europe. The fifth round took place on June 14–15, 2018, in a buoyant atmosphere just three days after the Trump-Kim Singapore summit. More than 150 attendees examined North-East Asian security from the perspectives of environment, energy, and humanitarian assistance.[49]

On June 5–6, 2019, the sixth UBD was held in the shadow of the stalemate in US-DPRK negotiations on nuclear disarmament. As part of the preparations, Mongolian State Secretary Damdinsuren Davaasuren visited North Korea in mid-April to meet officials from the Central Committee of the Workers' Party of Korea (WPK), Chairman of the Supreme People's Assembly Ri Su Yong, and Foreign Minister Ri Yong Ho.[50] The parties exchanged views on regional issues and expansion of bilateral relations and cooperation, DPRK's possible participation in the sixth UBD, and the October 2018 invitation of Mongolian President Battulga to Chairman Kim to make a state visit to Mongolia to celebrate the 70th anniversary of the establishing of diplomatic relations. In these discussions, Mongolia restated its offer to be the site of the next Trump-Kim summit, while firmly reiterating its desire for denuclearisation of the Korean Peninsula. A few days later, Davaasuren went to Washington DC for meetings with US Department of State and military officials, so it was possible that he was carrying a message from Kim to the Trump administration. In the end, the North Koreans did not attend the sixth UBD, but the Mongols still put a positive spin on the situation. Mongolian Foreign Minister Damdin Tsogtbaatar commented that "some changes had to occur at the last moment in the traditional cohort of participating countries, though commitments were pronounced earlier, which is reflective of the seriousness of the current status of the dialogue in the region."[51]

Non-nuclear proliferation efforts

Even though Mongolia has friendly relations with North Korea, this has not prevented it from vocally opposing Pyongyang's nuclear weapons programme. However, it would be a mistake to believe that opposition to nuclear weapons was a new position for Mongolia. During the communist era, it consistently advocated disarmament and non-proliferation of nuclear weapons. Following the end of the Cold War, it desired to keep its territory free of nuclear weapons in order to strengthen its national security. It was believed that re-affirming Mongolia's nuclear-weapon-free status at the highest policy level would link the country's national security to regional security and stability.[52] In 1992, Mongolia declared its territory a nuclear-weapon-free zone and obtained approval for its nuclear-free status from the UN General Assembly on December 4, 1998.[53] In February 2000, the Mongolian Parliament adopted a nuclear-weapon-free status law that included a ban on the manufacturing, stationing, testing, or transporting of nuclear weapons as well as the dumping or disposing of nuclear weapons-grade radioactive material or nuclear waste. The law stated that Mongolia would refrain

> from joining any military alliance or grouping, or allowing the use of its territory against any other State as well as banning the stationing on its territory of foreign troops and weapons, including nuclear and other weapons of mass destruction.[54]

It did permit the use of nuclear energy and technology for peaceful purposes, including in the fields of health care, mining, energy production, and scientific research.

Mongolia's nuclear-weapon-free status was affirmed in 2012 in a joint declaration of the permanent members of the UN Security Council (China, France, Russian Federation, United Kingdom, and United States).[55] In subsequent years, Mongolia sought unsuccessfully to expand its nuclear-weapon-free policy to make North-East Asia a nuclear-weapon-free zone, because of its conviction that such a regional commitment would ensure Mongolia's continuing nuclear-weapon-free status as well as increase the role and responsibilities of non-governmental organisations (NGOs) and other initiatives towards strengthening regional peace.[56] Nonetheless, Mongolia continues to be a broker and a site for a variety of regional security discussions. The Mongolian Ministry of Foreign Affairs and ISS organised a secret Track 1.5 meeting in Ulaanbaatar on May 21, 2014, among North Korean Deputy Foreign Minister Ri Yong Ho; Robert Einhorn, former Obama administration special adviser for non-proliferation and arms control at the State Department; Joel Wit, an ex–State Department official who was a senior fellow of the US-Korea Institute at the Johns Hopkins University School of Advanced International Studies; and Robert Carlin, a former Central Intelligence Agency analyst.[57]

Mongolia also has been very active in the Global Partnership for the Prevention of Armed Conflict (GPPAC)[58] North-East Asia Process. This is a pioneering initiative that is aimed at forging and strengthening cross-border ties between civil society organisations. The North-East network involves annual meetings and improving communication channels with governments that traditionally may not be responsive to civil society initiatives. In June 2015, Mongolia's Blue Banner[59] organisation established the Ulaanbaatar Process under the GPPAC umbrella. This promotes regional dialogue at the Track II level in order to consolidate the role of civil society in the peace-building process on the Korean Peninsula to develop a regional peace and security mechanism for North-East Asia. Mongolia's Ministry of Foreign Affairs and the "Tsenkher Suld" NGO,[60] a nuclear-weapon-free-status supporting group whose president is Punsalmaag Ochirbat, the first democratic-era president of Mongolia, actively support the GPPAC.

To date there have been four GPPAC conferences attended by peace organisations from the DPRK, South Korea, Japan, China, Russia, the United States, and Mongolia. At the fourth conference held in Beijing December 4, 2018, Mongolia was added officially to the six North-East Asian countries as "6+1" in the conference outcome document. Mongolian Major General Dovchin Myagmar remarked:

> As a result of our efforts, the role of Mongolia was recognized at the level of NGOs for peace. The stakeholders will further work to gain recognition of their governments. The participants also agreed that Ulaanbaatar is a convenient place to organize the meeting of leaders of DPRK and the USA.[61]

Conclusion

Diplomatic contacts between Mongolia and North Korea have intensified in recent years, as the North-East Asian peace process has faltered. Although their political systems have diverged since Mongolia's 1990 peaceful democratic revolution, Mongolia promotes the view that its transition could be a perfect model for Pyongyang's own eventual political reform. As ex-US official David Caprara has stated, "While Mongolian mediation may not be able to solve the nuclear issue, it can be an effective channel – among others – for increasing communication, finding common ground, and beginning to ease tension."[62] Mongolia's special role with regard to the DPRK continues to find favour among the Mongolian public because it reinforces the idea of Mongolia as a problem solver in Asia and as a non-nuclear-weapon state that is positioned to act as a peacemaker: "While neighboring countries, China, Japan, and South Korea are seeking deterrence, Mongolia may become an integral part of stabilizing the Korean Peninsula with its small country diplomacy."[63]

160　*Alicia Campi*

Mongolian efforts to find a way around the moribund Korean peace process by promoting cooperative trust-building through its UBD mechanism and by offering to be a summit venue[64] have gained the confidence of the Six-Party nations and especially been welcomed by the American administrations of Barack Obama and Donald Trump. It is no exaggeration to say that the UBD has reinvigorated the Korean Peninsula peace process. The success of the UBD in attracting the participation of the North Koreans over the years has elevated the UBD from its Track 2.0 origins to its present Track 1.5 status. Mongolia has reinforced the idea that it can act as a willing problem solver in Asia because it is a non-nuclear-weapon state that offers the parties a neutral meeting ground, which Mongols like to label as North-East Asia's Geneva or Helsinki. It is in this climate that Mongolia has proven that it can play a unique role as mediator in the North-South Korean dispute with the will and imagination to be an active force in the North-East Asian peace process and to create new mechanisms to contribute to regional connectivity.

Notes

1 The six parties are the ROK, the DPRK, Russia, China, the United States, and Japan. Discussions began in 2003 and were suspended in 2009.
2 "Foreign Policy," Embassy of Mongolia to the United States, May 21, 2013, at http://mongolianembassy.us/about-mongolia/foreign-relations-of-mongolia/#.W9dIfnpKii4 (accessed June 17, 2019).
3 Migeddorj Batchimeg, "Mongolia's DPRK Policy: Engaging North Korea," *Asian Survey*, 46 (2), March/April 2006, pp. 275–297.
4 Ambassador Mark Minton, speaking at a forum co-hosted by the Global Peace Foundation and the Center for Strategic and International Studies in Washington, DC, was quoted in J.C. Finley, "Mongolia Leverages Diplomatic Ties with North Korea," *upi.com*, December 4, 2014, at www.upi.com/Top_News/World-News/2014/12/04/Mongolia-leverages-diplomatic-ties-with-North-Korea/4921417633447/ (accessed April 20, 2019).
5 J. Battur, "A Glimpse into the History of the Mongolian-North Korean Relations in the XX Century," pp. 5–7 and Notes 12 and 13, at http://congress.aks.ac.kr/korean/files/2_1358236554.pdf (accessed June 18, 2019).
6 Balázs Szalontai, *Kim Il Sung in the Khrushchev Era: Soviet-DPRK Relations and the Roots of North Korean Despotism, 1953–1964*, Stanford University Press, Stanford, and Woodrow Wilson Center Press, Washington, DC, 2005, pp. 46–47.
7 J. Battur, No. 5, p. 10.
8 "North Korea, Mongolia Expand Economic Cooperation," Yonhap News Agency, in Korea Central News Agency, *North Korea Newsletter*, No. 271, July 18, 2013.
9 Sugirragchaa, "Ts. Elbegdorj: Our Two Countries Are Good Friends," *Montsame*, November 5, 2013.
10 "Mongolia Will Work with N. Korea to Promote NE Asia Stability: President," *Korea Herald*, October 29, 2013.
11 Choi Hyun-june, "Mongolian President Makes '"Unusual" Comments about Tyranny while in N. Korea," *Hankyoreh*, November 17, 2013, at http://english.hani.co.kr/arti/english_edition/e_northkorea/611452.html (accessed April 25, 2019).
12 "Mongolia's Elbegdorj Sees Trade Boost Through North Korean Ports," *Mongolian Economy and Finance*, October 31, 2013, at http://mongoliaeconomy.blogspot.com/2013/10/mongolias-elbegdorj-sees-trade-boost.html (accessed May 5, 2019).

13 "North Korea Takes First Steps towards Oil Exploration," *The Guardian*, July 1, 2014, at https://unleashmgr.wixsite.com/kird/single-post/2014/07/01/North-Korea-takes-first-steps-towards-oil-exploration (accessed May 5, 2019).
14 Located on the border with Russia, in the north-east corner of the country on the Tumen River, is the Tumangang-Khasan railroad crossing (42.415397 130.641489) in North Hamgyong province. North Korea's sole railroad crossing with Russia is of great potential importance due to its proximity to the port of Rajin, 33.5 km to the south-east. See Victor Cha, Joseph Bermudez, and Marie DuMond, "Making Solid Tracks: North Korea's Railway Connections with China and Russia, A CSIS Survey Study of Railway Cooperation and Connections on the Korean Peninsula," *Beyond Parallel*, January 7, 2019, at https://beyondparallel.csis.org/making-solid-tracks-north-koreas-railway-connections-china-russia/ (accessed April 24, 2019).
15 Ha-young Choi, "Mongolia to Send Coal Through N. Korean Port," *NK News*, February 25, 2015, at www.nknews.org/2015/02/mongolia-to-send-coal-through-n-korean-port/ (accessed May 5, 2019).
16 Comments made during DPRK Foreign Minister Ri Su Yong's February 22–25, 2015 official Mongolian visit, when the two countries finalised several cooperative agreements. "Mongolia, North Korea Sign MOU," *NK News*, February 25, 2015, at www.nknews.org/2015/02/mongolia-north-korea-sign-mou/ (accessed April 20, 2015).
17 Michael Kohn and Yuriy Humber, "Mongolia Taps North Korea Oil Potential to Ease Russian Grip," *Bloomberg*, June 18, 2013, at www.bloomberg.com/news/articles/2013-06-17/mongolia-taps-north-korean-oil-potential-to-ease-russia-reliance (accessed May 1, 2019).
18 Interview with DPRK Ambassador Hong Kyu by Sh. Batbold and N. Gantuya, "DPRK Ambassador Addresses Workforce Issue and Bilateral Relations," *Mongol Messenger*, November 25, 2016.
19 Hamish Macdonald, "HBOil Withdraws from North Korean Joint Venture due to Sanctions," *NK News*, January 23, 2017, at www.nknews.org/2017/01/hboil-withdraws-from-north-korean-joint-venture-due-to-sanctions/ (accessed May 5, 2019).
20 Thomas Mackie, "North Korea's New Trading Ally? Mongolia and Kim Hit Record High as China Tightens Trade," *Express*, January 6, 2018, at www.express.co.uk/news/world/900885/north-korea-kim-jong-un-world-war-3-mongolia-khaltmaagiin-battulga-tobacco-china (accessed April 30, 2019).
21 *North Korea Newsletter*, No. 271, July 18, 2013, at https://en.yna.co.kr/view/AEN20130717006100325 (accessed May 5, 2019).
22 Alastair Gale, "North Korea's Lucrative Labor Exports Come under Pressure," *The Wall Street Journal*, July 7, 2016, at www.wsj.com/articles/north-koreas-lucrative-labor-exports-come-under-pressure-1467916815 (accessed May 1, 2019).
23 "Mongolia: Protect Rights of North Korean Migrant Workers," *Human Rights Watch*, August 20, 2008, at www.hrw.org/news/2008/08/20/mongolia-protect-rights-north-korean-migrant-workers (accessed May 4, 2019).
24 "1,200 North Korean Workers to Leave Mongolia as UN Sanctions Bite," *South China Morning Post*, December 3, 2017, at www.scmp.com/news/asia/east-asia/article/2122637/1200-north-korean-workers-leave-mongolia-un-sanctions-bite (accessed May 5, 2019).
25 Resolution 2375 (2017): "The relevant authorities were instructed to close all joint ventures and cooperative entities operating in Mongolia by 8 February 2018 in accordance with paragraph 18 of resolution 2375 (2017)." Hamish Macdonald, "Mongolia Says It Granted 1221 North Korean Work Permits in 2017," *NK News*, February 13, 2018), at www.nknews.org/2018/02/mongolia-says-it-granted-1221-north-korean-work-permits-in-2017/ (accessed April 24, 2019).
26 "Report: Mongolia Could Host North Korean Refugee Camp," *Mongolia Web*, October 2, 2008 (accessed March 1, 2017).

27 "Mongolia Not Planning Camps for N. Koreans," *Gulf Times* (Qatar), November 24, 2006 (accessed from archives, January 27, 2009).
28 Mongolian Ministry of Foreign Affairs, p. 4, at www.mfa.gov.mn/wp-content/uploads/2015/12/Ulaanbaatar-Dialogue.pdf (accessed August 3, 2018).
29 A term coined by US Secretary of State James Baker when visiting Mongolia in August 1990. The "Third Neighbour" is a powerful nation that politically and economically could balance Mongolia's ties with its geographical neighbours, Russia and China.
30 "Mongolian President's Visit to North Korea Aimed at Increasing Ties," *South China Morning Post*, October 28, 2013, at www.scmp.com/news/asia/article/1341414/mongolian-presidents-visit-north-korea-aimed-increasing-ties (accessed May 5, 2019).
31 Robert Bedeski and Niklas Swanström, *Eurasia's Ascent in Energy and Geopolitics: Rivalry or Partnership for China, Russia, and Central Asia?*, Routledge, London and New York, August 6, 2012, p. 234.
32 Ts. Batbayar quoted in J. C. Finley, No. 4.
33 Ibid.
34 In 2002, Pyongyang admitted its agents had kidnapped Japanese nationals in the 1970s and 1980s to train its spies in Japanese language and customs.
35 "Japan, North Korea Agree to Continue Dialogue," *Bangkok Post*, November 16, 2012, at www.bangkokpost.com/news/asia/321622/japan-north-korea-agree-to-continue-dialogue (accessed April 25, 2019).
36 Colin Zwirko, "Mongolian President Invites Kim Jong Un to Ulaanbaatar," *NK News*, October 15, 2018, at www.nknews.org/2018/10/mongolian-president-invites-kim-jong-un-to-ulaanbaatar/ (accessed April 24, 2019).
37 Damba Ganbat, "National Security Concept of Mongolia: Basic Principle," in *Security Outlook of the Asia Pacific Countries and Its Implications for the Defense Sector*, National Institute for Defense Studies, Tokyo, 2014, p. 96.
38 Ts. Batbayar quoted in J.C. Finley, No. 4.
39 Charles Krusekopf, "North Korea and Mongolia: A New Partnership for Two Old Friends?," *Asia Pacific Bulletin*, No. 240, November 14, 2013, at www.eastwestcenter.org/sites/default/files/private/apb240.pdf (accessed June 17, 2019).
40 Ibid.
41 Track 2 diplomacy: non-governmental, informal, and unofficial contacts and activities among private citizens or groups, sometimes called non-state actors. Track 1 diplomacy: official, governmental diplomacy that occurs inside official government channels. Track 1.5: top leadership of one or both conflict parties are engaged in negotiations or conflict transformation activities in an informal setting and/or in their personal capacity, or as a consultation that attempts to generate new insights. The defining element distinguishing Track 1.5 process from a classic Track 2 dialogue is the composition of the participants' group, especially the involvement of decision makers. See Oliver Wolleh, "Track 1.5 Approaches to Conflict Management: Assessing Good Practice and Areas for Improvement," Berghof Foundation for Peace Support, May 2007, at http://peacemaker.un.org/sites/peacemaker.un.org/files/Track1.5ApproachestoConflictManagement_BerghofFoundation2007.pdf (accessed May 5, 2019).
42 "When a meeting, or part thereof, is held under the Chatham House Rule, participants are free to use the information received, but neither the identity nor the affiliation of the speaker(s), nor that of any other participant, may be revealed." It is now used throughout the world as an aid to free discussion. See "Chatham House Rule," Chatham House, at www.chathamhouse.org/about/chatham-house-rule (accessed October 25, 2018).
43 President Tsakhiagiin Elbegdorj, "Speech at the Opening Session of the Seventh Ministerial Conference of the Community of Democracies," Ulaanbaatar, Mongolia, April 29, 2013, at www.un.int/mongolia/mongolia/ulaanbaatar-dialogue (accessed June 18, 2019).

44 *Conference Proceedings, Ulaanbaatar Dialogue on Northeast Asian Security 2014*, Ministry of Foreign Affairs, Ulaanbaatar, September 2014.
45 Migeddorj Batchimeg quoted in *Conference Proceedings*, No. 44, p. 10.
46 "Nine Countries Participate in the 'Ulaanbaatar Dialogue,'" *Mongol Messenger*, June 20, 2014.
47 Nanjin Dorjsuren, "Why Mongolia Wants to be a Part of Traditional Security Framework in NEA," *Conference Proceedings, Ulaanbaatar Dialogue on Northeast Asian Security 2015*, Ministry of Foreign Affairs, Ulaanbaatar, September 2015, p. 16.
48 Niels Hegewisch, "Dialogue Is a Powerful Tool if It Leads to Cooperation," Friedrich-Ebert-Stiftung Office for Regional Cooperation in Asia, July 7, 2017, at www.fes-asia.org/news/dialogue-is-a-powerful-tool-if-it-leads-to-cooperation/ (accessed April 30, 2019).
49 See Mark Goleman, "5th Round of the Ulaanbaatar Dialogues," *New Eastern Outlook*, June 8, 2018, at https://journal-neo.org/2018/08/06/5th-round-of-the-ulaanbaatar-dialogues/ (accessed August 5, 2018); "Ulaanbaatar Dialogue on Northeast Asian Security Concludes," *The UB Post*, June 18, 2018.
50 5B. Misheel, "State Secretary of the Ministry of Foreign Affairs D. Davaasuren Paid Visit to the Democratic People's Republic of Korea (DPRK) on April 18–19, 2019," *Montsame*, April 19, 2019, at https://montsame.mn/en/read/1868 (accessed May 1, 2019).
51 R. Turmunkh, "Ulaanbaatar Dialogue Promotes Northeast Asian Security," *The UB Post*, June 7, 2019, at www.pressreader.com/mongolia/the-ub-post/20190607/281517932617878 (accessed June 17, 2019).
52 J. Enkhsaikhan, "Developing Nuclear Landscape in the Asian Heartland: Role of Nuclear-Weapon States," *Mongolian Journal of International Affairs*, no. 11, Ulaanbaatar, 2004, p. 32.
53 Resolution 53/77D, "Mongolia's International Security and Nuclear-Weapon-Free Status," stated that Mongolia's nuclear-weapon-free status represented a new international relations approach that constituted an important factor for ensuring Mongolia's security, which it considered a concrete contribution to strengthening the regime of non-proliferation of nuclear weapons.
54 Ambassador Od Och, "Declaration by Mongolia Regarding Its Nuclear-Weapon-Free Status," New York, September 17, 2012, at http://nautilus.org/wp-content/uploads/2012/09/signed-Mongolian-declaration.pdf (accessed May 5, 2019). See also "Memorandum from Mongolia Regarding the Consolidation of Its International Security and Nuclear-Weapon-Free Status," *2015 Review Conference of the Parties to the Treaty on the Non-Proliferation of Nuclear Weapons*, New York, April 27–May 22, 2015, at https://undocs.org/NPT/CONF.2015/8 (accessed May 5, 2019).
55 "The Joint Declaration of the People's Republic of China, France, the Russian Federation, the United Kingdom of Great Britain and Northern Ireland, and the United States of America on Mongolia's Nuclear-Weapon-Free Status," September 17, 2012, www.mfa.gov.mn/?p=29184&lang=en (accessed September 10, 2019).
56 D. Myagmar, executive director of the Global Partnership for the Prevention of Armed Conflict (GPPAC) Northeast Asia, quoted in *Mongol Messenger*, "Northeast Asian delegates Gather in Ulaanbaatar to Discuss Regional Issue," November 18, 2016.
57 Jee Abbey Lee, "Former US Advisor Meets with N. Korean Officials," *VOA News*, May 28, 2014, at www.voanews.com/a/former-us-advisor-meets-with-n-korean-officials/1924791.html (accessed May 5, 2019).
58 Headquartered in the Netherlands, the network was established in 2005 and consists of 15 regional networks, with priorities and agendas specific to their environment. "Who We Are," GPPAC, at https://gppac.net/who-we-are (accessed April 29, 2019).
59 Founded by Mongolian ambassador Jargalsaikhan Enkhsaikhan, Mongolia's leading specialist on nuclear disarmament issues.

60 Tsenkher Suld NGO, established in 2005, is a non-profit organisation aimed at promoting Mongolia's nuclear-weapon-free policy and its activities. See No. 55.
61 B. Misheel, "Mongolia's Role in Solving the Northeast Asian Security Recognized," *Montsame*, December 12, 2018, at https://montsame.mn/en/read/174159 (accessed April 29, 2019).
62 David L. Caprara, Katharine H.S. Moon and Paul Park, "Mongolia: Potential Mediator between the Koreas and Proponent of Peace in Northeast Asia," *Brookings East Asia Commentary*, January 20, 2015, at www.brookings.edu/opinions/mongolia-potential-mediator-between-the-koreas-and-proponent-of-peace-in-northeast-asia/ (accessed May 5, 2019).
63 Bolor Lkhaajav, "Mongolia's Small Country Diplomacy and North Korea," *The Diplomat*, September 29, 2016, at https://thediplomat.com/2016/09/mongolias-small-country-diplomacy-and-north-korea/ (accessed May 5, 2019).
64 Adam Taylor, "Why Mongolia Hopes to Host a Trump-Kim Jong Un Meeting," *The Washington Post*, April 20, 2018, at www.washingtonpost.com/news/worldviews/wp/2018/04/20/why-mongolia-hopes-to-host-a-trump-kim-jong-un-meeting/?noredirect=on&utm_term=.235625c456bf (accessed May 1, 2019).

10 India and the Korean Peninsula

Between dialogue, diplomacy, and denuclearisation

Jagannath P. Panda and Mrittika Guha Sarkar

Introduction

Albeit a peaceful and denuclearised Korean Peninsula may have many stakeholders to its interest and share, India is no exception in perceiving a change in the region crucial to its strategic interests. Such an assertion runs through the premise that other powers such as the United States, Russia, China, South Korea, and Japan are important actors in the peace and denuclearisation process, India remains a non-critical actor.

Objectively, issues such as major powers' presences in the Korean Peninsula, the significance of the denuclearization process, and the prospects of economic cooperation in North-East Asia, along with enhanced relations with the two Koreas, are significant factors that would certainly encourage India as much as other actors to view the evolving peace process positively. The same is being signified through an upward trajectory in the India-South Korea bilateral relations, which has the potential to progress towards a regional outlook with an ambition to cooperate in a range of fields from diplomacy to economic as well as people-to-people connectivity. On the other hand, India's relations with North Korea, though somewhat restrained, has been unrelenting since 1973. New Delhi's foreign policy manoeuvres through the current scenarios of the "four nos" of the Korean Peninsula, "no isolation of North Korea", "no regime collapse in North Korea", "no war-like situation in Korean Peninsula", and "no major nuclear proliferation" by the DPRK. These scenarios, after the inter-Korean summits in Panmunjom and Pyongyang in April and September 2018 respectively, throw light on India's keen desire towards a more innovative, sustained, and active engagement with North Korea. Further, the recent political and official visits from both sides reiterate a revitalization of the traditional diplomatic as well as strategic manoeuvres between both the countries.

To India, any outreach in Korean Peninsula should begin with the enrichment of its Act East Policy (AEP). Promoting dialogue and pursuing a more engaging diplomacy have been the key thrust to India's approach in the region. For instance, the recent dialogues of North Korea with South Korea and the United States, respectively, has brought the former out of the shadow of isolation into engagement, reiterating the approach India has been promoting for some time now. These dialogues have enriched the significance of India's diplomacy and increased the prospects of a greater engagement in the Peninsula. However, the dilemmas India faces regarding its engagement with the Peninsula remain the strengthening of relations with North Korea amidst the mounting sanctions by the UNSC, maintaining equi-cordial ties with the two Koreas without putting the India-RoK relations at risk, and not being caught up in major powers politics while pursuing its interests.

This chapter, therefore, assesses India's approach to the Korean Peninsula keeping in view New Delhi's growing interests, relations with key stakeholders in the region, and the recent developments in the Indo-Pacific. It essentially argues that, as a non-critical actor, the scope for India to play a constructive role on issues of significance, such as denuclearisation, through promoting dialogue in the region might be limited. Still, India's thrust on dialogue diplomacy, consistent engagement with the two Koreas evenly, and the subtle demand for a completely denuclearised Korean Peninsula have brought its foreign policy outreach to the core, which has become hard to ignore in a tightly balanced geopolitical equation.

India and the changing political equations in the Korean Peninsula

The security architecture of the Korean Peninsula is witnessing a shift with the rapid rise of China, growth of the middle power economies, and remodelling of the United States' approach towards North Korea in the region. A multi-textured foreign policy approach taken by major actors has further changed the politics in the region, leading it to become multipolar.[1] Further, alignment of the geopolitical and the geo-economic interests of the major powers has transformed it into one of the most dynamic regions in the world politics.[2] More importantly, unlike the Cold War period, North Korea is no longer an isolated country within the global affairs, that has often been portrayed. Instead, today, 164 countries have established diplomatic relations with North Korea, 47 host embassies of North Korea, and 25 have embassies in Pyongyang.[3] Such diplomatic connections of North Korea with the international community makes it one of the most significant political undercurrents of the region. The inter-Korean summits, major powers' frequent engagement with the Kim Jong-un administration, and the revival of hopes to address critical matters such as denuclearisation and reunification have brought in new dynamics that are impacting power balances in the region. Importantly, these newly arrived situations have given hopes and new contexts to both the Koreas to discuss the prospects of reunification even though it remains a complicated long-drawn matter.[4] Such developments in the region have encouraged many non-critical countries, including India, to see the region from a fresh strategic perspective. India's rising profile as a power, its growing outreach under Act East Policy

(AEP), and its historical presence in the region further make it a vital power that could envision to play a constructive role. In fact, a constructive role of India is not a far-fledged proposition since the Korean Peninsula requires a new model of cooperation which is based on mutual acceptance of each other's strategic stature and positive diplomacy to overcome the tensions. In this regard, any prospects for a constructive Indian role in Korean Peninsula could be envisioned by revisiting history.

Much has been written on the Korean War and its consequences. Hitherto, the world seems to overlook the role that many actors, including India, played to defuse such a war. India's efforts to put an end to the war with peace and cooperation were dismissed more often than not. Cold War tensions and the mood of the hour to respond with aggressive retaliation lead the two opposite blocs to shelve India's proposal, which aimed for a peaceful resolution to the crisis. The war ended thereafter, but with more than 2.5 million causalities and sustained enmity between both the Koreas.[5] The fallout of the war persists over the region even today, and tensions loom over the Korean Peninsula. Such has reiterated the reckoning for India's forgotten role in the resolution of the Korean War as a foundation for its growing engagement with the Peninsula.[6]

India, during the Korean War, held a unique position that allowed it, albeit not at all times, to influence the debates at the UN regarding the Korean war.[7] India acknowledged the importance of the Cold War situation in the Peninsula, which could transform into a severe dimension in Asia, even reaching India's vicinity. At the backdrop of nuclear tensions mounting with the Cold War, India realised that it had to play a constructive role in the Korean War to protect its security and national interests.[8] This could only be possible by preventing further aggression in the region and promoting collective peace and security. In this context, India's stance was persistent though understated – it wanted a peaceful unification of the two Koreas while observing neutrality towards the region. Such an approach often created friction between India and the United States, where the latter viewed India's foreign policy in the Korean Peninsula tilted towards the communists.[9] However, India's growing diplomatic role during the Korean War could be estimated, as just after three years of its state formation, K.P.S Menon from India was invited as the chairman of a nine-member UN Commission – UN Temporary Commission on Korea (UNTCOK) – that was set up to conduct elections in Korea. This commission successfully held elections in the southern part of the Peninsula, which then came to be known as the RoK.[10]

India then rendered support in the form of medical assistance to the injured in the war and tried to fulfil its aim of crisis resolution through two steps: containing the parties to go for the war and trying to prevent further escalation, and ensure unity amongst the critical stakeholders in the Peninsula.[11] In the context of the first step, there were many events which could be characterised as stimulus for the escalation of the war. Such were the North Korean forces crossing the 38th Parallel line; appointment of General Douglas MacArthur as the commander-in-chief of the UN Security Forces during the war and his aggressive nature leading the UN forces to cross the 38th Parallel Line in October 1950, overlooking the warnings by China[12]; and China, in turn, crossing the Yalu river in retaliation and subsequently crossing the 38th Parallel in November 1950. India, however, through all these developments maintained its commitments to peace and security, proposing to the UNSC to observe restraint from belligerence.

Characterising the second step, India believed that it is unfair for the UN to make decisions without the involvement of all the five major powers. China was not represented in the UNSC, and the Soviet Union had been proscribing the international body due to China's exclusion. India thus proposed to include China to the UNSC and resolve the war in collaboration.[13] However, India's balanced approached was not fully understated. This was reiterated by India's supportive stance towards the UNSC resolutions 82 and 83, which aimed at restoring the status quo and not escalating the war. However, it condemned the UN General Assembly resolution 377 V, which purported to unify the Peninsula without trying to resolve the tensions. At the same time, it denounced UNGA resolution 438, which targeted China as the aggressor for crossing the Yalu river and the 38th Parallel Line. According to India, such a step could provoke China into coercion and reduce the potentials for peace in the region (please refer to Table 10.1).

Further, its unique and independent stance on the Korean War could best be reiterated through a speech by KPS Menon to the Staff College, Wellington, in India in 1950 on "India's Foreign Policy". The speech stated:

> Over Korea, India did adopt an independent attitude, independent of both the United States and the Soviet Union. If we had wanted to placate the Soviet Union, we would have voted against the resolution of the General Assembly constituting the UN Commission on Korea. Not only did we refuse to do so, but we accepted the membership of the Commission and I, as delegate for India, accepted its Chairmanship. If, on the other hand, we wanted to placate the United States, we would have recognised the new Government in South Korea as the National Government, as the United States themselves, and China, have done. We declined to do so because we felt that this would be to betray the goal of Korean unity.... On the Whole, I think it is not unfair to say that, while the Great Powers looked at the Korean problem in its relation to their rivalries, we regarded it from one standpoint and one only, namely the welfare and the aspirations of the Korean people.[14]

This speech by K.P.S Menon demonstrated India's stance on the Korean War to be independent of the perspectives of both the Cold War blocs: the United States and the Soviet Union. The speech thus signified India's aspirations towards a unified Korea looking at the Peninsula beyond great power politics but through the lenses of benevolence and goodwill. However, India's concerns and initiatives were dismissed, and the resolutions were passed due to massive US

Table 10.1 India's stance on major UN resolutions and sanctions

S. No	Sanction	International Body/ International Platform	Date/Month/ Year	Key takeaways	India's stance
1	Resolution 82	UNSC	June 25, 1950	Aimed to restore status quo between DPRK and ROK; demanded end of North Korea's invasion of South Korea and withdraw the latter's forces from the 38th parallel.	Supported
2	Resolution 83		June 27, 1950		
3	Resolution 377 V	UNGA	November 3, 1950	Aimed to unify the two Koreas for peace in the region.	Condemned. India felt that the resolution was trying to unify the two Koreas without trying to stop the fight. Further, the agenda of the resolution was being shaped by the United States.
4	Resolution 498	UNGA	February 1, 1951	Condemned China as the aggressor in the Korean Peninsula; demanded Chinese troops to leave Korea; committed to continue supporting the UN troops in the region	Condemned. According to India, targeting China as the aggressor would, in turn, make China more aggressive and rigid.
5	Resolution 1718	UNSC	October 14, 2006	Condemned North Korea's nuclear tests on October 9, 2006 and imposed sanctions.	Supported
6	Resolution 1874		June 12, 2009	Condemned North Korea's nuclear tests on May 25, 2009 and imposed sanctions.	
7	Resolution 2087		January 22, 2013	Condemned North Korea's rocket launch on December 12, 2012; recalled all the previous relevant resolutions; and imposed sanctions.	
8	Resolution 2094		March 7, 2013	Condemned North Korea's third nuclear test on February 12, 2013; recalled all the previous relevant resolutions; and imposed sanctions.	

(Continued)

S. No	Sanction	International Body/ International Platform	Date/Month/ Year	Key takeaways	India's stance
9	Resolution 2270		March 2, 2016	Condemned North Korea's fourth nuclear test on January 6, 2016 and satellite launch on February 7, 2016; recalled all the previous relevant resolutions; and imposed sanctions.	
10	Resolution 2321		November 30, 2016	Unilaterally strengthen its sanctions regime against DPRK in response to September 9, 2016 nuclear test; and imposed sanctions.	
11	Resolution. 2356		June 2, 2017	Unanimously sanctioned a list of individuals and entities designated as being engaged in or providing support for Pyongyang's nuclear-related program; and imposed sanctions.	
12	Resolution 2371		August 5, 2017	Unilaterally strengthen its sanctions regime against DPRK in response to July 2017 nuclear tests; and imposed sanctions.	
13	Resolution 2375		September 11, 2017	Unilaterally strengthen its sanctions regime against DPRK in response to September 3, 2016 nuclear test; and imposed sanctions.	
14	Resolution 2397		December 22, 2017	Unanimously strengthened sanctions in response to the launch of Hwasong-15 intercontinental ballistic missile on November 28, 2017, and imposed sanctions.	

Source: Ministry of External Affairs, India (https://mea.gov.in/); United Nations Security Council (https://www.un.org/securitycouncil/); United Nations General Assembly (https://www.un.org/en/ga/)

support by its allies in the UN who were unwilling to challenge its hegemony. Ironically, India's proposal received a massive blow from the UN, and the country's prestige in the international forum took a hit. However, this did not dwindle India's commitment to peace and tranquillity. As the war was coming to an end, the issue of the prisoners of war (PoWs) surfaced. While, on the one hand, the UN favoured a non-forcible repatriation where the prisoners could choose the country to return to, on the other hand, the communists supported the opposite: PoWs would be returned to their respective country of origin, willingly or unwillingly.[15] As a result, India was made the head of the five-nation Neutral Nations Repatriation Commission (NNRC) where India's initiatives drew much appreciation.[16]

Nonetheless, India's engagement with the Peninsula during the war did not end the hostilities. Instead, the United States' approach remained the dominant voice guiding the policies of the UN, and frictions between the two blocs increased. While India persistently tried to prevent an escalation of the war, it could not do much. However, India's observations and experiences shaped its future foreign policy towards the region. Such could be reiterated through India's support for all future UNSC sanctions condemning North Korea's nuclear programmes, irrespective of India's sustained diplomatic relations with Pyongyang (Table 10.1). Thus, India's successes and failures did not deter it from playing a more significant role in the international community, despite criticisms from both the United States and South Korea. India instead utilized multilateral bodies such as the UN to mediate between the superpowers and aims to do so at present to resolve the crisis in the Korean Peninsula.

Strategic rendezvous after the Korean War

For India, the Korean Peninsula, with its current power balances and imbalances, has immense strategic importance. However, the record of India and Korean Peninsula strategic engagement in the region post the Korean War had been more of a deliberate disengagement than interaction. The Great Power politics during the Cold War, the geographical distance from the region, and the evolving regional politics reiterated this disengagement.[17] India's approach towards the Peninsula was marred by the politics of the power blocs, with a balanced approach which reiterated India's belief in the concept of non-alignment. This approach by India continued until 1990, even against the backdrop of India's diplomatic recognition to both the Koreas in 1973 and North Korea's full-fledged admission into the Non-Alignment Movement (NAM) two years later.[18]

It is in this context that the linkages between India and South Korea witnessed stagnation. India and South Korea's dependence on opposite power blocks (India-USSR and South Korea-United States) created ideological differences and accounted for mutual suspicion between them. However, the period of 1990–1991 witnessed a shift in India's foreign policy towards the Peninsula with the opening of its economy. It did away with its reticent approach and developed strong economic relations with South Korea through the channels of

India's new "Look East Policy". The growth and transformation of the "Asian Tigers" (Taiwan, Hong Kong, Singapore, and South Korea) attracted India towards South Korea, while the convergence of the growing concerns regarding the Pakistan-North Korea nexus and a rising China's strategic footprints in the region acted as catalysts.[19] India-South Korea relations witnessed an upward trajectory thereafter, from a "Long-term Cooperative Partnership for Peace and Prosperity" in 2004[20] to a "Comprehensive Economic Partnership Agreement" (CEPA) in 2009.[21] On the strategic front, New Delhi and Seoul signed the "Strategic Partnership", which focussed on an enhanced political and security cooperation between the two countries.[22]

However, unlike South Korea, which was gradually becoming a major actor in global affairs, North Korea was degenerating into isolation after the disintegration of the USSR, while increasingly depending on its strategic ally, China. Consequently, North Korea was left outside the purview of India's Look East Policy. Thus, India lacked a unified foreign policy for the entire Korean Peninsula. Nonetheless, what is important to note is that irrespective of any concrete foreign policy towards North Korea during this phase, India was one of the very few countries which maintained an understated but sustained linkage with the country since 1973.[23] This was reiterated through the Cultural Exchange Programme (CEP) Agreement signed by the two countries in 1976 and the agreement to cooperate in the field of science and technology in 1991.[24] What further highlighted the prolonged bilateral ties were the persistent official exchanges between India and North Korea, starting from 1991 and continuing till the present times.[25]

Nevertheless, while India in the post-Cold War period displayed a desire for a greater outreach towards the Peninsula, its focus was limited to the Republic of Korea (ROK). In this context, even though India maintained constant diplomatic contact with the Democratic People's Republic of Korea (DPRK), the ties between India and North Korea were primarily limited to a working-level relationship. Thus, the challenge for India was to develop strategic engagement with the Korean Peninsula as a whole, while rethinking its outreach to the DPRK. The task was also to strike a balanced approach towards the Peninsula without disturbing the bilateral relations with either the DPRK or the ROK. This was to be achieved amid the pressure of maintaining ties with the other stakeholders in the region, namely the United States, China, Russia, and Japan.

In this regard, in recent years, India's foreign policy under the Narendra Modi government has been attempting to strike the much needed strategically even-handed approach towards the region. Both India and South Korea are manoeuvring within a security architecture with independent foreign policies and are wary of China's rapid rise and the United States' remodelled strategic approach.[26] With no historical baggage to hinder their growing relationship, India and the ROK are capable of maintaining a greater balance between the powers in the region and prevent the Korean Peninsula to become a hub of power rivalries, if needed.[27] At the same time, having a multilateral approach to regional affairs would allow India and South Korea to neutralise any powers in the region with hegemonic agendas.

Further, India's prolonged engagement with North Korea is also increasingly being seen as strategically important, while diplomacy through dialogue is being used as an imperative. India has been cautiously manoeuvring between upholding stringent international sanctions against North Korea and preserving India's sovereignty in order to maintain diplomatic relations with Pyongyang. Most importantly, this development is taking place without hurting the growth trajectory of India-ROK relations. In fact, India and South Korea vision a collaboration that is future-oriented and factors *people*, *prosperity*, and *peace* as the locus of their "Special Strategic Partnership". While a regional outlook to the India-ROK relationship is yet to be achieved, a growing partnership through the convergence of India's AEP and South Korea's "New Southern Policy" (NSP) is being cemented, without deterring India's diplomatic engagement with the DPRK. This has, in turn, enabled major powers to better understand and acknowledge the prospects of India's role in denuclearisation of the Peninsula and recognise the country as a potential facilitator of the peace process in the region.

India's dialogue diplomacy between the two Koreas

In 2015, the then Indian minister of state for home affairs, Kiren Rijiju, participated in an event celebrating the North Korean national Independence Day in Embassy of North Korea in New Delhi.[28] Such attendance by an Indian minister was an intended diplomatic move that propounded a change in the bilateral relations between India and North Korea. It exhibited the political will to strengthen India's relations with North Korea, amidst all the international suspicion that was mounting on North Korea and its behaviour. The Indian minister of state for home affairs stated:

> North Korea is an independent country and a member of the United Nations and we should have good bilateral trade ties ... We have been discussing inside the government ways and means of upgrading bilateral ties with North Korea ever since the North Korean Foreign Minister visited Delhi last April. We feel that there should not be the usual old hurdles and suspicion in bilateral ties as North Korea is an independent country and also a member of the United Nations. A relationship based on greater trade and commerce between two sides is the way ahead.[29]

Such a statement enunciated the fact that India is unwilling to discard North Korea as a partner even though the international community remains quite sceptical of Pyongyang's international behaviour. Prior to the above event, the then railway minister of India, Suresh Prabhu, made an official visit to Seoul to seek enhanced collaboration with South Korea on high-speed rail networks in the same year.[30] This act, too, showcased India's desire to view the Korean Peninsula through a balanced approach, rendering equal diplomatic importance to both the Koreas, without thwarting bilateral relations with either.

A similar approach was demonstrated again during the visit by the then Indian minister of state for external affairs, V.K. Singh, to Pyongyang on May 15–16, 2018.[31] It was the first high-level visit by an Indian minister to the DPRK in about 20 years, and it served two purposes: one, the official visit aimed to nurture the bilateral relationship with North Korea. Two, this diplomatic step purported to advance India's strategic presence amid the rapidly evolving environment in the Korean Peninsula.[32] The meeting between the two counterparts further addressed the possibility of exploring areas of "mutual interests", while the official statement released after the visit restated India's support towards the joint initiative for restoring peace between the DPRK and the ROK.[33]

What is vital to note here is the timing of the visit – it was planned just ahead of the historic June 12, 2018, summit between the United States and the DPRK. The visit took place amidst tensions between the United States and the DPRK: there were reports of the summit being cancelled on account of an impasse between Donald Trump and Kim Jong-un regarding the denuclearisation of Pyongyang.[34] The success of the meeting between India and North Korea in such a scenario displayed the maturity in the bilateral relations between the two countries. Most importantly, this reiterated India's prospective role as a potential collaborating actor, to bridge the existing gap between the critical powers and DPRK, particularly to address matters pertaining to the process of denuclearisation in the Korean Peninsula.

Thus, after a successful Pyongyang outreach during the ministerial visit by V.K. Singh, India responded positively to the Trump-Kim summit in 2018.[35] The summit reiterated India's forward-looking diplomatic approach towards North Korea vis-à-vis the Korean Peninsula. Manoeuvring its foreign policy within the aforesaid four no's scenario, despite scepticism by the West, New Delhi visualised the "no isolation of North Korea" and "no regime collapse" as prospects to revitalise its traditional diplomatic linkages with Pyongyang and to bolster the dual-track approach by enhancing its presence in the Korean Peninsula.[36] In recent years, India, within the gambit of the UN mandate, has worked at nurturing its economic and cultural ties with North Korea. V.K. Singh's visit, too, was a step in this direction: both the countries focussed on "possibilities of cooperation", especially in the areas of agriculture, medicine, pharmaceuticals, yoga, and vocational training. The undertones of the visit were also the mutual desire to strengthen people-to-people contacts between the countries, which, in turn, would result in exemplifying India's stature as a peace-holder.[37]

The other two "nos" – "no war-like situation" in the Korean Peninsula and "no nuclear proliferation" – opened significant options for New Delhi to be portrayed as a more proactive actor in the inter-Korean denuclearisation dialogue and evolving peace process.[38] Further, not succumbing to any international pressure, an unrelenting India-North Korea relations provide New Delhi with diplomatic prospects to act as a neutral hand between both the Koreas.[39] The process for the same already seems to have begun with South Korea's encouraging stance towards a greater engagement of India in the region. In 2018, the Deputy Minister of Foreign Affairs of South Korea Enna Park stated that India could play an "influential role" towards establishing long-lasting peace in the Korean Peninsula.[40] The minister also urged New Delhi to persuade Pyongyang to recalculate its denuclearisation strategy in the region.

Looking at the current developments from a larger canvas, India's bolstered engagement with North Korea would only strengthen and further define the decade-old diplomatic relationship established in 1973, irrespective of the latter's military alliance partnership with China and continued missile and nuclear proliferation linkages with Pakistan. The same has not hindered the DPRK to establish diplomatic channels with India, nor has India apprehended to pursue an engaging approach even against the backdrop of strained relations with China. Besides, India sees its strengthened outreach towards North Korea as an opportunity for greater engagement of the latter in global affairs. India's special approach towards Pyongyang has shaped the India-DPRK relations, engendering mutual trust and confidence, amidst the growing uncertainty in the Korean Peninsula.

India's Act East and the Korean Peninsula

India's AEP under the Narendra Modi government has been the cornerstone of greater economic interactions with the countries in its extended neighbourhood, comprising powers in the Indo-Pacific region. While one of the major beneficiaries of this policy initiative has been the member countries of the Association of Southeast Nations (ASEAN), no relationship that India pursued in East Asia has augmented faster than the one with South Korea. While the latter was one of the first countries to respond to India's Look East Policy with vigour and invest in India with its consumer brands, India, too, did not hesitate to grant South Korea a special place in its AEP.[41] Further in the purview of the current scenario, South Korea has been playing a vital role in changing the trajectory of India's manufacturing industry and has been investing under the initiatives of "Make in India", "Start-up India", "Digital India", and more.

However, while the bilateral trade between both countries is witnessing progress, it is yet to reach its peak (see Figure 10.1). Besides, the various significant agreements, such as Strategic Partnership and CEPA, between South Korea and India, their relationship is yet to be scaled in the same length as that of other bilateral relationships in Asia, such as India-China, India-Japan, or Japan-China.[42] Further, India's relations with South Korea did not witness much advancement in the past, apart from some mutually beneficial economic arrangements, due to Seoul's suspicious approach towards India due to the latter's diplomatic linkages with Pyongyang.[43] Though Seoul did not ever clearly express its concern publicly, India's relations with South Korea remained mostly cold despite many promises to enhance bilateral ties. However, post the recent meeting between Prime Minister Modi and President Moon Jae-in in February 2019, both the countries have signed six pacts to enhance cooperation in

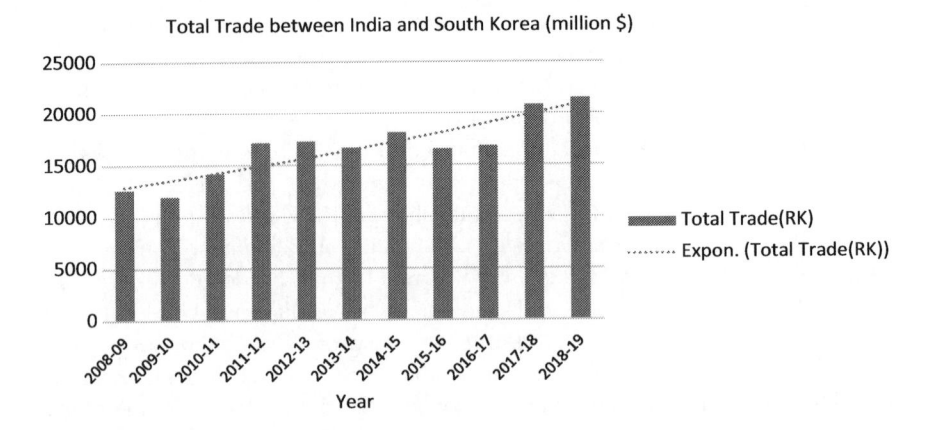

Figure 10.1 Total trade between India and South Korea.
Source: Ministry of Trade and Commerce, Government of India.

the areas of infrastructure, media, and start-ups, and combat international and transborder crimes.[44] Likewise, India and South Korea have taken note of their relatively slow-progressing bilateral trade and agreed to conclude the negotiations regarding the upgrade of their CEPA.[45] Further, by urging businesses to work on joint ventures, India and South Korea have targeted the bilateral trade to reach $50 billion by the year 2030.[46] Nonetheless, attaining economic and strategic goals, along with promoting the spirit of the "Asian Century", amid a rapidly evolving Indo-Pacific order would not be possible until the relationship imbibes a regional character in the future. In this regard, greater utilisation of India's AEP and South Korea's NSP would be vital to attain their regional goals. Besides, the synergy between the AEP and the NSP should factor the promotion of regional connectivity and infrastructure development as the main pillars of this engagement.[47]

Regarding connectivity and infrastructure, India and South Korea can explore many new areas of cooperation. They can both cooperate in the field of connectivity within the scheme of the Asian Infrastructure Investment Bank (AIIB). While India has decided not to be a part of China's Belt and Road Initiative (BRI), Prime Minister Modi has repeatedly emphasised on the importance of continuous engagement with China and the AIIB under a "development partnership" for sustainable infrastructure development in India and Asia.[48] India has been one of the founding members of the AIIB and one of its largest borrowers for infrastructural projects in areas of transportation, water supply, telecommunications, sanitation, rural and urban development, power, and energy.[49] On similar lines, South Korea, too, has been one of the founding members of the Multilateral Development Bank (MDB) and further has pledged $8 million for AIIB's special fund for enhancing infrastructure in developing countries.[50] South Korea also co-hosted AIIB's flagship annual meeting in 2017, which was centred around the theme of "sustainable infrastructure".[51] Therefore, the AIIB can act as an excellent platform for a more significant developmental partnership between India and South Korea.

Another multilateral organisation where India and South Korea can cooperate in the field of connectivity and infrastructure development, is the Indian Ocean Rim Association (IORA). As two major economies, both countries consider connectivity as an instrument for ensuring peace, security, and development in the Indo-Pacific region. India has time and again considered the IORA as an useful platform for the same.[52] India has been considerably supportive of the invigoration of IORA activities, including the blue economy and renewable energy. The focus of the IORA has been on promoting a shared understanding of maritime issues and helping develop cooperative mechanisms between the partner countries for maritime safety and security.[53] South Korea, on the other hand, is already seeking to collaborate on projects in order to improve regional cooperation and has expressed the intent to work with India in forums such as the ASEAN Regional Forum (ARF), East Asia Summit (EAS), and the IORA.[54] Further, engagement between India and South Korea in priority areas of communication, connectivity, agriculture, health, energy, environment, and economy seems viable, particularly in light of South Korea becoming a dialogue partner in the IORA.[55]

In view of multilateral engagements, both sides endorse an ASEAN vision of connectivity cooperation, and that could be the basis of their regional cooperation through their AEP and NSP. For instance, South Korea has recently developed a platform for cooperation with the ASEAN Connectivity Coordinating Committee (ACCC).[56] This platform can forge greater regional connectivity by bringing together South Korean and Indian connectivity initiatives. Since 2013, India has been continuously engaging with the ASEAN under the ACCC-India meeting to explore connectivity initiatives.[57] It is important to note that the ACCC-India meeting has been instrumental for the progress of the India-Myanmar-Thailand Trilateral Highway and the Kaladan Multimodal Project. Therefore, an India-South Korea connectivity cooperation in partnership with ASEAN could also be a plausible option for New Delhi and Seoul.

Besides, connectivity, infrastructure development; greater regional economic cooperation frameworks, such as the Regional Comprehensive Economic Partnership (RCEP); and the multilateral mechanisms, such as the ARF and ASEAN Defence Ministers' Meeting (ADMM) plus, are some of the common areas and mechanisms that could bring India and South Korea together through the ASEAN. For instance, while the NSP is yet to endorse the concept of Indo-Pacific officially, it is foraying into the Indo-Pacific region for strategic interests. A clear signal of the same was the joint exercise in April 2019, under the ADMM plus umbrella where Indian naval ships reached Busan, South Korea.[58] The exercise indicated the growing interactions and cooperation between India and South Korea through such regional platforms; at the same time, it also signified the Indian Navy's growing footprints and outreach in the Indo-Pacific. Further, South Korea's commitment towards connectivity and sustainable development was visible when its foreign ministry led the ARF inter-sessional meeting on disaster relief, proposing enhanced connectivity between disaster risk reduction and sustainable development as the ARF's priority area of cooperation.[59] Such initiatives could bring India and South Korea into closer cooperation to enhance infrastructural connectivity and sustainable development.

On similar lines, India's AEP could also look at North Korea as a prospect to further India's outreach in Korean Peninsula as a whole. The first step towards this potential development was the meeting between the former external affairs minister (Late) Sushma Swaraj and her North Korean counterpart Ri Su Yong in the year 2015. The meeting concluded with India's positive reassessment of its relationship with North Korea amid heavy sanctions by the UN and the Western countries.[60] The ministerial-level talks also assured enhanced humanitarian assistance by India to North Korea. In a statement after the meeting, the Ministry of External Affairs (MEA) said:

> The Foreign Minister level talks were held in a frank and friendly atmosphere where issues of mutual interest including India's security concerns came up for discussion. Ms. Swaraj conveyed to her Korean counterpart the significance of peace and stability in the Korean peninsula for India's Act East policy.[61]

Notwithstanding India's efforts to further dialogue and diplomacy with North Korea, an area that requires immediate attention is the decreasing trade between the two countries. The trade between India and North Korea has fallen considerably in the past decade from $993 million in 2008–2009 to a mere $30 million in 2018–2019 (see Figure 10.2).

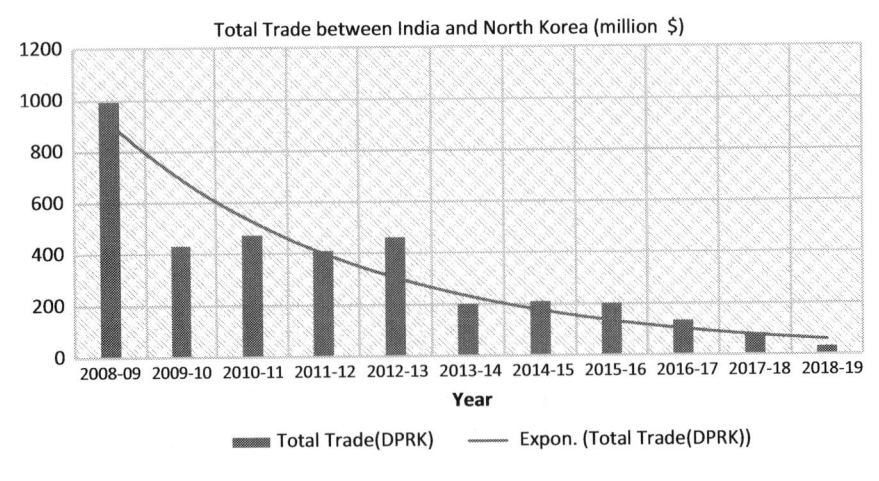

Figure 10.2 Total trade between India and North Korea.
Source: Ministry of Trade and Commerce, Government of India.

The decline in trade is mainly due to the sanctions imposed by the UN and the Western countries. In 2018, adhering to the sanctions, India supplied only food and medicines to the DPRK.[62] Further, training of North Koreans in advanced physics, aeronautical engineering, and nuclear engineering is banned in India, and Indian nationals were advised not to register ships in North Korea.[63] While India decided to abide by the sanctions amid the growing tensions between the United States and North Korea, there is a greater reason for India to engage in the Korean peace process. The strategic, as well as economic, imperatives for India to engage in North Korea are well foundational. Apart from an extended outreach for the AEP, a greater engagement with North Korea would also provide India with unexplored markets, once, or if, Pyongyang becomes a part of the East Asian economies.[64]

India's strategic moments in the denuclearisation impasse

As mentioned earlier, India's approach to the denuclearisation scenario in Korean Peninsula hinges on the following two no's: "no war-like situation" and "no nuclear proliferation". It is in this regard that this chapter argues for India's constructive role as a potential actor in the negotiation peace process through its long-standing diplomatic relations with both North Korea and South Korea.

India's historical role as a peacemaker during the Korean War has been well established. The ceasefire resolution, which was accepted by both North and South Korea, was sponsored by India and figured notably in the debates for the peace process in the region. Its relevance was further felt when the *Pyongyang Declaration* expressed the desire to "transform the Korean Peninsula into a land of permanent peace".[65] India's commitment to peace and stability has further been reiterated through its desire to ensure a denuclearized and peacefully unified Korean Peninsula by supporting the UNSC resolutions against North Korea's nuclear programme (please see Table 10.1).

Against this background, it is understandable that India wants to stay engaged with both the Koreas and not get isolated from the denuclearisation negotiation process. Moreover, India's approach of successive denuclearisation through dialogue and diplomacy distinguishes it from the perspectives of the other stakeholders in the process. At the same time, what complicates the process of denuclearisation and peaceful unification of the Peninsula, are the distinct approaches of major actors, which have eventually contributed to the power struggle in the region.

The approach of the United States is to exert maximum pressure on North Korea to denuclearise.[66] Along with the maximum pressure tactic, the United States also advocates a "no phased" approach, not wanting North Korea to denuclearise incrementally. This approach was demonstrated during the 2018 meeting between North Korea and the United States in Singapore, where, the

Trump administration demanded a unilateral disarmament by North Korea before the two countries could begin improving their bilateral relations.[67] This approach, however, did not achieve the desired aim, and the talks in Hanoi failed.[68]

On the other hand, China, like the United States, also wants complete denuclearisation but understands that it is a complicated process and cannot be achieved in the short term.[69] At the same time, it takes note of its role as a constructive actor in the region, where its alliance with North Korea provides China with a substantial amount of leverage.[70] However, even as China supports the US efforts to denuclearise, the former does not intend to use its leverage to apply undue pressure on North Korea.[71] Instead, it believes that the approach of maximum pressure would destabilise the region, and therefore, China supports a phased and step-by-step approach to denuclearisation. Russia, similarly, acknowledges the complications in the denuclearisation process and believes in a phased approach.[72] It also understands that its role, when it comes to crisis resolution, is very limited. Nevertheless, in a broader security architecture, Russia could still be an indispensable partner to North Korea through security guarantees, which Russia believes is the key to the crisis resolution process.[73] South Korea, too, acknowledges the lengthy and convoluted nature of denuclearisation and advocates patience to thaw the 70-year-old misunderstandings between the two Koreas.[74] It supports the recent ROK-DPRK and US-DPRK talks, seeing potential through diplomacy, and seeks to play the role of a mediator.[75] Japan also recognises the importance of denuclearisation, peace and stability in the region for its security. It is in favour of collective efforts by the stakeholders for crisis resolution in the Peninsula.[76]

In this context, it is essential to note that India is a non-critical actor in the crisis resolution on the Korean Peninsula and is not directly involved in the process, as not being a part of the Six-Party Talks.[77] India has time and again condemned DPRK's nuclear and missile tests, and has been demanding denuclearization of the Peninsula since the 1990s.[78] It has approached the DPRK nuclear tests through three broad premises: DPRK tests violate its international obligations; such tests affect regional peace and stability, and thus India's security as well; and DPRK must refrain from further tests.[79] This has been reiterated through India's press statement after North Korea's nuclear test on September 3, 2017. It stated:

> India deplores the nuclear test conducted by the DPRK this morning. It is a matter of deep concern that DPRK has once again acted in violation of its international commitments which goes against the objective of the denuclearization of the Korean peninsula, which has been endorsed by DPRK itself. We call upon DPRK to refrain from such actions which adversely impact peace and stability in the region and beyond. India also remains concerned about the proliferation of nuclear and missile technologies which has adversely impacted India's national security.[80]

However, India's approach has not yet served its purpose. Pakistan's assistance to the DPRK in the field of nuclear and missiles is an established fact, and their security linkages go back to the 1970s when the then prime minister of Pakistan, Zulfikar Ali Bhutto, visited North Korea. Subsequently, in the 1990s, Pakistan purchased long-range missiles from the DPRK and returned the favour by assisting the latter in the enrichment of its nuclear technologies.

India, through its repeated official statements, expressed concerns over the proliferation links between North Korea and Pakistan.[81] However, this has been overlooked by the major actors in the Peninsula. Nonetheless, India's concerns demand substantial attention, as reportedly North Korea, due to increasing international pressure, is renewing its missile and nuclear linkages with Pakistan, even after pledging to stop its proliferation activities post the Panmunjom and Pyongyang declarations.[82] In this regard, India's engagement in the process is particularly significant, as the "complete denuclearisation" of North Korea would not be possible without adequately addressing the proliferation linkages between North-East Asia and India's neighbourhood. Further, engagement in the reunification and denuclearisation process will allow India to put forward its concerns regarding the illegitimate nuclear technological nexus that exists between North Korea and Pakistan, with the possible consent of China, to international notice.

Thus, even though India's stance on most of the critical issues regarding the region does not hold as much weight as that of major powers – the United States, China, Russia, Japan, or South Korea, its positive and patient approach to the DPRK has enabled India's outreach to North-East Asia. Moreover, India is doing so by preserving its core values of peace, cooperation, and non-coercion without partaking into any alliances linked to the Korean Peninsula. Further, India's enhanced posture as a rising power in Indo-Pacific and its increasing strategic convergence with South Korea has enabled the latter to recognise India as a stakeholder in the Peninsular peace process. This has been reiterated by Prime Minister Narendra Modi's statement during the state visit by president of ROK, Moon Jae-In on July 11, 2018, too:

> Whole credit of accelerating the peace process in the Korean Peninsula, keeping it on track, and its progress goes to President Moon. I believe that the positive atmosphere which has been created is the result of the unremitting efforts of President Moon. I congratulate President Moon for this progress. In today's discussions I told him that the proliferation linkages of Northeast and South Asia are also a cause of concern for India. And therefore, India is also a stakeholder in the success of this peace process. We will definitely provide whatever support is required to ease the tension. And therefore, we have decided to speed up our consultation and coordination.[83]

As India witnesses a shift in its power status in the region, this progress contributes to the strategic enhancement of ties between India and South Korea: from bilateral to regional cooperation frameworks. As aforementioned, this has been a much-required development to prevent stagnation of the India-ROK relationship.

Further, improved relations between the two Koreas, as well as the two countries' bilateral ties with India, open up the opportunity to institute a neutral common platform for a trilateral collaboration and to instil a sense of cooperation and goodwill. In this regard, India can initiate common diplomatic dialogues among India, the ROK, and the DPRK, which would enhance the communication between India and the Korean Peninsula. This would also elevate India's diplomatic and strategic status in the global community. Thus, as aforesaid, India could play the role of a collaborating actor between North Korea and South Korea, or North Korea and the United States, to help facilitate the crisis resolution in the region. Here, it is essential to highlight the efforts by India to engage with the Peninsula through various meetings and discussions with the officials of the major stakeholders in the region. The discussions and joint statements signify the inclusion of India as an important actor in the Korean Peninsula peace and denuclearisation process (see Table 10.2).

Table 10.2 India's discussions on denuclearization with major stockholders in the Korean Peninsula

S. no.	Country	Official document	Date	Key takeaways
1	United States	Joint Statement	September 30, 2014	• Prime Minister Narendra Modi and President Barak Obama urged the DPRK to take concrete actions towards denuclearisation and comply with all the international obligations and relevant UNSC resolutions (UNSCRs). • Urged DPRK to fulfil its commitments under the 2005 Joint Statement of the Six-Party Talks.
2	United States	Joint Statement: Shared Effort; Progress for All	January 25, 2015	
3	Japan	Joint Statement: India-Japan Strategic and Global Partnership	September 1, 2014	• Focussed on the realisation of North Korea's Complete, Verifiable and Irreversible Dismantlement of all weapons of mass destruction and ballistic missiles of all ranges in accordance with the relevant UNSCRs, including the 2005 Six-Party Talks Joint Statement. • Addressed concerns related to North Korea's proliferation linkages. • Reaffirmed their commitment to the full implementation of the relevant UNSCRs.
4	Japan	Joint Statement: India and Japan Vision 2025	December 12, 2015	
5	Japan	Joint Statement	November 11, 2016	
6	Japan	Joint Statement: Towards a Free, Open and Prosperous Indo-Pacific	September 14, 2017	
7	Japan	Joint Vision Statement	October 29, 2018	

S. no.	Country	Official document	Date	Key takeaways
8	Russia	Joint Statement: An Enduring Partnership in a Changing World	October 5, 2018	• Reiterated support for lasting peace and stability in the region through diplomacy and dialogue. • Urged all the concerned parties to work together towards the goal.
9	Russia	Joint Statement: Reaching New Heights of Cooperation through Trust and Partnership	September 05, 2019	
10	South Korea	Joint Statement: Towards Strategic Partnership	January 25, 2010	Reiterated their common commitment on nuclear disarmament and the non-proliferation of weapons of mass destruction and their means of delivery.
11	South Korea	Joint Statement: India-Korea Strategic Partnership Deal	March 12, 2012	Reiterated importance of maintaining peace and stability on the Korean Peninsula including its denuclearisation
12	South Korea	Joint Statement: Expansion of Strategic Partnership	January 16, 2014	• Expressed concern over the development of the DPRK's nuclear weapons and ballistic missile programmes, violating international obligations and commitments. • Expressed importance for peace and stability in the Korean Peninsula. • Urged the DPRK to fully comply with all of its international obligations, including under the relevant UNSCRs, and to fulfil its commitments under the 2005 Joint Statement of the Six-Party Talks.
13	South Korea	Joint Statement: Towards Special Strategic Partnership	May 18, 2015	
14	South Korea	Joint Statement: A Vision for People, Prosperity, Peace and our Future	July 10, 2018	

Source: Ministry of External Affairs, India (https://mea.gov.in/).

A way forward

At the outset, it is crucial for India to express its concerns about the contentious issues in the region, in order to develop greater linkages with the Korean Peninsula. While India has been independently reaching out to the major stakeholders in the region bilaterally, an enhanced engagement in the Korean Peninsula would provide India with a common platform to interact with these major powers and negotiate its security interests. The process has started with the strengthening of economic, diplomatic, cultural, and strategic relations with South Korea, but India needs to upgrade the bilateral relations with a regional outlook. Simultaneously, it would be in India's interest that it should constructively enhance the networks of dialogues and communication with North Korea.

In fact, post the removal of the sanctions, India must facilitate exchanges with Pyongyang, mainly in the fields of educational exchanges, cultural and tourism promotion, and more. This would be a great way to enhance understanding between the two nations and their diverse thought processes. Cultural exchanges are a viable option, mainly as North Korea has remained culturally isolated from the rest of the world. India could be a great platform to showcase North Korea's rich heritage.

Furthermore, with the geopolitical locus shifting to the Indo-Pacific, it is imperative to understand the importance of the Korean Peninsula in the region. With proximity to major powers such as China, Japan, and Russia, the Korean Peninsula remains the balancer in the Indo-Pacific region. Subsequently, the Indo-Pacific has become the cornerstone of India's Foreign Policy. Thus, enhancing its footprints in the Peninsula can certainly aggrandise India's outreach in the region. More importantly, India should endeavour to utilise its historical card in the Peninsula and continue to pursue strong relations with the ROK and maintain continued lines of communication with the DPRK. Further, India must use its initial forays into North Korea to extend the outreach of its AEP and use it as a trump card trying to navigate its measured position in the reunification and denuclearisation process as a major actor, while becoming a facilitator of peace and stability in the region.

Notes

1 Lakhvinder Singh, "The Importance of South Korea: A Strategic Perspective on India's Engagement with Northeast Asia", *Korean Journal of Defense Analysis*, 20 (3), September 2008, pp. 285–286; Tae-Hwan Kwak and Seung-Ho Joo, "The Future of the Korean Peninsula: Unification and Security Options for the 21st Century," *Asian Perspective*, 23(2), Special Issue on the Dynamics of Northeast Asia and the Korean Peninsula (1999), pp. 179–180.

2 The Korean Peninsula is situated adjacent to the Korea Strait, which separates South Korea and Japan. This strait further connects the East China Sea, the Yellow Sea, and the Sea of Japan in the Pacific Ocean. Most importantly, several international shipping lanes pass through this strait, which houses a considerable amount of trade. This makes the Korean Peninsula extremely important in terms of security and economics. See, Ji Guoxing, "SLOC Security in the Asia Pacific", Center Occasional Paper, Asia-Pacific Center for Security Studies, Honolulu, Hawaii, February 2000, at https://apcss.org/Publications/Ocasional%20Papers/OPSloc.htm (accessed September 6, 2019); Lakhvinder Singh, ibid.

3 Tasha Wibawa, "North Korea: Diplomatic Life Inside Pyongyang Can Be 'Superficial, Difficult, and Controlled," *ABC News*, October 14, 2018, at www.abc.net.au/news/2018-10-14/diplomatic-relations-in-north-korea/10359848 (accessed September 27, 2019); please see, "North Korea and the World: North Korea's External Relations", *The National Committee on North Korea and East West Centre*, at www.northkoreaintheworld.org/diplomatic/dprk-embassies-worldwide (accessed September 27, 2019).

4 Nate Kerkhoff, "What to Expect in Inter-Korean Relations in 2019?" *The Diplomat*, January 16, 2019, at https://thediplomat.com/2019/01/what-to-expect-in-inter-korean-relations-in-2019/ (accessed September 6, 2019).

5 Jagannath P. Panda, "Indian Mediation in Korean War," *The Pioneer*, June 24, 2017, at www.dailypioneer.com/2017/columnists/indian-mediation-in-korean-war.html (accessed September 22, 2019).
6 Ibid.
7 Biswamohan Misra, "The Indian U.N. Policy During Korean Crisis," *The Indian Journal of Political Science*, 25(3/4), July–September–December 1964, pp. 146–147; Jairam Ramesh, "India's Role in Ending the Korean Crisis," *The Hindu*, May 3, 2018, at www.thehindu.com/opinion/op-ed/indias-role-in-ending-the-korean-war/article23750989.ece (accessed September 22, 2019).
8 Vineet Thakur, "India's Diplomatic Entrepreneurism: Revisiting India's Role in the Korean Crisis, 1950–1952", *China Report*, 49 (3), 2013, pp. 273–274; please read A. Torin, "The Hot Diplomatic Summer of 1950: Documents of the Early Period of the Korean War," *International Affairs*, 56 (4), 2010; A. Frolov, "War in Korea: Experience in Escalating a Conflict", *International Affairs*, 56 (4), 2010.
9 Robert Barnes, "Between the Blocs: India, the United Nations, and Ending the Korean War", *The Journal of Korean Studies*, 18 (2), Fall 2013, p. 265.
10 Vineet Thakur, No. 8, p. 276.
11 Jagannath P. Panda, No. 5; Nabarun Roy, "India's. Forgotten Links to the Korean War", *The Diplomat*, October 27, 2018, at https://thediplomat.com/2018/10/indias-forgotten-links-to-the-korean-war/ (accessed September 22, 2019).
12 Nabarun Roy, No. 11; Justin Kim-Hummel, "Diplomatic Relations with the DPRK: India as a Global Case Study", *Global Political Review*, 2 (1), April 2016, pp. 51–52.
13 Vineet Thakur, No. 8, p. 281; Nabarun Roy, No. 11.
14 "Speech by Mr. K.P.S. Menon, Foreign Secretary to the 'Government of' India on India's Foreign Policy at the Staff College, Wellington," 1950, at www.php.isn.ethz.ch/kms2.isn.ethz.ch/serviceengine/Files/PHP/94991/ipublicationdocument_singledocument/5a6fd963-3193-4dd7-a1c9-94a71d3124ac/en/Speech_Menon_1950.pdf (accessed September 23, 2019).
15 Jagannath Panda, No. 5.
16 Please see, "Armistice Agreement, Volume 1, Text of Agreement," *United Nations*, at https://peacemaker.un.org/sites/peacemaker.un.org/files/KP%2BKR_530727_AgreementConcerningMilitaryArmistice.pdf (accessed September 27, 2019).
17 David Brewster, "India's Developing Relationship with South Korea: A Useful Friend in East Asia", *Asian Survey*, 50 (2), 2010, pp. 403–405.
18 "India-Korea (ROK) Relations", Ministry of External Affairs, 2014, at www.mea.gov.in/Portal/ForeignRelation/Korea__ROK__June_2014_.pdf (accessed September 6, 2019).
19 Ranjit Kumar Dhawan, "India's 'Act East' Policy Towards the Two Koreas: Issues and Challenges", *Strategic Analysis*, 42 (5), November 11, 2018, p. 491, at https://doi.org/10.1080/09700161.2018.1523081 (accessed September 6, 2019); Thongkholal Hoakip, "India's Look East Policy: Its Evolution and Approach", *South Asian Survey*, 18 (2), 2011, p. 240; Archana Pandya and David M. Malone, "India's Asia Policy: A Late Look East", *ISAS Special Report*, No. 2, August 25, 2010, at https://mail.google.com/mail/u/0/#inbox (accessed September 27, 2019); Jagannath P. Panda, "DPRK's Nuclear Provocations and the Indian Response," *IDSA Comment*, September 27, 2016, at https://idsa.in/idsacomments/dprk-nuclear-provocations-and-the-indian-response_jppanda_270916 (accessed September 27, 2019).
20 "Joint Press Release on the visit of Minister of External Affairs of India to the Republic of Korea", Ministry of Foreign Affairs (MOFA), South Korea, September 17, 2007, at www.mofa.go.kr/eng/brd/m_5676/view.do?seq=303727 (accessed September 6, 2019).
21 India-Korea CEPA, Ministry of Commerce and Industry, August 7, 2009, at https://commerce.gov.in/writereaddata/trade/INDIA%20KOREA%20CEPA%202009.pdf (accessed September 6, 2019).

22 "India–Republic of Korea Joint Statement: Towards a Strategic Partnership", Ministry of External Affairs, January 25, 2010, at https://mea.gov.in/bilateral-documents.htm?dtl/3301/IndiaRepublic+of+Korea+Joint+Statement+Towards+a+Strategic+Partnership (accessed September 6, 2019).
23 Tanya Sen, "India and North Korea: A Strategic Friendship?" *The National Interest*, July 4, 2018, at https://nationalinterest.org/feature/india-and-north-korea-strategic-friendship-24947 (accessed September 6, 2019).
24 "India-DPR Korea Relations", Embassy of India, Pyongyang, at https://eoi.gov.in/pyongyang/?pdf4086?000 (accessed September 6, 2019).
25 Ibid.
26 Rajiv Kumar, "South Korea's New Approach to India", *ORF Issue Brief*, October 23, 2018, at www.orfonline.org/research/south-koreas-new-approach-to-india-45135/ (accessed September 6, 2019).
27 Lakhvinder Singh, "India and Peace-Building in Korea", *Asia Times*, July 31, 2019, at www.asiatimes.com/2019/07/opinion/india-and-peace-building-in-korea/ (accessed September 6, 2019); Lakhvinder Singh, No. 1.
28 Kallol Bhattacherjee, "India Reaches Out, Wants to Upgrade Ties with North Korea", *The Hindu*, September 16, 2015, at www.thehindu.com/news/national/india-reaches-out-wants-to-upgrade-ties-with-north-korea/article7656332.ece (accessed September 6, 2019).
29 Ibid.
30 "India Seeks South Korean Investments in Railways", *NDTV*, September 12, 2015, at www.ndtv.com/india-news/india-seeks-south-korean-investment-in-railways-1216913 (accessed September 6, 2019).
31 "Visit of Minister of State for External Affairs General Dr. V.K. Singh (Retd.) to the Democratic People's Republic of Korea", Ministry of External Affairs, May 16, 2018, at https://mea.gov.in/press-releases.htm?dtl/29899/Visit+of+Minister+of+State+for+External+Affairs+General+Dr+VK+Singh+Retd+to+the+Democratic+Peoples+Republic+of+Korea (accessed September 6, 2019).
32 Jagannath P. Panda, "What the Trump-Kim Summit Means for India", *The Diplomat*, February 26, 2019, at https://thediplomat.com/2019/02/what-the-trump-kim-summit-means-for-india/ (accessed September 6, 2019).
33 Ibid.
34 The meeting between Donald Trump and Kim Jong-un held in Singapore on August 1, 2018, was historic, because it was the first-ever meeting between the leaders of the two nations marred by nuclear tensions. While this meeting did not resolve the denuclearisation impasse, it ended with both sides signing an agreement that included security guarantees for North Korea and terms ensuring new peaceful relations between the two nations as well as denuclearisation of the Korean Peninsula. However, the purpose of this meeting was defeated, as the United States and North Korea are still locked in nuclear tensions. Nonetheless, the important takeaway of this meeting remains the start of the dialogue diplomacy approach, which India advocates as a measure towards crisis resolution in the Peninsula. See, Max Fisher, "What Happened in the Trump-Kim Meeting and Why It Matters", *The New York Times*, July 12, 2018, at www.nytimes.com/2018/06/12/world/asia/trump-kim-meeting-interpreter.html (accessed September 6, 2019).
35 "India Welcomes the U.S.-DPRK Summit," Ministry of External Affairs, June 12, 2018, at https://mea.gov.in/press-releases.htm?dtl/29973/india+welcomes+the+us+dprk+summit (accessed September 28, 2019)
36 Jagannath P. Panda, "Pyongyang and India: Strategic Choices on the Korean Peninsula", *Asia Pacific Bulletin*, February 20, 2019, at https://idsa.in/system/files/news/pyongyang-and-india.pdf (accessed September 6, 2019).
37 Ibid.
38 Ibid.

39 North Korea has been repeatedly penalised by the UN for flouting international norms, and its undemocratic nuclear behaviour has been condemned by the global community. Amid all the criticisms, India has, however, maintained its independence of approach and sustained diplomatic relations since 1973. Because of this stance, the Western countries, as well as South Korea, have often viewed India-DPRK relations through the lenses of suspicion. See, Rajaram Panda, "India-Republic of Korea Military Diplomacy: Past and Future Projections", *Journal of Defense Studies*, 5 (1), January 2011, pp. 16–38.

40 Subhajit Roy, "South Korea Dy Minister: 'India can play role for peace in Korean Peninsula'", *The Indian Express*, June 21, 2018, at https://indianexpress.com/article/india/south-korea-dy-minister-india-can-play-role-for-peace-in-korean-peninsula-5226386/ (accessed September 6, 2019). For the term "rogue" behaviour, see, Hunter Lovell, "North Korea: Pompeo Remarks Nations' 'Rogue Behaviour' Making Peace Talks 'More Difficult'", *Washington Examiner*, August 31, 2019, at www.washingtonexaminer.com/news/north-korea-pompeo-remarks-on-nations-rogue-behavior-making-peace-talks-more-difficult (accessed September 7, 2019).

41 Skand R. Tayal and Sandip Kumar Mishra, "India and the Republic of Korea: A Growing Strategic Partnership", *Indian Foreign Affairs Journal*, 7 (3), July–September 2012, pp. 324–326.

42 Soyen Park, "India-South Korea Relations Under the New Modi Government", *The Diplomat*, August 13, 2014, at https://thediplomat.com/2014/08/india-south-korea-relations-under-the-new-modi-government/ (accessed September 7, 2019).

43 Jagannath P. Panda, No. 32.

44 "India, South Korea Sign 7 Pacts to Enhance Cooperation in Infra, Start-ups", *Business Standard*, February 22, 2019, at www.business-standard.com/article/pti-stories/india-s-korea-sign-7-pacts-to-step-up-cooperation-in-infrastructure-combating-global-crime-119022200282_1.html (accessed September 7, 2019).

45 Ibid.

46 Ibid.

47 Infrastructure and connectivity remains a significant way to enhance trade relations, encourage foreign direct investment (FDI), facilitate regional integration, and hence lead to economic growth. While the India-South Korea bilateral relations have come a long way, enhancing their relationship to a "special strategic" level, infrastructural connectivity can provide the partnership the much-needed regional approach, important for further growth. Jagannath Panda, "South Korea in India's Indo-Pacific Vision: Impressions post-Moon Jae-In's Visit", *JPI PeaceNet*, July 14, 2018, at www.jpi.or.kr/eng/regular/policy_view.sky?code=EnOther&id=5341 (accessed September 22, 2019); please read, Jagannath P. Panda, "New Delhi's 'Act East' and the India-ASEAN Engagement: What They Mean for India-Korea Relations in the Indo-Pacific", *KIEP Working Paper*, 19:5, August 2019.

48 "Full Text: PM Narendra Modi's Speech at Opening Ceremony of Third AIIB Annual Meet", *Financial Express*, June 26, 2018, at www.financialexpress.com/economy/full-text-pm-narendra-modis-speech-at-opening-ceremony-of-third-aiib-annual-meet/1220855/ (accessed August 26, 2019).

49 "Approved Projects", Asia Infrastructure Investment Bank, at www.aiib.org/en/projects/approved/index.html (accessed August 26, 2019).

50 "S. Korea Agrees to Invest 8 Mln USD in AIIB's Special Fund", Xinhua, June 16, 2017, at www.xinhuanet.com//english/2017-06/16/c_136371548.htm (accessed August 26, 2019).

51 "AIIB and Republic of Korea Sign MOU to Launch AIIB 2017 Annual Meeting", Asia Infrastructure Investment Bank, February 27, 2017, at www.aiib.org/en/news-events/news/2017/20170227_001.html (accessed August 26, 2019).

52 "Remarks by External Affairs Minister at the 3rd Indian Ocean Conference, Vietnam", Ministry of External Affairs, August 27, 2018, at https://mea.gov.in/Speeches-Statements.htm?dtl/30327 (accessed August 26, 2019).
53 Ibid.
54 "Visit of Foreign Minister of Republic of Korea to India", Ministry of External Affairs, December 13, 2018, at https://mea.gov.in/press-releases.htm?dtl/30695/Visit+of+Foreign+Minister+of+Republic+of+Korea+to+India (accessed August 26, 2019).
55 "ROK Joins Indian Ocean Rim Association as Dialogue Partner", Ministry of Foreign Affairs, Republic of Korea, June 12, 2018, at www.mofa.go.kr/eng/brd/m_5676/view.do?seq=320267 (accessed August 26, 2019).
56 "Overview of ASEAN-Republic of Korea Dialogue Relations", ASEAN, August 16, 2018, at https://asean.org/wp-content/uploads/2012/05/Overview-ASEAN-ROK-Dialogue-Relations-as-of-16-August-2018.pdf (accessed August 26, 2019).
57 "India-ASEAN Relations", ASEAN India, August 2018, at http://mea.gov.in/aseanindia/20-years.htm (accessed August 26, 2019).
58 "Indian Ships Reach South Korea for Joint Exercise", *Business Standard*, April 28, 2019, at www.business-standard.com/article/news-ians/indian-ships-reach-south-korea-for-joint-exercise-119042800722_1.html (accessed August 26, 2019).
59 "Foreign Ministry Leads ARF Inter-Sessional Meeting on Disaster Relief", Ministry of Foreign Affairs, Republic of Korea, April 5, 2018, at www.mofa.go.kr/eng/brd/m_5676/view.do?seq=319772 (accessed August 26, 2019).
60 "North Korea Foreign Minister in India, Meets Sushma Swaraj", *Firstpost*, April 14, 2015, at www.firstpost.com/world/north-korea-foreign-minister-india-meets-sushma-swaraj-2195542.html (accessed August 26, 2019).
61 Ibid.
62 Dipanjan Roy Chaudhury, "India to Supply Only Food, Medicines to North Korea", *The Economic Times*, July 13, 2018, at https://economictimes.indiatimes.com/news/defence/india-to-supply-only-food-medicine-to-north-korea/articleshow/58406445.cms?from=mdr (accessed August 26, 2019).
63 This kind of exchange between India and North Korea was a part of an agreement signed between them in 1991 to cooperate in the field of science and technology. See, "India-DPR Korea Relations", Ministry of External Affairs, October 2017, at www.mea.gov.in/Portal/ForeignRelation/2_DPR_Korea_October_2017.pdf (accessed August 26, 2019); Dipanjan Roy Chaudhury, ibid.
64 "Peaceful North Korea Can Expand India's Act East Markets: Observers", *The Economic Times*, June 11, 2018, at https://economictimes.indiatimes.com/news/defence/peaceful-north-korea-can-expand-indias-act-east-markets/articleshow/64541906.cms?from=mdr (accessed August 26, 2019).
65 "Pyongyang Joint Declaration of September 2018", *The National Committee on North Korea*, September 19, 2018, at www.ncnk.org/node/1633 (accessed September 27, 2018).
66 Victor Cha and Katrin Fraser Katz, "The Right Way to Coerce North Korea: Ending the Threat Without Going to War", *Foreign Affairs*, May/June 2018, at www.foreignaffairs.com/articles/north-korea/2018-04-01/right-way-coerce-north-korea (accessed August 26, 2019).
67 Daniel Wertz, "The U.S., North Korea, and Nuclear Diplomacy", *NCNK*, November 2015, at www.ncnk.org/resources/briefing-papers/all-briefing-papers/history-u.s.-dprk-relations (accessed August 26, 2019).
68 One of the major reasons for a failed summit in Hanoi was the disagreements between the United States and North Korea, which has led to an impasse. On one hand, the United States, through its approach of maximum pressure, wanted complete denuclearization of North Korea without a phased approach. On the other hand, North Korea demanded sanction reliefs, which were passed by the UNSC in 2016 and 2017.

However, according to the US, these sanctions covered sources of revenue worth billions of dollars to the North Korean regime, while the North Korean side could consider denuclearisation only if the "corresponding measures were taken." Ankit Panda and Vipin Narang, "The Hanoi Summit Was Doomed from the Start," *Foreign Affairs*, March 5, 2019, at www.foreignaffairs.com/articles/north-korea/2019-03-05/hanoi-summit-was-doomed-start (accessed September 27, 2019); Joshua Stanton et al., "Getting Tough on North Korea," *Foreign Affairs*, May/June 2017, at www.foreignaffairs.com/articles/north-korea/2017-04-17/getting-tough-north-korea (accessed September 22, 2019); please read Andrea Berger, "From paper to practice: The Significance of New UN sanctions on North Korea", *Arms Control*, May 2016, pp. 8–15; Kim Jina, "UN Sanctions as the Instrument of Coercive Diplomacy Against North Korea," *The Korean Journal of Defence Analysis*, 26 (3), pp. 315–332.

69 "China's Role in North Korea Nuclear and Peace Negotiations", *USIP China-North Korea Senior Study Group*, May 6, 2019, www.usip.org/publications/2019/05/chinas-role-north-korea-nuclear-and-peace-negotiations (accessed August 26, 2019).
70 Ibid.
71 Ibid.
72 William Gallo, "After Meeting Kim, Putin Advocates Phased Denuclearization Approach", *VOA News*, April 25, 2019, at www.voanews.com/east-asia-pacific/after-meeting-kim-putin-advocates-phased-denuclearization-approach (accessed August 26, 2019).
73 Ibid.
74 Lee Jong Wha, "A Practical Approach to North Korean Denuclearization", *Project Syndicate*, May 29, 2019, at www.project-syndicate.org/commentary/north-korea-denuclearization-inter-korean-cooperation-by-lee-jong-wha-2019-05?barrier=accesspaylog (accessed August 26, 2019).
75 Ibid.
76 Nobumasa Akiyama, "A Japanese View on Necessary Conditions for the North Korean Denuclearization Challenge", *Carnegie Endowment for International Peace*, October 5, 2018, at https://carnegieendowment.org/2018/10/05/japanese-view-on-necessary-conditions-for-north-korean-denuclearization-challenge-pub-77679 (accessed August 26, 2019).
77 Six-Party Talks were a series of meetings which aimed to find a peaceful solution to the security concerns arising due to North Korea's nuclear programme. The meeting comprised of six members: North Korea, South Korea, United States, China, Japan, and Russia. These talks were the result of North Korea pulling out of the Nuclear Non-Proliferation Treaty in 2003 and witnessed considerable progress till 2009. However, the North Korea satellite launch in April 2009 prompted the UNSC to condemn the act and impose sanctions on North Korea. Subsequently, North Korea withdrew from the Six-Party talks and announced that it would continue with the strengthening of the nuclear programme. Please see Jayshree Bajoria and Beina Xu, "The Six Party Talks on North Korea's Nuclear Program," *Council on Foreign Relations*, September 30, 2013, at www.cfr.org/backgrounder/six-party-talks-north-koreas-nuclear-program (accessed September 27, 2019).
78 Please see the comment by Jagannath P. Panda in "The Curious Case on India-North Korea Relations," *DW*, June 1, 2018, at www.dw.com/en/the-curious-case-of-india-north-korea-relations/a-44042939 (accessed September 27, 2019).
79 Jagannath P. Panda, No. 19.
80 "Press Statement on Nuclear Test Conducted by DPRK," Ministry of External Affairs, September 3, 2017, at https://mea.gov.in/press-releases.htm?dtl/28911/press+statement+on+nuclear+test+conducted+by+dprk (accessed September 28, 2019).
81 "Official Spokesperson's Response to a Question on Reports of a Nuclear Test by DPRK", Embassy of India, Seoul, 6 January 2016, at www.mea.gov.in/media-briefings.

htm?dtl/26258/Official+Spokespersons+response+to+a+question+on+reports+of+a+nuclear+test+by+DPRK (accessed September 7, 2019).
82 Jagannath Panda, No. 19.
83 "Translation of Press Statement by Prime Minister during State Visit of President of the Republic of Korea to India," Ministry of External Affairs, July 11, 2018, at www.mea.gov.in/Speeches-Statements.htm?dtl/30042/Translation_of_Press_Statement_by_Prime_Minister_during_State_Visit_of_President_of_the_Republic_of_Korea_to_India (accessed September 28, 2019).

Part III
Competing and cooperating perspectives

11 Unification of Koreas and North Korea's changing political system

Models and movements

Jin Shin

Introduction

The people of the Korean Peninsula and its surroundings lived as citizens of the same country for more than 1,000 years, before the country became a Japanese colony from 1910 to 1945. After the defeat of Japan in World War II, and the subsequent liberation of Korea, North Korea established a totalitarian regime based on the communist ideology of its occupier, the Soviet Union. Concurrently, South Korea established a liberal democratic state, based on liberal democracy and capitalism with the support of the United States.

Of the 195 nations that constitute the United Nations (UN) as of 2019, South Korea features among the top 10 per cent most developed countries and is a liberal democracy. It is also a member of the Organisation for Economic Cooperation and Development (OECD), with a high standard of living and is a provider of foreign aid.

North Korea, on the other hand, is among the poorest 10 per cent, has been designated by the United States as a part of the axis of evil, and has been closed to the outside world under a dictatorship spanning three generations. Moreover, according to a recent human rights report of the UN, North Korea has the worst human rights record in the world, and countless North Koreans are being held in slavery.[1] Despite such a condition, similar to his father and grandfather, North Korean dictator Kim Jong-un, the representative of the Organizational Guidance Department of Korean Labor Party, enjoys god-like authority over his people. He has prioritised the development of nuclear weapons and Intercontinental Ballistic Missiles (ICBMs), threatening the international community with nuclear strikes, even as his people are dying of hunger. Such actions by the Kim forced the United States and the UN to strengthen economic sanctions against North Korea to force it to abandon the development of nuclear weapons. However, the years 2017 and 2018 witnessed a shift in the perspectives of not just the United States and the North Korea but also a portion of the international community. The last two years witnessed the Trump-Kim summit meetings, which failed to conclude the issues of denuclearization and unification but built a path towards crisis resolution in the peninsula through cooperation. Debates over complete denuclearisation have certainly been a major discussion point across the strategic spectrum of the world. Together, the significance of unification as an indigenous issue should not be overlooked in the context of the future of Korean Peninsula.

What is important to note is that the unification of North and South Korea would not only serve as a model for resolving conflicts worldwide but also lay the groundwork for the resolution of racial conflicts, religious conflicts, territorial conflicts, conflicts between democracy and totalitarianism, and conflicts between poor and rich countries. It would also have serious implications for the international political order. Thus, major powers such as the United States, Russia, China, and Japan, should join hands with the two Koreas to support the process of Korean unification.

Further, according to United Nations data, a comparison of North and South Korean per capita gross domestic products (GDPs) for 2017, 2016, and 2015 is as follows: $685 vs. $30,025; $666 vs. $27,855; and $648 vs. $27,855,. Thus, South Korea's per capita GDP is about 44 times that of North Korea. If the two sides can bridge this income gap and achieve unification, it will be an integration model for all conflicts. Yet, the question is: can these two extremely different political systems be integrated into one and whether the unification of two Koreas is a feasible proposition?

If North Korea's political system stays solid, the unification will take more time. On the other hand, if the North Korean political system is severely weakened, the process of unification can begin, in keeping with the will of the North Korean people. Thus this chapter examines the changing political system of North Korea after the collapse of the Hanoi talks and how this process of change will impact the process of the reunification of the Korean Peninsula. It also analyses the path and future direction of North Korea's nuclear policy – the base for Korean unification – by focussing primarily on Kim Jong-un's speech in April 2019 at the Supreme People's Assembly of North Korea. This chapter brings into account few analytical models by examining the possible movements of Kim Jong-un's regime in coming time. It reveals Kim's governing philosophy, strategies, rationale, and future direction at a time when the North Koreans were becoming aware of the failure of the Hanoi meeting – a landmark event that severely undermined Kim's status in North Korea.

North Korea's foreign policy decision-making process and strategic variables

Decision-making process model

Neo-realist and neoliberal theories explain cooperation and conflict among nations. According to neoliberal institutionalist theory, a state is only interested in gains acquired in international relations and not interested in the other's profit. However, according to the theories of structural realism and new realism, a state's interest is the magnitude of the gains achieved by its competitor country. So, it is very sensitive to how cooperation or conflict with other countries will change the current balance of power. The relative gains matter.

States essentially don't differentiate between seeking absolute gains and relative gains in the pursuit of national interests. Naturally, states pursue greatest profit at the lowest cost under normal circumstances. However, under certain conditions, that is, when the cost of war is relatively small compared to the benefits by war, they may choose war rather than cooperation. Thus, as Robert Powell emphasises, both theories of structural realism and neoliberal institutionalism should recognise the importance of the constraints of the system in which the states are located.[2]

A nation's top policy concern thus remains defence against security threats, which is one of the central elements of the theory of realism and the theory of balance of power. Stephen Walt explains that the motivation for states to pursue a balance of power is a means to defend against threats to their security. A state uses treaties with other countries to counter the military power of its opponents that threaten its security.[3] Moreover, experts like Kenneth Waltz argue that "the ultimate concern of states is maximizing security rather than profit".[4] In this regard, a state's security outweighs the profits of international cooperation. Paul Schroeder points out that states primarily pursue their survival by first using their own specialisation within the structure of international politics.[5] Randall Schweller also explains how a state determines its foreign policy by simultaneously considering security and interests in anarchy through his "balance of profit theory".[6] In other words, a state's top priority goal in the foreign policy decision-making is to eliminate security threats. And then it chooses cooperative foreign policies to maximise profits. In the course of pursuing these interests, the state also selects a policy to secure greater profits through a comparison between benefits from conflict and benefits from cooperation with the other country.

Figure 11.1 illustrates a state's preference model, which describes its process of policymaking.[7]

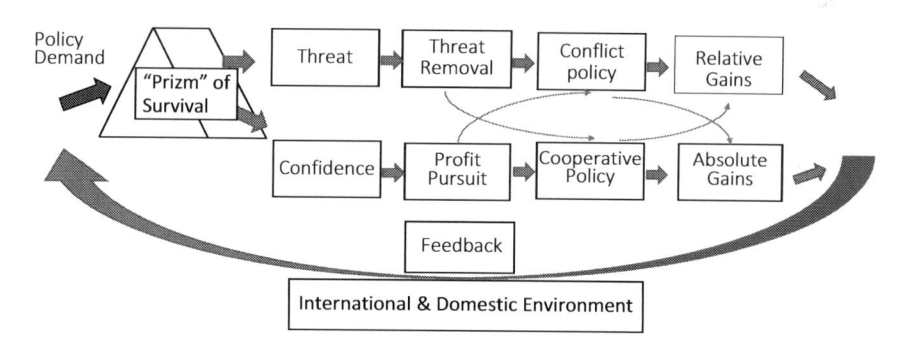

Figure 11.1 State's preference model.
Source: Jin Shin, "Korea's Sunshine Policy and its Structural Limits" *The Korean Journal of International Studies*, Vol. 43, No. 1, 2003, p. 300.

When a state faces certain policy demands threatening its security, it chooses conflict policy to get rid of the threatening factors (upper path in Figure 11.1). If a state confirms that the request of the opponent country does not threaten its survival, it chooses a cooperative policy (lower path in Figure 11.1). That is, if a state is confident in its survival, it pursues its own interests on the premise of trust in the opponent country.

According to this model (Figure 11.1), as long as the United States finds other ways to block North Korea's security threat, Washington may seek absolute gains through negotiations with Pyongyang. On the other hand, North Korea considers that the US demand "Complete, Verifiable and Irreversible Dismantlement (CVID)" of its nuclear weapons would pose a security threat to its political system. For North Korea, nuclear weapons do not only guarantee its national security but also act as means to conquer the Korean Peninsula. Therefore, North Korea will never accede to the US demand to give up nuclear weapons. Rather, Pyongyang is trying to eliminate crucial threats by using a mixed strategy of negotiations and military provocation seeking relative gains. Its strategy of eliminating threats depends on the balance of the degree of strength of the US sanctions on North Korea and the resilience of the North Korean political system.

Variables

In order to analyse North Korea's nuclear policy, this chapter uses two variables: "strength of the North Korean political system" and "pressure of international economic sanctions". At the intersection of these two variables is the indicator of the future of North Korea's nuclear policy and Korean unification. This also shows the direction of the unification process of the Korean Peninsula.

The North Korean political system can be described as totalitarian, as outlined by Carl J. Friedrich and Zbigniew K. Brzezinski.[8] The main characteristics of North Korea's political system can be classified into three categories: (1) Kim Jung-un's divine ideology and information control system, (2) exclusive planned economy, and (3) reign of terror through the police system and political prison camps.

The deification of Kim Jong-un and the information control policy play a key role in maintaining North Korea's dictatorial political system. North Korean authorities are brainwashing the residents into having an unquestioning faith in the perfection of the Kim regime by blocking the inflow of information from outside. Further, loyalty to anyone other than Kim Jong-un, who is considered a living god, is strictly forbidden. As reported by *Voice of America* (VOA):

> In North Korea, Ten Principles for the Establishment of a Monolithic Ideological System (also called Ten Principles of One-Ideology System), which are a set of ten principles and 60 clauses, control all of North Koreans' lives.[9]

All North Koreans have to memorise this text mentioned above. The citizens also have to get together at least once a week to openly criticise themselves and, at the same time, criticise others on the basis of the ten principles. These events function as a means to obliterate the sense of system, dissatisfaction, resistance, and dissent among the people.

The North Korean state also sponsors terrorism and uses arbitrary arrests, executions, and other inhumane acts to maintain control over its population and subdue any resistance. NBC News has featured the report on gross human rights violations and torture targeting more than 130,000 inmates imprisoned in North Korean political prison camps.[10]

Further, in 2014 the United Nations Commission of Inquiry (COI) report on human rights in the Democratic People's Republic of Korea (DPRK, North Korea) found the government committing heinous crimes against humanity, including extermination, murder, enslavement, torture, imprisonment, rape and other forms of sexual violence, and forced abortion. As a result, in December 2017, the UN's Sanctions 2397 (UNSC Res 2397) announced the egregious human rights violation of North Korea as a threat to international peace and security. Further, the UN General Assembly emphasised on mechanisms to ensure the improvement of the human rights scenario in North Korea as a human rights resolution.[11] However, the voices in North Korea are silenced irrespective of uncountable reports and the meetings between the United States, South Korea, and North Korea.[12]

The variables are further discussed in Figure 11.2, which represents the relationship between the aforementioned two variables – strength of the leadership of North Korea's political system and the pressure of international sanctions on North Korea. In this figure, it is illustrated that these two variables have a negative correlation, by describing the impact of the summit meetings in Singapore (2018) and Hanoi (2019) between the United States and the Democratic People's Republic of Korea (DPRK) on Kim's regime. Over the last several years, North

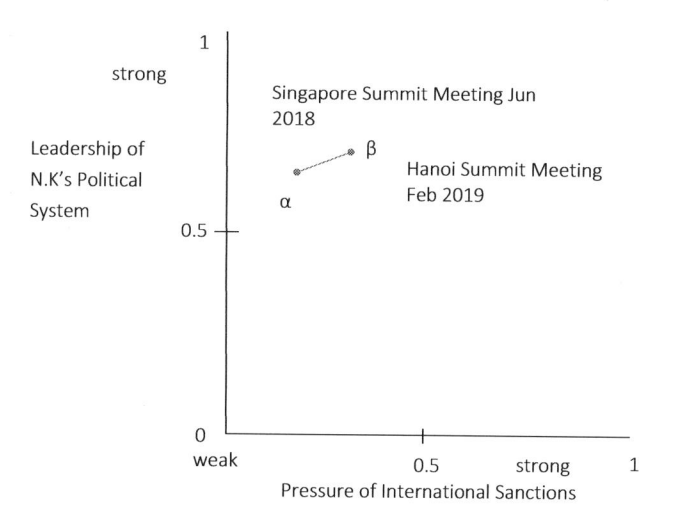

Figure 11.2 Conflict policy.

Korea's major foreign policy priorities have been a bilateral meeting between its leader and the US president and the withdrawal of the US troops from South Korea. So when a full-fledged US-DPRK summit was held in Singapore in June 2018 to resolve the North Korean nuclear issue, one of its objective was fulfilled.

The first presidential meeting in Singapore in 2018 was a harbinger of bonanza to North Korea. It was the first time that the leaders of North Korea and the United States were meeting since the founding of the North Korean regime. This meeting served Kim Jong-un's interests, which not only helped enhance his image but also gave him hope of having some control over South Korea through negotiations and the withdrawal of the US troops. Most importantly, this meeting gave North Korea the hope of relief against economic sanctions. In North Korea, they had evaluated the first summit meeting in 2018 so successful that Pyongyang could expect achievement of two goals at the same time: the lifting of economic sanctions and the possession of nuclear weapons. Thus, as shown in Figure 11.2, North Korea's political system became further strengthened following the US-North Korea summit meetings in Singapore (June 2018).

However, contradictory to predictions for progressive developments between the United States and North Korea, the Hanoi summit in 2019 failed. This occurred due to gaps between the approaches of Trump and Kim, where the former viewed the solution for crisis to be "maximum pressure" and complete disarmament, while the latter asked for the repeal of the UN security council sanctions billions of dollars.[13] This, moreover, undermined the strength of North Korea's political system and Kim's leadership (please see Figure 11.2).

Dynamic shift in North Korean political system

Undermining of Kim's leadership

According to a South Korean newspaper, *Chosun Ilbo*, Kim Jong-un, right before leaving for the Hanoi talks, said in a secret speech to senior North Korean officials that "North Korea would never give up the nuclear weapons that we had developed over the last few decades".[14] So, in this context, Pyongyang pursues a conflict policy (upper path, Figure 11.2) to defeat the US demand. Its strategy is to defend itself with nuclear missiles, characterising the US proposal for the elimination of nuclear weapons as a plot to overthrow the North Korean regime. According to *MK News*, Kim Jong-un argued that "the United States came to the talks and tried to create viable conditions for overthrowing our country (the Kim's regime)". Kim also asserted that "the US were seeking to eliminate North Korea's nuclear arsenal by improving relations between the two sides and lifting economic sanctions".[15]

As seen in Figure 11.2, North Korea and the United States choose conflict policies and lack mutual trust. For example, in 2017, North Korea threatened to attack the US territory of Guam with a nuclear missile.[16] As long as North Korea maintains its threats, there will be no trust between the United States and North Korea. The two countries regard each other's demands as threats to their security, which means that they are pursuing relative gains. Thus, the policy formulated by North Korea must strike a balance between the strength of the North Korean political system and the pressure of international sanctions against North Korea.

Figure 11.3 shows the dynamics of the policy-making process of North Korea's conflict policy. This diagram shows the direction of the two variables' balance point. If the North Korean political system is further strengthened after the Hanoi talks, North Korea's nuclear policy will be decided in quadrant A or B. Conversely, if sanctions are maintained or strengthened, North Korea's nuclear policy will be determined in A or D quadrants. Also, if the North Korean political system is strengthened and sanctions are strengthened, it will be in quadrant A, and if the North Korean political system and concurrent sanctions are weakened, it will be in quadrant C.

The failure of the Hanoi summit undermined Kim's authority very severely. The Korean newspaper *Joongang Daily* testifies that the regime's propaganda department ordered party officials to remain silent about the Hanoi talks:

> Don't ask questions about the Hanoi talks, and don't answer questions.[17]

North Koreans, however, came to know that the negotiations pursued by their supreme leader had failed. So, Kim's leadership position has moved to quadrant D in Figure 11.3.

The North Korean propaganda department had earlier exaggerated that the US president Trump would hold bilateral meeting with Kim Jong-un, because of Kim's bolstered political leadership and the fear of North Korea's nuclear weapons. Moreover, Kim Jong-un, too, had expected that an agreement would be reached with the United States, allowing Kim's demand for sanctions relief on the condition that Pyongyang scraps only one or two of its nuclear weapons facilities. Therefore, the failure hit harder.

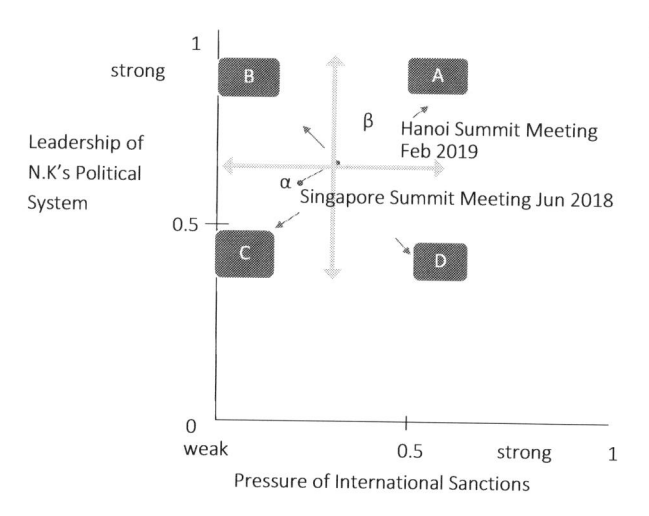

Figure 11.3 Dynamics of decision-making in conflict policy process.

Weakening of the divinity ideology

According to North Korea's official newspaper, *Rodong Shinmun*, "As long as the Labour Party makes a decision, we the people will do it". This slogan views "the party as the brain, and the people as the hands and feet, so people are commanded to believe in their leaders and create miracles".[18] Of course, it is well recognised in North Korea that the party and Kim Jong-un, the supreme leader, are one and the same. However, the supreme leader's authority is now weakening due to the continued policy failures following his rise to power. The first was the currency reform; second, the international community's economic sanctions and diminishing economic resilience; third, the surprise failure of the Hanoi summit; fourth, the international community's increasing economic sanctions and North Korea's diminishing economic resilience; and fifth, the collapse of information control.

Failure of the currency reforms

It is known that Kim Jong-un led the currency reform. On November 30, 2009, the North Korean authorities restricted the amount of money that could be exchanged to two months' living expenses and released it on a later date.[19] A 2016 Centre for Strategic and International Studies (CSIS) survey of North Korean refugees reported that when the North Korean authorities carried out the currency reform, confiscating entire life savings in the process, the common people expressed extreme hostility towards the Labour Party.[20]

The breakdown of the Hanoi talks in February 2019 was the biggest blow to the living god-like status of Kim Jong-un, which worsened the currency reform failure. Further the collapse of the Hanoi summit lead to a decrease in exports and hence North Korea has been witnessing a widespread inflation. At the same time, the failure of the summit resulted in a decline of food supply, which pushed the people of the country into malnutrition and starvation.[21]

It can be argued that North Koreans have begun to realise that their supreme leader can also make mistakes and fail to achieve results. When Kim's charisma collapses further, and people begin to perceive their supreme leader as a fallible figure, it will be difficult for the North Korean authorities to maintain their absolute authority. Such a realisation has also created growing unrest among the provincial population, given the gross disparity in the standard of living between citizens in and outside of Pyongyang.

Failure of the Hanoi talks

After all North Koreans became aware of the failure of the Hanoi talks, their "faultless leader" Kim had to offer an explanation at the Supreme People's Assembly meeting in April 2019. There, he laid the blame for the failure at the feet of the United States as well as his own aides. At the same time, in order to project himself as a relevant world leader, Kim spoke of his close relationship with Donald Trump by saying that he himself is "not hostile to the US President Trump and that he has an intimate friendship with U.S. President Trump by exchanging greetings anytime".[22]

In response to this speech, according to *Kyunghyang Daily*, the North Korean government quickly replaced Kim Young-chul, the minister of the unified front department, who led the US-North talks, along with Jang Geum-chul,[23] and also asked the United States to replace US secretary of state Mike Pompeo.[24] However, this was not viewed as a serious attempt to replace Secretary Pompeo for the upcoming talks. Rather, the propaganda department of the ruling Workers' Party of North Korea only tried to bolster Kim's attempts to lay the blame for the failure of the Hanoi meeting on the Americans.

These excuses are shaking the North Koreans' confidence in the Labour Party's teachings. Until now, North Koreans have been brainwashed into believing that the United States is the arch enemy of the North and that coexistence is impossible. They are taught that the Korean Peninsula was divided because of the United States and that unification failed because of the US intervention in the Korean War. However, as Kim officially declared his intimate relationship with President Trump, there seems a crack being developed in the prevalent belief among North Koreans regarding the United States. Trump also has become Kim's "interviewer" as no more will North Korean authorities target photos of President Trump at the shooting range!

However, Kim Jong-un's claim that he was close to President Trump was also proven to be false. This was reiterated when the United States seized the North Korean cargo ship, the *Wise Ernest*, on May 9, 2019.[25] The incident developed doubts in the minds of the citizens of North Korea as countries maintaining friendly relations would try to prevent such coercion. As a result, Kim's leadership took a further hit.

Nonetheless, to resolve this conflict with the United States and confirm his claim, Kim wrote a letter to Trump to commemorate the first anniversary of the Singapore talks on June 12, 2019. However, this letter contained nothing but the anniversary commemoration for Singapore meeting. Further, President Trump encouraged Kim and praised his cooperative will to participate in the next negotiation talks.[26]

Strengthening of sanctions against North Korea

According to Chanlett-Avery et al., the international community announced 10 UN sanctions to prevent North Korea from producing and testing weapons of mass destruction (WMDs) between October 2006 and December 2017. The UN Security Council Resolution 2397, passed in December 2017, banned most trade and financial transactions with North Korea. The United States imposed independent sanctions on North Korea to boost the effectiveness of the UN sanctions. From President George W. Bush to President Barack Obama and President Trump, they have continued to ban trade, including financial transactions, with North Korea.[27]

The imposition of sanctions by the UN and the United States and their continued tightening has made the economic situation in North Korea increasingly difficult. Most North Korean factories have ceased operations, and even the elite are experiencing economic difficulties. According to *Asia Press*, North Korean authorities have been continuously ensuring a distribution economy for the residents of Pyongyang, but this was stopped in April 2018, because of the sanctions.[28]

The Korean Statistics Bureau confirms North Korea's exports fell from $3.2 billion in 2013 to $1.8 billion in 2017 because of international sanctions. In addition, imports fell from $4.1 billion in 2013 to $3.8 billion in 2017.[29] According to KOTRA, North Korean exports in 2018 decreased by 30 per cent compared to 2017.[30] China accounts for 93.8 per cent of North Korea's foreign trade: while China's exports to North Korea dropped 31.6 per cent in 2018, North Korea's exports to China fell to 87.7 per cent.

Hence, after talks with the United States broke down, Kim Jong-un sought economic aid from the Chinese president Xi Jinping in early March 2019 and later visited Vladivostok, Russia, on April 25, 2019, to ask President Putin for assistance. However, according to Chosun Media, Putin announced his support towards the US nuclear policy to North Korea and insisted that the North should comply. Consequently, Russian food aid to the North remained only 50,000 tons of wheat – half of the requested amount.[31]

Limitations of North Korean economic resilience

The failure of the Hanoi talks was shocking given that Pyongyang had pinned considerable hopes on the summit. BBC reported that according to Foreign Minister Choi Sun-hee, Kim Jong-un, too, was in shock. She revealed that North Korea at Hanoi wanted only 5 of the 11 key UN sanctions to be lifted.[32] However, the United States refused North Korea's demand until the latter agrees to completely abandon its nuclear missiles.

MK News further reported that in 2019, Kim Jong-un confessed in a speech at the 14th Supreme People's Assembly, held on April 2019, that North Korea had been desperate for the lifting of sanctions. Further, Kim proclaimed, "I will no longer be obsessed with the question of whether hostile forces will lift sanctions or not, and I will open my way for recovery with our own strength".[33] After this declaration, North Korea fired medium-range missiles to demonstrate that Kim will not passively wait for the lifting of sanctions[34]; rather, it would take measure to restore Kim's position as the supreme leader with absolute power in North Korea.

Collapse of information control

Mobile phones and marketplaces are a double-edged sword for the North Korean regime. On the one hand, authorities have generated huge income by providing mobile phone services to the people. However, this has rendered impossible to prevent the spread of information that the authorities want to control. North Koreans are no longer isolated by their government's information blockade. The estimated 100,000 North Korean workers abroad in 2017,[35] scheduled to be repatriated home, have experienced the lives of people in their host countries. They are watching world news and entertainment programmes and are exposing themselves to the content restricted by the government of North Korea. This is enabling the people to become aware of the global scenario beyond the isolated North Korea. In this regard, once the North Korean citizens living abroad are repatriated home, they would be able to disseminate values of freedom, justice, and equality among the repressed people and introduce a sense of dissent.

NK Economy reports that in order to suppress the spread of information in North Korea, its information agency manufactured a Linux-based mobile phone operating system (Red Star 3 OS) which all North Korean computer and mobile phone users have been forced to install since June 2014. The Red Star 3 OS controls the registry of the mobile phone and records the insertion of any an external storage device, such as a Universal Serial Bus (USB) device, into a mobile phone.[36]

As of 2019, there are about five million mobile phones in use in North Korea. According to Cho Myung-kyun, South Korea's unification minister, there are close to six million active mobile phones in North Korea, with five million individual cell phones and about one million government phones.[37] According to *Insider*, the growth rate of mobile phones in North Korea is outpacing the North Korean authorities' information censorship and information control policy.[38]

North Korea's marketplace, where all information that North Korean authorities want to suppress is circulated actively, symbolises the changing political scene in the country. The North Korean government still denies its residents the freedom of movement. But since food shortages led to massive starvation in the North in the 1990s, the authorities have been overlooking trips made by merchants to procure food, which is another means of gathering and spreading information. The marketplace also reduces the economic control exercised by North Korean authorities on the people. The market is the only place in North Korea where the distribution economy has collapsed, where people can buy daily necessities and earn money. Markets have been formally approved by the regime at the rate of one per 50,000 people, and the number of smaller temporary markets is estimated to be greater still.

According to the CSIS project *Beyond Parallel*, based on satellite data collected from Google Earth in 2016, there were about 436 approved markets in North Korea.[39] The analysis of US satellite information by Curtis Melvin of the US-Korea Institute, on February 2018, showed that the number of marketplaces in North Korea were 482 in 2018, up from 468 in August 2017.[40]

Figure 11.4 shows the change in the leadership in the North Korean political system. It reiterates that the image of North Korean leader Kim Jong-un and the controlling power of the ruling North Korea Workers' Party are rapidly diminishing.

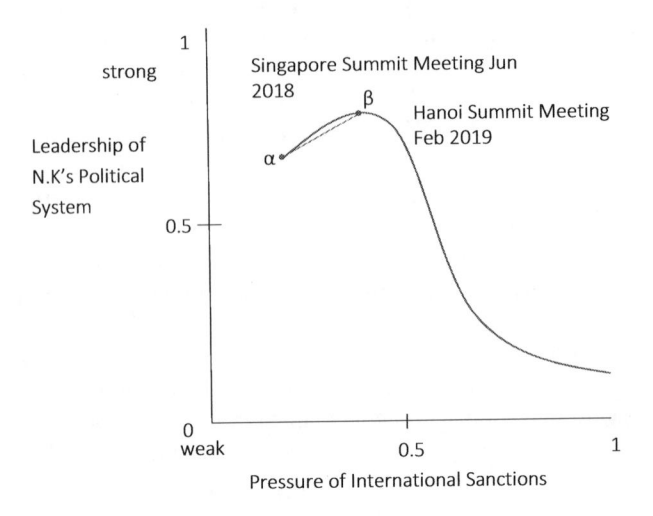

Figure 11.4 Leadership change of N.K's political system.

A way forward

The tougher the US sanctions against North Korea, the weaker the North Korean economy will become. Moreover, North Korea's economy will be brought to its knees if China and Russia join the United States in imposing sanctions on the North. Furthermore, since Hanoi, Kim Jong-un's leadership has weakened dramatically.

Thus, it can be assumed that the direction of North Korean policy will be determined by quadrant D of Figure 11.3. As shown in Figure 11.5, the robustness of the North Korean political system is like a curve (αθ), and its robustness will gradually weaken. Although the North Korean regime was highly cohesive until the Hanoi meeting (β), because of the Singapore meeting (α), the North Korean regime is believed to have rapidly weakened to the position of point δ due to the collapse of Kim Jong-un's authority and worsening economic situation. As the pressure of international sanctions on North Korea increases (p1 > p3), the North Korean political system gradually would weaken.

Despite the increasing international pressure on North Korea, the Singapore summit strengthened Kim's leadership in North Korea (α→β), and the country was hopeful that sanctions will be lifted while it still maintained possession of nuclear weapons. However, after the Hanoi talks failed, the sanctions imposed on North Korea continued to put pressure on the regime (p1→p2), resulting in a worsened North Korean economy and political system, and Kim's leadership dropped sharply to δ from β.

However, in a historic turn of events, Trump and Kim met at Panmunjum, in the Demilitarised Zone (DMZ), on June 30, 2019, after the former issued a surprise invitation (in a tweet) to the North Korean leader for a "handshake meeting".

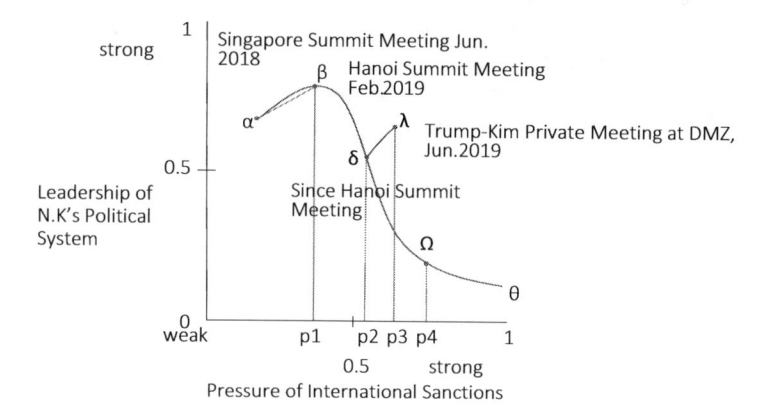

Figure 11.5 Strength-pressure curve.

Trump seems good at this kind of improvisational deal-making,[41] which may be helpful in bringing Kim to the negotiation table in the future as well.

The meeting gave North Korea an opportunity to officially confirm the "good relationship between two leaders", a claim Kim had made after the Hanoi failure.[42] And as a result, the status of Kim's leadership soared up to point λ dramatically (see Figure 11.5). This means Kim Jong-un now must make a decision whether to keep nuclear weapons and follow the downward slope to Ω or dismantle and continue upwards to λ. According to Figure 11.1, if North Korea changes its path from conflict policy (upper path) to cooperative policy (lower path), then a peaceful solution to the nuclear issue could be possible. As long as there is increasing economic pressure through international sanctions imposed on North Korea (increased to point p4), North Korea may reach point Ω, where it gives up its nuclear arsenal (see Figure 11.5).

Moreover, continued international sanctions will further squeeze the North Korean economy, completely paralyse its industry and exhaust the government's foreign exchange reserves. Consequently, Kim's regime will not only be unable to maintain its military and industry because of the shortage of foreign currency and national resources but will also lose the power to control its ruling class. North Korea's ruling elite are only vertically connected without horizontal interlinkages, so it is very hard to operate businesses, governments, or troops without resource support from their superiors.

On the contrary, if the international community lifts sanctions or begins to support North Korea, Kim's leadership will be strengthened and the North Korean nuclear issue will be determined in quadrant B or C (see Figure 11.3). In other words, North Korea's possession of nuclear weapons will be a *fait accompli*. In such a scenario, there is indeed a possibility that South Korea and the international community could be bullied by North Korea's nuclear threats.

Thus, strengthening of sanctions and accordingly weakening of the North Korean political system (particularly, Kim's leadership) will find a balance point in the fourth quadrant D (see Figure 11.3). As North Koreans get increasingly dissatisfied with the deteriorating economic conditions of their lives, they will begin to question the existing political system. As a result, Kim Jong-un's leadership, which has taken no measures to cope with the economic failure, other than oppressing its people, will be extremely weakened, which could lead to a power struggle among the elite groups. This power struggle will be the likely path for the unification of the Korean Peninsula.

Notes

1 "North Korea, Events of 2018", Human Rights Watch, at www.hrw.org/world-report/2019/country-chapters/north-korea (accessed May 25, 2019).
2 Robert Powell, "Absolute, and Relative Gains in International Relations Theory", *American Political Science Review*, 85 (4), December 1991, pp. 1303–1320.
3 Stephen M. Walt, *The Origins of Alliance*, Cornell University Press, Ithaca, 1987.
4 Kenneth Waltz, "The Origins of War in Neorealist Theory", in R. I. Rotberg and T. K. Rabb (eds.), *The Origin and Prevention of Major Wars*, Cambridge University Press, Cambridge, 1989, p. 40.
5 Paul Schroeder, "Historical Reality vs. Neo-realist Theory", *International Security*, 19 (1), Summer 1994, pp. 108–148.
6 Randall L. Schweller, "Bandwagoning for Profit: Bringing the Revisionist State Back", *International Security*, 19 (1), summer 1994, pp. 72–107.
7 Jin Shin, "Korean Sunshine Policy and Its Structural Limits", *The Korean Journal of International Studies*, 43 (1), 2003, p. 300.
8 Carl J. Friedrich and Zbigniew K. Brzezinski, *Totalitarian Dictatorship and Autocracy*, Harvard University Press, Cambridge, 1956.
9 "North Korea Revised 'Ten Principles of One-Ideology System'", *Voice of America*, August 12, 2013, at www.voakorea.com/a/1727952.html (accessed May 25, 2019).
10 Alexander Smith, "North Korean Gulags 'as Terrible, or Even Worse' than Nazi Camps, Auschwitz Survivor Says", *NBC News*, December 13, 2017, at www.nbcnews.com/news/north-korea/north-korean-gulags-terrible-or-even-worse-nazi-camps-auschwitz-n828751 (accessed May 18, 2019).
11 "North Korea: Events of 2018," *Human Rights Watch*, at www.hrw.org/world-report/2019/country-chapters/north-korea (accessed September 21, 2019); please see.
12 "North Korea: No Justice for Human Rights Crime," *Human Rights Watch*, January 17, 2019, at. www.hrw.org/news/2019/01/17/north-korea-no-justice-human-rights-crimes (accessed September 21, 2019).
13 Ankit Panda and Vipin Narang, "The Hanoi Summit Was Doomed from the Start," *Foreign Affairs*, March 5, 2019, at www.foreignaffairs.com/articles/north-korea/2019-03-05/hanoi-summit-was-doomed-start (accessed September 21, 2019).
14 "김정은, 어떤 광풍에도 핵 포기 없다고 하노이 가기 전 당간부들에 비밀 강연", *Chosun Ilbo*, May 2, 2019, at http://news.chosun.com/site/data/html_dir/2019/05/02/2019050200295.html (accessed May 4, 2019).
15 "Kim Jong Un's Address to North Korea's Supreme Representative Meeting at the 1st Session of the 14th Term", *MK News*, April 13, 2019, at www.mk.co.kr/news/politics/view/2019/04/228114/ (accessed May 2, 2019).
16 Brad Lendon and Joshua Berlinger, "Next Target Guam, North Korea Says", *CNN*, August 31, 2017, at https://edition.cnn.com/2017/08/29/asia/north-korea-missile-launch-guam-threat/index.html (accessed May 25, 2019).
17 Minjeong Baek, "'하노이, 입에 담지도 말라' 北 노동당 지침 내려왔다", *Joongang Daily*, April 10, 2019, at https://mnews.joins.com/amparticle/23436448 (accessed April 10, 2019).

18 *Rodong Shinmun*, July 24, 2009, at http://webcache.googleusercontent.com/search?q= cache:http://www.kcna.co.jp/calendar/2009/07/07-24/2009-0724-010.html (accessed May 20, 2019).
19 James M. Lister, "Currency 'Reform' in North Korea", at http://keia.org/sites/ default/files/publications/10January.pdf (accessed May 21, 2019).
20 Victor Cha and Lisa Collins, "The Markets: Private Economy and Capitalism in North Korea?" Beyond Parallel, *CSIS*, August 26, 2018, at https://beyondparallel. csis.org/markets-private-economy-capitalism-north-korea/ (accessed May 21, 2019).
21 Chan Young ban, "'Bright Future' in Rear-View Mirror: North Korea's Resurging Crisis After Hanoi," *The Globe Post*, April. 18, 2019, at https://theglobepost.com/2019/04/18/north-korea-crisis/ (accessed on September 21, 2019).
22 "[전문] 김정은 위원장, 최고인민회의 시정연설-2(끝)" *MK News*, April 13, 2019, at www.mk.co.kr/news/politics/view/2019/04/228119/ (accessed May 2, 2019).
23 Yoo-jin Kim, "북한 통일전선부장, 김영철에서 장금철로 교체…숙청은 아닌 듯", *Kyunghyang Daily*, April 24, 2019, at http://news.khan.co.kr/kh_news/khan_art_ view.html?art_id=201904242026001#csidxb79ad75af6283cc880deb802da6d885 (accessed April 24, 2019).
24 Jeong-won Kim, "북한 '폼페이오는 빠져라' 협상 파트너 교체 요구", Hankook Daily, April 18, 2019, at www.hankookilbo.com/News/Read/201904181834053291 (accessed April 18, 2019).
25 Ju-young Lim, "美, 北석탄운송 화물선 압류…'제재 위반' 北선박 압류 첫 조치(종합)", *The Korea Daily*, May 9, 2019, at www.koreadaily.com/news/read.asp?art_id= 7225881 (accessed May 21, 2019).
26 Kylie Atwood, "Kim Jong Un's 'Beautiful' Letter to Trump Contained No Details on Way Forward, Source Says", *CNN*, June 13, 2019, at https://edition.cnn. com/2019/06/12/politics/kim-trump-letter-lacked-details/index.html (accessed June 29, 2019).
27 Emma Chanlett-Avery et al., "North Korea: U.S. Relations, Nuclear Diplomacy, and Internal Situation", *Congressional Research Service*, July 27, 2018, pp. 6–8.
28 "<북한내부>평양시민도 경제 악화로 반발… 배급 악화와 전정으로 "먹을 것도 전기도 주지 않는다" Asia Press, May 14, 2018, at www.asiapress.org/korean/2018/05/ nk-economys/pyongyang-economic-depravation/2/ (accessed May 21, 2019).
29 Please see Korean Statistics Bureau, 2017, at http://kosis.kr/bukhan/bukhanStats/ bukhanStats_03_02List.jsp?menuId=03&NUM=28&LIST_NM=%EB% 8C%80%EC%99%B8%EA%B2%BD%EC%A0%9C (accessed May 21, 2019).
30 "Analysis of 2018 Korea-China Imports and Exports Under Sanctions," *World Market News*, Kotra, April 9, 2019, at http://news.kotra.or.kr/user/globalBbs/kotranews/ 786/globalBbsDataView.do?setIdx=247&dataIdx=174264&pageViewType=& column=&search=&searchAreaCd=&searchNationCd=&searchTradeCd=& searchStartDate=&searchEndDate=&searchCategoryIdxs=&searchIndustry CateIdx=&searchItemCode=&searchItemName=&page=1&row=10 (accessed May 18, 2019).
31 "Yomiuri: Putin Urges Kim Jong-un to Final and Complete Denuclearization" *Chosun Media*, May 5, 2019, at http://news.chosun.com/site/data/html_dir/2019/ 05/04/2019050400431.html (accessed May 4, 2019); *Joongang Daily*, May 3, 2019, at https://news.joins.com/article/23457720 (accessed May 4, 2019).
32 "북한 리용호 외무상 기자회견: '전면적 제재 해제 아닌 일부 해제' 원했다", *BBC News Korea*, March 1, 2019, at www.bbc.com/korean/news-47404051 (accessed May 1, 2019).
33 MK News 2019.04.13., www.mk.co.kr/news/politics/view/2019/04/228119/ (accessed May 2, 2019).
34 "북한:'경고한다', '협상준비 안됐다'…잇따른 미사일 발사에 한미 대응 수위도 높아졌다", *BBC News Korea*, May 10, 2019, at www.bbc.com/korean/news-48223605 (accessed May 10, 2019).

35 "2017 Country Reports on Human Rights Practices: Democratic People's Republic of Korea", *Bureau of Democracy*, Human Rights, and Labor, US Department of State, pp. 24–25.
36 "White Paper on Human Rights in North Korea", Seoul, *2018*, Korea Institute for National Unification, *NK Economy*, June 25, 2018, p. 174, at www.nkeconomy.com/news/articleView.html?idxno=90 (accessed May 20, 2019).
37 Young-kwonKim, "북한 휴대폰, 보급 대수와 사용자 수 구분해야", *VOA*, January 28, 2019, at www.voakorea.com/a/4761619.html (accessed May 20, 2019).
38 Yonho Kim, "North Korea's Mobile Telecommunications and Private Transportation Services in the Kim Jong-un Era", *Insider,* January 10, 2019, at www.hrnkinsider.org/2019/01/north-koreas-mobile-telecommunications.html (accessed May 20, 2019).
39 Victor Cha and Lisa Collins, No. 20.
40 Benjamin Katzeff Silberstein, "North Korean Market Update", *North Korean Economy Watch*, February 5, 2018, at www.nkeconwatch.com/2018/02/05/north-korean-market-update/ (accessed May 21, 2019).
41 Scott Horsley, "Trump Tweets an Invitation to North Korea's Kim – Meet in the DMZ?" *NPR*, June 29, 2019, at www.npr.org/2019/06/28/737209058/trump-tweets-an-invitation-to-north-koreas-kim-meet-in-the-dmz (accessed June 30, 2019).
42 조은정, "트럼프대통령 북한에서 연락받아..매우 흥미로울 것", *VOA*, June 30, 2019, at www.voakorea.com (accessed June 30, 2019).

12 Negotiating mechanisms in the Korean Peninsula

What has worked? Any lessons for the Indo-Pacific?

Manpreet Sethi

The majority view on how best to handle the difficult issue of a nuclear North Korea favours negotiations and not military action. There are, however, differences of opinion on which forum to use, who should be involved, what to negotiate, how to sequence priorities, etc. Over the past three decades or so, a time period over which many attempts at halting North Korea's nuclear weapons and missile programmes have taken place, several kinds of negotiating mechanisms – bilateral, trilateral, quadrilateral, and even multilateral negotiations – have been experimented with. Each one has had a limited impact, but overall, none of the negotiating mechanisms has yielded any long-lasting or really substantive, successful outcomes. As a result, North Korea's nuclear and missile capability has steadily grown over the decades.

There was a particular spurt in Pyongyang's nuclear and missile activities between 2016 and 2018. The country restarted its nuclear testing in 2016, after a gap of three years, when two tests were conducted. Another test of a claimed thermonuclear weapon followed in September 2017. This prompted, primarily the United States and, reluctantly, China, to impose ever more stringent sanctions on the country that was already under heavy sanctions. The United States also made it clear that it was open to considering military action to stop North Korea, from furthering its nuclear activities. However, caution was advised by all international players who reiterated that the only real solution to the issue lay in negotiations and not military action.

Nevertheless, the United States and Democratic People's Republic of Korea (DPRK)[1] continued to make highly belligerent noises in 2017–2018, threatening to impose a bloody war, with nuclear overtones, upon each other. Tempers finally cooled down, to the relief of all, when owing to the backchannel diplomatic work of many countries, the presidents of the US and DPRK consented to hold a summit meeting at Singapore in June 2018. This was preceded by a bilateral meeting between the North and South Korean heads of state at the heavily fortified Demilitarised Zone (DMZ) between the countries in April 2018. The ensuing Panmunjom declaration signed between the two laid the ground for the Singapore summit.

The two aforementioned bilateral meetings in 2018 signified a major breakthrough. Given that the DPRK had always been keen on direct bilateral negotiations, especially with the United States, Kim Jong-un could claim his meeting with President Trump as a diplomatic victory. President Trump, too, proclaimed that the talks would quickly lead to North Korea's denuclearisation. Unfortunately, nothing really concrete in terms of denuclearisation of the DPRK followed the Singapore Summit. In fact, the interactions after the June summit between officials of both countries yielded little. Nevertheless, the two leaders decided to meet once again in Hanoi on February 28, 2019. This second summit, however, ended earlier than expected, with both countries maintaining intransigent positions on how to handle the issue of the DPRK's nuclear and missile programme. President Trump walked away from the meeting, though he described it as "productive time", since the two got to know each other better. He also indicated that he had not given up on the prospect of future negotiations and continues to describe Kim Jong-un as "'quite a guy'". Since then, the DPRK has conducted two missile tests and it seems to be yesterday once more, notwithstanding another short meeting between the American and North Korean heads of state in July 2019.

This chapter examines the various forums that have been used for negotiating a resolution of the difficult issue of North Korea's nuclear weapons. It briefly traces the evolution and conduct of the various negotiating mechanisms in order to understand what has worked in the past and could be used again to make it work in the future. The chapter begins by highlighting some principles on which negotiations must be anchored to have any chance of success. Thereafter, it provides an overview of the limited achievements of the negotiating mechanism at different points of time. The chapter concludes by drawing some inferences from these negotiating mechanisms in the Korean Peninsula for the situation in the Indo-Pacific.

The Indo-Pacific has emerged in recent times as an arena for Chinese assertiveness, and hence the United States has indicated its desire to activate other countries in the region to contain China. However, the idea of the Indo-Pacific – as a geographical or a conceptual entity– is still pretty diffused. Negotiations will be the order of the day to keep the situation in the region peaceful and beneficial for all. How could these be structured and what lessons can one learn about conducting meaningful dialogue in tense times, from the long experience of the Korean negotiations? The chapter briefly examines this question, too.

International negotiations – principles and modalities

International relations are mainly about the pursuit of self-defined national interests in a game of power politics. International negotiations, by extension, involve a process of power-based dialogues intended to achieve certain goals or ends, where each actor seeks to maximise his gains and minimise his losses.[2] The process involves a display or play-out of power equations as they exist between the negotiators. Influence and coercion are, therefore, an inherent part of the process. International negotiations can be bilateral or multilateral, public or secret, and can involve different forms of negotiation among states or between a state and one or more non-state actors, or even anti-state actors, such as individual terrorists and terrorist organisations.

The differing cultures of the negotiators add to the complexity of differing styles of engagement, differences of priorities, and varying assessments of the levels of dangers of failure of negotiations. This leads to different expectations from the negotiations and asymmetries, in the desire to sustain them despite all odds. Obviously, respect for, and understanding of, cultural differences can have considerable impact on the outcome of the negotiations. Other important factors that play a role in negotiations are domestic considerations; personalities of individual leaders; the value ascribed by the involved parties to the issue being negotiated; the trust the sides repose in each other; and lastly, the credibility of the outcome and its sustainability in the future irrespective of government or leadership changes.

Negotiations may take different forms based on their objectives. For instance, they may aim for conflict management, conflict transformation, or conflict resolution. Conflict management negotiations would seek to limit or minimise tensions and disputes to the extent possible, without necessarily seeking to change the status quo or power equations between disputing parties. Meanwhile, negotiations aimed at conflict transformation would, particularly, seek to alter the status quo and to transform relations between the negotiators in order to push hitherto disparate interests towards a more "positive" and less controversial direction, even if some points of difference persist. On the other hand, conflict resolution would aim to completely resolve the dispute through an agreement on the content and the modalities of how to do so. This would generally be expected to be a long-drawn-out process, as attempts to reach a common and complete agreement among parties engaged in a power tussle can never be easy.

The negotiations for finding a solution to the North Korean nuclear issue represent all three types of processes – conflict management, transformation, and resolution – that have been attempted through many kinds of negotiating mechanisms. With little success, though. The issue has been neither contained nor managed through negotiations (except for short periods). Nor has it led to any change in the situation or relationship between the main negotiating participants. Conflict resolution, of course, appears to be a distant dream at this juncture.

It is clear that the art and science of creating negotiating mechanisms and processes calls for a fair amount of preparation by all parties involved. For the negotiations to be successful, it is important for all sides to have a good understanding of not only their own strengths and leverages but also the psyche, behavioural patterns, cultural affinities, and personal afflictions of the other side. Negotiations literally call for cooperation between adversaries. A respect for differing perspectives and a readiness to compromise need to be part of the package.

Given all of the above imperatives, international negotiations are by nature a complex process. In the case of the DPRK, it is even more so because of the many stakeholders involved and the long-standing hostility between the two sides. Though the main hostility is between the United States and the DPRK, and the latter has always insisted on the need for purely bilateral negotiations, the involvement of the Republic of Korea (ROK) and Japan as US allies, and that of China as the closest friend and supporter of North Korea, cannot be discounted. These nations have their own individual interests and relationships with the DPRK, which impinge on other dimensions, too. Efforts at resolving the North Korean nuclear issue have involved negotiations between all permutations and combinations of the nations. Four such mechanisms are briefly discussed in the following section. Though these have yielded only limited and episodic success, an examination of the negotiating mechanisms does offer an insight into what has or has not worked.

Bilateral negotiating mechanisms – DPRK-ROK and DPRK-US

Two major bilateral relations have dominated the negotiation mechanisms in the North Korean crisis. These are the relations between North and South Korea and those between North Korea and the United States. Though the DPRK-Japan relations are also important and have their share of issues, such as the kidnapping of Japanese citizens by North Korea, this relationship has largely been handled through the United States. Tokyo depends on its alliance with the United States and lets Washington take the lead in handling North Korea.

On the other hand, while the ROK, too, is an American ally, it has allowed Washington to take the lead in its relationship with DPRK only a few times. This happened, for instance, in 1996, after the incursion of the North Korean submarine into the ROK territorial waters. It was through talks between the United States and DPRK that the issue was resolved, after a public apology was rendered by Pyongyang to Seoul. Despite some such instances, however, Seoul's sense of being part of the same peninsula, with historical, cultural, and familial ties, have motivated it to take several political initiatives to engage in direct negotiation – especially when the United States has turned its back on talks. The current South Korean administration of President Moon Jae-in is particularly keen on negotiations to resolve the problem of North Korea's nuclear weapons and improving relations between the two Koreas. He rather effectively played the role of a facilitator in bringing the United States and DPRK to Singapore in 2018. He ensured that the summit took place even when, it seemed, yet again, to be getting derailed. Therefore, the ROK-DPRK bilateral track has been important, not just for itself but also for helping the DPRK and the United States to stay focussed.

It is not the purpose of this section to recount the historical relations between the two Koreas. Given the scope of this chapter, the significant start point of bilateral negotiations came at the end of 1991, when a round of meaningful negotiations between the two Koreas resulted in an Agreement on Reconciliation, Non-aggression and Exchanges and Cooperation between the South and the North. The agreement called for economic, scientific, and cultural exchanges between the two, reopening rails and roadways to allow free access to divided families on the two sides. This agreement was followed up next year with a "Joint Declaration of the Denuclearisation of the Korean Peninsula". However, neither of these agreements was implemented. Over the years, many other accords have followed and met largely the same fate. The biggest breakthrough in recent times happened in 2018, when Kim Jong-un crossed over to South Korea for the first time, and then president Moon Jae-in followed suit in September 2018 with a visit to Pyongyang. This exercise not only helped to soften their bilateral relationship but also augured well for the US-DPRK summit meet.

According to the North Korean rationale, it is the conventional and nuclear threats made by the United States and the military confrontation along the demilitarised zone that makes it necessary for them to possess nuclear weapons. The United States, however, places the onus of provocation on the other side. For a long time, the United States maintained the position that DPRK did not "deserve direct bilateral talks because of its track record of cheating, blackmail and brinkmanship".[3] This position, however, changed in the first half of the 1990s. In fact, the one agreement that followed the direct negotiations between the United States and DPRK, and that did get partially implemented holding out a real ray of hope for the possibility of eventual elimination of the North Korean nuclear weapons ambitions was the 1994 Agreed Framework.

The Agreed Framework sought to freeze the DPRK's nuclear weapons programme and place its key nuclear facilities and spent fuel rods under International Atomic Energy Agency (IAEA) monitoring, in exchange for heavy fuel oil and the construction of Light Water Reactors(LWRs) in the DPRK, to meet is electricity requirements. The agreement lasted from 1995 until 2002 and largely managed to block the plutonium route to nuclear weapons. The LWRs were to be built by a consortium called Korean Peninsula Energy Development Organisation (KEDO), and the task was to be undertaken by the ROK, with Japan as the essential partner and financier. However, eight years into the implementation of the agreement, both sides had started making allegations of violations of the agreed terms. The United States accused the DPRK of building a capability that would allow it to access highly enriched uranium in order to continue developing nuclear weapons. The DPRK accused the United States and KEDO of not living up to their part of the bargain and dragging their feet on the construction of the two LWRs. By the end of 2002, Pyongyang had asked the IAEA inspectors to leave the country and put the international community on notice, with regard to its withdrawal from the Treaty on the Non-Proliferation of Nuclear Weapons (NPT). The KEDO was formally terminated in 2006 after much tension and mistrust.

Thereafter, the United States tried to activate the Six-Party architecture up to 2013, but once that hit a stalemate, the United States, around 2015, once again began to favour bilateral engagement. Backed by Seoul and Tokyo, Washington indicated its willingness to talk if the DPRK were to demonstrate its commitment to denuclearisation. As always, the United States insisted that the resolution of the nuclear issue was a prerequisite for diplomatic normalisation. For the DPRK, however, as stated by a foreign ministry official in January 2009, these are two different issues, and Pyongyang made it clear that "North Korea would not give up its status as a nuclear weapon state even after normalisation as long as it is exposed to the slightest US nuclear threat".[4]

While holding this stand publicly, Pyongyang did, in January 2009, informally indicate that it was prepared to suspend its nuclear and missile tests, and halt fissile material production in return for the scaling down of the US-South Korea military exercises.[5] After many ups and downs, direct talks between the two bilateral tracks did achieve some success in 2018, at least in terms of toning down the nuclear rhetoric and getting Pyongyang to put a halt to its missile and nuclear testing. A second summit planned between Presidents Trump and Kim for February 2019 had more expectations riding on it. But the involvement of all other parties in a primary agreement between the United States and DPRK will nevertheless be necessary as providers of complementary support or as guarantors of its implementation. In fact, lessons in this context can be drawn from the partial success of Agreed Framework of 1994.

Notwithstanding the lack of complete success of the Agreed Framework, this negotiating mechanism showed promise on two fronts: one, given the direct talks between the DPRK and United States, it proved to be more satisfactory for both sides; and two, since the implementation of the agreement required involvement of the ROK and Japan, it seemed to be the most effective way of securing a meaningful participation of the relevant parties. In the future, too, something like this would be necessary, in order to get everyone to feel that they have a stake in the process. Obviously, the DPRK believes that its main threat is from the United States, and it is with Washington that it hopes to achieve an agreement. There is also the prestige factor of a small country being able to negotiate with the world's most advanced nation on an equal basis. For a leader like Kim Jong-un, this imagery is of great value at the domestic and international level. It is only through engagement with the United States that it hopes to overcome its pariah status and get the respect of other nations. This also gives it leverage over China.

Trilateral negotiating mechanism

A trilateral engagement between the United States, DPRK, and China was briefly attempted in 2003, soon after Pyongyang had announced its withdrawal from the NPT. Angered by the move, the United States tried to involve Beijing in getting Pyongyang to the table. Beijing tried to do so by secretly promising the DPRK an opportunity for direct engagement with the United States, as part of the trilateral talks, but the United States refused to engage with them directly. This refusal led North Korea to opt out of this mechanism. During this brief phase, however, China established itself as the lead arbiter, by taking control of all conversations between the two sides. One US diplomat, who was President Bush's top aide in the negotiations with North Korea, described this as Beijing's "benign deception".[6] Beijing became the official and only channel of communication with Pyongyang. However, the DPRK's insistence on bilateral engagement with the United States was spelt out clearly on every occasion.

Though the trilateral mechanism could not really take off, President Trump, over the past year or so, has focussed heavily on the role that China should play as a core participant in the resolution of the issue. Holding out a carrot to China, he even suggested greater accommodation with Beijing on other contentious bilateral issues, if it would be more assertive with Pyongyang. A similar point was made in a recent article in *South China Morning Post* wherein the author argued that

> [i]f Washington and Beijing can cooperate to defuse the decades-old hostility on the Korean peninsula, it will help them work together to solve, or at least soften their rhetoric, on other issues, such as trade, Taiwan and the South China Sea.[7]

China, however, has maintained a studied distance from the issue, insisting that it has little leverage with North Korea and has no direct role to play between the two main interlocutors. Several scholars though have pressed China to have a "new conversation with the DPRK that stresses both its commitment to ensuring that the DPRK gets a good and fair deal but also its new resolve that the status quo on the peninsula cannot endure".[8] That China has the ability to influence Pyongyang is clear from the fact that Kim Jong-un has been seen to visit Beijing before every major summit with the United States. It remains to be seen, however, whether China will play the role of an honest broker in resolving the US-DPRK tensions, as also the nuclear issue. Given that the state of US-China relations is not very good in these times, Pyongyang's ability to discomfit Washington should not be particularly unwelcome to Beijing. Be that at it may, there is little hope or scope for a trilateral negotiating mechanism comprising the United States, DPRK, and China in the current circumstances.

Four-party talks

The DPRK, US, ROK, and China held talks for first time in April 1996 to negotiate a more permanent peace mechanism. As is evident, this initiative came from Washington and Seoul two years after the conclusion of the Agreed Framework. Three preliminary rounds and six formal plenary sessions of talks took place. However, they failed to reach a consensus on the agenda. The only achievement of these talks was to provide a platform for the regular engagement of the four nations – all together, as well as bilaterally and trilaterally. The 2000 summit between Pyongyang and Seoul was one successful outcome of these talks. This was a historic first when South Korea's then president, Kim Dae-jung, who won a Nobel Peace Prize for his Sunshine Policy of engagement with the North, visited Pyongyang for an unprecedented inter-Korean summit with late leader Kim Jong-il.[9] The two agreed on a joint peace declaration which promised to facilitate reunification of families separated since the Korean War and humanitarian and economic cooperation. However, the process collapsed with the demise of the Agreed Framework in 2002.

Six-Party Talks

The United States chose to broaden the field of players after the failure of the Agreed Framework. In any case, with the change of administration in the United States in 2001 and following 9/11, which created new security concerns for the United States, President George W. Bush, Jr. chose not to follow the trend set into motion by his predecessor, Bill Clinton, whose administration had concluded the 1994 agreement. Moving far away from that position, Bush included North Korea in his "axis of evil" formulation. No direct contact between the two sides looked possible under these circumstances. However, the efforts to negotiate a path for peaceful resolution was not completely abandoned. The United States initially offered a P-5 plus 5 (the ROK, Japan, the European Union, Australia, and the DPRK) setting, which the North Koreans rejected. Pyongyang maintained the position that this was a DPRK-US bilateral nuclear issue that did not merit the participation of multiple actors.

Subsequently, and after considerable Chinese persuasion, the DPRK relented and agreed to the creation of a forum consisting of six parties – US, China, ROK, Japan, Russia, and DPRK. Nevertheless, it insisted on direct talks with the United States on the sidelines of the larger multilateral meeting. So, when the first round of talks was held in August 2003, the opportunity was also used for 30 minutes of direct talks between the United States and DPRK. However, no joint statement followed this meeting. In fact, the DPRK dismissed the US offer for multilateral written security guarantees as a "laughing matter, which is not worth even a glance, if the US gives us a certain security assurance within the multilateral framework in return for an end to our nuclear weapons programme".[10] It eventually led US vice president Cheney to remark, in December 2003, "We don't negotiate with evil; we defeat it". The year 2003, therefore, ended with no remarkable achievement for the Six-Party Talks except that it re-launched an institutionalised dialogue framework to deal with the nuclear concerns.

The next round of talks under this mechanism took place in February 2004. But, yet again, it ended without a joint statement. A third round took place in June 2004 and registered a little more progress than the previous two. At this meeting, both sides, the United States and DPRK, presented their proposals for resolution of the issue. While the American proposal outlined steps to be taken by North Korea towards the dismantlement of its nuclear programme over three months, Pyongyang called for the United States to first give up its hostile policy against the country, withdraw demand for Comprehensive Verifiable Irreversible Disarmament (CVID), and accept its demand for reward. Obviously, the proposal made by one side was not accepted by the other. But the very fact that proposals were being made was considered to be a sort of success in this round of talks.

Subsequently, a joint statement signed on September 19, 2005, opened a window of opportunity for the DPRK to consider denuclearisation, in return for energy and food assistance and security guarantees. Pyongyang also agreed to consider returning to the NPT and to allow re-entry of IAEA inspectors.

But, this hope collapsed just a month later when the United States placed restrictions on North Korean bank accounts, including the Banco Delta Asia of Macau, accusing them of being involved in counterfeit currency and money laundering.

In 2006, Pyongyang conducted its first nuclear test, which led to almost a year's stalemate, confrontation, and crisis. The Six-Party Talks, however, revived somewhat with a sixth round of negotiations in 2007 that produced the "Initial Actions for the Implementation of the Joint Statement", on February 13, 2007. This was a plan with two phases of implementation. The first phase required North Korea to freeze its nuclear programme at Yongbyon, invite IAEA inspectors back for verification, and declare all its nuclear programmes. The agreement also set up working groups involving all six countries for issues relating to denuclearisation of the Korean Peninsula, normalisation of the US-DPRK and DPRK-Japan relations, economy and energy cooperation, and a North-East Asia peace and security mechanism. In exchange for implementing this phase, the DPRK insisted on the unfreezing of its Banco Delta Asia funds. The terms of the agreement were upheld by the DPRK on its part, by shutting down and sealing its Yongbyon reprocessing facility.

In the second phase of implementation, which was articulated in the Six-Party Agreement of October 2007 and had a 60-day deadline, North Korea pledged to declare all nuclear materials and disable the fuel fabrication plant, chemical reprocessing facilities, and a five MW nuclear reactor. The United States was to reciprocate by removing the country from the list of terrorist-sponsoring nations and improve diplomatic relations. North Korea was also promised one million tons of heavy oil or its equivalent in aid. However, this phase could not go very far since the United States and DPRK disagreed on the issue of nuclear declaration. While the United States insisted on the inclusion of its uranium enrichment programme in the list of declared facilities, North Korea denied its very existence. A tentative compromise was finally reached in April 2008, whereby the DPRK only agreed to acknowledge US concerns about the programme. In exchange, the White House initiated the process of removing the DPRK from the list of state sponsors of terrorism but made it contingent upon the DPRK agreeing to a verification system to check out the declarations. This turned out to be problematic since Pyongyang failed to agree to a verification protocol that included US proposals for visits to facilities, reviews of documents, and interviews of technical personnel. There were also differences over the sequencing of acceptance of verification and the US delisting of the state from the list of sponsors of terrorism. Ultimately as a compromise solution, the United States delisted the state in exchange for North Korea agreeing to a more limited verification system.

Consequently, despite a promising start, the year 2008 ended with North Korea agreeing to only limited inspections, restricted to Yongbyon, while retaining its right to block access to undeclared sites. It categorically refused to accept "international standards", claiming that these would be an "infringement on their sovereignty without taking into consideration the present level of confidence in relations between the two countries that are technically at war".[11]

The year 2009 began with the change of administration in Washington and low trust levels. Though President Obama had indicated his willingness to adopt a two-track approach to bilateral talks and keep intact the framework of the Six-Party Talks, little progress was anticipated as the DPRK once again resumed its nuclear enrichment programme and conducted another nuclear test and multiple missile tests in 2009. It also announced withdrawal from the Six-Party Talks. Belligerence continued through 2010, with the DPRK sinking a South Korean navy ship and unveiling a new uranium enrichment facility.

Bilateral discussions in 2011 between the United States and North Korea to restart the Six-Party process proved difficult, since Pyongyang insisted on returning to the framework only if all preconditions were removed. On the other hand, the United States and South Korea demanded a tangible demonstration of the DPRK's commitment to abandon its nuclear programme before resuming talks. In 2013, China once again stepped up its efforts to re-launch the talks. A nuclear envoy was sent to Pyongyang, and an informal meeting between the other five participants was proposed. But the United States insisted on the DPRK honouring its past commitments before any new negotiations could begin. Meanwhile, North Korea went ahead with more nuclear and missile tests. In March 2013, the United Nations (UN), led by the United States and China, imposed severe restrictions on North Korean banking, travel, and trade. Obviously, the hostility increased, as also the nuclear capability of North Korea. The Six-Party Talks have since not been convened. Some cautious stirrings became visible in 2018, but the mechanism has not yet been revived.

This forum of negotiations, like all others with the DPRK, has had its share of ups and downs, and its stop and go phases. It came into being as an informal structure to facilitate dialogue. No secretariat to facilitate implementation of agreements or preserve any institutional memory of the meetings was set up. The purpose of the forum, largely steered by China, was to get the actors together to discuss issues and possible solutions.

With all six parties pushing for their vested interests, it also gave enough room to the DPRK to play one against the other. While Japan and the United States have traditionally pushed for strong sanctions, China, South Korea, and Russia have generally been in favour of less stringent action owing to the fear of the sudden collapse of the country. This, they believe, would create instability in the region. Such differences of views have been exploited by the DPRK. Meanwhile, the allies have also had their share of troubles. For instance, in 2008, there was disquiet in Japan when the United States agreed to remove the DPRK from the list of terrorism-sponsoring states. Tokyo had insisted on linking the delisting with the resolution of the issue of the kidnapping of Japanese nationals. The United States had initially accepted this linkage as part of the Six-Party Talks. But after the North Korean nuclear test in 2006, it changed its policy and became more keen to seek the disabling of the Yongbyon facility, in order to prevent the DPRK from increasing its nuclear capability. Japan viewed this as its "diplomatic defeat".[12] At another level, Japan and South Korea have also had their share of differences. The ROK, for instance, has sometimes sided with Japan and favoured stern action and, at other times, been more accommodating with regard to the DPRK, playing mediator between Washington and Pyongyang while shutting out Tokyo's concerns.

On balance, therefore, five parties of the Six-Party Talks have not always presented a united front. Consequently, individual concerns and priorities have weakened their hand.

Inferences and lessons

After its two nuclear tests in 2006 and 2009, North Korea seemed to have gained a sense of achievement that allowed it to engage in negotiations, as part of the Six-Party Talks. As was expressed by a North Korean party worker, Kim Jong-il's desire was to make the DPRK a "strong and prosperous great nation".[13] Having demonstrated its nuclear capability, he believed that he had made his country strong. The DPRK also believed that its nuclear capability had helped it to balance the "military equilibrium on the Korean peninsula through the acquisition of asymmetric military capabilities".[14] Meanwhile, for the Kim regime, the acquisition of nuclear weapons has also helped bolster the ruling Workers' Party of Korea's domestic legitimacy and coalition building, besides the added benefit of enhancing the country's international status and prestige.

Having accomplished all these objectives with its nuclear weapons programme, it is not surprising that Kim Jong-un is now ready for some meaningful negotiations to achieve prosperity. It was in 2013 that Kim Jong-un announced the *Byunglin* policy, which envisaged the parallel advance of economic growth and nuclear capabilities. The same thought was echoed once again in April 2018 at a Workers' Party plenum, where President Kim announced the victory of the nuclear path and the new strategic path of Economy First.[15]

The Supreme Leader of North Korea now hopes to leverage his nuclear capability to win economic and energy concessions. In that sense, the time is ripe for negotiations. However, any plan that seeks to deprive the country of its nuclear capability is unlikely to be successful. Kim would want the negotiations with President Trump to allow his nuclear programme to be retained, even if it is a bit constrained. It should be evident to Kim that neither abandoning the capability nor furthering it beyond the present level where it poses a credible threat is in the best interest of the nation.

As far as North Korea is concerned, it would prefer to talk directly with the United States, and that too with President Trump. Kim Jong-un has rightly sensed that a more instinctive and business-like US president such as Donald Trump would be a better interlocutor than bureaucratic and old-style conservative diplomacy. In any case, the economic possibilities of an open North Korea should greatly appeal to the businessman in Donald Trump. Kim, however, would certainly be sure to hold on to his prized crown nuclear jewels, giving up the least possible to gain economic benefits for his nation. The biggest achievements for Pyongyang would be to gain an end to American hostility, seek an assurance for regime security through recognition of its identity, and have cooperation for its economic growth and development.

But this requires a modicum of trust and the acknowledgement that the DPRK is a sovereign equal. Innovative diplomacy will be necessary to work out a multifaceted deal that has something for every stakeholder: security assurances and economic assistance for the DPRK; a freeze, if not the abandonment, of its nuclear and missile programmes for the United States and its allies; diplomatic success for China; and guarantees from other involved parties to take on a commitment for fulfilment. It is only through such an interlocking set of commitments that a direct agreement between the United States and DPRK will yield something meaningful and lasting.

Moreover, the negotiations will have to be a process, not a one-off event. However much President Trump may desire a quick victory, the agreement will require long and tedious negotiations if it has to capture all the complex dimensions of the North Korean nuclear issue. No easy or quick solutions will be possible and should not even be expected or accepted. Negotiations will need to get heavy on specifics with each meeting even if the first ones are vague and more by way of ice-breaking meetings.

The various negotiating mechanisms have revealed the complexities of interplay of national interests. It is obvious and not surprising that the United States and North Korea, who are in opposite camps, have divergent goals and differ on how to attain them. The DPRK is certainly most concerned about regime survival. The United States, on the other hand, has denuclearisation as its utmost priority. So, while North Korea seeks normalisation of diplomatic relations as a precondition for disarmament, the United States has set denuclearisation as a precondition for abandoning its hostile policy. This makes for a diplomatic catch-22, with each expecting the other to demonstrate good faith as the starting point for success. Meanwhile, the other actors add their own priorities to the negotiations. Balancing regional security and stability with non-proliferation makes political consensus difficult to achieve.

The mechanism of Six-Party Talks evolved at a time when the United States and North Korea were unwilling to engage bilaterally. Now that President Trump has agreed to directly meet his North Korean counterpart, it may be more effective to pair the bilateral approach with a multilateral one. The latter could serve as a guarantee for the agreements reached at the bilateral level. Also, soon after the creation of this mechanism, in 2004, some liberal Japanese scholars expressed the hope that the talks could "develop into a North-East Asian multilateral security framework".[16] This could still happen but only if the United States and North Korea can reach an agreement to normalise their relations. Backing for this bilateral arrangement could come from the other four parties. The creation of such a new regional security environment could enable the US alliance or even the extension of nuclear umbrella to be reconsidered.

Lessons for the Indo-Pacific[17]

China's behaviour and actions have been a trigger for the revival of the Indo-Pacific, since the countries spearheading the concept have felt, if not threatened, then certainly uncomfortable with the emerging situation. The United States, as the driver of this version of the Indo-Pacific, has not shied away from terming China an adversary in its *National Security Strategy of 2017* and the *Nuclear Posture Review* of early 2018. The idea of the Indo-Pacific is Washington's way of dealing with China. Nearly all other countries, big and small, that have shown interest in the Indo-Pacific are also influenced by shared geopolitical concerns posed by China's "rise".

In fact, the reason why the Indo-Pacific in its first avatar faded away was largely because none of the participants felt the gravity of China's growth to power. In 2007, China's assertive behaviour was yet to be seen. In fact, in the initial stages of the Indo-Pacific, all the major powers, such as the United States, Japan, Australia, and India (the Quad), had different perceptions of China.[18] It may be recalled that India had celebrated 2006 as a friendship year with China, with a series of large-scale political, economic, and cultural engagements. The bonhomie continued for a while, and in 2008, China agreed to India's exceptionalisation by the Nuclear Suppliers Group (NSG). But, within a couple of years, China's nationalism and assertive behaviour had begun to be felt.

A decade down the line, China seems to have had a brush of sorts with many countries of the Indo-Pacific. Japan has its issues with China in both the East and South China seas; Australia is wary of its interference in its domestic arena; India has had a showdown at Doklam and differences over the Belt and Road Initiative (BRI), NSG, terrorism, and Pakistan; and the United States is engaged in a tug of war on trade issues, as also about Beijing's military activities in South China sea. China's rapid military and nuclear modernisation is changing the balance of power that could have implications for its nuclear doctrine, which until now has been inclined towards minimum and defensive deterrence. Changing capabilities could add new dimensions that could appear threatening to others, not the least to India.

So, China is a factor in the formulation of the concept of the Indo-Pacific. For now, Beijing has refrained from expressing any strictly official view on the concept. But it has certainly taken note of the development. China's foreign minister Wang Yi in March 2018 dismissed the Quad and Indo-Pacific as a "headline grabbing idea", which would dissipate like "foam on the sea". Several Chinese strategic analysts, too, have expressed their scepticism about the sustainability of the "formless" concept and have predicted that differences in capabilities of countries would lead to coordination problems among them.

Meanwhile, editorials in *Global Times* have, on the one hand, been characteristically caustic about the prominence being accorded to India and, on the other hand, seem to be cautioning India against becoming a US pawn in its China containment strategy. They contend that US support for India's rise as a global power is meant to check China's movements in the Indian Ocean, since Washington has no reliable alliances here. Another editorial on May 31, 2018, described the concept of the Indo-Pacific as a trap set by Washington: one, to "instigate China and India into long-term infighting"; and, two, to cope with the inevitable rise of India and strengthen Washington's control over the Indian

Ocean. It warns India that its phase of "smooth diplomacy" with the West will soon run its course, and like China, India's rise, too, will be perceived as a threat by the West. So, as per this Chinese view, the Indo-Pacific strategy of the United States is meant to drive a wedge between China and India and drag them into a conflict that would hamper the rise of both.[19]

As far as India is concerned, it certainly does not want a zero-sum relationship with either China or the United States. In fact, the present-day multipolarity allows states to simultaneously engage in competition and cooperation. India would certainly not want to sharpen the rift with China. The Wuhan summit was an indication of this, and despite their differences, both consider each other as important players in the region.

In the Indian formulation, the idea of the Indo-Pacific offers an alternative model of infrastructure development that is based on the principles of respect for sovereignty and territorial integrity, international law, financial transparency, environmental sustainability, and mutually beneficial trade and investment. Therefore, without getting into a direct confrontation with China, the bilateral, trilateral, or multilateral arrangements among nations of the Indo-Pacific are meant to offer a starkly different approach to quality infrastructure development, as compared to Chinese projects under the BRI.

For India, the Indo-Pacific is not only a geographical space for politico-economic maritime partnerships and the strengthening of regional frameworks but also a platform to showcase an alternative development model in which nations are bound by a vision of shared prosperity underpinned by a common interest in maritime order and strategic stability. Whether this idea will remain a loose economic, maritime, and political relationship or whether it would lead to a tight military alliance anchored in the Quad wholly depends on China's own behaviour and actions in the future. These will determine the future shape and trajectory of the Indo-Pacific and the Quad.

While all geographical regions and the geopolitical circumstances prevailing therein are unique, lessons learned from one can always make for the better understanding and adaptation of another. Negotiating mechanisms such as the Six-Party Talks have shown that in a multilateral setting, all states have their individual national interests and priorities. This not only leads to creation of mini groups within the larger group, on the basis of shared interests, but also provides an opportunity for one nation to play off the other. The Indo-Pacific is also likely to see the interests of nations in the region either coalesce or clash.

If the Indo-Pacific is to remain peaceful and open for all, negotiations between all relevant stakeholders must be regularly held to avoid misperceptions and misadventures. While such negotiating mechanisms might have their imperfections and limitations, they nevertheless are the only worthwhile tool in international relations and are necessary for international security, peace, and prosperity.

Dialogue diplomacy, therefore, is a major lesson to be learned from the North Korean issue for the Indo-Pacific before relations are vitiated. As pointed out by an Indian scholar, "The world had overlooked the importance of both 'dialogue' and 'diplomacy' in the Korean Peninsula for many years now, contrary to India's continuous advocacy that dialogue diplomacy should be the real pathway to attain peace".[20] Even in the case of the North Korean nuclear crisis, India has always supported all negotiating mechanisms, as a way of lowering the risk of military action. Continuing engagement between the stakeholders, irrespective of whether there are path-breaking results after each such meeting, is necessary for avoiding a crisis. It is also clear that all kinds of negotiations are important – bilateral and multilateral – in order to keep miscommunications at bay.

If India wants the Indo-Pacific to be a forum for cooperation among likeminded countries, rather than as a platform for isolating another country, it should be open to the idea of negotiations with all parties. While there is little doubt that some of China's policies, with regard to India's border or Pakistan, lead to misgivings in India, New Delhi still emphasises bilateralism with Beijing, even as it participates in the Indo-Pacific. This explains India's traditional belief in the concept of strategic autonomy and pluralism in international relations. India has always maintained that strategic outreach to many allows for better positioning for pursuing its interests rather than boxing itself into a tight alliance. In fact, India's continuance of diplomatic relations with the DPRK, despite US efforts to isolate the country, reflects the thinking that channels for dialogue should be kept open for when the time is right. It would be prudent for India to continue to emphasise this important lesson that stands out from the long experience of negotiations, through many mechanisms, in the case of North Korea.

Notes

1 The chapter uses the nomenclature of DPRK and North Korea interchangeably.
2 For more on this see, Robert Powell, "Absolute and Relative gains in International Relations Theory", *American Political Science Review*, 85 (4), December 1991, pp. 1303–1320.
3 Chung-in Moon, "Managing the North Korean Nuclear Quagmire: Capability, Impacts and Prospects", in John Ikenberry and Chung-in Moon (eds.), *The US and Northeast Asia: Debates, Issues and New Order*, Rowman & Littlefield, Lanham, 2008, pp. 231–262.
4 *Korea Times*, January 23, 2009.
5 For more, see, Leon V. Sigal, "Getting What We Need with North Korea", *Arms Control Today*, April 2016.
6 Charles L. Pritchard, "The Korean Peninsula and the Role of Multilateral Talks", *Disarmament Forum*, 2, 2005, p. 28.
7 Cary Hunag, "How North Korea Could Be the Balm that Soothes Tensions Between China and the US", *South China Morning Post*, January 17, 2019.
8 Ron Huisken, "One Way to Step Back from the Brink on North Korea", *The National Interest*, May 15, 2017.
9 Hyonhee Shin, "Fact Box: History of Inter-Korean Summits", *Reuters*, February 10, 2018.
10 Charles L. Pritchard, No. 6, p. 30.
11 Sachio Nakato, "Six Party Talks: The Sixth Round Talks and Its Future Prospect", *Ritsumeikan Kokusai Kenkyu*, 22 (1), June 2009, p. 92, at www.ritsumei.ac.jp (accessed May 3, 2019).
12 *The Daily Yomiuri*, October 15, 2008.

13 As cited in Chung-in Moon, "The North Korean Nuclear Dilemma and the Six Party Talks: A South Korean Perspective", *North Korea's Nuclear Issues: Toward Peace and Security in Northeast Asia*, Proceedings of the 10th Symposium, The National Institute for Defense Studies, December 13, 2007, p. 25.
14 Ibid., p. 28.
15 R. Carlin, "Kim Jong Un's New Strategic Line", *38 North*, April 23, 2018.
16 Kang Sung Jung, *The Asahi Shimbun*, December 31, 2004, as cited in Nakato, No. 11.
17 Parts of this section are derived from an article on the subject by the author in 2018 for the IPCS website.
18 For detailed analyses of these differences, see Jagannath Panda, "India's Call on China in the Quad", *Rising Powers Quarterly*, 3 (2), 2018, pp. 83–111, at http://risingpowersproject.com/wp-content/uploads/2018/10/vol3.2-panda.pdf (accessed 3 May 2019).
19 "Indo-Pacific Strategy a Trap by Washington", Op-ed, *Global Times*, May 31, 2018, at www.globaltimes.cn/content/1105064.shtml (accessed May 20, 2019).
20 Jagannath Panda, "What the Trump-Kim Summit Means for India", *The Diplomat*, February 26, 2019, at https://thediplomat.com/2019/02/what-the-trump-kim-summit-means-for-india/ (accessed April 30, 2019).

13 Geoeconomics of the Indo-Pacific

Competing economic architectures and South Korea

Seonjou Kang

Introduction

The "Indo-Pacific" has only recently gained currency as a strategic concept. The Indo-Pacific as a strategic concept was first floated more than a decade ago,[1] but it was not until US president Donald Trump referred to "Free and Open Indo-Pacific" (FOIP) multiple times during his visit to Asia in November 2017 that it became an established strategic concept. The *National Security Strategy* of 2017 (released in December) affirmed this by adopting the term "Indo-Pacific", instead of the Asia-Pacific, to describe the United States' new strategic sphere across Asia. This new strategic concept, which has overtones of countering the rise of China, is based on the fact that the western Pacific Ocean is conjoined with the eastern Indian Ocean and the United States is moving its strategic pivot westward from the Asia-Pacific and expanding it to include India and the Indian Ocean Rim. This westerly shift in the US strategic pivot not only ends the Obama administration's "Pivot to Asia" but also heralds an era of new strategic partners and measures.

The US Indo-Pacific Strategy initially tended to be confused as a regional scheme because of its geographical bounds, but its purpose and function is hardly regional. The Strategy is a manifestation of a hegemonic competition with China, which transcends the geographical boundaries of the Indo-Pacific. It is a global geopolitical scheme to counterbalance, if not to contain, China, which is extending its influence over a wide region with its rising military and economic capabilities. The United States views China's rise, especially its maritime rise, as building a Chinese sphere of influence from the Eastern China Sea to the Indian Ocean, thereby limiting the US global power projection and leadership in the international system over the longer term.[2] The Indo-Pacific region is a new arena where the US hegemony is being challenged.

While the US Indo-Pacific Strategy is geopolitically motivated, it should also be noted that the Strategy is a geoeconomic scheme as well. Geoeconomics implies employing economic measures to strengthen national security or using geopolitical instruments to promote national economic goals.[3] In Harris and Blackwill's words, geoeconomics is "war by other means".[4] The US Indo-Pacific Strategy is a geoeconomic scheme because it employs economic tools for counter-balancing

China and maintaining US dominance in the world. In a concrete sense, the Strategy is a geoeconomic scheme because it attempts to achieve its hegemonic goals by countering China's "Belt and Road Initiative (BRI)". China's BRI itself is a geoeconomic scheme because it would establish a Chinese sphere of influence spanning Central Asia and the Indian Ocean Rim, through economic ties with China. The US Indo-Pacific Strategy would function in a similar fashion.

As the United States and China execute their respective geoeconomic strategies in the Indo-Pacific, the outcome is, among other things, competing economic architectures led by these two countries. The presence of competing economic architectures in the Indo-Pacific, however, creates a strategic conundrum for countries in the region. For three decades, Asian countries have been used to a single Asia-Pacific economic architecture led by the United States, but now they may have to choose between two competing architectures. They may even find themselves "worse off because of 'institutional balancing', like its more well-known power balancing counterpart", in the Indo-Pacific.[5]

This chapter intends to examine the competing economic architectures in the Indo-Pacific region and their effects. More specifically, it explores how the US Indo-Pacific Strategy, starting as geopolitics, transforms itself into a geoeconomic construct in the face of the rise of China. It then compares the two architectures and analyses their effect on the region as a whole, and South Korea in particular.

The US Indo-Pacific Strategy as geopolitics

New security challenges in Asia

The US Indo-Pacific Strategy merges formerly two separate regions into one arena for the purposes of hegemonic competition, owing to the changes in the balance of power in the 21st century. Since 1945, the United States has been the hegemonic power and set its strategic pivot where its strategic vision of the day saw fit. The US strategic pivot also tended to be aligned with the world's economic centre of gravity. For instance, when the Cold War ended, the United States shifted its strategic pivot from the Atlantic to the Pacific, which coincided with the world economic centre of gravity, moving from west to east.[6] For three decades since then, the United States has been dominating the Pacific basin as the centre of the security and economic network of Asian countries.

In the wake of the 1997 Asian financial crisis and the wars in Afghanistan and Iraq in the 2000s, the United States remained relatively distant from the Asia-Pacific. In the meantime, China emerged as a world economic power and even led Asian regionalism, from which the United States was excluded. Upon taking office in 2009, President Obama announced the US foreign policy "Pivot to Asia" in order to regain its dominant position in the Asia-Pacific. This strategy included a diverse range of measures, such as reinforcing US troop strength in allied countries, redefining the Asian maritime space to include the Indo-Pacific littoral, and participating in East Asian Summit (EAS) for the security domain while negotiating the Trans-Pacific Partnership (TPP) for the economic domain. The "pivot" was an indication that, although in a quiet and engaging manner, the United States aimed to deal with the rise of China as a matter of vital interest and win back the Asians' trust in the United States.[7]

Against this backdrop, the Trump administration has formulated a new US foreign policy that is centred around openly and actively countering China as a strategic rival. The Trump administration views the maritime security threats emanating from the rise of China as particularly problematic for the United States.[8] The factors threatening maritime security are as follows:

- China's military modernisation, including the increasing capabilities of the People's Liberation Army Navy (PLAN) and concerns that this may upset the existing security balance in Asia.
- The escalation of long-running territorial disputes in the region, particularly those in the South China Sea, which also relate to China's military modernisation.
- The increasing need to secure the Sea Lines of Communication (SLOCs) stretching from the Middle East to the western Pacific, through which much of the world's seaborne trade and oil supply passes.[9]

The essence of the US Indo-Pacific Strategy is to build a "Free and Open Indo-Pacific" by upholding the rule of law and freedom of navigation, improving connectivity, fostering economic growth and forging multi-layered cooperation with the countries that share those values. A free Indo-Pacific implies all nations being able to protect their sovereignty against coercion by other countries; an open Indo-Pacific implies all nations enjoying access to seas and airways, and the peaceful resolution of territorial and maritime disputes as the basis for international peace and for each country's pursuit of its own national aims.[10] And in this, the US stands ready to maintain the peace and stability of the region and keep the region free from coercion or great power domination, through cooperation with regional partners.

Since the US Indo-Pacific Strategy is a geopolitical construct, it is natural for the United States to modify its military doctrine accordingly. Among other things, the United States renamed the United State Pacific Command (USPACOM) as the US Indo-Pacific Command (USINDOPACOM) in May 2018. Before the renaming, the USPACOM had been deployed for force projection in the Pacific basin, which now extends to the Indian Ocean region. After the renaming, there has been no immediate sign that the United States is increasing its military assets in the region. Nevertheless, this renaming indicates the reinforced connection between the Pacific and the Indian Oceans in its military doctrine; and the rising military importance of India for the United States.[11] In other words, the Trump administration links the implementation of the Indo-Pacific Strategy with India, to a considerable degree.

New security network: the Quad

The US Indo-Pacific Strategy highlights a new security model, the so-called "Quad" composed of Australia, India, Japan, and the United States. These four countries have shared concerns about the security threats arising from the growing assertiveness of China and the necessity to respond to these perceived security threats. The Quad is an informal security network of the four countries and supplements, not supplants, the half-century-old US-centric hub-and-spokes security model in the Asia-Pacific.[12] The Quad reinvigorates the existing US alliance partnerships with Australia and Japan and develops a new security relationship with India, for countering China's growing assertiveness.[13] The formation of the Quad effectively elevates India to key partner status in the US Indo-Pacific Strategy.

To a considerable degree, Japan played a major role in propelling the concept of Indo-Pacific and Quad. For five decades or so, Japan had adopted a passive security posture in the US-Japan alliance. In the face of a rising China, however, Japan moved to "normalise" its security posture and took on a more active role in regional security affairs.[14] In so doing, Japan prioritised incorporating India into its existing security relations, based on the US alliance system. In 2012, Prime Minister Shinzo Abe proposed the formation of a "Democratic Asian Security Diamond" of Australia, India, Japan, and the United States,[15] which was an expression of Japan's will to contain China and preserve the existing regional order.

Australia's 2009 and 2013 *Defence White Papers* showed that the Indo-Pacific region was at the centre of its strategic thinking.[16] Besides the fact that Australia has two-ocean geography, systemic and structural factors led Australia to embrace the concept of Indo-Pacific.[17] The Indo-Pacific is important for Australia as a trade route for energy resources and as a region of economic activity. The region also poses non-traditional security challenges such as migration, piracy, organised crime, natural disasters and food security.[18] And equally important, the Indo-Pacific is the potential site of a strategic and geopolitical rivalry between India and China. Thus, for Australia, the Indo-Pacific is the framework within which to expand its security relations beyond the US and Japan and address a range of security issues it shares with India.

In India, the concept of Indo-Pacific was first floated as early as 2007 and gradually incorporated into Indian foreign policy. In 2012, Prime Minister Manmohan Singh at a commemorative Association of South East Asian Nations (ASEAN) summit noted that a stable, secure and prosperous Indo-Pacific region is crucial for India's own progress and prosperity.[19] This is unsurprising because India has emerged as a regional security actor that desires to protect its own maritime space in the Indian Ocean, and the Indo-Pacific provides an ideal framework within which India can take on the role of a regional security actor, befitting its size and regional importance.[20] And the Indo-Pacific is also useful for India's other foreign policy objectives, that is, "strategic autonomy".[21] While India's long-standing external doctrine has been non-alignment, anxieties about a potential maritime conflict with China may lead India to veer away from non-alignment to counterbalance China. Thus, the Indo-Pacific is an ideal framework that allows India to engage with the United States, Japan, and Australia to offset China's geopolitical rise.

All in all, the US Indo-Pacific Strategy is founded on the geopolitical interests shared by Australia, India, and Japan in dealing with the rise of China. With India on board, the US Indo-Pacific Strategy as a geopolitical construct becomes a more credible response to China's maritime rise in the Indo-Pacific region.

The US Indo-Pacific Strategy as geoeconomics

The US Indo-Pacific Strategy is unambiguously a geopolitical construct. Its fundamental purpose is to manage complex security threats caused by the rise of China and develop security ties within the Quad. At the same time, however, the US Indo-Pacific Strategy is, and needs, to become a geoeconomic construct. Because a (military) strategic concept alone would not be sufficient for achieving the security goals set for a vast region. Ideally, a well-designed strategic concept has economic components that approximately match the spatial scale it seeks to encompass. A strategic concept becomes complete when it manages both security and economic interdependence among participating countries. Economic components within a strategic concept do not necessarily compromise security goals but complement and strengthen them.[22] Economic components in a strategic concept incentivise cooperation, as they internalise positive externalities from security cooperation to participating countries.[23] In that regard, the US Indo-Pacific Strategy would not be an exception. The US Indo-Pacific Strategy can achieve security goals vis-à-vis China more effectively and efficiently by linking security to economic interdependence.

The geoeconomic rationales for the US Indo-Pacific Strategy

Responding to China's BRI

The US Indo-Pacific Strategy incorporates economic components because it is, first and foremost, a response to China's BRI. The BRI is, in and of itself, a geoeconomic construct in that it would change the political landscape of Central Asia and the Indian Ocean Rim and establish a Chinese sphere of influence, through economic ties with China. If the United States intends to counter or at least neutralise the Chinese expansion in the Indo-Pacific region, the United States needs to deploy economic measures similar to those of the BRI.

The BRI is a long-term investment project announced in 2013 to construct the network of roads, ports, oil pipelines, and telecommunication that connect China to Europe through Central Asia, the Middle East and Africa. It includes the "Silk Road Economic Belt", which builds roads and railways to connect China to Europe via Central Asia; the "21st Century Maritime Silk Road" stretching from southern China across the Indian Ocean to Africa and the Mediterranean;

and the "Digital New Silk Road" for building information and communication infrastructure along the land and maritime infrastructure. China is developing land and maritime infrastructure in nearly all the countries that are covered by the BRI. The entire BRI is estimated to cost between $4–8 trillion,[24] which the Chinese government channels from policy banks such as the China Development Bank (CDB) and the Asian Infrastructure Investment Bank (AIIB), which was initiated by the Chinese and established in 2015. In a nutshell, the BRI is a massive China-centric connectivity project.

What makes the BRI a geoeconomic construct is its potential, if successful in full, or even part, to bring a considerable part of the world within the Chinese sphere of influence. The BRI covers about 65 per cent of the world's population and one-third of the world's gross domestic product (GDP). The BRI could become a trade bloc even without a multi-lateral trade agreement, where China is dominant. Moreover, it would contribute to internationalising the yuan and promoting its reserve currency status as well. BRI projects, by forcing the international use of the yuan, will make for a yuan bloc that covers one-third of the world's GDP.[25]

The BRI is a geoeconomic construct because the infrastructure built under the BRI has dual purpose, that is, both economic and military. This has led some to criticise the BRI as being China's "debt trap diplomacy", meaning that China intentionally extends excessive credit to small countries in order to extract political and military concessions from them when they are unable to honour their debt obligations.[26] China is also criticised for undermining the Rules-Based International Order (RBIO) with the BRI, because China's financing practices for BRI projects are incompatible with the international guidelines for upholding the rule of law, social and environmental sustainability, and global standards for transparency.

Thus, the US Indo-Pacific Strategy is likely to be ineffective against the BRI if it relies only on military measures or rhetoric. Tangible economic benefits need to be delivered to countries in the region in order to make them indifferent to China's BRI. The question is, what economic benefits can the United States deliver under the Indo-Pacific Strategy and how effective will they be compared to those offered by China? This could turn out to be no small challenge for the United States because of its resource constraints and its professed position toward the RBIO. Obviously, the United States is more constrained by self-imposed restrictions than China, in delivering economic benefits to the region.

Providing a substitute for TPP

The US Indo-Pacific Strategy becomes a geoeconomic construct because it can provide the United States with means to restore its economic, and even political, clout in Asia, which has been shaky in the wake of the US withdrawal from the TPP. The economic components of the US Indo-Pacific Strategy would reassure Asian countries of the US commitment to the region, though not exactly in the same manner as the TPP.

The TPP was a US-led multi-lateral Free Trade Agreement (FTA) for the Asia-Pacific region. The United States' decision to join the TPP was motivated by political, security, and economic considerations. President Obama declared "Pivot to Asia" as US foreign policy in order to restore its influence in the Asia-Pacific region, and the TPP was incorporated into the "Pivot to Asia" as an economic pillar, to secure its leadership role in Asian regional integration.[27] The TPP, which claimed to be a model for 21st-century trade agreements, was signed by 12 Asia-Pacific countries in February 2016. However, in January 2017, the United States under President Trump withdrew from the TPP. President Trump's decision to withdraw was regarded by many Asia-Pacific countries as a signal that the United States was retreating from the region, yielding a strategic advantage to China.

In the meantime, China's economic leadership in the Asia-Pacific has been playing out on the trade front, through Regional Comprehensive Economic Partnership (RCEP) as well as the BRI. Though the RCEP was launched by ASEAN, China has been leading the RCEP negotiations since 2013, to counter the TPP, which China perceived as a US attempt to contain China economically. The RCEP as a mega FTA in the Asia-Pacific aims at consolidating the existing FTAs between ASEAN and its "Plus Six" partners (Australia, China, India, Japan, South Korea, and New Zealand) into a single agreement. Since the United States has weakened the TPP considerably by abandoning it, the RCEP would be the world largest trading bloc, if the negotiations are completed in 2019, and, given its size, the trade rules set by the RCEP could become the accepted global standards. What is significant in the context of the Indo-Pacific is that the RCEP has an Indo-Pacific-style membership, including all the ASEAN countries and India.[28] The RCEP would be the first economic institution to be established for the Indo-Pacific region and would become another channel for China to spread its influence in the Indo-Pacific region.

Considering these possibilities, the United States needs to overcome the perception that China is the economic leader of the region. The Indo-Pacific Strategy is one way for the United States to signal its comeback to lead the region both politically and economically. Especially by incorporating economic components in the Indo-Pacific Strategy, the United States could hope that the Indo-Pacific Strategy functions as a substitute for the TPP, although it lacks a multi-lateral FTA.

Mobilising support from the region

Integrating economic components into the Indo-Pacific Strategy is necessary for the United States to garner support and cooperation for the Indo-Pacific Strategy, from potential regional partners. Small and medium countries in the region are concerned that the United States would form a security-oriented forum for the Indo-Pacific and ask them to join it to counterbalance China. They believe that if the Indo-Pacific remains primarily a security region, it would have deleterious implications not only for the stability and security of the region but also for its prosperity.[29] ASEAN countries are particularly apprehensive about the expansion of the Quad for counterbalancing China. They have close economic ties with China and worry about being forced to choose between the United States and China. For instance, the Singaporean foreign minister Vivian Balakrishnan made it clear that Singapore would not participate in the US Indo-Pacific Strategy if it was intended to exclude particular countries.[30]

On the United States' part, the support and cooperation of the small and medium countries in the region is essential for the Indo-Pacific Strategy to succeed. By bringing as many countries as possible into the Indo-Pacific Strategy, the United States can achieve its geopolitical goals vis-à-vis China while reducing the possibility of resorting to military measures. Thus, in order to incentivise the small and medium countries in the region to participate in the Indo-Pacific Strategy, the United States is toning down its security orientation and playing up the economic orientation of the Indo-Pacific Strategy.

Protecting US economic interests

The US Indo-Pacific Strategy is necessary for the United States to secure its own economic interests. It allows the United States to deploy diplomatic tools to establish a foothold in the fast-growing Indian Ocean Rim. The Indian Ocean region has great potential for economic growth. The countries in the region are home to roughly 2.7 billion people, or 30 per cent of the world's population, with the lowest percentage of elderly population among all other regions. They have the potential to be a promising market in the future. The economic components incorporated in the US Indo-Pacific Strategy would enable the United States not only to have a strategic presence in the region but also to gain trade and investment opportunities for US firms.

The Indian Ocean is also vital for the US international commerce in that it is home to critical sea lanes used for transportation of energy and goods. Almost two-thirds of the world's oil tankers and half of the world's container vessels pass through the Indian Ocean. Thus, the United States as a trading nation has a stake in keeping the Indian Ocean free and open. The Indo-Pacific Strategy is designed to protect US economic security as well as national security.[31]

The US Indo-Pacific economic vision

Eight months after its initial announcement, in July 2018, the United States announced a more economically oriented Indo-Pacific Strategy. Overall the Indo-Pacific Economic Vision is founded on the concept of economic openness. "Open" in economic terms means fair and reciprocal trade, a free competition and investment environment, transparent agreements between nations, and improved connectivity to drive regional ties as the paths for sustainable growth in the region.[32]

The US Indo-Pacific Economic Vision has three prongs: Digital Connectivity and Cybersecurity Partnership, Enhancing Development and Growth through Energy (EDGE), and the Infrastructure Transaction and Assistance Network (ITAN). The United States will start with a $25 million initial investment to improve partner countries' digital connectivity. It will support communications infrastructure and cybersecurity capacity through technical assistance, market-driven digital regulatory policies, and public-private partnerships. Through Asia EDGE, the United States will invest nearly $50 million to help Indo-Pacific partners import, produce, move, store, and deploy their energy resources, while the ITAN will boost infrastructure development in an environmentally sustainable and financially transparent manner. For infrastructure development, the United States will establish a new inter-agency body to coordinate, strengthen, and share US tools for project scouting, financing, and technical assistance.

The US government will initially allocate $113 million for economic engagement in the Indo-Pacific. Its development finance capacity is expected to be more than doubled to $60 billion with support from the Congress under the Better Utilisation of Investment Leading to Development (BUILD) Act of 2018.[33] Also, public funding for Indo-Pacific Economic Vision projects is likely to be matched by private sector investment, in which Overseas Private Investment Corporation (OPIC) is to play a catalytic role.

A comparison of the economic architectures in the Indo-Pacific

As geoeconomic constructs, China's BRI and the US Indo-Pacific Economic Vision are both similar and dissimilar. These characteristics help in assessing their respective viability and future evolution.

Emphasis on infrastructure

The US Indo-Pacific Economic Vision emphasises infrastructure development as does China's BRI, although it is, in both scale and scope, much smaller than the BRI. This appears unavoidable given that the US Indo-Pacific Strategy is, among other things, a response to the BRI. Since infrastructure development is a significant part of the BRI, the United States follows suit. Moreover, there exists real demand for infrastructure in the region, which is hard to ignore. According to the Asian Development Bank (ADB), the Asia-Pacific will need to invest $1.7 trillion per year in infrastructure, from 2016 until 2030 to maintain its growth momentum.[34] China understands the importance of infrastructure from its own development experience and uses it to legitimise the BRI. Similarly, the United States has adapted the Indo-Pacific Economic Vision to this reality. By accommodating local needs for infrastructure, the United States would be able to garner support for the Indo-Pacific Strategy more easily and facilitate trade and investment for US businesses.

Value-based cooperation

The US Indo-Pacific Economic Vision is different from China's BRI in terms of emphasising values. The US Indo-Pacific Economic Vision operates on the extension of the principles underlying the FOIP, which are rooted in the rule

234 *Seonjou Kang*

of law and the RBIO. Applying those principles to the Indo-Pacific Economic Vision has three effects. Firstly, they define the programmes that the United States will be involved in. For example, because of its professed position towards the rule of law and the RBIO, the US Indo-Pacific Economic Vision will support institution building that is conducive for trade and investment and provide policy and technical assistance. Such programmes find no place in the BRI.[35] Secondly, institution building and technical assistance usually form part of development cooperation, using foreign aid. Hence the US Indo-Pacific Economic Vision also includes development cooperation.[36] Lastly, those principles, in practice, would have the effect of keeping certain countries out of the US Indo-Pacific Strategy, although the United States professes to exclude no country. Participation in the US Indo-Pacific Strategy requires sharing the US vision for the region rooted in the rule of law and the RBIO, but not all countries in the region would find it easy to share those principles.

Public-private partnership

The United States implements the Indo-Pacific Economic Vision through bottom-up and market-driven processes, in contrast to the BRI, which is characterised by a top-down approach. The BRI is less driven by economic fundamentals than China's political and strategic concerns, and accordingly BRI projects are government-driven and dependent on public funds.[37] Only recently has the Chinese government started to encourage the private sector to invest in BRI projects, but the private sector risk perception of the opaque BRI projects appears to hold them back.[38]

In contrast, the United States admits to limited public resources and actively invites private capital to participate in the Indo-Pacific Economic Vision. The role of the US government in the Indo-Pacific Economic Vision is to be confined to promoting productive capitalism and channelling public funds through public-private partnership. This, in turn, will have the region ready for private investment, which is welcome by US businesses.

Multi-lateral approach

The United States mobilises its allies, partner countries, and multi-lateral organisations for implementing the Indo-Pacific Economic Vision. This is the third aspect in which it differs from the BRI. The BRI operates in a closed and bilateral manner in that it is implemented through government-to-government agreements between China and participating countries. In the US multi-lateral approach to the Indo-Pacific Economic Vision, the Quad is likely to form the core for economic cooperation as well as security. The United States, Australia, and Japan have formed a trilateral partnership to mobilise investment for Indo-Pacific projects.[39]

The multi-lateral approach of the US Indo-Pacific Economic Vision also involves support for regional institutions. ASEAN is literally at the centre of the

US Indo-Pacific Economic Vision. The $113 million package includes support for ASEAN and the ASEAN Connect Initiative, APEC, and the Lower Mekong Initiative. In the Indian Ocean Rim, the United States chooses to support the Indian Ocean Rim Association (IORA). The IORA is a regional institution established in 1997, to promote economic and social cooperation, among the 22 coastal states bordering the Indian Ocean. By working through regional institutions, the United States would be able to mobilise collective support for the Indo-Pacific Strategy more easily.

On the other hand, it should be noted that, multi-lateral as it may seem, the US Indo-Pacific Economic Vision does not involve a multi-lateral trade agreement, while the architecture led by China does. The RCEP was launched independent of the BRI and is not an integral part of the BRI. Nevertheless, since the RCEP excludes the United States, China has naturally come to dominate the RCEP. The multi-lateral approach of the US Indo-Pacific Economic Vision would become more credible and functional if it also included a multi-lateral trade agreement.[40]

Limitations of the economic architectures in the Indo-Pacific

The geopolitics of coping with the changing balance of power in Asia is morphed into geoeconomics. Geoeconomics is competitive, but it has the advantage of making competition less conspicuous and intense than raw geopolitics while producing tangible results. If the hegemonic rivalry between the United States and China remains predominantly geopolitical, it would lead to more volatility and risk of miscalculation, so geoeconomics is more tolerable than geopolitics.

While the United States and China turn geopolitical competition into geoeconomic one in reliance on the Indo-Pacific Economic Vision and the BRI, they still have limitations in managing competition in the Indo-Pacific region. The US Indo-Pacific Economic Vision and China's BRI need to overcome the following challenges in order to produce desirable results:

First, both the United States and China's Indo-Pacific economic architectures should include more Indian Ocean countries. In the China-led architecture, only India is included from the Indian Ocean region, while major Asian powers are excluded. In the US-led architecture, membership still remains fluid. Candidates for both architectures include countries on the Indian Ocean Rim and major Asian economic powers, such as China, Japan, and South Korea, and the United States. Until these countries participate as full members in both architectures, neither architecture can be truly Indo-Pacific. Furthermore, the bifurcated membership in the Indo-Pacific economic architectures would hamper them from fulfilling the economic potential of the region and only solidify the respective spheres of influence for the United States and China.

Second, both economic architectures in the Indo-Pacific need multi-lateral trade agreements to encompass the entire Indian Ocean region. Given trade and investment data, economic ties between the Asia-Pacific and the Indian Ocean region are weak.[41] This is also indicated by the scarce cross-regional membership in the existing trade agreements. Within the China-led RCEP, India is the only Indian Ocean member. The US Indo-Pacific Economic Vision does not even feature a multi-lateral trade agreement yet. This means that both fast-growing regions are missing out on opportunities to develop mutually beneficial economic relationships. The Indo-Pacific needs to institute cross-regional trade agreements with a broad membership to realise its potential.

But this is problematic as Indian Ocean countries are less trade-oriented and less involved in FTAs, whether bilateral or multi-lateral, unlike the Asia-Pacific countries. The possible ways for instituting cross-regional FTAs in the Indo-Pacific would be that Indian Ocean countries join the existing Asia-Pacific FTAs, and/or Indian Ocean countries negotiate FTAs between themselves first and merge them with the Asian-Pacific FTAs later.

In both cases, however, the question still remains as to which Asia-Pacific FTA the Indian Ocean countries will join. As things stand, the RCEP is poised to emerge as the first and largest multi-lateral FTA in the Indo-Pacific, especially if the United States does not return to the TPP or initiate a fresh multi-lateral trade agreement under the Indo-Pacific Economic Vision. The RCEP is not an ambitious FTA in that it aims for a low level of tariff reduction and contains few WTO-Plus provisions.[42] However, in the context of the Indo-Pacific, where the levels of economic development and trade liberalisation vary wildly, the RCEP could be convenient for developing countries from the Indian Ocean Rim to join, or for the Indian Ocean FTAs to merge with, so that a cross-regional trade agreement with a broad membership could emerge in the Indo-Pacific. If things develop in this direction after the RCEP takes effect some time in 2020, it would be a significant development for global trade and Chinese leadership in the Indo-Pacific.

Lastly, both the US Indo-Pacific Economic Vision and the BRI need to overcome an institutional deficiency. If the Indo-Pacific is to be less confrontational and more stable and cooperative, it needs a regularised dialogue body for not only economic issues but also security. This would provide an institutional space that facilitates consultation, builds trust, and mitigates geopolitical tensions. One example of this is APEC, which has ensured a cooperative relationship between the United States and China, which might, in the absence of economic interdependence, otherwise be security rivals.[43] Similarly, the Indo-Pacific region needs to establish an umbrella institution where dialogues on diverse issues at diverse levels, including summits, can take place.

What kind of an umbrella institution would be appropriate for the Indo-Pacific? A G20-style inter-governmental institution might work for the Indo-Pacific. The G20 is an inter-governmental institution, known for efficiency and flexibility while retaining its major stakeholders. The reason that a G20-style inter-governmental institution is desirable for the Indo-Pacific region is that a realistic institutional goal for the Indo-Pacific would be to manage geopolitical competition but not to eliminate it or to impose binding rules. Furthermore, an umbrella institution for the Indo-Pacific should be developed by design, not by accident. Such an institution would be indicative of the will and consensus of the concerned parties to manage geopolitical competition in the Indo-Pacific.

An umbrella institution could follow two courses, as in the case of a cross-regional trade agreement, for the Indo-Pacific. One, to expand Asia-Pacific institutions by admitting interested Indian Ocean countries; or two, to expand Indian Ocean institutions by admitting interested Asia-Pacific countries. Which of the two courses is more feasible would depend on three factors: expected benefit (distribution), participants (number of actors), and uncertainty.[44] In both cases they have to cast their geographical net beyond their current membership and function. Having said that, the East Asia Summit (EAS) could be a candidate for expansion, if the first course is adopted. The EAS is the region's premier forum for strategic dialogue. The advantage of the EAS is that it is, in a sense, already an Indo-Pacific institution, because India is a member. More Indian Ocean countries can be admitted over time. Also, the EAS has the merit that it is a leader-led forum where the full range of political, security, and economic issues can be discussed.

On the other hand, the IORA could be a potential platform in case of option two. India and South Africa led the establishment of the IORA in 1997, to address development issues shared by countries on the Indian Ocean Rim. In recent years, the IORA has actively promoted economic cooperation initiatives, though they are neither a specific cooperation nor legally binding agreements.[45] The reason that the IORA has the potential to house an umbrella institution for the Indo-Pacific is its malleability. Although the Council of Ministers is the highest decision-making body for the IORA, the latter is flexible enough to upgrade it to summit level. For instance, in 2017, the IORA held a Leaders' Summit to commemorate its 20th anniversary. In addition, the IORA seeks to bolster its presence on the international stage, as it has recently launched dialogue programmes with the major countries of the world. The IORA membership is only open to countries on the Indian Ocean Rim, but it accepts non-regional countries as dialogue partners albeit with a limited role in the Association. However, the fact that the IORA is expanding its engagement with major countries indicates that, given sufficient incentive, the Association has room for expanding its function from an economic to a strategic organisation for the Indo-Pacific region.

Competing economic architectures in the Indo-Pacific and South Korea

The geoeconomic competition unfolding in the Indo-Pacific has significance for South Korea. As a trading nation, about 99.7 per cent of South Korea's energy resources and cargoes use sea-borne transportation. The country's economic prosperity depends on the freedom of navigation, the open market system, and the assurance that the RBIO is upheld in the Indo-Pacific region. In addition, President Moon Jae-in has launched a new diplomatic initiative called "New Southern Policy" (NSP), which targets the Indo-Pacific region. The NSP aims to diversify South Korea's economic relations and expand its diplomatic horizons to

ASEAN and the Indian Ocean Rim. However, given South Korea's geographic location and strategic constraints, its NSP would not be immune from US-China competition in the Indo-Pacific. Thus, it necessitates South Korea to deal with the complex situation in the Indo-Pacific.

A challenge, potentially emerging from the geoeconomic competition between the United States and China, that South Korea may face, will be to navigate the Indo-Pacific trade system. Prior to the emergence of the Indo-Pacific trade system, the United States and China vied to establish a template for the Asia-Pacific trade system with the TPP and the RCEP, respectively. As the United States withdrew from the TPP in January 2017, Japan and Australia reinvented the weakened TPP as the Comprehensive and Progressive Agreement for the TPP (CPTPP) in 2018. The CPTPP retains most of the original TPP agreements and keeps a door open for the United States and other countries to join the CPTPP in the future, although the Trump administration has made clear that it has no intention of joining the CPTPP. However, the United States has more than enough incentive to remain a critical player in a trade system for the fast-growing Indo-Pacific region. A multi-lateral Indo-Pacific trade architecture would therefore be essential if the United States is to establish an economic leadership, comparable to that of China in the region. Future administrations with different trade preferences than that of the Trump administration may see strategic and economic value in launching a new multi-lateral trade agreement similar to the TPP.

On the other hand, unlike the CPTPP, the China-led RCEP does not seek trade liberalisation at levels high enough to satisfy developed countries in the Indo-Pacific region. However, the RCEP as a trade agreement has the merit of offering member countries vast value chains and an opportunity to negotiate preferential trade agreements with a rising India. The RCEP aims at concluding negotiations by the end of 2019, in spite of multiple postponements arising from disagreements between China and India over tariff reduction. If the RCEP is concluded on schedule, it will become the first Indo-Pacific multi-lateral trade architecture.

As long as the United States continues to neglect forming a multi-lateral trade system in the Indo-Pacific region, it is likely that the China-led RCEP will establish itself as the main Indo-Pacific trade system. There exists a so-called first-mover advantage in international relations. No matter how low the level of trade liberalisation under the proposed RCEP, the institutional effect of the RCEP, once established, would not allow room for late-coming multi-lateral trade agreements to stand, even if they are US-led. Therefore, under the circumstances, it seems to be in South Korea's interest to adopt a forward-looking approach towards the RCEP that advocates open membership and higher liberalisation, which would potentially leave the door open for future US participation.

As a way of carrying out the NSP amid geoeconomic competition in the Indo-Pacific, South Korea seeks to cooperate with the United States and China on Indo-Pacific projects, where there is compatibility. Having said that, the US Indo-Pacific Economic Vision appears to allow more room for South Korea than the BRI. The BRI is thus far much less multi-lateral and allows less room for third-party countries to participate.[46] The emphasis of the US Indo-Pacific Economic Vision on infrastructure, digital economy, and energy cooperation is similar to what is emphasised by the South Korean NSP. For South Korea's NSP to have a cooperative relationship with China's BRI, BRI projects first need to become more multi-lateral, which could take place, to a certain extent, through the AIIB's financing decisions.

Further, South Korea chooses to join international organisations in the Indo-Pacific region to operationalise the NSP. International membership would give South Korea more strategic space to execute the NSP. Thus, South Korea joined the IORA as a dialogue partner in November 2018. Its dialogue partnership with the IORA will provide South Korea with multi-dimensional and multi-level opportunities for carrying out the NSP. The IORA is a suitable forum where South Korea implements the NSP because key players in both the Indo-Pacific competition and the NSP, such as Australia, China, India, Indonesia, Japan, Singapore, and the United States, are participating as full members or dialogue partners. Especially since India and Indonesia, which South Korea views as key partners for the NSP, place great emphasis on the IORA, its dialogue partnership with the IORA will help South Korea to obtain the cooperation of the two countries for the NSP. The geographical horizon and scope of the NSP can expand too, as the IORA focusses on maritime and non-traditional security issues (e.g. piracy and maritime terrorism, and human and drug trafficking).

Lastly, implementing the NSP in the competitive environment of the Indo-Pacific requires South Korea to support an inclusive architecture rather than joining divisive ones and engaging in bilateral or trilateral diplomacy for that purpose. An inclusive architecture for the Indo-Pacific would enable South Korea to carry out the NSP. In relation to this, it would be important for South Korea to cooperate with ASEAN. Over the years, ASEAN has been playing a bridging role in Asia by providing institutional mechanisms, which, however, is in danger of being reduced due to the westerly shift in US strategy and the competition unfolding in the Indo-Pacific. South Korea and ASEAN have a common interest in building an inclusive architecture for the Indo-Pacific and thus should cooperate to achieve this objective.

Notes

1 The concept "Indo-Pacific" was first formally introduced and explained in Gurpreet S. Khurana, "Security of Sea Lines: Prospects for India-Japan Cooperation", *Strategic Analysis*, 31 (1), 2007, pp. 139–153.
2 Shane C. Tayloe, "Crossover Point: How China's Naval Modernization Could Reverse the United States' Strategic Advantage", *Journal of Asian Security and International Affairs*, 4 (1), 2017, pp. 1–25.
3 Edward N. Luttwak, "From Geopolitics to Geo-Economics: Logic of Conflict, Grammar of Commerce", *National Interest*, 1990, pp. 17–23.
4 Jennifer M. Harris and Robert D. Blackwill, *War by Other Means: Geoeconomics and Statecraft*, Belknap Press, Cambridge, 2016.

5 Mark Beeson, "Asia's Competing Multilateral Initiatives: Quality versus Quantity", *Pacific Review*, 2019, 32 (2), pp. 245–255.
6 Philip Chr. Ulrich, *The US Pivot Towards Asia-Pacific: Third Time's the Charm?* Royal Danish Defence College, Copenhagen, 2013.
7 Kenneth G. Lieberthal, "The American Pivot to Asia: Why President Obama's Turn to the East Is Easier Said than Done", *Foreign Policy*, December 21, 2011.
8 Shane C. Tayloe, No. 2.
9 Gurpreet S. Khurana, No. 1; David Michel and Ricky Passarelli (eds.), *Sea Change: Evolving Maritime Geopolitics in the Indo-Pacific Region*, Stimson Center, Washington, DC, 2014.
10 US secretary of state Michael Pompeo, "America's Indo-Pacific Economic Vision", Address at Indo-Pacific Business Forum, July 30, 2018.
11 Idrees Ali, "In Symbolic Nod to India, U.S. Pacific Command Changes Name", *Reuters*, May 31, 2018.
12 Gordon Flake et al., *Realising the Indo-Pacific: Tasks for India's Regional Integration*, USAsia Centre, Perth, 2017.
13 David Brewster, *Australia, India and the United States: The Challenge of Forging New Alignments in the Indo-Pacific*, United States Studies Centre, Sydney, 2016.
14 John Nilsson-Wright, *Creative Minilateralism in a Changing Asia: Opportunities for Security Convergence and Cooperation Between Australia, India and Japan*, Chatham House, London, 2017.
15 Shinzo Abe, "Asia's Democratic Security Diamond", *Project Syndicate*, December 27, 2012.
16 John Nilsson-Wright, No. 14.
17 Andrew Phillips, *From Hollywood to Bollywood? Recasting Australia's Indo/Pacific Strategic Geography*, Australian Strategic Policy Institute, Barton, 2016.
18 Andrew Carr and Daniel Baldino, "An Indo-Pacific Norm Entrepreneur? Australia and Defence Diplomacy", *Journal of the Indian Ocean Region*, 11 (1), 2015, pp. 30–47.
19 Melissa Conley-Tyler and Aakriti Bhutoria, "Diverging Australian and Indian Views on the Indo-Pacific", *Strategic Analysis*, 39 (3), 2015, pp. 225–236.
20 Jeffrey D. Wilson, *Investing in the Economic Architecture of the Indo-Pacific*, USAsia Centre, Perth, 2017.
21 Monish Tourangbam, "Indo-Pacific and the Practice of Strategic Autonomy", *Indian Foreign Affairs Journal*, 9 (2), 2014, pp. 119–124.
22 Robert D. Blackwill, "Indo-Pacific Strategy in an Era of Geoeconomics", Keynote Speech at Japan Forum on International Relations, July 31, 2018.
23 David A. Lake, *Entangling Relations: American Foreign Policy in Its Century*, Princeton University Press, Princeton, 1999, pp. 49–51.
24 There are diverse estimates of the total cost of the BRI. It is hard to have a single, fixed estimate for the BRI because different assumptions about project numbers and duration lead to different estimates for the BRI's size.
25 Sarah Chan, "The Belt and Road Initiative: Implications for China and East Asian Economies", *The Copenhagen Journal of Asian Studies*, 35 (2), 2017, pp. 52–78.
26 Brahma Chellaney, "China's Debt-Trap Diplomacy", *Project Syndicate*, January 23, 2017.
27 Nina Silove, "The Pivot Before the Pivot: U.S. Strategy to Preserve the Power Balance in Asia", *International Security*, 40 (4), 2016, pp. 45–88.
28 Jeffrey D. Wilson, No. 20.
29 Ibid.
30 Vivian Balakrishnan, "ASEAN: 2018 and Beyond", International Institute for Strategic Studies Fullerton Lecture Series, May 14, 2018.
31 Michael Pompeo, No. 10.
32 Ibid.

33 The BUILD Act sets up the US International Development Finance Corporation (USIDFC). The USIDFC will be in charge of mobilising private sector investment for low- and lower-middle income countries, giving loans or loan guarantees, providing technical assistance, and administering special projects.
34 *Meeting Asia's Infrastructure Needs*, Asian Development Bank Institute, Tokyo, 2017.
35 China appears to relegate, if not ignore altogether, such programmes to multi-lateral development banks with which China signed Memoranda of Understanding (MOUs) at the 2017 Belt and Road Forum.
36 This could be related with the Trump administration's foreign aid reform, which has moved such functions from the United States Agency for International Development (USAID) to the USIDFC.
37 Jonathan E. Hillman, "China's Belt and Road Is Full of Holes", *CSIS Briefs*, September 4, 2018.
38 Sarah Chan, No. 25.
39 Australia, Japan, and the United States signed a Trilateral MOU on November 12, 2018, to operationalise the Trilateral Partnership for Infrastructure Investment in the Indo-Pacific. See, "Joint Statement of the Governments of the United States of America, Australia, and Japan", Statements & Releases, The White House, November 17, 2018, at www.whitehouse.gov/briefings-statements/joint-statement-governments-united-states-america-australia-japan/ (accessed December 1, 2018).
40 Robert D. Blackwill, No. 22.
41 Jeffrey D. Wilson, No. 20.
42 Jeffrey D. Wilson, *Beyond TPP: Maintaining US Engagement in Asia's Emerging Trade Architecture*, United States Studies Centre, Sydney, 2017.
43 Jeffrey D. Wilson, No. 20.
44 Barbara Koremenos et al., "The Rational Design of International Institutions", *International Organisation*, 55 (4), 2001, pp. 761–799.
45 These include the IORA Economic Declaration of 2014 (committing members to trade and investment liberalisation), the Mauritius Declaration on the Blue Economy of 2015 (focussing on cooperative management of shared marine resources), and the Jakarta Concord in 2017 (focussing on strengthening maritime cooperation in the Indian Ocean).
46 According to a study by the Centre for Strategic and International Studies, 89 per cent of China-funded transport infrastructure projects in 34 Asian and European countries were awarded to Chinese contractors. In contrast, 173 projects in Eurasia funded by two western Multi-lateral Development Banks (MDBs) between 2006 and 2017 were evenly distributed among local contractors where the infrastructure was built (41 per cent), Chinese contractors (29 per cent) and third-party contractors (30 per cent). See, Jonathan E. Hillman, "China's Belt and Road Initiative: Five Years Later", Centre for Strategic and International Studies, January 25, 2018, at www.csis.org/analysis/chinas-belt-and-road-initiative-five-years-later-0 (accessed December 10, 2018).

14 Between security and insecurity

Resource politics in North-East Asia

Atmaja Gohain Baruah

Introduction

In an increasingly competitive world, it is inevitable for countries to compete for control over energy, seas, and resource-rich territories. Control and access to these resources becomes heavily politicised and has in fact become a crucial determining aspect of the global developmental agenda at both regional and global levels.[1] It can involve competition and cooperation amongst states – based on broadly either a realist or a liberal perspective – over concerns pertaining to environmental issues, climate change, energy security, and maritime security. Thus, there are historical, territorial, economic, political, and geopolitical elements that all fall within the purview of resource politics. In order to understand the challenges facing countries with regard to the management of resource politics, it is crucial to understand their context and critically evaluate the domestic compulsions, that is, how resource efficient or resource dependent a country is. As demand grows and resources deplete, the nature of the relationship between two countries can keep oscillating between resource cooperation and competition.[2]

Intense resource politics has become particularly salient in the Indo-Pacific. There are, however, differences among countries depending on whether they benefited from the "global resource boom" or suffered through the "global resource crisis" in the early 2000s. For instance, resource-rich countries like Russia, Australia, and the United States saw tremendous growth and development during the "global resource boom" – which not only enhanced their revenues but also their diplomatic influence. However, the situation was different in resource-poor regions and countries such as the Korean Peninsula, Japan, and Mongolia in North-East Asia. As the boom turned into a crisis, these countries struggled to maintain their relationships with the profit-seeking resource suppliers.[3] In the face of mounting import bills and the growing threat to their energy security, they sought trade and investment ties with the resource-rich producers. Thus, global resource politics in the Indo-Pacific became extremely charged. For instance, Russia's East Siberia has one-third of the world's natural gas reserves. The diplomatic tussle between China and Japan over East Siberia's pipeline supplies has been on since the 2000s, ending with China finally winning the bid and acquiring Gazprom's Power of Siberia natural gas pipeline.[4]

Geographically, North-East Asia comprises the Russian Far East, the Chinese North-East, Japan, the Korean Peninsula, Mongolia, the West Sea/Yellow Sea, and the East Sea/Sea of Japan. Geopolitically, however, it includes other stakeholders, such as the United States, India, and the Association of Southeast Asian Nations (ASEAN). Resource politics in this region is complex because of the various motives that fuel inter-state competition. These include lack of domestic energy sources, historical territorial and maritime disputes, excessive reliance on the Middle East, and risky shipping lanes.[5] According to many scholars, such resource insecurity can certainly lead to a crisis in the future. For example, Kent E. Calder shows how a potential energy shortage can lead to a scramble for overseas resources, a naval arms race, and, ultimately, chaos in terms of North-East Asian security.[6] Xuanli Liao, too, argues that growing competition between China and Japan for oil and gas will generate antagonism, rather than cooperation.[7]

Scholars have often depicted countries as following either of the two resource security strategies – a state-led neomercantilist approach or a market-led liberal approach.[8] While the state-led neomercantilist approach focuses on inter-state competition led by fiercely nationalistic states to acquire resources, the market-led liberal approach focuses on creating suitable conditions for healthy competition based on neutral market variables. While the former instigates competition among "rivals", the latter fosters cooperation among "partners".[9] According to neomercantilists, it is important to use strategies and economic measures to pursue economic objectives and national interests.[10] This is now new but can be seen from long before. For instance, during the Cold War, Western states expanded their foreign trade by offering aid to potential emerging partners, and their foreign aid strategies were mostly shaped by their geostrategic deliberations. Today, countries seek to diversify their holdings of international reserves through sovereign wealth funds and by boosting outward foreign direct investments (FDIs) in resource regions and for infrastructure services.[11] Emerging markets of Africa, Latin America, Asia, and Europe are particularly targeted.

While North-East Asian countries, too, have adopted resource security strategies that favour resource mercantilism, it is always not so simple. The resource crisis and acute competition have certainly involved these countries in an intense inter-state rivalry, resulting in a low motivation for deeper regional cooperation.[12] Nonetheless, arguing that countries strictly follow either of the two approaches would be inaccurate. As shall be seen later, most countries are adopting a combination of cooperative development strategies, along with state-controlled mercantilist policies, while engaging with one another. China, because of its political and economic might, wields a lot of power in Asian resource politics. Though the Chinese government somewhat follows a market-led liberal strategy for commodities, it uses its party-state authority to create state-centric oil policies and ensure a stable and convenient oil supply. The institutional capacity and the policy instruments of the central party-state are such that central planning agencies and National Oil Companies (NOCs) have the maximum role in allocating oil resources.[13] The Japanese, South Korean, and Russian governments, too, over the past decade, have formulated their own resource security strategies, to strengthen their position in Asia.[14] In fact, energy acquisition has become a major driver of their foreign policy since the mid-2000s.

What causes resource insecurity

While time and again countries in North-East Asia have sought to develop regional resource interdependence, intergovernmental disputes as well as hawkish national policies have locked them in a tight struggle for control over resources. All forms of economic and diplomatic capital have been leveraged to expedite privileged access to energy supplies and marine resources. This follows the argument that, these countries rely less on resource cooperation with fellow regional countries but more on inter-state competition for acquiring resources.[15]

Some countries like Russia and China have made effective use of resources as a diplomatic weapon – using their power over resource supply to extract concessions from the dependent countries. Disputes are more prominent in the maritime zone, particularly in the East China Sea and the South China Sea, which are teeming with subsea hydrocarbons.[16] The resolve to exercise control over the maritime zone stems from three reasons: first, an overall lack of resources; second, competition over the ownership of maritime resources in the East China Sea (over delimitation and gas fields) and the Yellow Sea (over delimitation and fishery resources); and finally, safeguarding the maritime routes.

As resources are becoming such a critical factor in great power rivalry and diplomatic clashes in the Indo-Pacific, it is crucial to analyse the patterns of cooperation and competition for ensuring peaceful accommodation. While North-East Asia has had some record of resource interdependence, it is not very strongly followed by all the regional governments. Political motivation is low, and resource competition is invariably the more dominant factor.[17] Moreover, there is no binding, permanent negotiating, security, or consultative mechanism for North-East Asia, though it comprises three of the world's biggest economies and is the largest consumer of resources.[18]

Approaches to resource security

The strategy for maximising resource security is to be better placed in the global energy market. Governmental policies and funds are directed towards assisting national firms in gaining better access to global resource suppliers through Free Trade Agreements (FTAs). China has fared exceptionally well in this respect. It has an economic edge over its competitors, through its financial assistance and infrastructure projects. China's financial aid policies – through which it offers loans to its state firms on certain preferential terms – are directed towards setting up state-owned resource projects abroad. Its state-owned enterprises (SOEs) have been instrumental in stimulating China's "going out" strategy. Particular attention was given to oil and gas, energy, shipping, and telecommunications. This was mainly for the purpose of fast acquisition of limited resources, building global market chains, creating access to global markets, and finding lucrative investments for China's immense foreign currency reserves.[19]

Resource diplomacy is high in North-East Asia.[20] In order to secure shipping routes and maintain a stable supply of energy from resource-rich countries, they are engaging in proactive resource diplomacy both at the leaders' level and ministerial level with countries in the Middle East, Latin America, North America, and the Indo-Pacific region. Their assistance through infrastructure development, technical support, and human resource development has been central in creating resource networks that further resource competency.[21]

However, competitive resource politics triggered by the countries' individual mercantilist strategies have aggravated the region's resource insecurity.[22] It has not only undermined the openness and efficiency of a free market but also created exclusive supply chains that are ultimately detrimental to the cohesiveness of the region's resource security. While there are certain regional multilateral institutions that facilitate resource cooperation, they are relatively weak and ineffective in generating consensus. In this regard, cooperating in the non-traditional security sphere could prove useful in improving general good neighbourliness in North-East Asia.

Environment: a zone of conflict and cooperation

North-East Asia is plagued by transboundary environmental issues such as air pollution, dust storms, sandstorms, over-fishing, contamination of transboundary rivers, and marine pollution through oil spills. Apart from jeopardising environmental and human health, these irritants have created diplomatic complications between neighbouring countries. For instance, air pollution from China and Mongolia blowing into Japan and South Korea has raised serious concerns over the last decade. Dust and sandstorms, too, from Mongolia and China's Inner Mongolia Autonomous Region, carry huge amounts of harmful dust particles and have heightened tensions.[23]

Such transboundary environmental irritants fall within the scope of multilateral institutions, as they are not just limited to one country. A cooperative and inclusive intergovernmental approach is required to create an effective regulatory structure and set binding targets. South Korea is especially dependent on China for the scientific predicting of dust storms and for reducing their impact.[24] The first environmental forum in North-East Asia was the Symposium of South Korea-Japan Environmental Science organised in 1988. It evolved into Northeast Asian Conference on Environmental Cooperation (NEAC) in 1992, which China, Russia, and Mongolia also joined. As awareness about environmental protection grew after the 1992 Rio Earth Summit, other regional cooperative bodies were set up. The most prominent of these being the North-East Asian Subregional Programme for Environmental Cooperation (NEASPEC), Acid Deposition Monitoring Network in East Asia (EANET), the Northwest Pacific Action Plan (NOWPAP), and the Tripartite Environment Ministers Meeting (TEMM).[25]

The NEASPEC, which includes all the North-East Asian countries, has set for itself a multi-sectorial approach towards addressing transboundary environmental problems, the priority areas being transboundary air pollution, conserving biodiversity, protecting the marine resources, promoting low carbon cities, and preventing desertification.[26] By sharing real-time emissions and meteorological data, the NEASPEC aims to reduce pollution and give reliable pollution forecasts to create better living conditions.[27]

Comparatively, NOWPAP has been more proactive in creating awareness and using new forms of technology for preservation of marine ecology. Set up in 1994 by China, South Korea, Russia, and Japan, NOWPAP is focused on managing marine resources in North-East Asia[28] and has played a major role in uniting the North-East Asian countries. Some of its achievements include the establishment of the NOWPAP Regional Coordinative Unit in 2000 and several regional activity centres (RACs); adoption of the Regional Oil Spill Contingency Plan in 2003, Regional Oil and Hazardous and the Noxious Substance Spill Contingency Plan in 2008 and the NOWPAP Policy on Data and Information Sharing in 2006; and signing of memoranda of understanding (MoUs), such as for Regional Cooperation Regarding Preparedness and Response to Oil Spills.[29] Algae blooms, commonly known as red tides, due to the accumulation of excessive nutrients from industrial and agricultural wastes, have led to serious damage of the marine ecosystem. The Yellow Sea and the East China Sea are particularly prone to them. Most recently, NOWPAP brought together marine scientists from China, Japan, South Korea, and Russia to create the Northwest Pacific Action Plan Eutrophication Assessment Tool (NEAT). NEAT uses cloud computing technologies to analyse multispectral satellite images of the ocean and to avoid further degradation.[30]

TEMM was first initiated by South Korea, China, and Japan in 1999 to facilitate cooperation on environmental issues such as air quality, resource-waste circulation, and climate change through annual meetings.[31] For over 15 years, the body has been monitoring and analysing transboundary pollutants through large-scale joint environmental projects and by creating working groups and monitoring networks. The EANET is focused on monitoring acid deposition caused by acid rain in North-East Asia. At present, over 13 countries are participating, including China, Japan, Russia, South Korea, Mongolia, Malaysia, Indonesia, Philippines, Vietnam, Cambodia, Thailand, Myanmar, and Laos. There are about 56 monitoring sites that have standardised techniques to monitor and compare acid deposition. However, there is less focus on joint-policy development. Since the scope of the EANET does not include air pollution, countries do not take it as seriously as other institutions like the NEASPEC and TEMM.

Apart from multilateral mechanisms, there is also bilateral cooperation between these otherwise competitive North-East Asian countries. For instance, China, Japan, and South Korea (and India) are particularly active in fighting piracy in the Gulf of Aden. Since 2012, they have been rather successful in deploying Combined Maritime Forces (CMF), participating in counter-piracy missions and securing the Sea Lines of Communication (SLOCs).[32]

The multilateral institutions are mostly focused on managing transboundary air and water pollution, desertification, and nature conservation. They focus on information sharing, technical monitoring, and other functional aspects like capacity building rather than on problem-solving. So far, TEMM has been the main platform to discuss dust storm-related issues. Despite coordination at the government level, no substantial progress has been made in regional cooperation. Regional insecurities run high, and environmental issues are embedded in a wider security agenda.[33] While these associations have succeeded in launching a few joint monitoring projects for data sharing, the outcome is inadequate. Hindering effective cooperation are conflicting national priorities and inadequate coordination.[34] Moreover, none of the associations have binding environmental targets for the member countries, which slows down decision-making. North Korea also does not participate, which limits the overall impact.

Fuelling maritime tensions

According to Admiral Alfred T. Mahan, an American historian and strategist, a country's naval strength determines its national security and the strategic influence it observes over other nations.[35] This naval strength, or "sea power", has both a military/strategic and historical/cultural dimension and can even be traced back to the 17th and 18th centuries when European and American navy vessels were most powerful. Such heavy securitisation of the maritime domain is reflected in the ongoing maritime tensions in Asia.

The North-East Asian maritime region, comprising the Yellow Sea, the East China Sea, and the Sea of Japan (East Sea), is increasingly vulnerable to marine degradation, specifically toxic algal blooms in the form of red and green tides, and environmental accidents, like oil spills and marine litter, all of which threaten the biodiversity.[36] North-East Asia especially has coastal zone management issues as well as conflicts over maritime resources, fishing, and overlapping claims (e.g. in the East China Sea and the South China Sea). Given that 50 per cent of world's busiest port traffic takes place in the South China Sea, any act of maritime terrorism is going to cost everyone heavily.[37] Moreover, China's modernisation of its area denial weapon or Anti-Access and Area-Denial (A2AD) capabilities and the building of artificial reefs have attracted much public scrutiny. Japan, too, is steadily pursuing a naval strategy, gaining military control, and enhancing its naval combat system, for making better strategic use of its sea power. The Japan Maritime Self-Defence Force (JMSDF) is actively engaged in improving its sea-lane defence to counter China's rise. For South Korea, enhancing sea power is all about developing blue water operations, extending overseas investments, and protecting its SLOCs. The threat posed by North Korea also makes it a defensive national necessity.[38]

Viewed from a neo-realist perspective, this naval modernisation has created much insecurity; more so, because the trade and energy shipping also passes through the same maritime zone – the Straits of Malacca, the Indian Ocean, and the South China Sea. The maritime disputes festering between the North-East Asian countries can actually be traced much back to history and politics. The disputes between China and Japan involve mainly the East China Sea, its resources, and islands, particularly the Senkaku (Diaoyu钓鱼岛) islands.[39] Both want to maximise control over the maritime domain and the offshore oil and gas reserves in the East China Sea. According to the United Nations (UN) International Law of the Sea, a country has exploration rights up to 200 nautical miles off its coast. China and Japan are thus making overlapping claims in the

East China Sea, which is just 360 nautical miles wide. Japanese claims are based on its jurisdictional boundary, while the Chinese claim is based on its continental shelf.[40] Japan and South Korea are competing over Takeshima/Dokdo, an island in the Japan Sea (or East Sea), known for its fishing. While Japan claims Takeshima on the basis of the feudal rights bestowed on Japan in the 17th century, South Korea claims the Dokdo Island, citing an even older claim, going back to the 6th century. Russia and Japan are disputing over four islands, known as the Northern Territories, situated north of Hokkaido. They were seized by the USSR in 1945, but Japan claims them on the basis of international law.[41]

All these countries, however, agreed on the security of the SLOCs.[42] Dealing with maritime piracy and launching anti-piracy operations is therefore significant, particularly discussed in forums such as the G20, the Asia-Pacific Economic Cooperation (APEC), ASEAN plus 3 (China, Japan, and South Korea), the East Asia Forum, and the ASEAN Regional Forum (ARF).[43] The Regional Cooperation Agreement on Combating Piracy and Armed Robbery against Ships in Asia (ReCAAP) is one such instance of maritime cooperation.

Securitisation of energy resources

As all countries in this region, except Russia, are resource consumers, they are inherently competitive, and cooperation is bogged down by geopolitical and economic constraints.[44] Instability in supplier countries of the Middle East also creates political concerns and economic backlash. The Cold War hostility and political distrust still continues;[45] for instance, the East Siberia Pacific Ocean (ESPO) oil pipeline project was a bone of contention between China and Japan for a long time.[46] There are disputes in the Yellow Sea and the East China Sea over the development of the Chunshao gas field (also known as the Shirakaba gas field). The Yellow Sea has substantial petroleum deposits, and this has stirred rivalry between China and the two Koreas.

The race for energy security in North-East Asia stems from rapid economic development and hunger for more energy supply, which has taken on an economic and strategic dimension.[47] What has contributed heavily to the resource crisis is the dependency on the Middle East – over 80 per cent in the case of Japan, China, and South Korea.[48] Even their energy transportation routes, particularly the Straits of Malacca, are unstable, as they are affected by piracy and marine terrorism. Energy cooperation in North-East Asia is expected to improve their economic interdependence, and hence, the focus is on joint development projects and oil and gas pipelines. These pipelines are favourable for the environment as well since they do not produce any greenhouse gases. One potential option is a pipeline from East Siberia's Kovykta gas field, through China to South Korea via the Yellow Sea. Another option is the Sakhalin I gas field, connecting the Russian Far East, the Korean Peninsula, and China's North-East.[49]

Considering this from a neoliberal perspective, forming multilateral and bilateral forms of cooperation has the ability to not only enhance sustainable energy flow across the region but also create conditions for regional integration and stability. Some areas could be particularly useful for cooperation, such as developing joint explorations for protecting vital SLOCs, offshore resources, oil stockpiling, and developing clean energy technologies. China and Japan issued a joint communiqué to further the development of marine resources in 2007. More than reducing costs of investment, it was expected to create a favourable condition for maritime peace and stability.

Several intergovernmental mechanisms have been set up to hasten the dialogue process for energy cooperation since the mid-2000s. For instance, the two Koreas, Russia, and Mongolia are involved in Intergovernmental Collaborative Mechanism on Energy Cooperation in North-East Asia (ECNEA) since it was initiated by the UN Economic and Social Commission for Asia and the Pacific (UNESCAP) in 2005.[50] Another UNESCAP-initiated proposal is the Trans-Asia Energy System (TAES) for better energy transactions. There is also a trilateral mechanism between South Korea, Japan, and China called the Korea-China-Japan Trilateral Energy Dialogue. On a broader level, APEC Energy Working Group (EWG) meetings and the East Asia Summit Energy Cooperative Task Force have been useful in creating mechanisms to discuss energy efficiency, alternate energy sources, and market integration. There are programmes with ASEAN, too, such as the Asia-Pacific Partnership on Clean Development and Climate. Sub-regional energy connectivity has gained momentum lately, particularly in the field of renewable energy-based power interconnectivity. The Gobitec, supported by the Mongolian government, and Asia Super Grid initiatives have been in focus since 2013. The Chinese and Russian administrations, too, have stressed on forming a Global Energy Interconnection mechanism and a Northeast Asia Super Energy Ring to facilitate cooperation. President Moon Jae-in of the Republic of Korea also spoke of the importance of an interconnected power network based on a super grid at the Eastern Economic Forum in 2017. New studies are being conducted on the viability of having a joint connectivity grid in terms of capacity building, investments, and environmental cost, in the backdrop of China's Belt and Road Initiative (BRI), Mongolia's Gobitec Project, South Korea's New Northern Policy, and Russia's New Far Eastern Policy.

However, renewable energy resources require huge investment, technical know-how, and a tilt towards neoliberal cooperation. An inability to develop common clean energy infrastructure and the lack of political will delay cooperation. South Korea, Japan, and China are more interested in furthering their national priorities – economic and geopolitical interests superseding regional cooperation. Multilateral security cooperation, backed up by a strong institutional framework and binding commitments, is required to secure energy cooperation.

Conclusion

There has always been a lack of trust in North-East Asia because of historical antagonism. The current geopolitical and economic scenario, with China striving to attain global power status, has only exacerbated this trust deficit. This region has become a battleground for major powers, like China, Russia, Japan, and the United States, which are competing not only for overlapping maritime resources but to ensure energy security as well.

Resource politics in North-East Asia is a double-edged sword – it has the potential to instigate rivalry over scarce resources but also for generating shared priorities to create opportunities for closer integration. A common perception of threat and vulnerability can be a good and powerful basis for collaboration. Long-term cooperation, however, depends on effective institutional mechanisms and a strong political will. If the region does not succumb to geopolitical rivalries and focuses on bilateral and multilateral cooperation, resource politics can become a means of promoting regional integration, instead of being an irritant.

However, cooperation at the regional level in North-East Asia is abysmal – there is no binding institutional security mechanism.[51] While the countries can act to ensure regional peace and stability, legally binding agreements can strengthen cooperation at a regional and global level. Beyond the constrained limits of regional institutes, it will be instrumental to reconceptualise and broaden the scope to include non-governmental agencies and civil societies. Cooperation at the non-traditional security level not only deconstructs traditional ways of cooperation but finds common ground to reduce regional tension and form new mechanisms to further integration. Furthering environmental and health security is one. Another is for these countries to utilise their complementarities in energy use, especially in the renewable sector. China has a high renewable energy capacity, while Russia and Mongolia have massive wind, solar, and hydropower capacities. An interconnected power grid, as suggested by South Korea, Japan, and Mongolia, called the Asia international grid connection, will not only create a reliable and closer source of renewable energy but also support energy transition in North-East Asia and ensure energy security. The "Asian Super Grid" proposal is also an area of interest, which will unite the power network in the region, harnessing renewable energy from Mongolia, China, and Russia.

Albeit natural gas trade between Russia and South Korea has been going on for years, Russia is still not a top gas exporter to the latter.[52] So, the Russia-Korea natural gas pipeline connecting Russia Far east to South Korea through overland pipes in North Korea could act as a "bridging fuel" between these countries and also bring certain stability to the North Korean energy crisis.[53] While these projects will require utmost political resolve, huge investments, and regular feasibility tests, it shall be highly conducive for energy cooperation and diversification in the region. Problems may nonetheless persist in the form of sanctions on North Korea and Russian businesses and conflict of interest with China. In this regard, developing joint energy grids can be a good incentive for cooperation that could lead to regional détente as well.

Notes

1 Jeffrey David Wilson, *International Resource Politics in the Asia Pacific: The Political Economy of Conflict and Cooperation*, Edward Elgar, Cheltenham, 2017.
2 Shunji Cui, "Beyond History: Non-Traditional Security Cooperation and the Construction of Northeast Asian International Society", *Journal of Contemporary China*, 22 (83), 2013, pp. 868–886.
3 Jeffrey David Wilson, No. 1.

4 Tsvetana Paraskova, "Russia's Huge Natural Gas Pipeline to China Nearly Complete", *Oil Price*, September 6, 2018, at https://oilprice.com/Latest-Energy-News/World-News/Russias-Huge-Natural-Gas-Pipeline-To-China-Nearly-Complete.html# (accessed July 17, 2019).
5 Jae-Seung Lee, "Energy Security and Cooperation in Northeast Asia", *The Korean Journal of Defence Analysis*, 22 (2), 2010, pp. 217–233.
6 Hyun Jin Choi, "Fuelling Crisis or Competition? The Geopolitics of Energy Security in Northeast Asia", *Asian Affairs: An American Review*, 36 (1), 2009, pp. 3–28.
7 Ibid.
8 Jeffrey David Wilson, "Northeast Asian Resource Security Strategies and International Resource Politics in Asia", *Asian Studies Review*, 38 (1), 2013, pp. 15–35; J. Aizenman, Y. Jinjarak, and N. Marion, "China's Growth, Stability, and Use of International Reserves", *Open Economies Review*, 25 (3), 2014, pp. 407–428.
9 Jeffrey David Wilson, No. 1.
10 David N. Balaam and Bradford Dillman. *Introduction to Political Economy*, 5th ed., Pearson Education, New York, 2011, p. 57.
11 Joshua Aizenman, Yothin Jinjarak, and Huanhuan Zheng, "Chinese Outwards Mercantilism: The Art and Practice of Bundling", *Vox*, May 4, 2015, at https://voxeu.org/article/chinese-outwards-mercantilism (accessed July 17, 2019).
12 Daewon Ohn and Mason Richey, "Cooperation on Counter-Piracy in the Gulf of Aden among China, Korea and Japan: Implications for Trilateral Security Cooperation in Northeast Asia", *The Korean Journal of Defense Analysis*, 26 (1), 2014, pp. 81–95.
13 Monique Taylor, *The Chinese State, Oil and Energy Security*, Palgrave Macmillan, London, 2014, pp. 1–30.
14 Min Gyo Koo, "Embracing Free Trade Agreements, Korean Style: From Developmental Mercantilism to Developmental Liberalism", *The Korean Journal of Policy Studies*, 25 (3), 2010, pp. 101–123.
15 Raimund Bleischwitz et al., "International Resource Politics: New Challenges Demanding New Governance Approaches for a Green Economy", *Heinrich Boll Stiftung Publication Series on Ecology*, 26, 2012.
16 Christian Wirth, "Ocean Governance, Maritime Security and the Consequences of Modernity in Northeast Asia", *The Pacific Review*, 25 (2), 2012, pp. 223–245.
17 Suk Kyoon Kim, "Marine Pollution Response in Northeast Asia and the NOWPAP Regime", *Ocean Development and International Law*, 46, 2015, pp. 17–32.
18 Ibid.
19 Mark Grimsditch, "The Role and Characteristics of Chinese State-Owned and Private Enterprises in Overseas Investments", Friends of the Earth, June 2015, at https://1bps6437gg8c169i0y1drtgz-wpengine.netdna-ssl.com/wp-content/uploads/2018/01/Role-and-Characteristics-of-SOEs-Overseas-1.pdf (accessed July 17, 2019).
20 "Unpacking China's Resource Diplomacy", *The Herald*, September 25, 2018, at www.herald.co.zw/unpacking-chinas-resource-diplomacy/ (accessed July 17, 2019).
21 "Japan's Foreign Policy to Promote National and Worldwide Interests", *Diplomatic Bluebook 2017*, Ministry of Foreign Affairs of Japan, at www.mofa.go.jp/policy/other/bluebook/2017/html/chapter3/c030303.html (accessed July 23, 2019).
22 Fiona Hill, "Energy Integration and Cooperation in Northeast Asia", *NIRA Policy Research*, 15 (2), 2002, at www.brookings.edu/wp-content/uploads/2016/06/20011001.pdf (accessed July 17, 2019).
23 Ken Wilkening, "Dragon Dust: Atmospheric Science and Cooperation on Desertification in the Asia and Pacific Region", *Journal of East Asian Studies*, 6, 2006, pp. 433–461.
24 Ibid.
25 Matthew A. Shapiro, "Regionalism's Challenge to the Pollution Haven Hypothesis: A Study of Northeast Asia and China", *The Pacific Review*, 27 (1), 2014, pp. 27–47.

26 *Strategic Plan 2016–2020*, North-East Asian Subregional Programme for Environmental Cooperation, at www.neaspec.org/sites/default/files/NEASPEC%20Strategic%20Plan_after%20SOM20.pdf (accessed July 17, 2019).
27 Hun Park, "Tackling Climate Change Could Bring North and South Korea Closer and Help Stabilise the Region", MENAFN, July 10, 2019, at https://menafn.com/1098741726/Tackling-climate-change-could-bring-North-and-South-Korea-closer-and-help-stabilise-the-region (accessed July 17, 2019).
28 Lorraine Elliott, "Environmental Regionalism: Moving in from the Policy Margins", *The Pacific Review*, 30 (6), 2017, pp. 952–965.
29 Christian Wirth, No. 16, pp. 223–245.
30 "NEAT – A Satellite-Based Technique to Keep an Eye on Growing Eutrophication Threat to Oceans", UN Environment, May 5, 2019, at www.unenvironment.org/news-and-stories/story/neat-satellite-based-technique-keep-eye-growing-eutrophication-threat-oceans (accessed July 20, 2019).
31 Ken Wilkening, No. 23, pp. 433–461.
32 Daewon Ohn and Mason Richey, No. 12.
33 Suk Kyoon Kim, No. 17.
34 Shin-wha Lee, "Environmental Regime Building in Northeast Asia: A Catalyst for Sustainable Regional Cooperation", *Journal of East Asian Studies*, 1 (2), 2001, pp. 31–61.
35 A.T. Mahan, *The Influence of Sea Power Upon History: 1660–1783*, Dover Publications, New York, 1987.
36 Christian Wirth, No. 16, pp. 223–245.
37 Ibid.
38 Jae-Seung Lee, No. 5.
39 Hyun Jin Choi, No. 6.
40 Thomas J. Schoenbaum (ed.), *Peace in Northeast Asia: Resolving Japan's Territorial and Maritime Disputes with China, Korea and the Russian Federation*, Edward Elgar, Cheltenham, 2008.
41 Ibid.
42 Pawel Behndt, "Maritime Strategy in Northeast Asia", *The Maritime Executive*, June 24, 2019, at www.maritime-executive.com/editorials/maritime-strategy-in-northeast-asia (accessed September 11, 2019).
43 Kyunghan Lim, "Non-Traditional Maritime Security Threats in Northeast Asia: Implications for Regional Cooperation", *Journal of International and Area Studies*, 22 (2), 2015, pp. 135–146.
44 Jae-Seung Lee, "Towards Green Energy Cooperation in Northeast Asia: Implications from European Experiences", *Asia Eurasia Journal*, 11, 2013, pp. 231–245.
45 Jae-Seung Lee, No. 5.
46 David von Hippel et al., "Northeast Asia Regional Energy Infrastructure Proposals", *Energy Policy*, 39, 2011, pp. 6855–6866.
47 Jae-Seung Lee, No. 5.
48 Thomas J. Schoenbaum (ed.), No. 40.
49 David von Hippel et al., No. 45; Hyun Jin Choi, No. 6.
50 Jae-Seung Lee, No. 5.
51 Daewon Ohn and Mason Richey, No. 12.
52 Valentin Voloshchak, "A Closer Look at South Korea's Plan for Cooperation with Russia", *The Diplomat*, January 9, 2019, at https://thediplomat.com/2019/01/a-closer-look-at-south-koreas-plan-for-cooperation-with-russia/ (accessed July 25, 2019).
53 "South Korea and Russia to Conduct Joint Study for Natural Gas Pipeline Running Through N. Korea", *Hankyoreh*, October 26, 2018, at http://english.hani.co.kr/arti/english_edition/e_business/867575.html (accessed July 25, 2019).

Index

3Es (energy security, economy, and environment) 2
21st Century Maritime Silk Road 229
38th Parallel line 167–168
1967 Six-Day War 127
1973 Yom Kippur War 127
1982 Lebanon War 127
1988 Summer Olympics 73
1992 Joint Declaration of the Denuclearisation of the Korean Peninsula 96
2005 joint statement 88
2012 Korea Trade-Investment Promotion Agency 125
2018 *New York Times* 126
2018 *Nuclear Poster Review Report* 117
2018 *Nuclear Posture Review Report* 117

A2AD *see* Anti-Access and Area-Denial (A2AD)
Abe administration 61, 64–65, 67–68; security cooperation policy 67
Abe, Shinzo, Prime Minister of Japan 2, 6, 47, 50, 57, 61, 63–65, 67–68, 155, 228
ACCC *see* ASEAN Connectivity Coordinating Committee (ACCC)
Acheson line 64–65
Acid Deposition Monitoring Network in East Asia (EANET) 245–246
Act East Policy (AEP) 165–166, 173, 175–179, 184
Action for action 80, 97
Act on the Protection of Specially Designated Secrets 60
ADB *see* Asian Development Bank (ADB)
ADMM *see* ASEAN Defence Ministers' Meeting (ADMM) plus
Aegis-Ashore system 60
Aegis destroyer 66

Aegis destroyers 57, 59–60
AEP *see* Act East Policy (AEP)
Africa 126, 229, 237, 243
Agreement on Reconciliation, Non-aggression and Exchanges and Cooperation 212
AIIB *see* Asian Infrastructure Investment Bank (AIIB)
aircraft 6, 61–63, 66, 109; carriers 61–62, 109; patrol 63; transport 66
alliance treaty 73
American Global Defence Posture Review 5
Amphibious Rapid Deployment Brigade (ARDB) 62
animosity 50
Anti-Access and Area-Denial (A2AD) 115, 247
anti-China rhetoric 6
anti-Japanese resistance 41
anti-nuclear sentiment 2
AN/TPY-2 *see* Army/Navy Transportable Radar Surveillance (AN/TPY-2)
APEC 235–236, 248–249
APEC Energy Working Group (EWG) 249
Arbatov, Alexey 72
ARDB *see* Amphibious Rapid Deployment Brigade (ARDB)
Arirang 78
Armed Forces of the Philippines 62
Armstrong, Charles 51
Army/Navy Transportable Radar Surveillance (AN/TPY-2) 46
Asahi Shimbun 58
ASEAN *see* Association of Southeast Asian Nations (ASEAN)
ASEAN Connectivity Coordinating Committee (ACCC) 177
ASEAN Defence Ministers' Meeting (ADMM) plus 177

Index

ASEAN Regional Forum (ARF) 177–178, 248
Asghari, Ali Reza 128
Asia 1–6, 11–13, 21, 31, 33, 39–42, 45–49, 51, 58–59, 63, 73, 75, 82, 98, 102, 107, 115–116, 122, 126, 131, 137–143, 146, 149, 151–160, 165, 167, 175–177, 181, 202, 217, 225–231, 233, 235–239, 242–250; security challenges in 226
Asian Development Bank (ADB) 233
Asian Financial Crisis 42
Asian Infrastructure Investment Bank (AIIB) 176–177, 230, 239
Asian Institute for Policy Studies 131
Asia-Pacific Economic Cooperation (APEC) 248
Asia-Pacific Partnership on Clean Development and Climate 249
Asia Press 202
Asia Super Grid 249
Asmolov, Konstantin 72
Assad, Bashar 128, 131
Association of Southeast Asian Nations (ASEAN) 175, 177, 228, 231–232, 234–235, 238–239, 243, 248–249
Australia 59, 63, 67, 216, 221, 228–229, 231, 234, 238–239, 242; *Defence White Papers* 228
Axe murder 24

B-1 65
B-52 65
Bagabandi, Natsag, Mongolian President 150
Balakrishnan, Vivian 232
Ballistic Missile Defence (BMD) 58–60
ballistic missile(s) 58–61, 66, 80–81, 92, 110, 113, 115, 121, 124, 126–127, 129, 131, 144, 170, 182–183; intercontinental 60; intermediate-range 60–61, 124; medium-range 59; South Korean 66; threat of 61; warning exercise 66
Barracuda-class (5,300 tons) nuclear submarine 66
BCP *see* Business Continuity Planning (BCP)
Bedeski, Robert 154
benign deception 214
Bethtol, Bruce 127
Better Utilisation of Investment Leading to Development (BUILD) Act 233
Beyond Parallel 203
Bhutto, Zulfikar Ali, the then prime minister of Pakistan 181

Biegun, Stephen 35
bilateral: agreement 102; arrangement 138, 220; cooperation 182; diplomacy 239; diplomatic relations 151; economic ties 151; engagement 213–214; issues 12, 88, 215; meetings 198–199, 209; negotiating mechanisms 212; negotiations 212; nuclear issue 216; political alliances 154; relations 27, 57, 72–76, 78, 82, 137, 149, 157, 165, 172–175, 180, 183, 212–213; talks 91, 213, 218; ties 76, 141, 172–173, 175, 182; tracks 214; trade 80, 151–152, 154, 173, 175–176; training activities 7; treaty 75
bilateralism 223
Blue Banner 159
Blue Chromite 62
Blue House 33
BMD *see* Ballistic Missile Defence (BMD)
Bolton, John, National Security Adviser 29, 33–35, 49
Bong-Guen Jun 51
BRI *see* Belt and Road Initiative (BRI)
Brooks, Vincent, General 29, 31
Brzezinski, Zbigniew K. 196
buffer zone 8, 40, 48, 50, 59, 65, 68
BUILD *see* Better Utilisation of Investment Leading to Development (BUILD) Act
Bush, George W., US 27, 75, 126, 201, 214, 216
Business Continuity Planning (BCP) 61
Byung jin Policy 87, 219

C-130 transport aircraft 66
Calder, Kent E. 3, 123, 243; *Making of Northeast Asia* 3
Camp Humphreys 41
Canada 12, 63–64, 67
Canadian Army 63
Candlelight Revolution 30, 33
Cargo ship 51, 60, 201
Catch-22 220
CBMs *see* Confidence building measures (CBMs)
CBS News 25
CDB *see* China Development Bank (CDB)
Central Asia 226, 229
Central Intelligence Agency (CIA) 123, 128, 159
Central link theory 93
Centre for Strategic and International Studies (CSIS) 200, 203
CEP *see* Cultural Exchange Programme (CEP) Agreement

Index   255

CEPA *see* Comprehensive Economic Partnership Agreement (CEPA)
Charter of the United Nations (UN) 75
Cha, Victor 42, 72, 126
Cheonan 77, 130
Cheong Wa Dae 77
China 1–8, 10–13, 32–34, 39–51, 59–68, 76, 78–81, 88–89, 94, 101–102, 106–107, 109, 112–113, 115–117, 124, 127–130, 140, 143–145, 149, 151–154, 156, 158–159, 165–166, 168–169, 172, 175–176, 180–181, 184, 194, 202, 204, 209–210, 212, 214–216, 218, 220–223, 225–236, 238–239, 242–250; as resident power in North-East Asia 5; Belt and Road Initiative (BRI) 176, 221–222, 226, 229–231, 233–236, 239, 249; "debt trap diplomacy" 230; deterrence against 65, 67; diplomatic success for 220; economic entanglements in North-East Asia 40, 45; economic interests 48; "freeze for freeze" initiative 40; geopolitical influence of 10; implications on 43, 45; influence on Korean Peninsula 10; market economy 44; military power 61; missile activities 46; missile tests 46; neighbourhood policy 40, 42; North-East Asian policy 40; "one-Korea" (pro-Pyongyang) policy 46; policies 48, 223; policy in South Korea 5; reform push in 1978 44; rise of 40, 42, 166, 225–227, 229, 247; role and interest in Korean Peninsula 5; role as a protector of North Korea 5; security, implications on 45, 67; security concerns 67; strategic community 47, 48; strategic dilemma for 48; strategic thinking 40; "Three Oppositions" 47; two-Koreas "de-facto and de-jure" policy 8, 46
China and DPRK 3, 4
China and India 175, 221–222, 238
China and Japan 45, 47, 102, 175; confrontation 11, 67; maritime boundary 47; relations 46–47; trade 45
China and Korea
China and North-East Asia 40, 41; economic entanglements 40, 45; relations 40
China and North Korea 3–5, 39, 40, 42–44, 47–48, 68, 79; 1961 "alliance treaty" 4; alliance 4; friendship 43; military aid 43; relations 39–40, 42, 44, 47–48, 79; secret pact on the shared boundary 40; shared socialist ideology 43; strategic allies 43; trade 43; Treaty of Friendship, Cooperation and Mutual Assistance 4, 40, 73, 143
China and Russia: cooperation 101; relations 76
China and South Korea 45–47; economic ties 46; exports 46; military alliance 10; relations 45
China and United States 5, 40, 58, 115–116, 215, 238; bilateral dialogues 5; confrontation 58; relations 64, 251, 236; strategic competition 115; strategic stability 106; trade war 40
China Development Bank (CDB) 230
China-Korea industrial parks 45
China-North Korea Treaty of Friendship 5, 48
China-South Korea Free Trade Agreement (CKFTA) 45
Chinese coast guards 61
"Chinese Dream" 8
Choe Ryong-hae 79
Choi Sun-hee 202
Chosun Ilbo 198
CIA *see* Central Intelligence Agency (CIA)
CKFTA *see* China-South Korea Free Trade Agreement (CKFTA)
Clemens, Walter 123, 124
climate change 2, 242, 246
Clinton, Bill 74, 216
CMF *see* Combined Maritime Forces (CMF)
CNN 35
Coast guards 61
COI *see* United Nations Commission of Inquiry (COI)
Cold War 64, 72, 109, 113–115, 124, 128, 137, 150, 158, 166–168, 171–172, 226, 243, 248
colonisation 41, 47, 50, 109
Combined Maritime Forces (CMF) 246
Comfort Women 66
communism 40, 153
Communist Party of China (CPC) 48
Community of Democracies Governing Council 154
complete denuclearisation 2–3, 11, 25–26, 28, 40, 50, 87, 129, 180–181, 193; commitment to 25
Complete, Verifiable and Irreversible Dismantlement (CVID) 3, 11, 24–25, 27, 33, 50, 57, 77, 80, 90, 143, 196, 216
Comprehensive and Progressive Agreement for the TPP (CPTPP) 238

256 *Index*

Comprehensive and Progressive Trans-Pacific Partnership 50
Comprehensive Economic Partnership Agreement (CEPA) 172, 175–176
confidence-building 88, 97, 102, 145
confidence building measures (CBMs) 88, 100, 102
confidence-building process 102
conflicts 7, 10, 13, 65, 107, 110, 112, 127, 129, 140, 142, 154–155, 159, 194–199, 201, 205, 211, 222, 228, 247, 250; large-scale 142; low-intensity 110; management 211; military 127, 129, 140; of interest 250; policy 196–199, 205; racial 194; religious 194; resolution 10, 211; territorial 194; transformation 211
Congressional Research Service 33
contestation 9, 11
cooperation 10–13, 23, 44–46, 50, 58, 63, 66–68, 74, 76, 79, 81–82, 88–89, 91, 96–102, 113, 115, 117, 126–128, 137–140, 142–146, 149, 151–152, 156–157, 165, 167, 172, 174–178, 181–182, 193–195, 211, 215, 217, 219, 222–223, 227, 229, 231–235, 237, 239, 242–250; bilateral 246, 250; economic 44–46, 76, 88, 96–99, 101, 138–139, 142, 146, 149, 165, 177, 215, 234, 237; energy 217, 239, 248–250; forms of 248; humanitarian 215; institutionalisation of 102; inter-Korean 58; Japanese 50; military 79, 100, 126–127, 143; multilateral 82, 102, 250; regional 156, 177, 182, 243, 246, 249; security 63, 66–68, 117, 156, 172, 229, 249; socio-economic 88; technological 91; tri-country 66; trilateral 128, 139; value-based 233
Copeland, Dale 45; theory of trade expectations 45
cost-sharing deal 5
CPC *see* Communist Party of China (CPC)
CPTPP *see* Comprehensive and Progressive Agreement for the TPP (CPTPP)
Crimea 78
CSIS *see* Centre for Strategic and International Studies (CSIS)
Cultural Exchange Programme (CEP) Agreement 172
Cultural Revolution 43
CVID *see* Complete, Verifiable and Irreversible Dismantlement (CVID)
Cybersecurity 116, 233

Daily Beast 25
Davydov, Oleg 72
defence 6–7, 9, 22, 24–25, 47, 58–62, 65–67, 98–100, 113–116, 125–126, 128, 195, 247; burden 59; capabilities 6, 9, 59; island 62, 67; missile 47, 58–60, 67, 114, 116; national 61, 98; South Korean 66
defence treaty 100
Demilitarized Zone (DMZ) 21–22, 26, 35, 41, 59, 87, 100, 204, 209
Democratic People's Republic of Korea (DPRK); economy 125, 130; enrichment programme 121, 123; ICBM programme 125; illicit proliferation activities 122; missile programme 124; nuclear and ballistic missile programmes 81; nuclear and missile capabilities 125, 128; nuclear and missile issues 131; nuclear and missile programmes 122; nuclear weapons programme 122, 213; proliferation activities 121, 127–129, 131; UN sanctions imposed on 77
Denisov, Valery 72
denuclearisation 1–3, 6–7, 9–12, 21–29, 32–33, 35, 40, 49–51, 57–58, 62, 64–65, 68, 77, 82, 87–102, 106–108, 111–112, 117–118, 121–122, 129, 131–132, 142–143, 145–146, 149, 157, 165–166, 173–175, 179–184, 193, 210, 213, 216–217, 220; China's proposal for 107; complete 2–3, 11, 25–26, 28, 40, 50, 87, 129, 180–181, 193; concept of 95; definition and scope of 91; diplomacy 129, 132; implementation of 88; importance of 145, 180; negotiations 7, 12, 58, 68, 97, 101, 106, 108, 112, 117–118, 122, 129, 131, 179; North Korean 2, 122; process of 88, 145, 174, 179; progress in 101; sanctions versus 23; scope of 91, 112; successive 179; unilateral and gangster-like demand for 27; verification and procedures for 88
denuclearisation talks 57, 58, 62, 64, 77, 88–89, 90–92, 97, 101–102, 121; four hypotheses 89; proposal for 91
denuclearization 3, 89, 100, 165, 180, 182, 193
deterrence 12, 45, 51, 60, 65, 67, 87, 89–91, 99, 107–108, 110, 112–117, 129, 159, 221; architecture 113, 115, 117; extended 12, 107, 110, 112–117; nuclear 45, 87, 91, 108, 129; power 60; regional 107, 115

development: Chinese model of 44; economic 9, 59, 90, 93–94, 108, 131, 137, 139–140, 154, 236, 248; nuclear and ballistic missile 60; nuclear weapons 45, 93, 95; sustainable 91, 177–178
dialogue(s) 1, 5, 7, 10, 12–13, 21, 25, 27, 32, 34, 63–64, 74–76, 78, 80–81, 90–91, 93, 96–97, 115, 149, 154–159, 165–166, 173–174, 177–179, 182–183, 210, 216, 218, 222–223, 236–237, 239, 249; bilateral 5; constructive 78, 157; diplomacy 1, 10, 166, 173, 222–223; diplomatic 182; institutionalised 216; multilateral 97; power-based 210; regional 159
Digital New Silk Road 230
diplomacy 1, 7, 9–10, 13, 35, 39, 42, 46, 48–49, 63–64, 75, 79, 98, 129, 132, 144–145, 149, 156, 159, 165–167, 173, 178–180, 183, 219–220, 222–223, 230, 239, 244; American 35; bilateral 239; coercive 144; conservative 219; cooperative 98; debt trap 230; denuclearisation 129, 132; dialogue 1, 10, 166, 173, 222–223; innovative 220; Northern 46; nuclear 48; President Trump's 49; President Xi's 49; proactive 42; regional 42; resource 244; responsive 42; Russian 79; smooth 222; summit 75; triangular 145; trilateral 239
diplomatic: capital 244; catch-22 220; channels 49, 175; clashes 244; complications 245; connections 166; contacts 159, 172; defeat 218; dialogues 182; efforts 142; engagement 102, 129, 173; failure 129; influence 106, 242; initiatives 67; isolation 79; issues 12, 88; leverage 46; linkages 174, 175; methods 80; normalisation 111–112, 115, 213; option 102; outreach 80; overtures 89; policy 68; process 82, 87, 142, 145; relations 13, 39, 67, 73, 88, 93, 96, 111, 123, 151, 157, 166, 171, 173, 175, 179, 217, 220, 223; settlement 80; stalemate 39; tack 11, 35; tightrope 39; top-down track 106; tussle 242; weapon 244
disarmament 99, 100, 102, 157–158, 180, 183, 198, 220; conventional 99–100; nuclear 102, 157, 183
dispute(s) 11, 13, 30, 47, 75, 101, 116, 154–156, 160, 211, 227, 243–244, 247–248; maritime 11, 13, 227, 243,

247; North-South Korean 13, 160; regional 155; territorial 47, 154, 227
distrust 6, 34, 51, 57, 248
DMZ *see* Demilitarized Zone (DMZ)
Doklam 221
Dosan Ahn Chang Ho (SS 083) 66
double freeze 50, 80
DPRK *see* Democratic People's Republic of Korea (DPRK); North Korea
DPRK and Japan 155, 212, 217; negotiations 155; relations 154–155, 212, 217
DPRK and ROK 174; bilateral track 212; diplomatic process 82
DPRK and Russia ties 141
DPRK and United States 26–27, 81–82, 155, 212–214, 216–217, 220; bilateral nuclear issue 216; détente 82; first summit 93, 129; negotiations 157; relations 25–26, 49; second summit 87, 129; summit in Singapore 93; summits 2, 81, 87, 93, 155, 129, 198, 213; tensions 215
DRPK 142, 143
DTT *see* US-ROK-Japan Defence Trilateral Talks (DTT)

EARC *see* East Asian Railway Community (EARC)
EAS *see* East Asia Summit (EAS)
East Asia Forum 248
East Asian Railway Community (EARC) 49
East Asia Summit (EAS) 177, 227, 237
East Asia Summit Energy Cooperative Task Force 249
East China Sea 47, 62–63, 244, 246–248
East Sea 140, 243, 247–248
East Siberia 140, 242, 248
East Siberian Oil Pipeline project (ESPO) 248
Eberstadt, Nicholas 72
ECNEA *see* Intergovernmental Collaborative Mechanism on Energy Cooperation in North-East Asia (ECNEA)
economic: aid 11, 73, 202; architectures 13, 225–226, 233, 235, 237; bait 22, 50; blessings 35; burden 47; capability 121; change 11; connectivity 139; contraction 49; cooperation 44–46, 76, 88, 96–99, 101, 138–139, 142, 146, 149, 165, 177, 215, 234, 237; crisis 74, 131; development 9, 59, 90, 93–94, 108,

258 *Index*

131, 137, 139–140, 154, 236, 248; drive 94; engagement 42, 46, 144, 146, 233; entanglements 40, 45, 48; goals 225; impact 61; interdependence 49, 229, 236, 248; interests 42, 48, 145, 166, 232; issues 6, 236–237; leverage 48; partners 4, 40, 46, 137; policy 153; projects 80, 141; reforms 44; relations 67, 96, 171, 236–237; resilience 199, 202; sanctions 8, 93, 106, 111–112, 117, 125, 130–131, 142, 146, 193, 196, 198–199; significance 3; summits 154; ties 46, 78, 151, 174, 226, 229, 232, 235; vision 232

economy 2, 7–8, 11, 22–23, 39–40, 42, 44, 46, 51, 77, 87, 89–91, 94, 108, 110–111, 122, 125, 129–131, 144, 149, 154, 166, 171, 177, 179, 196, 202–205, 217, 239, 244; China's 51; East Asian 154, 179; global 11, 131; impoverished 8, 125; market 44; market-based 7; North Korean 77, 91, 122, 125, 130, 144, 204, 205; South Korean 46

EDD *see* Extended Deterrence Dialogue (EDD)

EDGE *see* Enhancing Development and Growth through Energy (EDGE)

EDPC *see* Extended Deterrence Policy Committee (EDPC)

Egypt 44, 124, 126

Einhorn, Robert 158

Elbegdorj, Tsakia, Mongolian President 151, 153, 155–156; visit to Pyongyang 151

emergency information network system (EM-net) 61

EM-net *see* Emergency information network system (EM-net)

end-of-war declaration 27, 29, 33, 94, 100, 112

energy: connectivity 156, 249; cooperation 217, 239, 248–250; nuclear 2, 96, 122, 143, 158; requirement 2; resources 2, 140, 228, 233, 237, 248–249; security 2, 13, 140, 242, 248–250; supply 2, 140, 248

Energy Working Group (of APEC) (EWG) 249

Enhancing Development and Growth through Energy (EDGE) 232–233

Enkhbayar, Nambar, Mongolian Prime Minister 150–151

Enkhbayar summit 151

Enkhbold, Miyeegomb, Mongolian Prime Minister 153; trip to China 153

entrapment dilemma 48

environmental irritants 245

environmental issues 242, 245–246

Environmental Protection and Disaster Management in NEA 157

espionage 46, 125

ESPO *see* East Siberian Oil Pipeline project (ESPO)

EU *see* European Union (EU)

European Union (EU) 8, 79, 130

evacuation drills 61

EWG *see* Energy Working Group (of APEC) (EWG); *See* APEC Energy Working Group (EWG)

Extended Deterrence Dialogue (EDD) 115

Extended Deterrence Policy Committee (EDPC) 115

F-35B 62

F-35s 62

Fakhrizadeh-Mahabadi, Mohsen 127

Far Eastern region 138–140

FDI *see* Foreign Direct Investment (FDI)

FE *see* Foal Eagle (FE)

FFVD *see* Final, Fully Verified Denuclearization (FFVD)

Final, Fully Verified Denuclearization (FFVD) 106

fire and fury 21, 34, 90

Fissile Material Cut-off Treaty (FMCT) 101

Flying Horse Movement 43

FMCT *see* Fissile Material Cut-off Treaty (FMCT)

Foal Eagle (FE) 65

FOIP *see* Free and Open Indo-Pacific (FOIP)

FOIPS *see* Free and Open Indo-Pacific Strategy (FOIPS)

Foreign Direct Investment (FDI) 156, 243

foreign ministerial conference 63

foreign policy 12, 35, 42, 48, 72–74, 76, 80, 106–107, 118, 137–139, 142, 146, 149, 154, 165–167, 171–172, 174, 194–195, 198, 226–228, 231, 243; establishments 73, 107; negative attitude of 76; North Korean 74; principles 72; priority 106; Russian 74, 138–139; USSR 73, 137

Foreign Policy Concept of the Russian Federation 74

Four-party talks 215

France 12, 63, 67, 113, 158

Frantz, Douglas 127

Free and Open Indo-Pacific (FOIP) 225, 233

Free and Open Indo-Pacific Strategy (FOIPS) 63
Freedom House 22, 27
Free Trade Agreement (FTA) 45, 231, 236, 244
Freeze-for-freeze 50, 94
French Navy 66
Friedrich, Carl J. 196
Friedrich Ebert Foundation 157
FTA *see* Free Trade Agreement (FTA)
Fukushima nuclear disaster 2
Funabashi, Yoichi 48

G8 75
G20 236, 248
Gaddafi, Muammar, late Libyan Leader 35, 51, 109, 143
Galushka, Alexander 79
Ganbat, Damba 157
GDP *see* Gross Domestic Product (GDP)
General Security of Military Information Agreement (GSOMIA) 6, 66, 68
Geneva agreement 29
geoeconomics 225–226, 229–230, 233, 235, 237–238
geopolitics 13, 226, 235; US Indo-Pacific strategy as 226
geostrategy 3
Ghauri-1 missile 128
GLF *see* Great Leap Forward (GLF)
Global Partnership for the Prevention of Armed Conflict (GPPAC) 159
Global Times 221
Gorbachev, Mikhail, Soviet President 72–73, 137, 138; policy of 72
GPPAC *see* Global Partnership for the Prevention of Armed Conflict (GPPAC)
Great Leap Forward (GLF) 43
Great Wall of China 39, 41
GRIPS *see* National Graduate Institute for Policy Studies (GRIPS)
Gross Domestic Product (GDP) 194, 230
GSOMIA *see* General Security of Military Information Agreement (GSOMIA)
Gwangmyeongseong-1 60
Gwangmyeongseong-2 60

Haggard, and Stephen 72
Hamas 131
Hankook Ilbo 66
Hanoi talks 194, 198–200, 202, 204; failure of 200, 202
Harris, Harry, US ambassador to South Korea 29, 31

Hezbollah 131
Honecker, Erich 73
Hostile policy 111, 216, 220
Hu Jintao, Chinese President 39; visited North Korea 39
human resource development 245
human rights 10, 100–101, 118, 193, 197; improvements 100; violations 10, 197
hunger crisis 49
Hwasong-5 124
Hwasong-6 124
Hwasong 12 61
Hwasong-15 45, 60, 125, 170
hydrogen bomb 45, 124

IAEA *see* International Atomic Energy Agency (IAEA)
ICAS *see* Institute for Corean [sic] American Studies (ICAS)
ICBM *see* Intercontinental Ballistic Missile (ICBM)
ICCSR *see* Indian Council of Social Science Research (ICCSR)
ideology 9, 43, 72, 145, 193, 196, 199; communist 193; divinity 199; juche 43; self-reliance 9; socialist 43
Ignatius, David 35
illicit proliferation 122, 131
IMF *see* International Monetary Fund (IMF)
IMSS *see* India's Maritime Security Strategy (IMSS)
India 3, 13, 43, 62–63, 67, 157, 165–184, 221–223, 225, 227–229, 231, 235–239, 243, 246; Act East Policy 175, 178; approach to the Korean Peninsula 13, 166; dialogue diplomacy 173; diplomacy 166; diplomatic recognition 171; foreign policy 167, 171, 172; stance on major UN resolutions and sanctions 169
India and Japan 175
India and Korean Peninsula 165, 182
India and North Korea: economic and cultural ties 174; relations 174; trade 178
India and South Korea 171–173, 176–178, 181; relations 166, 173, 182; trade 176
India and two Koreas, dialogue diplomacy 173
Indian Ocean 62, 141, 177, 221, 225–229, 232, 235–238, 247
Indian Ocean Rim Association (IORA) 177, 235, 237, 239
Indo-Asia Pacific region 122
Indo-Pacific 1, 3, 5–7, 11–13, 63, 65–67, 106–108, 112–118, 121, 129, 131, 166,

175–176, 177, 181–182, 184, 209–210, 220–223, 225–239, 242, 244–245; economic architectures in 226, 233, 235, 237; geoeconomics of 225; lessons for 209, 220; power politics 1; resource politics in 242; security in 3, 121, 129; strategic stability in 106; United States' military commitments in 5; US interests in 6; US strategy 226; volatile zone in 3
Indo-Pacific Economic Vision 232–236, 238–239
Indo-Pacific Strategy 13, 62–63, 66–67, 225–235
information control 196, 199, 202–203; collapse of 199, 202
information-sharing 103, 246
infrastructure 81, 91, 114, 121, 140, 153, 176–177, 222, 230, 233, 239, 243–245, 249; investment in 91
Infrastructure Transactional Assistance Network (ITAN) 232–233
insecurity 13, 67, 242–247; regional 67, 246; resource 13, 243–245
Insider 203
Institute for Corean [sic] American Studies (ICAS) 33
Institute of International Education's Scholar Relief Fund 153
institutionalism 195
intellectual theft 46
intelligence-sharing pact 6
interconnectivity 151, 249
Intercontinental Ballistic Missile (ICBM) 9–10, 24, 90, 93, 110, 115, 121, 125, 127, 129, 193
Intergovernmental Collaborative Mechanism on Energy Cooperation in North-East Asia (ECNEA) 249
Intergovernmental Commission on Cooperation in Trade, Economy, Science and Technology 80
Inter-Korean: first summit 87; accord 99; denuclearisation dialogue 174; dialogue 91, 97, 174; economic cooperation 99; exchanges and cooperation 58, 88, 97 Inter-Korean 99, 102; Joint Declaration on the Denuclearisation of the Korean Peninsula 96; meetings 2; Nuclear Control Joint Commission 96; reconciliation 57; relations 57, 90, 96, 99, 102, 106; summits 4, 10, 28, 58, 87, 94, 97, 129, 165–166, 215; talks 97
International Atomic Energy Agency (IAEA) 29, 96, 123, 213, 216–217

internationalism 74
international relations 72, 137, 139, 194, 222–223, 238; norms and principles of 72
international sanctions 1, 89, 108, 122, 127, 153, 173, 197, 199, 202, 204–205
IORA *see* Indian Ocean Rim Association (IORA)
Iran 3, 10, 44, 123, 126–128, 131; missile system 127; nuclear deal 10; nuclear weapons programme 126
ISS *see* Mongolia's Institute for Strategic Studies (ISS)
ITAN *see* Infrastructure Transactional Assistance Network (ITAN)
Ivanov, Igor 74

JADIZ *see* Japan's Air Defence Identification Zone (JADIZ)
J-Alert 47
J-ALERT *see* National instantaneous warning system (J-ALERT)
Jang Song Thaek incident 44, 79
Japan 1–3, 5–8, 11–12, 26, 34, 40–42, 45–47, 49–50, 57–68, 75–76, 88, 100, 102, 109–110, 115–116, 118, 124, 130, 140–141, 149, 154–156, 159, 165, 172, 175, 180–182, 184, 193–194, 212–214, 216–218, 221, 228–229, 231, 234–235, 238–239, 242–243, 245–250; ballistic missile defence capability of 59–60; coast guards 61; defeat in World War II 193; defence capability 59; dependency on nuclear energy resources 2; economic growth 46; energy requirement 2; Indo-Pacific strategy 67; intelligence capacity 60; Korean Peninsula strategy 12, 68; militarisation 50; military relations 67; national interest 68; perception of North Korea 57; re-militarisation of 47; scepticism 57; security policy 67; security threat to 67; threat to 57, 67
Japan Air Self-Defence Force (JASDF) 59, 60
Japan and Korean Peninsula: security pledge 57
Japan and North Korea 47, 58, 64; relations 47; summit 64
Japan and South Korea 5–7, 45, 50, 60, 65–66, 68, 118, 141, 154, 218, 245, 248; military information 66; relations 65, 68; security cooperation 66, 68; ties, challenges in 65; trade war 50
Japan and United States 3, 5–6, 57–61, 64, 228; alliance 6, 58–60, 64, 228; joint

naval ballistic missile warning exercise 66; relations 59
Japanese government 57, 60, 61, 64, 65, 66
Japanese hegemony 42
Japanese Ministry of Defence 62
Japan Ground Self-Defence Force (JGSDF) 62
Japan Maritime Self-Defence Force (JMSDF) 57, 60, 62, 247; Izumo (DDH-183) 60; Sazanami (DD-113) 60
Japan Ministry of Defence 62
Japan-North Korea Pyongyang Declaration 58
Japan's Active Promotion of Security Cooperation 67
Japan's Air Defence Identification Zone (JADIZ) 61
Japan Self-Defence Forces (JSDF) 58–62
Japan's National Defence Programme Guidelines 62–63, 67–68
Japan-South Korea agreement 68
Japan's White Paper on Defence 47
Japan-US-Australia military exercises 63
Japan-US Defence Cooperation Guidelines 67
Japan-US-India military exercises 63
JASDF *see* Japan Air Self-Defence Force (JASDF)
JASSM *see* Joint Air-to-Surface Standoff Missile (JASSM)
JGSDF *see* Japan Ground Self-Defence Force (JGSDF)
Jie Shun 126
JMSDF *see* Japan Maritime Self-Defence Force (JMSDF)
Joint Air-to-Surface Standoff Missile (JASSM) 61
Joint Declaration on the Denuclearisation of the Korean Peninsula 50, 96
Joint Security Area 24, 27, 87
Joongang Daily 199
JSDF *see* Japan Self-Defence Forces (JSDF)

Kaesong Industrial Complex (KIC) 30, 44, 49, 51, 130
KAMANDAG 2 62
Kang Kyung-wha, South Korean foreign minister 32
KCNA *see* Korean Central News Agency (KCNA)
KEDO *see* Korean Peninsula Energy Development Organisation (KEDO)
KGB *see* USSR Committee for State Security (KGB)

Khan, A.Q., Pakistani nuclear physicist 44, 121, 122, 123, 126
Khorramsharh 127
KIC *see* Kaesong Industrial Complex (KIC)
Kidnappings 47
Kim and Trump 10, 21, 24–25, 27–28, 33–34, 157, 174, 193, 198, 204, 214; first summit in Singapore 11, 22–23, 26, 33, 48–48, 93, 157, 204, 209; Hanoi summit 23, 91, 98, 198–200; joint statement 25; second summit 22, 28, 33, 48–49; statement 27; third meeting 21
Kim Dae-jung 74–75, 150, 215
Kim Eui-kyeom 33
Kim Il-sung 43–44, 72–73, 75, 92, 109, 150–151
Kim Jong-il 23, 30, 43–44, 47, 75–77, 150, 215
Kim Jong-un 2–3, 8–10, 12–13, 21–35, 39, 43–44, 47–48, 57, 75–79, 81–82, 87–88, 90–94, 106, 108–111, 125, 131, 141, 145, 149–151, 155, 157–158, 166, 174, 193–194, 196–206, 210, 213–215, 219; New Year's speech in 2018 23; nuclear programme for defence against enemies 22
Kim Jong-un and Moon Jae-in 24, 28, 31; Pyongyang joint declaration 31; summit 24
Kim and Putin, Vladimir, President: first summit 34
Kim, Samuel 42, 46
Kim Yo-jong 23
Kim Yong-chol 26–30; letter to Pompeo 30
Kitamura, Shigeru 64
Klinger, Bruce 72
Koda, Yoji 57
KOEC *see* Korea Oil Exploration Corporation (KOEC)
Koizumi, Junichiro, Japanese prime minister 47; visit to Pyongyang 47
Korea-Chinese Friendship Year 45
Korea formula 97
Korean Armistice Treaty 39, 100
Korean Central News Agency (KCNA) 26, 34
Korean Journal of International Studies, 195
Korean nuclear issue 81, 102, 198, 205, 211–212, 220
Korean Peninsula 1–13, 21, 24–25, 27, 39, 49, 50, 57–65, 67–68, 72, 74–79, 81–82, 87–93, 95–100, 102, 106–107, 109–110, 112, 116–118, 123, 128–129, 131,

137–146, 149, 153, 155–157, 159–160, 165–167, 169, 171–175, 178–184, 193–194, 196, 201, 206, 209–210, 213, 215, 217, 219, 223, 242–243, 248; 1992 Joint Declaration on 95; alliance management in 9; Americanisation of 92; America's strategy for 21; China's role and interest in 5; complete denuclearisation of 2–3, 26, 87; denuclearisation of 2–3, 9, 50, 87, 91–92, 95–96, 146, 157, 217; hostilities on 76–77, 79; implications for 117; influence of China on 10; issue, political solution to 39; mediation initiatives for peace on 153; military balance on 92, 100; nuclear issue 81; nuclear-weapons-free 96, 102; peace and stability in 9, 183; peace regime on 49, 57, 88, 96–97, 102; problem of 68, 143; prospects of peace in 2; reunification of 7, 194; Russian approach to 77; Russia's position on 78; Russia's role in 72; security architecture of 59, 64, 166; tensions on 61, 90, 96, 139; unstable pivot 3; US military presence on 100; US policy on 21
Korean Peninsula Energy Development Organisation (KEDO) 96, 213
Korean Peninsula of Peace and Prosperity 98
Korean People's Army (KPA) 43
Korean question 142, 145
Korean reunification 8
Korean Statistics Bureau 202
Korean War 4, 8, 22–25, 27–28, 30, 39–43, 58, 65, 78, 90, 100, 109, 122, 150, 167–168, 171, 179, 201, 215; return of some of the remains of Americans missing in 27
Korea Oil Exploration Corporation (KOEC) 152
Korea Trade-Investment Promotion Agency (KOTRA) 152, 202
KOTRA *see* Korea Trade-Investment Promotion Agency (KOTRA)
Kozyrev, Andrey 74
KPA *see* Korean People's Army (KPA)
Krusekopf, Charles 156
Kumamoto earthquake 66
Kunadze, Georgy 72
Kwon Jong-gun 34
Kyunghyang Daily 201
Kyung-seo, Park, president of the South Korean Red Cross 30

labour 50, 73, 153; camps 73; forced 50
Lankov, Andrei 40
Latin America 243, 245
Lavrov, Sergey 81
Leap Day Deal 77
Lee Myung-bak, South Korean president 65, 76, 153
Legislation for Peace and Security 60–61
Liberal Democratic Party (LDP) 50
Libya 3, 44, 51, 109, 122–123, 128, 143
Light Water Reactor (LWR) 213
Li Nan 43, 45–46, 49
Long-term Cooperative Partnership for Peace and Prosperity 172
Look East Policy 172, 175
Los Angeles Times 127
Lukin, Alexander 72
LWR *see* Light Water Reactor (LWR)

MacArthur, General Douglas 167
Mahan, Admiral Alfred T. 247
Malabar 2017 62
Manchus 41
Manoeuvres 11, 165
Mao 43
Mao Anying 43
Mao Zedong 43
maritime 11, 13, 47, 60, 62–63, 115, 141, 177, 222, 225–230, 239, 242–244, 247–249; boundary 47; disputes 11, 13, 227, 243, 247; patrol aircraft 63; tensions 247; zone 47, 244, 247
market(s) 140–141, 179, 203, 243–244; Asian 140; economy 44; South Korean 141
Mattis, Jim, Trump's defence secretary 24, 26, 65, 125
Matvienko, Valentina 81
Maximum-pressure campaign 98
MDB *see* Multilateral Development Bank (MDB)
MEA *see* Ministry of External Affairs (MEA)
Medvedev, Dmitry 76, 77, 113
Memorandum of Understanding (MOU) 151, 246
Memorial of the War to Resist America and Aid Korea 43
Menon, K.P.S 167–168
MFA *see* Ministry of Foreign Affairs (MFA)
Micheev, Vasily 72
Michishita, Narushige 68
Middle East 9, 122, 126, 131, 140, 227, 229, 243, 245–248; victim of aggression 9

Militarisation 47, 50, 142, 156; Japan's 50
Military: Alliance, trilateral 67; provocations 10–11, 67, 108; aid 43, 126; alliance 10, 24, 67, 129, 158, 175, 222; ally 40; balance/balancing 5, 92, 100; base 5–6, 41, 94; capabilities 100, 114–115, 126, 219; confidence building measures 88, 102; conflicts 127, 129, 140; confrontations 138; cooperation 79, 100, 126–127, 143; demarcation line 24; drills 80; power 59, 61, 100, 195; provocations 10–11, 67, 108; realignment programme 5; relations 12, 47, 67; tension 58, 68
Military exercises 10, 25–26, 33, 50, 63, 65, 92–93, 107, 109, 111–112, 144, 214; Foal Eagle (FE) 65; Japan-US-Australia 63; Japan-US-India 63; joint 10, 25–26, 50, 65, 80, 92, 107, 109, 111–112, 144; Key Resolve (KR) 65; multilateral 62–63, 67
Military-to-military action 5
Ming Wan 45
Ministry of External Affairs (MEA) 178
Ministry of Foreign Affairs (MFA) 48
Ministry of Trade and Commerce, Government of India 176, 178
Min Ye 3; *Making of Northeast Asia*, 3
missile-and-nuclear tests 22
missile(s) 4–6, 12, 22–23, 26, 28–29, 31–34, 40, 44–47, 49–51, 57–62, 64, 66–67, 75, 77–81, 87, 90, 92–94, 106–107, 109–110, 112–116, 121–122, 124–132, 142–144, 170, 175, 180–183, 198, 202, 209–210, 214, 218, 220; alert 61; cruise 60; defence 47, 58–60, 67, 114, 116; detection capabilities 59; ground-to-air 62; ground-to-ship 62; interception system 59; interceptor 60; long-range 23, 31–32, 34, 49–50, 87, 181; short-range 40, 49–51, 124; technology 44, 124–125, 128; tests 45, 46, 75, 79–80, 87, 90, 130, 180, 210, 214, 218
missile(s) testing 4, 214
Missile Technology Control Regime (MTCR) 44
MK News 198, 202
Modi, Narendra, Indian Prime Minister 172, 175–176, 181–182
Mongolia 12–13, 49, 64, 149–160, 242–243, 245–246, 249–250; foreign economic policy 153; mediation initiatives 153

Mongolia and North-East Asia 149, 159; historical contacts 150; peace process 149
Mongolia's Diplomacy with the Two Koreas 149
Mongolia's Institute for Strategic Studies (ISS) 156–158
Mongols 41, 151, 153, 158, 160
Moon administration 66, 67, 140
Moon Jae-in: policy objectives of 97; visited North Korea 49
Moon Jae-in, President of Republic of Korea 2, 5, 10, 22–24, 26, 28–33, 46, 49, 57, 63, 66–67, 87, 90, 97–98, 106, 139–140, 175, 181, 212–213, 237, 249
MOU *see* Memorandum of Understanding (MOU)
Mount Kumgang Tourist Zone 44
MTCR *see* Missile Technology Control Regime (MTCR)
Multilateral Development Bank (MDB) 176
Musharraf, Pervez, Pakistani president 123
Musudan 124, 127
mutual defence treaty 100
mutual exchanges and cooperation 88
mutual interests 10, 91, 102, 174, 178
mutual suspicion 29, 171
mutual trust 93, 113, 175, 198
mutual trust-building measures 93
Myagmar, Dovchin 159

NAM *see* Non-Alignment Movement (NAM)
National Graduate Institute for Policy Studies (GRIPS) 58, 68
National instantaneous warning system (J-ALERT) 61
nationalism 11, 145, 221
National Security Council (NSC) 67
National Security Strategy (NSS) 64, 67, 68
National Security Strategy of 2017 221, 225
NATO *see* North Atlantic Treaty Organisation (NATO)
natural resources 79, 143
navigation 66, 227, 237; rule of law and freedom of 66, 227
NDRC *see* National Development and Reform Commission (NDRC)
NEA 157
NEAC *see* Northeast Asian Conference on Environmental Cooperation (NEAC)
NEASPEC *see* North-East Asian Sub-regional Programme for Environmental Cooperation (NEASPEC)

NEAT *see* Northwest Pacific Action Plan Eutrophication Assessment Tool (NEAT)
negotiation(s) 2–3, 7–10, 12, 31, 34, 58, 64, 68, 74, 76, 82, 88–90, 91, 94, 97, 100–102, 106–108, 112, 117–118, 122, 129, 131–132, 150, 155, 157, 176, 179, 196, 198–199, 201, 205, 209–214, 217–220, 222–223, 231, 238; bilateral 212; denuclearisation 7, 12, 58, 68, 97, 101, 106, 108, 112, 117–118, 122, 129, 131, 179; failure of 211; international 210–211; Korea-to-Korea 150; modalities for 3; multilateral 209; peace process 179; strategy of 196; talks 64, 201; unification 8; United States and North Korea 82; US-DPRK 157
NEO *see* Non-combatant Evacuation Operation (NEO)
Neutral Nations Repatriation Commission (NNRC) 171
New Northern Policy 139–141, 249
New Southern Policy (NSP) 67, 173, 176–177, 237–239
New Zealand 63, 231
NGO *see* Non-Governmental Organisation (NGO)
Niksch, Larry 33
NK Economy 203
NNRC *see* Neutral Nations Repatriation Commission (NNRC)
NOC *see* National Oil Company (NOC)
Non-Alignment Movement (NAM) 171
Non-combatant Evacuation Operation (NEO) 47, 61; execution of 61
Non-Governmental Organisation (NGO) 99, 158–159
non-nuclearization 49
non-nuclear proliferation 158
Non-Proliferation of Nuclear Weapons 143, 213
Nordpolitik (Northern Diplomacy) 46
North America 245
North Atlantic Treaty Organisation (NATO) 35
North-East Asia 1, 3, 5–6, 11–12, 13, 21, 39–42, 45–49, 51, 58, 63, 65, 75, 82, 98, 102, 107, 115–116, 118, 137–143, 146, 149, 153–160, 165, 181, 217, 220, 242–250; China as resident power in 5; China's economic entanglements in 40, 45; DPRK's participation in 82; dramatic changes in 48; economic significance 3; importance of 40; peace and security arrangement in 82; peace and security in 75, 157; progress in 48; regional stability in 6, 155; resource politics in 242, 250; security 155–157, 243; security alliances in 5; security dilemma in 58; significance of 40; US interests in 6; US-led missile defence system in 47
Northeast Asian Conference on Environmental Cooperation (NEAC) 245
North-East Asian Sub-regional Programme for Environmental Cooperation (NEASPEC) 245, 246
Northern Sea Route 140
North Korea 1–13, 21–35, 39–51, 57–68, 72–82, 87–103, 106–112, 116–118, 121–128, 130–131, 138–139, 141, 143–146, 149–160, 165–167, 169–175, 178–184, 193–194, 196–206, 209–220, 222–223, 247, 250; as a nuclear neighbour 44; as a strategic shield 42; behavioural pattern of 1; bellicose attitude 9; complete denuclearisation in 3; concessions to 65; currency reforms 199; debt problem of 78; demand for the lifting of sanctions 88; denuclearisation of 2–3, 6, 9, 12, 40, 50, 57–58, 64, 68, 88, 91, 107–108, 111–112, 117–118, 122, 210; dynastic succession 44; economic crisis in 74; economic problems in 44; economic resilience 202; economic sanctions 8; effective deterrent against 63; emergence as a nuclear power 4; energy needs 29; first nuclear test 44; foreign policy 74, 194; ICBM launches 10; international sanctions 1, 89, 108, 122, 127, 153, 173, 197, 199, 202, 204–205; intrusions into Japanese waters 47; military provocation by 60, 66–67; military provocations 11, 67; missile and nuclear tests 26, 40, 77, 169, 180; missiles or missile technology 44; nuclear activities 96; nuclear and ballistic missile development 60; nuclear arsenal 49, 198; nuclear capability of 218; nuclear policy 194, 196, 199; nuclear problem 74; nuclear programme 24–25, 34, 91, 101, 106, 116, 171, 179; nuclear reprocessing facility in 95; nuclear weapons 45, 90, 97, 199, 209–210, 212; nuclear weapons capability 101; nuclear weapons development 45; nuclear weapons programme 97; pattern of behavior 95; policies regarding concessions on 6; political goals and

aspirations 74; political system 194, 196, 198–199, 203–205; politics of 109; pressure on 64, 68, 78, 141, 179–180, 204; propaganda 73, 199; reforms in 44; research and development 101; return of Japanese people abducted by 64; sanctions against 101, 173, 193, 199, 201, 204; sanctions and pressure policy against 80; satellite launch 48; security guarantees for 10, 82; security threat 196; settlement of debt 76; siege mentality 108, 109; Sinuiju Special Administrative Region (SAR) 44; Soviet-backed 21; threats 47; understanding of denuclearisation 40; UN mission 29; UNSC sanctions resolutions against 4, 10, 23–24, 26, 30, 63; urgency of denuclearising 5; US policy on 29; US unilateral sanctions against 101
North Korea and Pakistan 3, 181; nuclear technological nexus 3
North Korea and Russia: bilateral relations 76; relations 12, 72, 74–80, 139
North Korea and South Korea 23, 25, 28, 194, 209; dispute 13, 160; reconciliation, hope of 61; relations 99; summit 28, 81
North Korea and United States 12, 24–25, 27–29, 39, 50–51, 57–58, 61, 64–65, 68, 77, 81–82, 87–88, 91–92, 96–97, 99, 101–102, 106–107, 111–112, 117, 179, 182, 198, 212, 218, 220; bargain 99; bilateral issue 12, 88; bilateral talks 91; deal 50; denuclearisation talks 58; diplomatic process 87; diplomatic relations 88, 111; diplomatic stalemate 39; negotiations 82; political and economic relations 96; relations 24, 88, 111; summits 28, 57, 61, 64–65, 81, 107, 198; talks 64, 201
North Korean Factor 141
North Korean national Independence Day 173
North-South line 21–22, 24, 26, 30, 35
North-South reconciliation 30
Northwest Pacific Action Plan Eutrophication Assessment Tool (NEAT) 246
Northwest Pacific Action Plan (NOWPAP) 245, 246
Norway 59
NOWPAP *see* Northwest Pacific Action Plan (NOWPAP)
NOWPAP Policy on Data and Information Sharing 246

NPT *see* Treaty on the Non-Proliferation of Nuclear Weapons (or Non-Proliferation Treaty) (NPT)
NSC *see* National Security Council (NSC)
NSG *see* Nuclear Suppliers Group (NSG)
NSP *see* New Southern Policy (NSP)
NSS *see* National Security Strategy (NSS)
nuclear: ambitions 23, 128; arms race 45; arsenal 49, 111–112, 114, 117, 198, 205; capability 2, 111–112, 114, 116, 118, 218–219; crisis 29, 43, 51, 57, 59, 143, 223; debate 2; deterrence 45, 87, 91, 108, 129; device prototype 73; diplomacy 48; disarmament 102, 157, 183; disaster 2; energy 2, 96, 122, 143, 158; facilities 33, 44, 49, 81, 109, 127, 213; inspections 31; issues 64, 81, 96–97, 102, 143, 159, 198, 205, 211–213, 215–216, 220; might 8; missiles 59; neighbour 44; North Korea 2, 4, 5, 40–41, 44, 143, 209; power 1–2, 4, 8, 41, 47, 87, 110, 112–114; problem 74, 143; programme 22–25, 28, 34–35, 73, 80, 82, 91–92, 101, 106, 108–110, 116, 126, 128, 130, 143, 179, 216–219; proliferation 101, 121, 129, 158, 165, 174–175, 179; reactors 2, 128; relations 115; reprocessing facilities 96; security standings 1; standoff 30, 114; strike capability 50; submarine 66; talks 10, 97, 99; technological nexus 3, 181; tests 4, 22, 26, 29, 40, 44, 48, 78, 87, 93–95, 97, 108–109, 112, 121, 124, 127, 130, 144, 169–170, 180, 209, 214, 217–219; threat 3, 93, 96, 109, 122, 205, 213–214; umbrella 9, 50, 92, 96, 116, 143, 220; warheads 23–25, 29, 112, 121, 124; zone 1; umbrella 9, 50, 92, 96, 116, 143, 220
nuclear and missile: capabilities 12, 121–122, 125, 128, 130–131; facilities 26, 127, 129; tests 79–80, 130, 180, 214, 218
nuclear, biological, and chemical weapons 92
Nuclear Non-Proliferation Treaty 29, 47
Nuclear Posture Review 114, 115, 117, 221
Nuclear Suppliers Group (NSG)
Nuclear Weapon Free Zone 3, 158
nuclear weapons 3, 8–9, 22–23, 29, 32, 44–45, 49–51, 61, 73, 76, 87, 89–90, 92–97, 99, 101–102, 109–115, 117, 121–123, 126–127, 131–132, 143–144, 153, 158, 183, 193, 196, 198–199, 204–205, 209–210, 212–213, 216, 219;

266 *Index*

capability 101; development of 87, 122–123, 193; elimination of 102, 198; non-use of or not to use or threaten to use 92, 96; possible use of 8; production, introduction, and use of 92; tactical 114
Nuclear Weapons Free Zone (NWFZ) 92
Nuclear weapons state 44, 87, 89, 92, 94, 121
Nuclear Weapons State Law, North Korea 44
nukes and missiles 28–29, 31–32, 34
NWFZ *see* Nuclear Weapons Free Zone (NWFZ)
Nye, Joseph 28

Obama, Barack, US President 22, 113, 115, 117, 158, 160, 182, 201, 218, 225–226, 231
ODA *see* Official Development Assistance (ODA)
OECD *see* Organisation for Economic Cooperation and Development (OECD)
Okinotorishima 47
OPCON *see* Operational Control (OPCON)
Operational Control (OPCON) 63, 98
OPIC *see* Overseas Private Investment Corporation (OPIC)
Organisation for Economic Cooperation and Development (OECD) 193
Organisation for Security and Cooperation (OSCE) 157
Organizational Guidance Department of Korean Labor Party 193
OSCE *see* Organisation for Security and Cooperation (OSCE)
Overseas Private Investment Corporation (OPIC) 233

P-5 plus 5 216
PAC-3 *see* Patriot Advanced Capability (PAC-3)
Pacific Dragon 2016 66
Pacific Partnership 2017 62
Pakistan 3, 43–44, 121, 123, 126, 128, 172, 175, 181, 221, 223
Pakistan-North Korea nexus 172
Panmunjom Declaration 4, 7, 26, 49, 181, 209
Panmunjom Declaration for Peace, Prosperity and Unification of the Korean Peninsula 7, 49
Paris Climate Agreement 10
Park, Enna 175

Park Geun-hye, South Korean president 30, 48, 62, 63, 130, 153; convicted on abuse of power and corruption charges 31
Park Hahnkyu 50
Patriot Advanced Capability (PAC-3) 58, 59
peace 2, 4, 7, 9, 11–13, 22, 24–25, 27–29, 31–33, 42, 49, 51, 57–58, 60–61, 67, 75–76, 80, 82, 87–88, 90, 92, 94–100, 102–103, 106, 111–112, 128–129, 131, 142, 146, 149, 151, 153, 155–160, 165, 167–169, 171–175, 177–184, 197, 215, 217, 222–223, 227, 249–250; arrangements 88, 98; declaration 28–29, 31–33, 100, 215; permanent 28, 88, 98, 179, 215; process 4, 13, 97, 146, 149, 159–160, 165, 173–174, 179, 181; regime 27, 49, 57, 87–88, 90, 96–98, 102; regional 158–159, 180, 250; treaty 27, 33, 58, 90, 94, 99–100, 111–112
Peace and Development Debate 42
People's Liberation Army Navy (PLAN) 227
People's Liberation Army (PLA) 43, 48
People's Republic of China (PRC) 42 *see* China
People's Volunteers Army (PVA) 43
perestroika 72
Philippines 62, 246
Pivot to Asia 225–226, 231
PLA *see* People's Liberation Army (PLA)
PLAN *see* People's Liberation Army Navy (PLAN)
PMD *see* Possible Military Dimension (PMD)
Pobeda 79
polarisation 11
political: alliances 154; configurations 39, 40; controversies 75; differences 46; dynamism 30; equations 166; impasse 41; instability 43; means 82; overtones 28; powers 39; process 81; scandal 62; settlement 49; situation 48, 67; solution 39; stability 42; support 74
politics 1, 3–4, 7–8, 11, 13–14, 49, 68, 109, 149, 166, 168, 171, 195, 210, 242–243, 245, 247, 250; alliance 1, 4; domestic 68; great power 168, 171; international 13, 195; North Korean 109; of power blocs 171; power 1, 7–8, 13, 166, 168, 210; regional 149, 171; resource 242–243, 245, 250; world 3, 166
Pompeo, Mike, US secretary of state 24, 26–30, 32–35, 93, 201; mission to Pyongyang 29, 32

Index 267

Powell, Robert 195
power blocks 171
power(s): Asian 41; asymmetry of 49; balance of 107, 118, 194, 195, 221, 226, 235; Chinese 40, 115; competition 113, 115; configuration of 40; deterrence 60; military 59, 61, 100, 195; nuclear 1 2, 4, 8, 41, 47, 87, 110, 112–114; political 39; politics 1, 7–8, 13, 166, 168, 210; regional 12, 107–108, 121; rivalry 12, 244; socialist 11, 42; sources 2; struggle 1, 179, 206
POW/MIA *see* Prisoner of War/Missing in Action (POW/MIA)
PPP *see* Purchasing Power Parity (PPP)
Prabhu, Suresh 173
PRC *see* People's Republic of China (PRC)
preventive strikes 6
Primakov, Yevgeny 74
Prisoner of War/Missing in Action (POW/MIA) 49, 171
Propaganda 73, 199, 201
provocations 10–11, 60, 66–67, 76–78, 80, 94, 108, 110, 118, 130, 144, 196, 213; North Korean 77, 80
public awareness 102
public-private partnership 234
Putin and Kim summit meeting 82, 145
Putin, Vladimir, President 34, 74–76, 78–80, 82, 138, 141, 145, 202; visit to Pyongyang 75
PVA *see* People's Volunteers Army (PVA)
Pyeongtaek military base 5
Pyongyang Declaration 4, 58, 75, 179, 181

Quad *see* Quadrilateral grouping of Australia, India, Japan, and the US (Quad)
Quadrilateral grouping of Australia, India, Japan, and the US (Quad) 63, 221–222, 228–229, 232, 234
Quadrilateral Security Dialogue 117

RAAF *see* Royal Australian Air Force (RAAF)
RACs *see* Regional activity centres (RACs)
radars 59
Rajin-Hasan project 80
rapprochement 10, 21, 106, 144
RasonConTrans 76, 81
Rason Special Economic Zone (RSEZ) 151–152
RBIO *see* Rules-Based International Order (RBIO)
RCEP *see* Regional Comprehensive Economic Partnership (RCEP)

realism 194–195
realpolitik 46, 48
ReCAAP *see* Regional Cooperation Agreement on Combating Piracy and Armed Robbery against Ships in Asia (ReCAAP)
regional: activity centres (RACs) 246; adversaries 114; affairs 150, 154, 172; balance of power 107; commitment 158; concerns 154; connectivity 13, 154, 160, 176–177; cooperation 156, 177, 182, 243, 246, 249; deterrence 107, 115; dialogue 159; diplomacy 42; disputes 155; economic cooperation 139, 177; goals 176; insecurity 67, 246; integration 149, 154, 231, 248, 250; issues 157; nuclear arms race 45; organisations 146; peace 158–159, 180, 250; politics 149, 171; power 12, 107–108, 121; scope of denuclearisation 112; security 4, 59, 63, 117, 138, 143, 154–156, 158, 220, 228; stability 6, 155–156; strategic stability 12, 107; tension 13, 250; ties 232
Regional Comprehensive Economic Partnership (RCEP) 177, 231, 235, 236, 238
Regional Cooperation Agreement on Combating Piracy and Armed Robbery against Ships in Asia (ReCAAP) 248
Regional Cooperation Regarding Preparedness and Response to Oil Spills 246
regionalism 226
Regional Oil and Hazardous and the Noxious Substance Spill Contingency Plan 246
Regional Oil Spill Contingency Plan 246
repression 11
Republic of Korea and United States 24; alliance 34
Republic of Korea Marine Corps (ROKMC) 62
Republic of Korea (ROK) *see* ROK
resource(s) 2, 11, 13, 140, 144, 205, 230, 242–246, 248, 250; diplomacy 244; fishery 244; human 245; insecurity 13, 243–245; nuclear energy 2; overseas 243; politics 242–243, 245, 250; regions 243
reunification 1, 7–8, 11, 40, 47, 81, 109–110, 166, 181, 184, 194, 215; demand for 1; forceful 8
Revere, Evans 34
Richard E. Byrd (T-AKE-4) 60

Rijiju, Kiren 173
Ri Su Yong 79, 157, 178
rivalry 12–13, 41, 228, 235, 243–244, 248, 250; power 12, 244
Ri Yong-ho, North Korea's foreign minister 35, 81, 157–158
Rodong 28, 95, 124, 127–128, 199
Rodong-1 124
Rodong Shinmun 28, 95, 199
rogue state 9, 144
Roh Moo-hyun, late South Korean President 23
Roh Tae-woo 73, 95
ROK *see* Republic of Korea (ROK)
ROKMC *see* Republic of Korea Marine Corps (ROKMC)
Royal Australian Air Force (RAAF) 63
RSEZ *see* Rason Special Economic Zone (RSEZ)
Rules-Based International Order (RBIO) 230, 234, 237
Russel, Daniel, vice president of the Asia Society 32–33
Russia 1–2, 7–8, 10, 12, 34, 40–41, 43, 49–51, 63, 72–82, 88, 94, 101, 112–113, 124–125, 127, 137–146, 149, 151–152, 154, 156, 159, 165, 172, 180–181, 183–184, 194, 202, 204, 216, 218, 242, 244–246, 248–250; foreign policy 74, 138–139; influence on North Korea 74; role in Korean Peninsula 72; strategic interests of 72; "Turn to the East" policy 139
Russia and Two Koreas 137–138, 141; foreign policy strategy 138
Russian card 34, 78
Russian Federation 72, 74, 137–138, 140, 141, 158
Russia-North Korea Trading House 79

Sakhalin Island 140
sanctions 1, 4, 8, 10, 22–24, 26, 30–32, 34–35, 49, 58, 63, 77–78, 80–82, 88–89, 93–94, 98–101, 106, 108, 111–112, 117, 122–123, 125–131, 142, 144–146, 152–153, 157, 166, 169–171, 173, 178–179, 184, 193, 196–199, 201–202, 204–205, 209, 218, 250; economic 8, 93, 106, 111–112, 117, 125, 130–131, 142, 146, 193, 196, 198–199; international 1, 89, 108, 122, 127, 153, 173, 197, 199, 202, 204–205; removal of 184
Sankei Shimbun 62
SAR *see* Special Administrative Region (SAR)

Schweller, Randall 195
Scud missiles 127–128
SDF *see* Self Defence Forces (SDF)
Sea Lines of Communication (SLOCs) 227, 246–249
Sea of Japan 60, 243, 247
secondary boycott 89, 130
security 1–7, 9–10, 12–13, 22, 25–28, 31, 34, 41–42, 45–46, 48–51, 57–59, 62–68, 73, 75–76, 80, 82, 87, 90–92, 96, 98–99, 102, 107–108, 110–111, 115, 117–118, 123, 128–129, 131, 138–144, 149, 154–159, 166–168, 172, 177–178, 180–181, 183, 195–198, 216–217, 219–220, 222, 225–229, 231–232, 234, 236–237, 239, 242–245, 247–250; architecture 58–59, 62, 64–65, 107, 117–118, 166, 172, 180; assurances 9, 220; challenges 226, 228; collective 82; concerns 67, 111, 178, 216; cooperation 63, 66–68, 117, 156, 172, 229, 249; energy 2, 13, 140, 242, 248–250; external 42; guaranteeing 28; guarantees 9–10, 26, 34, 76, 82, 87, 180, 216; Indo-Pacific 3; international 34, 82, 131, 222; multilateral 10, 117, 220; national 49, 59, 111, 141, 158, 180, 196, 225, 232, 247; North-East Asian 155, 156–157, 243; nuclear 1; perceptions 46; pledge 57; problems of 82; regional 4, 59, 63, 117, 138, 143, 154–156, 158, 220, 228; riddle 49; risk 46; trainings 7
Sejong the Great (DD-991) 66
self-defence 6, 9, 61, 67; collective 61, 67; rights 67;
self-defence capabilities 6, 9
Self Defence Forces (SDF) 47
self-reliance 9, 43
self-reliance ideology 9
Senkaku Islands 11, 47, 61, 67, 116
Senkaku Islands dispute 116
Seoul Foreign Correspondents' Club 29
Shahab-3 127
Shahab-4 127
Shambaugh, David 42
Shangri La dialogue 25
Shevardnadze, Eduard 73, 74
Shevardnadze, Shevardnadze 73
Shin Sang-bum 28
ship-to-ship cargo transfer 63
Short Take-Off and Vertical-Landing (STOVL) 62
siege mentality 51, 108–112
signature foreign policy project 48
Silk Road Economic Belt 229
Singapore agreement 88

Singh, Manmohan, Prime Minister 228
Singh, V.K. 174
Sino-Korean Friendship bridge 43
Sino-North Korean border 44
six-party conference 74
Six-Party Talks 1, 34, 47, 51, 76–77, 88, 94, 96, 142, 149–150, 154–156, 180, 182–183, 216–220, 222
SLBM *see* Submarine-Launched Ballistic Missile (SLBM)
SLOCs *see* Sea Lines of Communication (SLOCs)
SM-3 *see* Standard Missile-3 (SM-3)
SM-6 60
social change 11
social interest 61
socialism 73
SOEs *see* State-Owned Enterprises (SOEs)
South Asia 3, 122, 126, 181
South China Morning Post 215
South China Sea 62, 215, 227, 244, 247
South-East Asian countries 63, 67
South-East Asian countries and India 67; economic relations 67
South Korea 2–8, 10, 12–13, 21–30, 33, 39–43, 45–51, 57–68, 73–77, 80, 82, 87–93, 95–102, 106–107, 109–111, 115, 118, 124–125, 129–130, 137–138, 140–144, 146, 149, 152–154, 159, 165, 168–169, 171–183, 193–194, 197–198, 203, 205, 212–215, 218, 225–226, 231, 235, 237–239, 245–250; aggressive attitude 57; Americanised 21; China policy in 5; concept of denuclearisation 95; domestic politics in 68; importance of 59, 67; intelligence 74; National Intelligence Service 30; nuclear weapons deployed in 92; policy 96, 98; policy towards North Korea 98; pressure on Russia 73; strategic significance 41; US military assistance to 6–7; US troop deployment in 27; *see also* ROK
South Korea and North Korea 8, 96, 212
South Korea and Russia 139–141
South Korea and United States 3, 6, 12, 24–27, 29–31, 48, 50–51, 59, 65, 68, 80, 89–90, 93, 100, 102, 107, 111–112, 115, 129, 171, 218; 1953 Mutual Defence Treaty 41; alliance 5–6, 27, 31, 62–63, 68, 92, 94, 99; dispute 30; joint military exercises 26, 65, 92; military activities 6; military exercises 25, 33, 63, 65, 214; relations 24; Special Measures Agreement 6

South Korea and USSR relations 73
South Korea-Japan Environmental Science 245
South Korean Air Force 66
South Korean government 95, 98–99, 101, 106
South Korean Navy 66
South Korean president Korean Peninsula, 76
sovereignty 82, 91, 94, 173, 217, 222, 227
Soviet internationalism 74
Soviet Union 4, 40, 42, 72, 109, 113, 115–116, 121–123, 125, 137–139, 150, 168, 193; collapse of 40; dissolution of 72; fall of 4; foreign policy 137
Soviet Union and US nuclear relationship 115
Spain 59
Special Administrative Region (SAR) 44
SSBN *see* Strategic Submarine Ballistic Nuclear (SSBN)
SS-N-6 124
State-Owned Enterprises (SOEs) 244
STOVL *see* Short Take-Off and Vertical-Landing (STOVL)
strategic : ally 5, 40, 43, 172; asset 67; attacks 114; burden 47; communication 62, 67; community 47, 48; competition 12, 107–108, 115, 117–118; dilemma 40, 48; interests 11–12, 72, 107, 113, 165, 177; liability 4, 40, 44, 47; partnership 77, 172–173, 175, 183; relations 65; rendezvous 171; shield 40, 42; significance 41; stability 12, 106–108, 113–116, 222; thinking 40, 228
Strategic Submarine Ballistic Nuclear (SSBN) 65
strategy 6–7, 9, 11–12, 21, 30, 35, 58–59, 62, 64, 67–68, 97, 107–108, 111, 115, 117, 138–140, 142, 154, 175, 196, 198, 221–222, 226, 239, 243–244, 247; *Byung jin* 108, 111; conflicted 21; hedging 59; India-Pacific 62; mercantilist 245; military-first 9; non-involvement 58; pressure 9;
strike capability 50, 115–116
Submarine-Launched Ballistic Missile (SLBM) 66, 124
submarine(s) 6, 43, 66, 109, 115, 143, 212; North Korean 43; nuclear 66; Type-33 (Romeo Class) 43
Suga, Yoshihide 57
Sunshine Policy 30, 195, 215
sustainability 97, 98, 211, 221–222, 230
Switzerland 124

270 Index

Synder, Scott 45
Syria 3, 44, 122, 126–128, 131; military conflicts 127
Syrian issue 79

Taepodong 124, 127
Taepodong-1 127
TAES *see* Trans-Asia Energy System (TAES)
Taiwan 42, 45–46, 172, 215
Tanaka, Akihiko 58
TCS *see* Trilateral Cooperation Secretariat (TCS)
Team Spirit 92
technology 2, 43–46, 103, 113–114, 121–129, 139, 158, 172, 180–181, 246, 249; gas-centrifuge 123; leaks 46; missile 44, 124–125, 128; nuclear 181; Russian 139
TEMM *see* Tripartite Environment Ministers Meeting (TEMM)
tension 7, 11, 13, 27, 49, 58, 61, 63, 67–68, 79, 87, 90, 96, 99, 112–113, 123, 129, 138–139, 142, 146, 155, 157, 159, 167–168, 174, 179, 181, 211, 213, 215, 236, 245, 247, 250; maritime 247; military 58, 68; regional 13, 250; US-DPRK 215
Terminal High Altitude Area Defence (THAAD) 5, 10, 45–47, 60, 67, 109; deployment of 47
terrorist organisations 131, 211
THAAD *see* Terminal High Altitude Area Defence (THAAD)
threat(s) 3, 6, 8, 11, 21, 47, 50, 57–61, 66–67, 73, 90–93, 96, 98, 100–101, 106, 108–109, 112, 114, 122, 129, 131, 141, 195–198, 205, 213–214, 219, 222, 227–229, 242, 247, 250; consciousness 61; military 61, 91; North Korean 59, 66; nuclear 96, 109, 122, 205, 213
Tillerson, Rex 24
Torkunov, Anatoly 72
Total Construction of North Korean Economy 91
totalitarianism 194
TPNW *see* Treaty on the Prohibition of Nuclear Weapons (TPNW)
TPP *see* Trans-Pacific Partnership (TPP)
TPY-2 *see* Transportable Radar Surveillance (TPY)-2
Track 1.5 meeting 158
trade agreements 230–231, 235–238; cross-regional 236–237; multi-lateral 235, 238

trade(s) 4–5, 32, 40, 43, 45, 50, 64, 79–80, 88, 94, 111, 123, 126, 128, 131, 140–141, 151–152, 154, 156, 173, 175–176, 178–179, 201–202, 215, 218, 221–222, 227–228, 230–238, 242–243, 247, 250; bilateral 80, 151–152, 154, 173, 175–176; expectations 45; indirect operations 79; issues 80, 221; nuclear and missile 126; resumption of 50; war 40, 50; weapons 126
Trans-Asia Energy System (TAES) 249
Trans-Pacific Partnership (TPP) 5, 10, 227, 230–231, 236, 238; United States' withdrawal from 5
transparency 44, 113, 115, 222, 230; financial 222; lack of 44
Transportable Radar Surveillance (TPY)-2 59
Treaty of Friendship, Cooperation and Mutual Assistance 40, 73, 143
Treaty on Friendship, Good-Neighbourliness and Cooperation 74
Treaty on the Non-Proliferation of Nuclear Weapons (or Non-Proliferation Treaty) (NPT) 96, 101, 143–144, 213–214, 216
Treaty on the Prohibition of Nuclear Weapons (TPNW) 101
Trilateral Cooperation Secretariat (TCS) 102
Tripartite Environment Ministers Meeting (TEMM) 245–246
triumvirates 11
Trump administration 5–6, 21, 79, 92, 106, 117, 158, 180, 227, 238; foreign policy priority 106
Trump, Donald, US President 5–6, 10–11, 21–35, 39, 48–49, 51, 65, 79, 87–88, 90, 92–93, 106–107, 117–118, 129–130, 145, 155, 157–158, 160, 174, 180, 193, 198–199, 201, 204–205, 210, 214–215, 219–220, 225, 227, 231, 238; cost-sharing mechanisms with Japan and South Korea 5–6; foreign policy 35; letter to Kim 29; selective and business-oriented military strategy 6
Trutnev, Yury 79
Tsenkher Suld 159
Tsushima Strait 62, 65
Turkey 128
Two Koreas 1, 3, 6–13, 21–23, 25–26, 34, 41, 46, 49–50, 81, 87, 89, 95, 98–99, 106–107, 110, 129, 137–142, 145–146, 149, 165–167, 169, 171, 173–174, 179–180, 182, 193–194, 212, 248–249; colonisation of 41, 47; formula 97;

identity of 1, 7–8; Japanese colonisation of 41; negotiation for unification of the two 8; partition of 41; reunification of 1, 47; Soviet policy towards 137; unification of 193; unification of the two 7–8, 142, 167
Two Koreas, unification of 7–8, 13, 143, 194, 196
two-track policies 34

UBD *see* Ulaanbaatar Dialogue on Northeast Asia Security (UBD)
Ukraine 44, 125
Ukrainian crisis 78, 146
Ukrainian issue 79
Ulaanbaatar 150–151, 153, 155–159
Ulaanbaatar Dialogue on Northeast Asia Security (UBD) 155–158, 160
Ulaanbaatar Process 159
Ulchi-Freedom Guardian (UFG) 65, 94
UN *see* United Nations (UN)
UNC *see* United Nations Command (UNC)
UN Command 28–30, 64, 90
UN Commission on Korea 168
UNESCAP *see* United Nations Economic and Social Commission for Asia and the Pacific (UNESCAP)
UN Forces 63
UNGA *see* UN General Assembly (UNGA)
UN General Assembly (UNGA) 34, 158, 168–169, 197; Resolutions, 82 168–170, 201
Unha-3 rocket 77
Unha-3 satellite 124
unification 7–8, 10, 13, 23, 50–51, 77, 97–98, 100, 110, 142–144, 167, 179, 193–194, 196, 201, 203, 206; causes of 7; issue of 10; negotiation 8; peaceful 7, 97, 144, 167, 179
Unified Korea 7–8, 41, 143–144, 168
United Arab Emirates 2
United Kingdom 63, 67, 123–124, 158
United Korea 10
United Nations Command (UNC) 58, 62–63, 90, 100
United Nations Commission of Inquiry (COI) 197
United Nations Economic and Social Commission for Asia and the Pacific (UNESCAP) 249
United Nations Security Council (UNSC) 8, 10, 27, 33, 63, 67, 80–81, 108, 126, 130, 140, 144, 146, 158, 166, 168–171, 179, 182, 197, 201. Resolutions, 80; sanctions resolutions against North Korea 10; violations of the resolutions 10; *see also* United Nations Security Council (UNSC);
United Nations (UN) 4, 8, 23–24, 26–32, 34, 58, 63–64, 75, 77–78, 80–81, 90, 99, 101, 108–109, 126, 128, 130, 144–145, 154, 157–158, 167–171, 173–174, 178–179, 193–194, 197–198, 201–202, 218, 247, 249; sanctions 32, 77–78, 81, 99, 130, 144, 157, 201–202
United Nations (UN) International Law of the Sea 247
United State Pacific Command (USPACOM) 227
United States Forces Korea (USFK) 6, 12, 58, 61, 63, 65, 68, 90, 92, 100; withdrawal of 12, 65, 68, 90, 92
United States Indo-Pacific Command (USINDOPACOM) 227
United States Marine Corps (USMC) 62
United States (US) 1–13, 21–35, 39–51, 57–68, 73–82, 87–94, 96–102, 106–118, 123–127, 129–130, 138, 142–145, 149, 151, 154–159, 165–169, 171–172, 174, 179–182, 193–194, 196–204, 209–223, 225–236, 238–239, 242–243, 245, 249. commitment towards Japan's security 6; declaration of the non-use of nuclear weapons against the North 92; demand for complete denuclearisation of North Korea 40; disengagement 62; double-dealing attitudes 30; economic interests 232; foreign policy 226, 227, 231; Indo-Pacific strategy 226; intelligence agencies 28; interests in Indo-Pacific 6; interests in North-East Asia 6; military assistance to South Korea 6; military bases in Japan 63; military commitments in Indo-Pacific 5; missile defence network 67; nuclear umbrella 9, 50, 96, 143; policies 10; policy on Korean Peninsula 21; policy on North Korea 29; pressure tactics 4; rotational policy 6; seizure of the cargo ship 51; Seventh Fleet 6, 41; shifting policy on Korea 21; strategic attacks against 114; strategy for Korean Peninsula 21; troop deployment in South Korea 27; withdrawal from Trans-Pacific Partnership (TPP) 5; withdrawal of troops 28, 50, 96; see United States (US);
UN military 63
UNTCOK *see* UN Temporary Commission on Korea (UNTCOK)
UN Temporary Commission on Korea (UNTCOK) 167

Uranium 28–29, 44, 49, 75, 96, 107, 122–123, 127, 213, 217–218; crisis of 2002 75; enrichment facilities 96; production 49
US administration 6, 9; military approach 6
USAID *see* United States Agency for International Development (USAID)
US Army 60, 63; 38th Air Defence Artillery Brigade Headquarters 60
US base 41
US-DPRK Agreed Framework 96
USFK *see* United States Forces Korea (USFK)
USIDFC *see* United States International Development Finance Corporation (USIDFC)
US Indo-Pacific Strategy 13, 225–230, 232–234
USINDOPACOM *see* United States Indo-Pacific Command (USINDOPACOM)
US–Japan partnership 5
US–Korea-Japan military relations 47
USMC *see* United States Marine Corps (USMC)
US military 6, 34, 42, 59–60, 63, 65, 93, 100, 108, 115–116, 118, 143–144; strategic base for 60
US National Security Strategy 114
US Navy 60
US Nuclear Posture Review 114
US nuclear umbrella, removal of 50, 96, 143
USPACOM *see* United State Pacific Command (USPACOM)
US-ROK-Japan Defence Trilateral Talks (DTT) 102
US-South Korea partnership 5, 33, 62–63, 65, 68, 80, 92, 100, 214
USSR 72–73, 171–172, 248; collapse of, 72–73; foreign policy 73; *see also* Soviet Union
USSR Committee for State Security (KGB) 73
US troops 24, 41, 43; presence in South Korea 43

Vanin, Yuri 72
Vietnam 44, 64, 155, 246
Voice of America (VOA) 196
volatile zone 3
Vorontsov, Alexander 72

war/missing in action 22, 49
Washington Post, 35

weapon(s) 3, 8–9, 22–23, 29, 32, 34, 44–45, 49–51, 60–61, 66, 73, 76, 87, 89–90, 92–97, 99–102, 109–117, 121–124, 126–128, 131–132, 143–144, 153, 158–160, 182–183, 193, 196, 198–199, 201, 204–205, 209–210, 212–214, 216, 219, 244, 247; chemical 92, 128; conventional 96, 100, 126–127; destructive 122; non-nuclear 114; nuclear 96; space-based 116; thermonuclear 209; trade 126
Weapons of Mass Destruction (WMD) 9, 22, 92–95, 101, 108–109, 111, 131, 139, 143, 157, 158, 182–183, 201; dismantlement of 92;
Wedge 26–27, 29, 64, 222
Western policy 78
West Sea 243
Winter Olympic Games 23, 57
Winter Olympics 78, 87
Wise Ernest 201
WMD *see* Weapons of Mass Destruction (WMD)
Workers' Party of Korea (WPK) 26, 43, 87, 92, 93–95, 108, 111, 157, 201, 203, 219
World Tribune 127
World War II 72, 150, 193
WPK *see* Workers' Party of Korea (WPK)
Wu Jianmin 42

Xi Jinping, China's President 5, 32, 39, 46, 48–49, 51, 79, 202; visit to North Korea 39, 49; visit to Pyongyang 48

Yachi, Shotaro 65
Yang Xiyu 51
Yanukovych, Viktor, Russian President 125
Yellow Sea 243–244, 246–248
Yeltsin, Boris 73, 74
Yeonpyeong Island 77
Yomiuri Shimbun 64
Yongbyon 22–23, 28–29, 31–34, 49, 87–88, 122–123, 128, 217–218
Yongbyon nuclear facility 29, 31, 87, 128
Yongbyon Nuclear Research Centre 122
Yongnam, Kim 73
Yongsan Garrison base 5
You Ji 44, 48
Yun, Joseph 35

Zero-sum game 46, 49
Zhebin, Alexander 72
Zone of Peace 92